Radical ESSEX

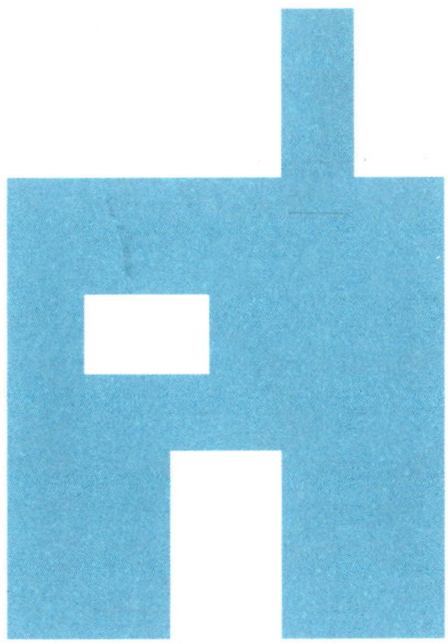

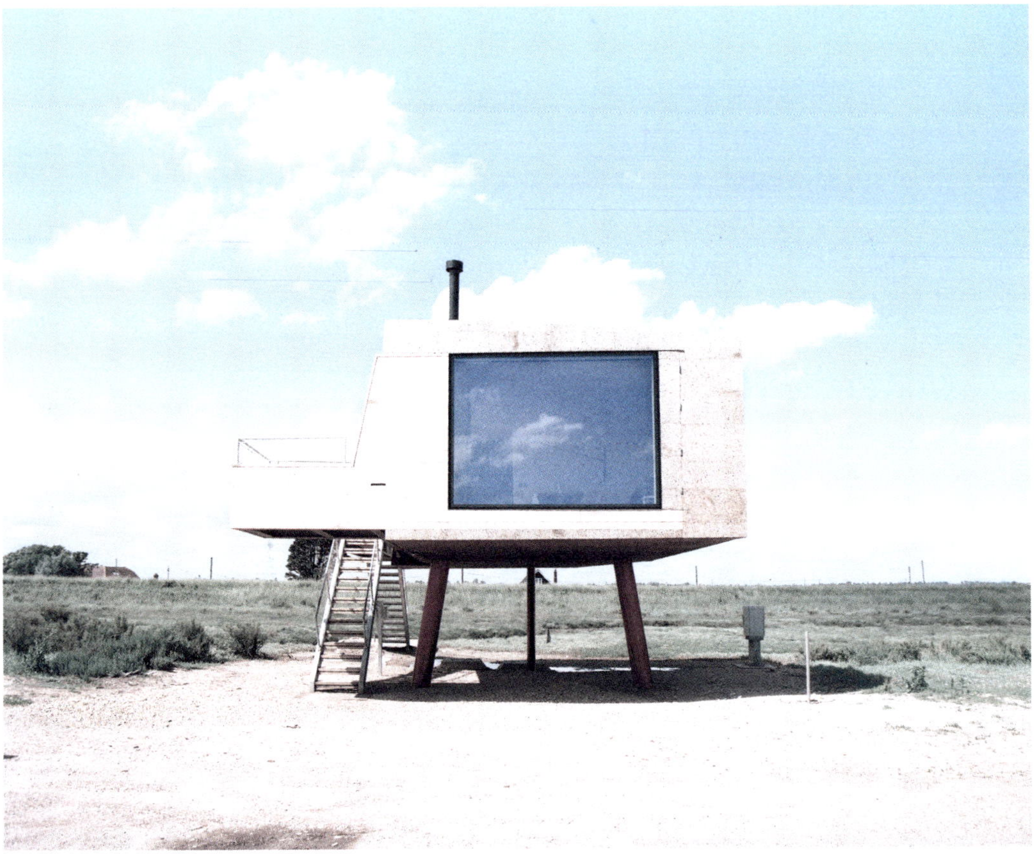

Redshank, Lee-over-Sands

Foreword

The Radical ESSEX project set out to redefine the county in relation to radicalism in thought, lifestyle, politics and architecture. Throughout 2016 and 2017, a diverse range of talks, screenings, exhibitions, tours and performances took place across the county, celebrating the extreme social landscape of Essex from the late-nineteenth century onwards.

The proximity of Essex to London, particularly to some of the poorest parts of the capital, is key to understanding how the county has developed. The writer and broadcaster Jonathan Meades describes Essex as 'the East End gone a roving', home to a cockney diaspora moving out from London. This permeable relationship with the city, along with the distinctive landscape, have encouraged innovators to view Essex as a testing-ground for radical thought and experimental lifestyles, incorporating often conflicting political ideologies, religious practices and social structures.

Throughout the county, communities have rejected traditional approaches of formalised occupation and embraced a 'new start' approach. From Tolstoyan communes, to the worker colonies and plotland settlements, these communities promoted a life of transience and experimentation. The dynamic between these community practices and the creeping urban spill of the suburban commuter belt, creates an ideological interspace that can make Essex notoriously difficult to define. These tensions were played out politically during the late 1980s with the rise of 'Basildon Man', a concept engineered by Thatcherism. Defined as a Tory supporter who had previously been expected to vote Labour, *The Sunday Telegraph* described him as 'young, industrious, mildly brutish and culturally barren' and 'breathtakingly right-wing'. This characterisation later made Basildon and Essex a political barometer for the rest of the country.

For Essex writer Ken Worpole, this mercurial character can be understood not only politically and socially, but geographically; he states that Essex is 'neither part of East Anglia nor one of the Home Counties; it contains both radical and conservative elements, and is therefore open to all possibilities'. This open and progressive nature has been a guiding principle throughout the Radical ESSEX project, moving away from a gallery environment and into homes, community halls, pubs, colonies and even the tidal swell of the Thames Estuary. Indeed, it is the geographical and social context of Essex that lies at the centre of this project.

As someone not from the area, I'm always surprised by how at odds the county is with the stereotypes associated with it. I believe the ultimate aspiration for Essex is to be self-guided in its desires – to seek, experiment and redefine.

The project is indebted to writers Dennis Hardy, the late Colin Ward, Ken Worpole and Jonathan Meades for initially inspiring us to delve deeper, and I would especially like to thank all of the individuals and communities that opened their doors to us, as well as Hayley Dixon, Hannah Rose Whittle, Riah Pryor, Stephanie Sutton, Warren Harper and the team at Focal Point Gallery for their continued vision, enthusiasm and support throughout the project.

Joe Hill
Director, Focal Point Gallery

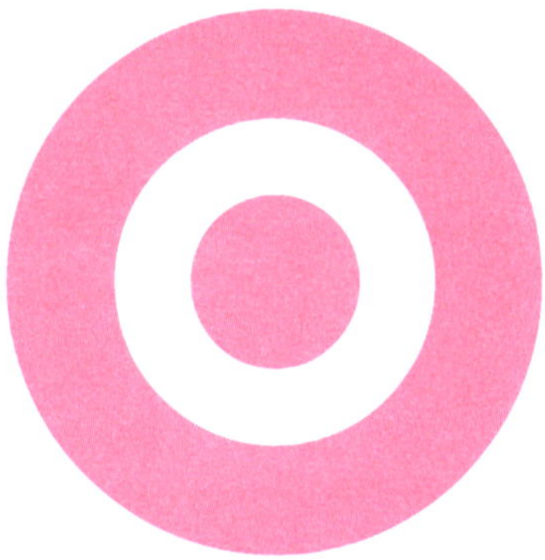

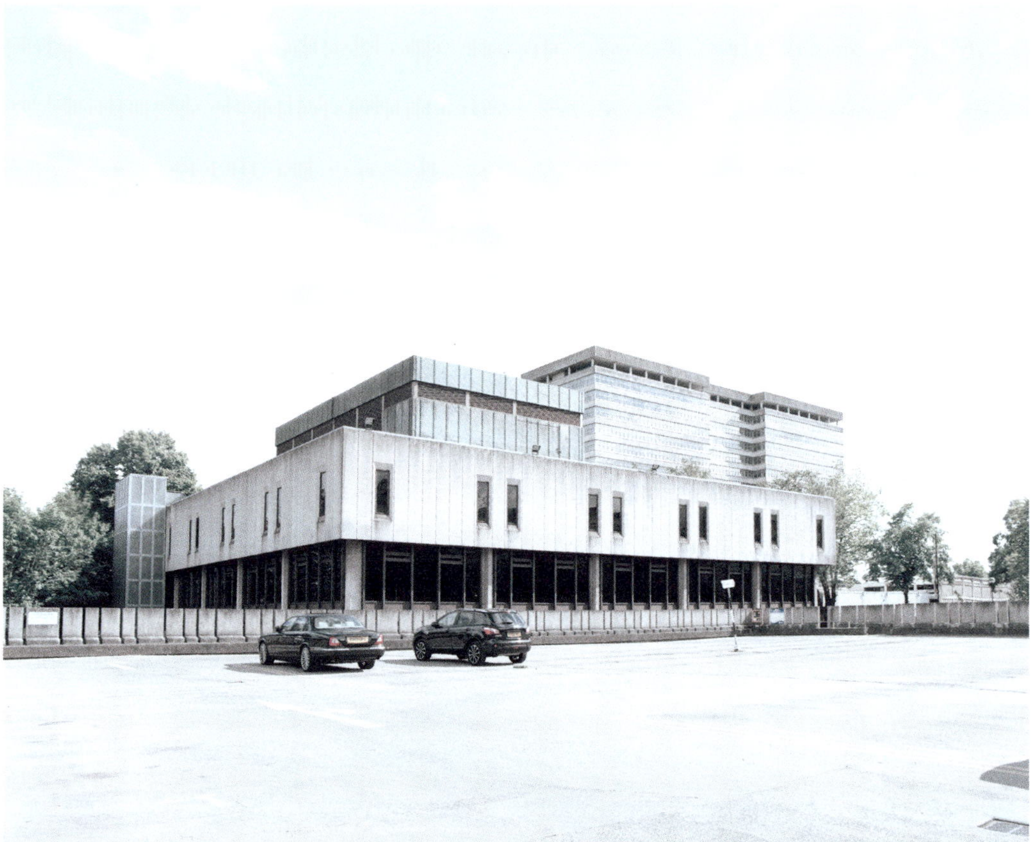

Beecroft Art Gallery, Southend-on-Sea

The Essex Escape

A Partial History

Tim Burrows

Walking in Essex, whether through metropolitan borderland or by far-flung saltmarsh, it is still possible to feel decidedly outside of things. There is a particular feeling when I find myself suddenly alone, whisked out of London's intensity and into the (dis)quiet of the open field or marsh; I have started to refer to this feeling as 'the Essex solitary'. It is a condition that thrives on incongruity; despite the county's closeness to the city, it is still possible to feel the eeriness a sudden emptying of urban markers brings. It's not always pleasant: being unprepared for such a sharp state of solitude can induce great fear. But it is always an escape.

The last time I experienced the Essex solitary, I took a wrong turn around Wanstead Park on a walk bound for Dagenham via Ilford, and ended up on a long, barren path ensconced between the City of London cemetery and the River Roding and its tributary Alders Brook. Administratively this metropolitan edgeland ceased to be part of Essex in 1965, when it was subsumed by the Greater London borderland of Redbridge and Newham. But as I walked on with scant evidence of other people, aside from distant shapes of golfers over the other side of the brook and the north circular rumbling out of sight, this slither of deserted London was the outsider realm of Essex once more.

Essex has, of course, been characterised as the UK's brashest county, one of in-yer-face aggrandisements and aggro niceties. But its more established characteristic is one of muteness. 'Essex is a queer country', wrote H. Cranmer-Byng, who compiled Essex folk stories in the early twentieth

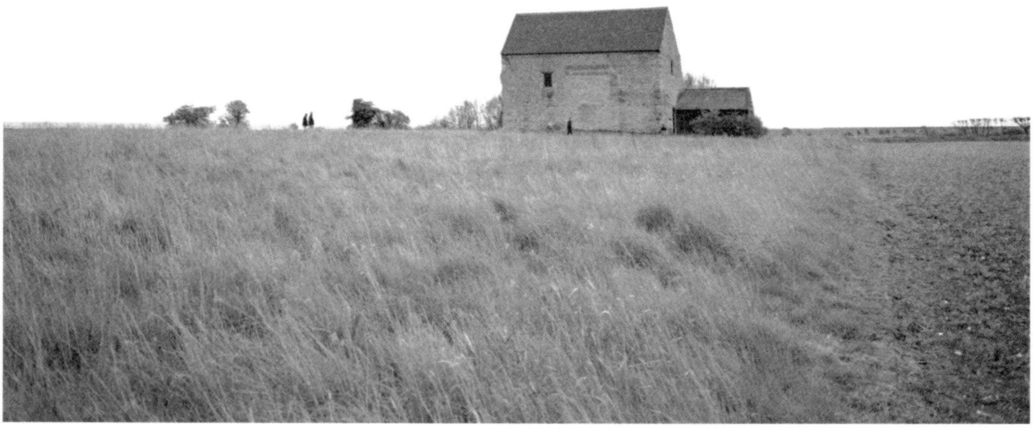

Chapel of St Peter-on-the-Wall, Bradwell-on-Sea

century. 'A famous writer who lived for some time on the fringe of Roding country once said to me he had a curious feeling that Essex was completely deaf. I recall that he could not explain it. It was just a feeling, a sudden personal insight into something too subtle for analysis or explanation.'

Walter Besant, Victorian-era writer and friend of Charles Dickens and Wilkie Collins, offered a good account of the Essex solitary in his book *East London* (1901). He takes the train to Barking, then an 'ancient village… on the little river Roding' and not the bustling slice of East London it is today. He takes a walk down to the wall on the north bank of the Thames, built to protect the land in this part of the Thames Estuary, and marvels at his sudden switch in surroundings. 'No one ever walks upon this wall; once beyond the chemical works we are in the most lonely spot in the whole of England […] you will see no one in the meadows protected by the wall; you may walk mile after mile in a solitude most strange and most mysterious […] If one were to tell of a murder, this would be a fitting place for the crime.'

Later in the same book, Besant travels to Bradwell Juxta Mare (Bradwell-on-Sea) on the Dengie Peninsula, between the rivers Blackwater and Crouch in Essex. He comments on how it protected the lowlands from the saline attentions of the North Sea, noting the ruined seventh century Chapel of St Peter-on-the-Wall that overlooked another ruin, the Roman fort of Othona, and other churches along Essex's estuarial coastline, positioned as if asking for divine intervention to help keep the floods at bay.

My shadow grew longer as I approached St Peter's, now a restored ecclesiastical and sometime civic site, on the way to a reading that formed part of the Radical Writing Retreat organised by Essex Book Festival and Radical ESSEX, followed by dinner at the Othona Community next to the old chapel. Wind turbines were a majestic presence on the horizon; the decommissioned Bradwell nuclear power station seemed to hover incongruously in the other direction.

In my bag I carried an issue of *Direct Action* from 1966, signed by Tom Driberg, a gift given to me by John Lyons, an ale enthusiast with a wispy beard I'd met a few years previously at The Station Arms in Southminster. Born in Walthamstow back when it was still an Essex edgeland, John worked at free presses in London and was a postman until he somehow ended up out here in the Dengie. When I first met him he convinced me Dengue fever first originated from these parts (it didn't, but the malarial Essex ague, referenced by Daniel Defoe, was once apparently rife). Since our first meeting we'd formed a loose friendship, meeting up every now and then for clear and frothy pints in the same Southminster public house.

We'd spent the day catching up; I was passing through on the way to the event at Bradwell. John told me how as a child he used to camp with the Othona Community when it was in its infancy in the 1950s. It was set up by Norman Motley to 'foster peace and reconciliation between people of different nations, beliefs and outlooks' in the aftermath of the Second World War. Although his mother wasn't particularly impressed with the reality of camping, John loved it. It's part of the reason he ended up back here.

John, who's long identified as an anarchist, had been trying to find the signed copy of *Direct Action* since the day we met and I mentioned I found Driberg a fascinating figure. Driberg was an openly left wing but not openly gay Labour MP for Maldon and later Barking and Dagenham, a sometime commie-columnist, whose dalliances with male Cabinet members in the House of Commons toilets were well known in political circles but kept away from public knowledge.

Desiring a safe bolthole from city life, Driberg moved to Bradwell Lodge, a Tudor-Georgian hybrid. The migration was a radical act in itself. He pointed out how the county was 'consistently underestimated by Victorian romantics, who wallowed [in] the melodrama of mountain and torrent. They called it "flat and uninteresting".' For Driberg, who had been lustful for the metropolis during his youth, it was the counter to a city he had grown tired of: 'you may walk for miles along a sea-wall track, raised between rich marsh pastures and mysterious saltings, and see no sign of human activity but the white fleck of a sail out in the turbulent estuary'.

The flamboyant aristocratic artist, composer, novelist and aesthete, Lord Berners, was an early visitor and congratulated Driberg on his new residence: 'It is, as far as I can see, without a flaw – save possibly Liverpool Street – but that is made up for by the delightful rurality of the railway – and even Liverpool Street has a certain Monet-esque charm on a foggy morning.'

After the Lodge was requisitioned during the Second World War to become an RAF officers' mess, Driberg wrote poetry about the injection of armed servicemen into his erotic life. 'The stroking of muscle – the contours of silk – the terminal jets of passion.' Yet he married Ena Mary Binfield in 1951, largely for show, it was a union rarely more than miserable.

Driberg would get blind drunk with his secretary and drive back to the darkness of the Dengie; they'd both be thankful of waking up alive the next day. A gangster certified as a psychopath during a stretch in prison who Driberg had a thing for started hanging around towards the end. Bradwell Lodge was sold in the early 1970s and Driberg became Lord Bradwell of Bradwell Juxta Mare a few months before his death in 1976. On the way to St Peter's I pass The Cricketers pub, where Driberg used to sit towards the end of his life, pining after the pot boy to such a degree that he left him a portion of his estate after he died.

In the 1980s, writer and novelist Jonathan Raban chose the Dengie Peninsula to write his Falkands War-chronicling travelogue around the British Isles, *Coasting* (1986), renting a seventeenth-century farm labourers' cottage to write the book. *Coasting* documented Raban's adventures sailing around the British Isles, trying to find temporary respite from the populist warmongering emanating from the Palace of Westminster that was embraced by the tabloid press and espoused by armchair generals up and down the country in 1982, towards the end of the first term of Margaret Thatcher's government, during which she solidified popularity thanks in part to her sabre rattling.

The Dengie is 11,000 acres of reclaimed marshes, land won through struggle. What appealed to Raban about this amphibious Essex backwater – a marshy outpost ridden with malaria in Defoe's day, and lived in by 'bog people', the males of which were said to have multiple wives – was its ad-hoc nature, where cottages were built from the wreckages of ships. It was all decidedly un-English: 'When I moved in, it was like finding a neglected loophole in the English system... There were no braying gentry voices, no taint of dry sherry in the air after church on Sunday morning, none of the quashed and deferential manners which I had thought inseparable from English village life.'

In his 1974 book, *Soft City*, Jonathan Raban posited Victorian East London as an intricate city apart, armed with its own logic. Of social reformer and writer Henry Mayhew's groundbreaking study of the diverse segmentation of East Enders, *London Labour and the London Poor* (1851), Raban wrote: 'The people Mayhew saw were invincibly alien – untempted by the charms of evening institutes, self-help, union organisation or edifying tasks with missionary clergymen. They were pagan, superstitious, hostile and fatalist... spoke in a thieves' slang that sounded frighteningly like the beginning of some primitive foreign language.' Reading *Soft City* you can feel Raban, the son of a Church of England vicar, rejoicing in the renunciation of his stuffy and ordered public-school upbringing, finding another country within his own made up of outsider stock. His account of the cockneys of the East End presented them as an entirely more diverse and stratified band than popular lore suggests: 'a honeycomb mix of caste groups, each one circumscribed by the commodities in which it dealt, living in a state of thievish animosity towards a society of hostile others'. This wilful

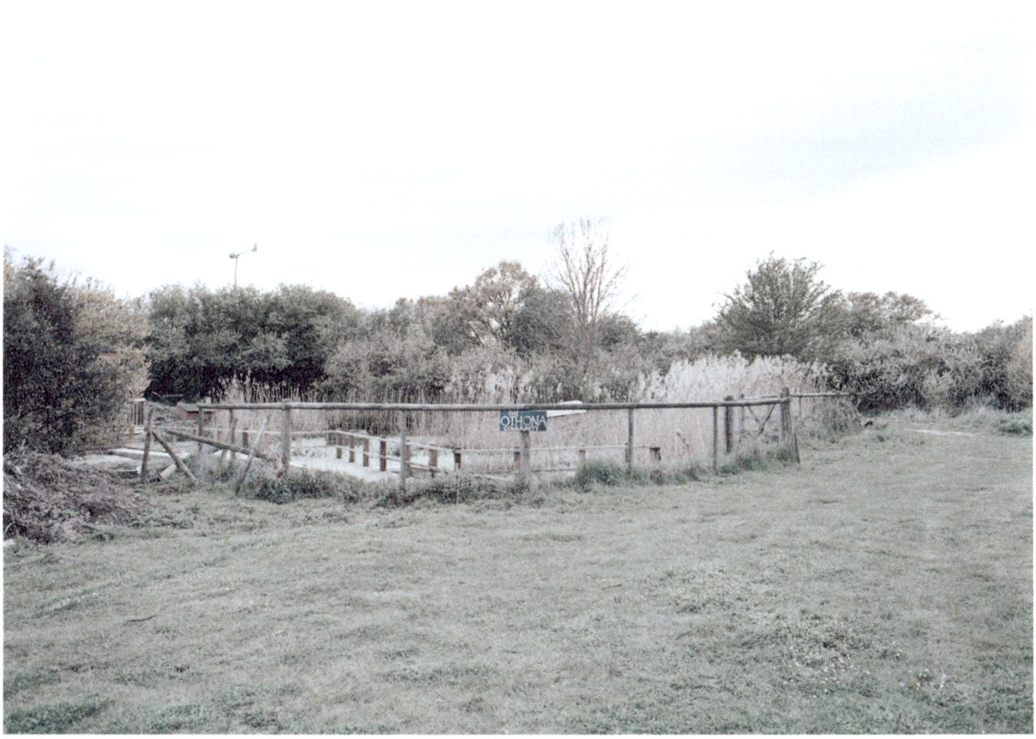

Othona Community, Bradwell-on-Sea

ignorance of the stultifying practices that made up British life fired Raban right up: the way that the Victorian cockney's position seemed 'dangerously indifferent to the systems of deference and order by which English society had been traditionally maintained'.

Essex was populated by this tribe of dangerous indifferents, in one way or another. Often the Londoner-into-Essex was working class. As a result, there is no other county in England that carries the weight of assumptions quite as readily as Essex. Nor is there one that is in quite as much need of reappraisal. To infer anything intellectual from the county has at times seemed like a radical act.

Gustav Holst wrote part of his orchestral suite *The Planets* (1914–16) in a 300-year-old cottage between two cornfields on top of a hill a few miles from Thaxted, north Essex. The village is where the Roding Valley begins its descent all the way to Barking on the Thames. The thatched-roofed Monk Street Cottage belonged to the writer S.L. Bensusan and dated back to 1614. Horses ambled between hedges where the A130 is now. 'It was the first time he had known what it felt like to be living in the depths of the country, where the everyday things that he had always taken for granted became suddenly transformed into matters of vital importance', wrote his daughter Imogen Holst in a biography of her father. 'Water had to be pumped, and when the rain-water butts were empty the sky would be anxiously scanned for clouds of the right shape. And when the rain fell, day after day, it would prove a calamity for having interfered with the hay-making or the harvest.'

Holst delighted in the 'quiet dignity' of Thaxted's fifteenth-century cottages. He had been a member of the Hammersmith Socialist Society, attending meetings at the house of William Morris when he was a twenty-one-year-old compositional student. The vicar of Thaxted Church was Conrad Noel, a socialist who organised folk dances on the village green and flew the red flag from the church spire to mark May Day.

Declared unfit to serve in the First World War, Holst put on a four-day festival of amateur music every Whitsun between 1916 and 1918 at Thaxted Church. He described the first event in a letter to a friend: 'It was a feast, an orgy. Four whole days of perpetual singing and playing, either properly arranged in the church or impromptu in various houses or still more impromptu in ploughed fields during thunderstorms, or in the train going home.'

In his book on the visionary music of Britain, *Electric Eden* (2010), Rob Young describes the first Whitsun event as 'the moment English music lost its inhibitions and erupted into a cascade of spontaneous music-making. In this remote village, Holst created a four-day temporary autonomous zone, an orgy of colour, music and movement on the village green, during which William Morris's desire for an art that would fill all corners of life and spill over into the common experience was realised.'

But Holst wasn't always treated with quite the same enthusiasm in return. At first, neighbours were suspicious at his solitary walking and his Germanic family name, Von Holst, and notified the police. 'Many rumours are current about this man, but nothing can be traced against him', read their report. Later Holst moved into Thaxted proper. 'The only sounds were the arguments of swallows at the end of the garden, and the clamour of ducks on the other side of the wall.' He remained connected to the village until his death in 1934.

Holst's perennially ominous and ireful *Mars, the Bringer of War* (1914) opened the 1950s BBC radio production of H.G. Wells's *War of the Worlds*. The works make a fitting pairing, and their creators were part of the same milieu. Wells was also known to attend the Hammersmith Socialist Society, and was a tenant of the left-wing patron of Conrad Noel,

Daisy, Countess of Warwick (Holst was also a tenant of the countess, some years after Wells).

As one of this publication's contributors Rachel Lichtenstein points out in her book, *Estuary* (2016), the Essex coast features in Wells's alien invasion story. He describes the panicked rush of people eastwards from alien attacks in London and the Home Counties to Southend and Shoeburyness. As the enormous throng of escapees gathered on the shoreline, the Martians advanced towards them: 'the low Essex coast was growing blue and hazy, when a Martian appeared, small and faint in the remote distance, advancing along the muddy coast from the direction of Foulness [...] Then, far away beyond the Crouch, came another, striding over some stunted trees, and then yet another, still farther off, wading deeply through a shiny mudflat that seemed to hang halfway up between sea and sky. They were all stalking seaward, as if to intercept the escape of the multitudinous vessels that were crowded between Foulness and the Naze.'

It has been written, in Todd Kuchta's *Semi-Detached Empire* (2010) and elsewhere, that Wells's terrifying and fantastical vision of the despoliation and destruction wrought by his fictional Martians had roots in his preoccupation with the very real suburban developments blanketing the South East. As a child, Wells reeled from the destruction of some of his much-loved rural surroundings in Bromley in Kent; later on he posited in a paper to the Fabian Society that the railways were creating a new type of 'delocalised' person who was bleeding dry the old ways of life: 'Every tramway, every new twopenny tube, every light railway, every improvement in your omnibus services [...] increases the proportion of your delocalised class, and sucks the ebbing life from your old communities into the veins of the new.'

In some ways this was the fate of Essex commuter towns and designer villages, with their mobile coffee vendors and Marks and Spencers placed near the station. The tensions coursing through Essex could be said to be between the bohemian, or even utilitarian, bucolic fantasist and the onset of modernity in the form of suburban developments and the wires and pipes attached to them, characterised as creeping into Essex from the capital like tentacles from some alien life form.

Great Bardfield was protected from becoming a commuter town when Edward Bawden and Eric Ravilious came to look around it as a potential place to start an artist colony, as it didn't have a bus or train service. In 1931, the two Royal College of Art design school alumni cycled there from Great Dunmow. Bawden grew up in Braintree and they settled on Essex as they wanted to avoid the mountainous landscapes that had been done to death by the Romantics. Essex, on the other hand, had not. They started the colony at Brick House in Great Bardfield, which had no gas, no electricity, no drains, no indoor toilets and no piped water.

The artists were attracted to the rugged nature of rural life, but part of the reason for decamping to Essex was financial. A familiar process: the metropolis empties of artists who can no longer afford its resource-sucking embrace. Studio space was cheaper, air was cleaner, and the city – where careers were tended to – not that far.

The Bawdens and the Raviliouses gardened and played and swam together. There was a sort of realism, a making do, in their work. An exploration of the delights of the everyday, of the muted, of the sometimes overlooked and the plain forgotten. Artist and writer Thomas Hennell was a presence at Brick House after he stopped off there en route to Suffolk for a rest and was told he could wash in the kitchen. He made watercolour illustrations that depicted country trades in light of mechanisation. Artist Tirzah Garwood, wife of Eric Ravilious, also made work, including wood engravings displaying kitchen scenes and pubs.

Eventually the Bawden–Ravilious arrangement faltered. The Raviliouses moved to Castle Hedingham in 1934. But Great Bardfield was making a name for itself. The artist John Aldridge moved there, to the annoyance of the Bawdens as he constituted a threat to their hold on the place. Art as marking territory. Aldridge bought Place House in the village, which attracted its own bohemian visitors, and he and Tirzah Garwood became lovers.

During the Second World War the house took in German refugees and men fleeing from the Spanish Civil War; evacuees came to the village. Bawden and Ravilious became official war artists, the former posted to France and the Middle East. Aldridge and Hennell also went to war. Michael Rothenstein, the creator of lively and savage prints inspired by the Essex countryside, was too ill to serve, so took part in the project Recording Britain, which documented the country's landscape before a feared flattening by the Luftwaffe.

In 1942 Eric Ravilious's aircraft disappeared off the Icelandic coast during an air-sea rescue mission at dawn to find an RAF aircraft lost the day before. Hennell never came back to Great Bardfield either: he was killed in Indonesia in 1945. Bawden survived, and after the war contributed a great asset to the documentation of rural Essex living in the form of the sixteen lithographs that make up *Life in an English Village*, published in 1949. A contributor to this book, Gillian Darley, noted in the *London Review of Books* that one of the strengths of village life was to show 'public spirit in any common effort', but the 'touching of caps' was over and so too was the boredom and the 'rheumatism from damp floors'. Noel Carrington's introduction to Bawden's *Life in an English Village* argued, somewhat optimistically, 'that the village "cannot remain for the benefit of the tourist a shell of its vanished social life. The agricultural engineer cannot be housed in the village smithy".'

The story of another example of communal artistic living in Essex, Tilty Mill house near Great Dunmow, shows the potential outfall of the bohemian dreams. The photographer Christopher Barker has detailed his unconventional upbringing. His father was the poet George Barker, who was championed by his patron T.S. Eliot. He frequently disappeared from the family abode for weeks on end after tempestuous rows with Barker's mother, the Ottawa-born writer Elizabeth Smart. 'Typically, every Friday my mother would trawl the watering holes of Soho, gathering a weekend party for our tumbledown house', he wrote in an essay for *Granta*. He went on to comment, 'This photo celebrates a fine catch – my father.'

Barker's analysis of his upbringing in 1950s Essex is withering at times. His parents' milieu was often where bohemianism met alcoholism. On the poet Paul Potts: 'Often a figure of fun as he grew older, he would eventually be barred from Soho pubs for incontinence as he bummed his drinks.' On the half-blind poet John Heath-Stubbs: 'much later I watched [him] fumble with a curtain in a pub for ten minutes before I realised he was trying to find the door.'

Tilty Mill had no electricity; it was lit by oil lamps. George contributed nothing financially to the family, and so Elizabeth took a job as a copywriter in London, caught between the two poles of Soho, where she conversed with artists Frank Auerbach, Lucian Freud and Francis Bacon, and the Essex countryside where she raised a family. Barker and his brother and two sisters were often looked after by 'the two Roberts' Colquhoun and MacBryde, the Scottish painters involved in the neo-Romantic movement that loved William Blake and was filled with young gay men. Barker dreamed of a hungry wolf howling across the Essex countryside when the two Roberts had their inevitable rows after they had been to the local pub The Rising Sun: 'Ye snivin' shite, I'll faaak'n keel ye!'

Barker eventually wrote a book about his and his siblings' upbringing, partly to unpick a disdain for his father that was baked into a childhood of explosive, violent rows and blatant affairs (George Barker had fifteen children with four different women). In 1982, Barker's youngest sister Rose died of an

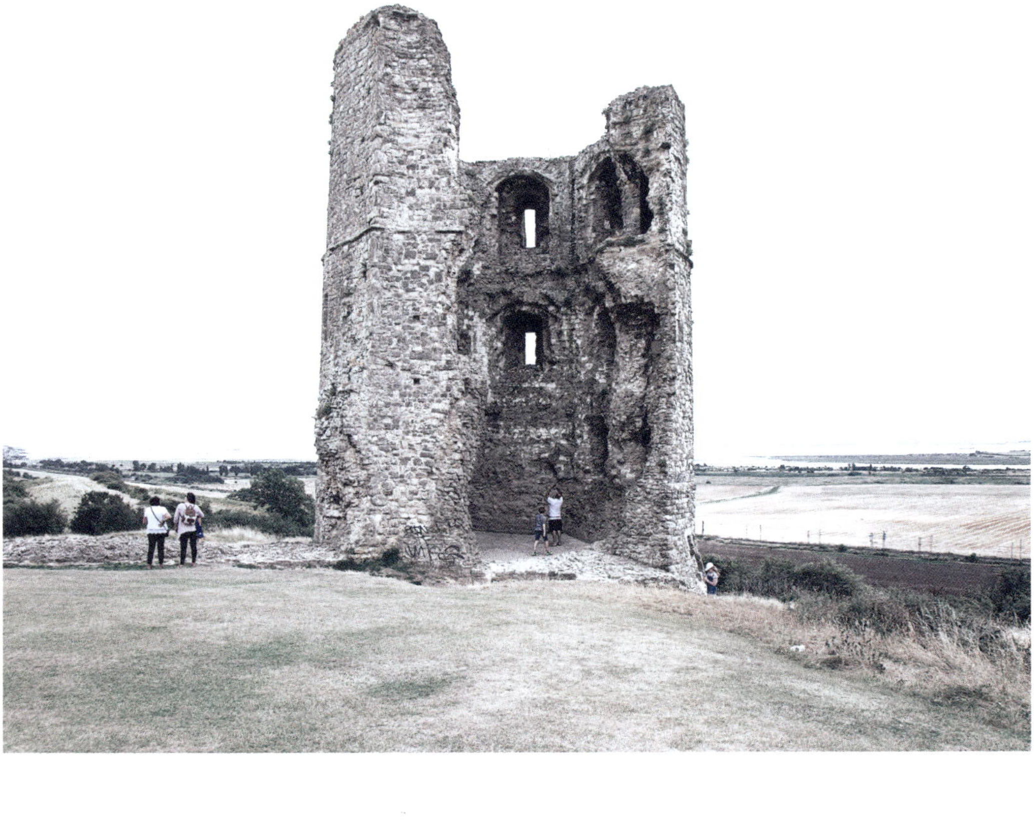

Hadleigh Castle, Hadleigh

accidental paracetamol overdose after years of drug addiction, a habit she had formed on trips to Soho with Elizabeth. When Barker entered the operating theatre to view the body, his father declined to join him.

The two Roberts were notable kilted additions to the carousel of Denis Wirth-Miller and Richard 'Dicky' Chopping's Soho drinking pals in the 1940s and 50s. Six decades later in 2005, when Denis was 90 and Dicky wasn't far off, they became one of country's first civil partnerships on the first day it was legal. They had spent the majority of their years together in Wivenhoe in north Essex, moving there over two decades before such relationships were decriminalised.

Chopping was born in Colchester. The Bloomsbury Group fired his imagination, the stories of experimentation in literary form as much as in sexual relationships. He longed for the bohemian, the radical; he found it in London and then took it back to Essex in 1944 when he moved to Wivenhoe with the more forthright Denis, who had worked in Walter Sickert's studio. Chopping designed the front covers of Ian Fleming's James Bond novels; Denis painted landscapes. Always smartly attired in this old shipbuilding town, the latter painted estuarial paintings depicting the shifting light and beguiling marshland of this corner of the Colne. Their friend Francis Bacon visited and later took residence in Wivenhoe.

The explosiveness of Denis and Dicky's relationship became the stuff of legend. Sue, owner of Wivenhoe Bookshop tells me there are stories of one of them chasing the other with a knife down the street where they lived. They were barred from every pub in Wivenhoe before dementia and death enveloped them. They lived a glamorous life of temper and promiscuity offset by a deep love.

Modernity struck Essex hard in the twentieth century. Marconi established the first regular radio broadcasting company in the world on Valentine's Day in 1922 in a humble hut in Writtle, near Chelmsford. In Southend in 1926, Eric Cole set up EKCO, to manufacture radio devices with cutting-edge techniques and rounded, modernist design from Wells Coates, made from Bakelite and exported all around the world.

Silver End saw a sea of white-painted flat-roofed houses set back behind front gardens in wide, tree-lined streets built over 220 acres of farmland, when Crittall Windows expanded from Braintree to this unpopulated place on the way to Witham in the 1920s. People came from all over to Silver End for work. Indoor bathrooms and toilets and all the electricity you needed. It had the lowest death rate and highest birth rate in England for its first decade. During the Second World War the factory put Crittall Windows into sea forts and manufactured parts for Bailey bridges to be erected around Europe, and after the war the company employed people who had been injured and had lost arms and legs.

The whole place was built to work in a self-sufficient manner. People didn't need to leave. They grew produce on their allotments. There were flower shows, knitting, cakes. There was a print works and newspaper, a dancehall and a cinema, and the pride of the village, the Silver End department store. The store had two entrances, with pillars and big windows that displayed furniture and drapery. The store housed chemists, offices, a post office, bakery counter, sweet counter, tobacco counter, provisions, grocers, green grocers, butchery. It was destroyed by a fire in 1952. Steel girders were 'twisted like putty'.

The Crittall dream is over, but its architectural traces still survives. The village hall, where Radical ESSEX's ESSEX Architecture Weekend took place, is the largest in the UK. Its hotel – now a care home – had the 'longest bar' in Essex. Poplars line the path to the large property once lived in by 'the guv'nor' Francis Henry Crittall. The former warden's office is also a care home. Preservation orders keep Silver End largely in architectural check.

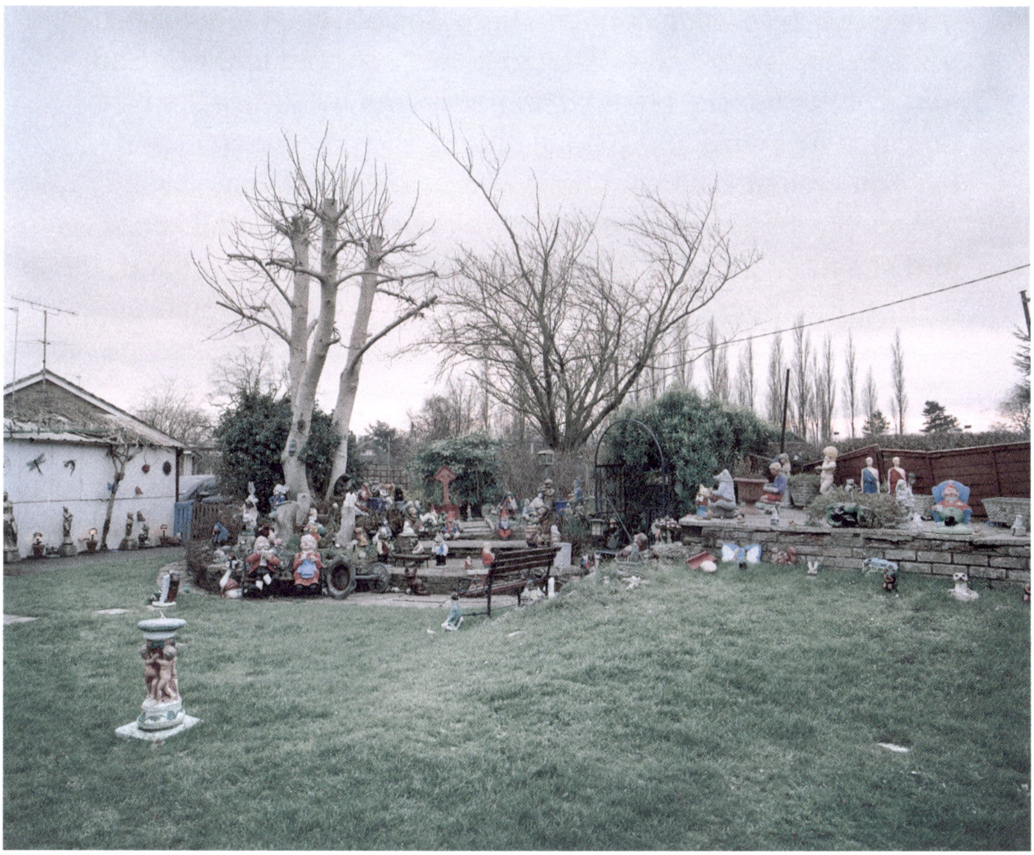

Garden Gnomes in Silver End

The clean lines of East Tilbury's modernist estate were built at the behest of Czech shoe magnate Tomas Bata to house workers at the local shoe factory. The effect of walking around it feels even more incongruous than Silver End's somehow quainter and self-contained rows of boxes, in that it was built against the backdrop of these numinous Thames marshlands. Bata had a line in utopian Fordism, caring for his workers (in order to make them more productive). And they loved it, by all accounts. There was a Bata supermarket, a Bata shoe shop and a Bata farm that supplied bacon, eggs and milk for guests' breakfasts at the Bata hotel. Leisure was provided by tennis and netball courts, a swimming pool and full-size football pitches. There was an espresso bar, which opened in 1963 complete with a coffee machine and jukebox, and scooters and motorbikes lined up outside.

East European migration to Essex did not stop at Bata's foothold here. After the war, the RAF army base at Rivenhall near Silver End became home to a Polish camp, which housed Poles, Czechs and other East Europeans displaced by the war. 'Over the years the Poles gradually became integrated into the East Anglian scene, marrying local girls and working alongside Essex workers in fields and factories', wrote local historian B.A. Stait. 'Some families emigrated to the Colonies with government assistance and a number returned to Poland. By the mid 1950s the process of integration had been so successful that the need for the Polish Camp disappeared entirely and it was finally closed down.'

Families lived in Nissen huts provided with electricity and running water. 'The relative isolation and "ready-made" camp infrastructure created for these people an illusion of a tiny Polish state, nestled within a benevolent but alien English landscape. It was a welcome and largely happy little world for people who had been through a good deal during the war', recalled Kaz Janowski whose family lived at the Kelvedon camp near Silver End.

Essex has long been a place that people can find a home of sorts. I had a correspondence with a Royal College of Art student, Isabel Taube, who told me her Estonian grandfather is believed to have arrived at Tilbury in 1946. 'He spent nearly all his life in Essex, living in a house overlooking West Mersea and the marshes', she said. 'Estonia has a high concentration of bog land and its flatness is reminiscent of Essex in so many ways.'

Tilbury, of course, is where the SS Empire Windrush docked in 1948. Lord Kitchener performed for an insistent Pathé news journalist: 'London is the place for me', he now famously sang. 'London, this lovely city.' The Windrush carried under 500 migrants from the Caribbean, but as a symbolic moment, the perceived marker the UK became multicultural, it might as well have held 500,000. Yet twenty years after the Windrush arrived at Tilbury, the port's dockers marched to Westminster in support of Enoch Powell's Rivers of Blood speech. Elsa James, a Southend-based artist, has made work resurrecting forgotten stories of black people in Essex. One of the protagonists is Princess Dinubolu of Senegal. After being barred from a beauty contest in Great Yarmouth in 1908, Dinubolu sent a telegram from there to Mr Bacon, manager of the Kursaal amusement park in Southend. 'Have you a rule barring me? I am light chocolate', the telegram read. 'Don't enter. Local prejudice', read the curt reply from Mr Bacon. The Kursaal manager was put off, reported the *Standard*, by the scarring memory of a baby show at the Kursaal. 'One of the competitors was a black ugly little nigger', Bacon flatly told the *Evening Standard* in London. 'I permitted the entry. Nobody could dream it was likely to win.' But the baby did win. The prize was judged on audience reaction and the crowd at the Kursaal whooped hardest for the infant of colour. 'It came out right on top and for weeks afterwards I was absolutely mobbed whenever I went out: "Why couldn't you give the prize to a baby of your own colour? What do you mean by it? How could you dare?"' Bacon passed the decision of whether

Dinubolu would be allowed to enter and, in August, she did so. But she didn't win, and James isn't even sure if Dinubolu was a princess – but these details aren't the point. In pursuing beauty on her own terms, in an atmosphere of violent monoculture, Dinubolu's story is held up as an early example of black resistance. 'Princess Dinubolu, you did not win the Southend beauty show, but I know you were strong, witty and confident', says James in her video work. 'Princess Dinubolu, I salute you.' That the idea of a 'black Essex' still feels a somehow radical addition to the region's cultural zeitgeist tells its own story of demographic and generational tensions, betraying the Essex of white flight and fear of immigrants. Yet twenty-first century Essex is neither the racist enclave reported by some nor some kind of harmonious utopia. Essex is disparate, conflicted and up for grabs. But the pertinent truth is the lives of Essex people of colour are still under-represented in the arts, and in the press and politics at large. This must, and surely will, change.

Wivenhoe musician and writer Martin Newell knew Denis and Dicky and met Francis Bacon once or twice. 'The marsh light is very good, it's always attracted artists. The light and the birds and the flatness imbues the place with something which there is probably a name for in German.'

Newell calls himself the 'wild man of Wivenhoe'. He has written and published thousands of poems, stories, articles, songs about the area he has lived in since the mid 1970s. He has been befriended by the hip, avant-garde cassette crowd of the US, artists such as Mac DeMarco and Ariel Pink, who create a woozy and febrile bedroom music in a similar way as Newell did in the 1980s, depicting Wivenhoe with an ad hoc impressionistic approach.

'I'm renting a room, you can see the moon in the factory yard at night', he sings on the wistful *Wivenhoe Bells* (1980);

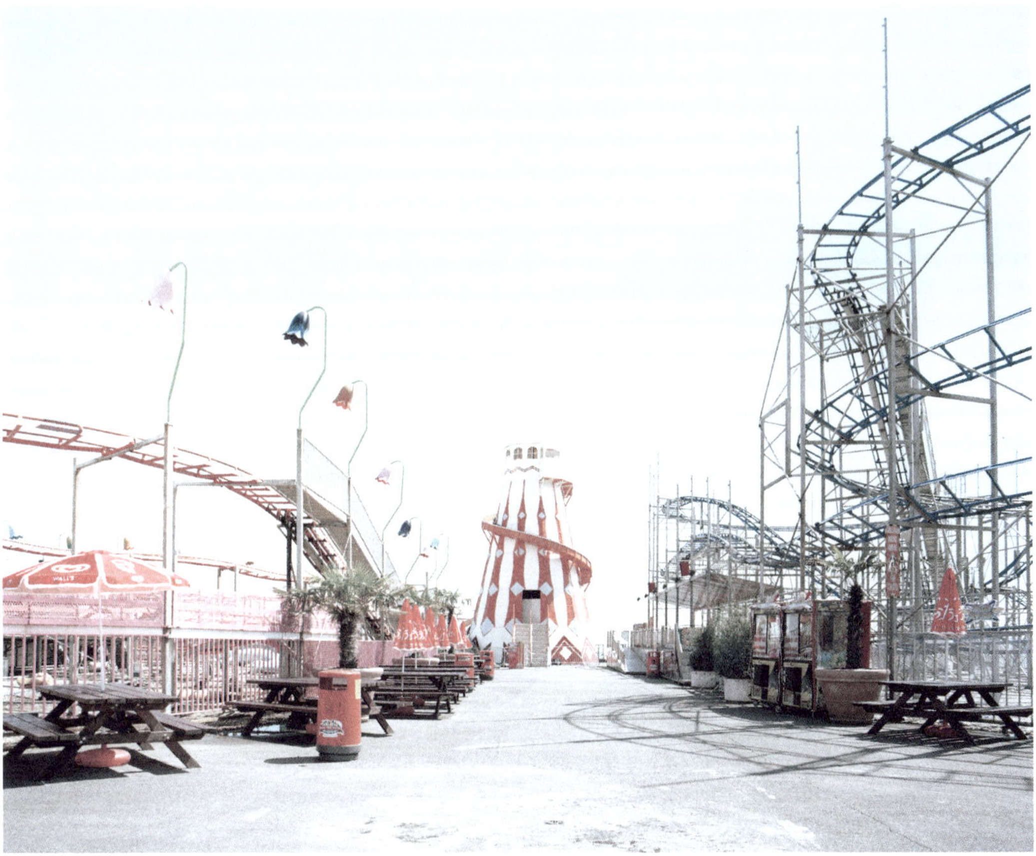

Clacton Pier Amusements, Clacton-on-Sea

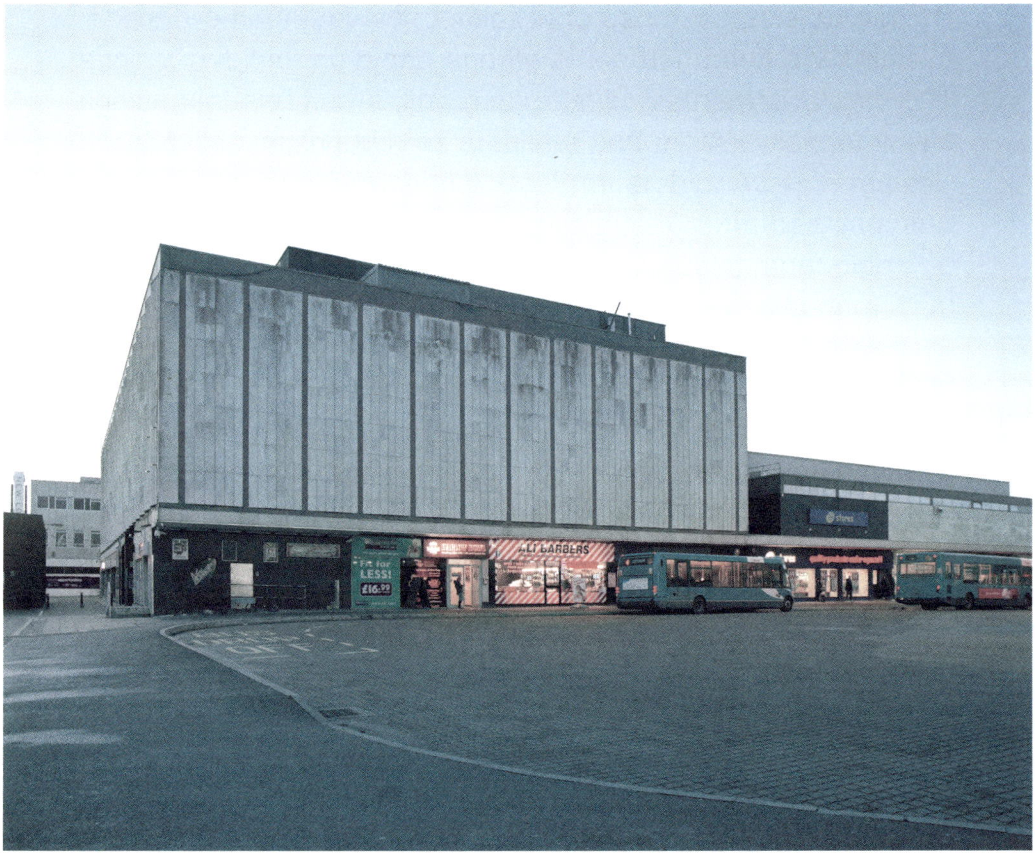

Harlow

a soaring, infectious vocal over an old out-of-tune piano and steady beat: 'Terraced houses very near the railway, hear Sunday church bells.' The song documents time spent in a room overlooking the old Wivenhoe dockyard from his flat. 'It was a working town when I first got here: there were docks, there was a fishing fleet and there was a shipyard', Newell tells me. 'And then there was the farmers. They've really thinned away now, they have.'

When Newell moved to Wivenhoe, 'it was very much still a village then. You had to play dommies in the bottom bar of The Station Hotel before they even acknowledged you. It was all run by old families.' Newell still sees Essex as wilderness – 'It's 70 per cent rural' – but laments London using it 'as a dumping ground'. In recent years he's noticed the influx of Londoners moving from the capital to start families. 'They've built an estate where my old flat by the docks used to be and it's full of people doing "wild writing" courses. They're all right but the place is a little less punchy. They are being forced out because the oligarchs bought the posh bits and the people who couldn't afford that bought in Southwold and the people who couldn't afford that came here.'

Newell tells me how on 16 August 1960, The Beatles left Harwich for Hamburg. He emails me a picture of the group's first manager Allan Williams's Commer van being hoisted by crane onto the ferry at Parkeston Quay. The Fab Four's Hamburg trip is a crucial part of British pop mythology. That the Essex coast is the site of this famous departure into a coming of age myth is fitting. In Essex, the pop boom happened off shore, in the form of the pirate radio ships such as Radio Caroline off Harwich, Radio London off Frinton and Radio Luxembourg in the Thames Estuary.

Some years after the band's return and subsequent explosion, Jean-Luc Godard's *British Sounds* (1969) depicted University of Essex students doctoring lyrics to The Beatles's *Hello, Goodbye* and *Revolution* to make them more aggressive and political, adding lines about Mao and Nixon and Ho Chi

Minh, and discussing the reactionary qualities of Paul McCartney's 1920s-indebted *Honey Pie*. University of Essex was one of the first to value social sciences. When Enoch Powell was invited in 1968 by the Essex student Conservative Association, one student recalled, an anarchist placed a black-painted grapefruit with a candle stuck in it on the lectern at the front of the hall. The Conservative students panicked, perhaps mistaking it for a bomb, and plunged it into water, while Powell was escorted from the building.

Godard opens *British Sounds*, a Marxist polemic paid for by London Weekend Television (LWT), at Dagenham's Ford plant, and in one of its most effective scenes the workers at the plant are seen describing working conditions. The film closes proclaiming solidarity with the masses and the strikers at Dagenham against the 'fascist laws of Barbara the scab' over a montage of fists punching through the Union Jack flag. Disappointingly but unsurprisingly, LWT shelved it.

The avant-garde sound poet Henri Chopin moved to Essex after the failure of the student uprisings in Paris in May 1968, moving to Ingatestone, between Chelmsford and Brentwood. He was born in Paris in 1922, and was deported to Germany in 1943 by the Nazis but repatriated and ended up fighting against them. Chopin lived in my hometown of Leigh-on-Sea during the early 1980s. The death of his wife Jean Ratcliffe-Chopin spurred a return to his native France in 1985, the same year my family moved there from neighbouring Southend when I was a young baby.

Focal Point Gallery has exhibited an archive invite for a 1971 event from when Chopin lived at Ingatestone:

HENRI ET JEAN chopin
INVITE you
to
INGATESTONE essex
station lane
the gate house.

OFF THE A12 NEAR CHELMSFORD
OR BY TRAIN from LIVERPOOL STREET STATION.

The invite promised a 'living museum' filled with 'NEW LANGUAGES, SENSORIAL and ELECTRONIC REVIEWS – PUBLICATIONS for this century' and promised appearances by a roll call of the literary avant-garde: Brion Gysin, William Burroughs (who called Chopin an 'inner space explorer') and Raoul Hausmann, who all contributed to Chopin's avant-garde music publication *Revue OU*. Chopin published works by Burroughs from Ingatestone. As with Dial House, the Epping anarchist open house synonymous with Penny Rimbaud and Crass, here was a muted, forgotten semi-rural corner of the county utilised to make culture from the outside in.

'People are people so why should it be / You and I should get along so awfully' Depeche Mode, *People Are People* (1984)

Before her first Top of the Pops performance with Yazoo, Alison Moyet went to Basildon Market. Vince Clarke had asked her to form the duo with him after he left the initial Basildon synth-pop hitmakers Depeche Mode with no little acrimony. A few years ago I talked to Moyet about it for an interview I conducted for the *Daily Telegraph*. 'My mum lent me 20 quid and I bought the cheapest fabric I could find and my mate who was on the dole whipped me up a dress from a sewing machine', she said. 'That's what I wore on the show.'

Watching the footage of that first show today, it's obvious how unprepared she is for fame: just laughing at the start of the performance of breakthrough single *Only You*, coming in on the second line. She hadn't seen any money from her new stardom yet; she was still living on pocket money at home. But she soon bosses the stage and the screen, tapping into her 'Alf' persona already carved on the pub rock circuit stages of The Greyhound, the Vortex, The Hope and Anchor, the Marquee and Dingwalls. 'I still had an opportunity to use the pub rock blues singing that I was doing while I was at college, there was a band called The Screamin' Ab Dabs and we supported Dr Feelgood with Wilko Johnson and stuff like that – that was the musical area that I was moving in, that Thames Delta kind of vibe.'

The Basildon set were tight, and Moyet already knew Depeche Mode's Dave Gahan, Martin Gore and Andy Fletcher. 'Dave was a market boy, a cheeky chappy, so to see the band then so coiffed was a quite a surprise – we were all boracic, just local people, so that was interesting. Seeing anyone come from your background and do well is confusing and wonderful at the same time. It is really weird, you are seeing your schoolmates on the television but at the same time you're thinking there is possibility, there were things that you can do without exams from school, from our background. You don't expect it and it's good to see.'

Looking back, Yazoo were a fascinating cultural proposition: ephemeral yet solid, twinkling, self-taught synths allied with a butch blues-trained vocal emanating from a striking frontwoman in Basildon Market fabrics but achieving long-term pop worth. According to Moyet the experience wasn't the warmest she's had in music. When she joined Yazoo, Clarke still seemed an unknown quantity to her, the boy who went to the school they used to fight with across town. And he was still smarting from leaving Depeche Mode. Clarke had already earned his position as a pop enigma in the pages of the music press principally by not being that happy to talk to them, and so press duties fell to Moyet.

'There's something about being a pop star that unmans you. Coming from Basildon, being the kind of person I was, I did become very strong. I found it very easy to square up to people, I wasn't intimidated, I had this supernatural braveness. I grew up in a peasant family, I never had a dress, never had dolls – we were taught to mend and to fix and to build. I was hard', she said. 'In Basildon we were all brought up on council estates. There wasn't a big history of home ownership. Funnily enough my parents bought a council house in Laindon [later on] but it wasn't as good as the council house they had before. There was a greater sense of community in Basildon and when people did start to leave I was absolutely gutted. When I was in Yazoo I still lived in Basildon but it got to the point when my milkman used to bring people round. "Go on then, tell 'em who you are", while you are in your nightgown and your eyes are bleary at 7am.'

In the end Moyet had to leave the pressure-cooker environment of her hometown, swapping Basildon for Hertfordshire, where pop stars move to (at least they move there more than they do Basildon). The Essex I know is built on a two-way desire for escape; the escape from London by the cockney pioneers, and the escape of their ancestors back to London for work.

It could be said that it is the Essex plotlands at places like Canvey, Laindon and Jaywick that most offered glimpses of freedom. Since the mid-nineteenth century, farming had declined in Essex to a crippling degree after bad harvests and the advent of American grain and New Zealand meat leading many farms to ruin. The land around what is now Basildon – Laindon, Langdon Hills, Dunton, Vange, Pitsea – was sold off plot by plot to make way for dream homes away from the city in the form of little more than shacks. Looking back from an atrophied twenty-first century vantage point, the Essex plotland years seem to have played host to a kind of anarchy.

During their heyday, plotlands acted as a much-needed verdant open external space, a literal relief to the grimy conditions of slum-living cockneys. The railways made the area accessible for weekend trippers, areas with such names as Gumboot Hill; Dodge City. But they were seen as unruly by the authorities: tens of thousands of people started new lives there, without sewers or proper roads or running water. Of course it could not last. Following the plotlands was the New Town of Basildon, which came into being in 1949. The emblem of Basildon's first residents' association was a pioneer wagon. 'People who came thought there was something to aspire to in Basildon', said Eric Moonman, MP for Basildon between 1975 and 1979. 'They could do more, better and faster. It was like a little bit of America in Essex.'

I grew up in south Essex, in suburbia built over field, marsh and forest. The weight of assumptions around Essex is what makes the act of scrubbing them away so necessary. It's there as other to London; it's there as an escape valve, alleviating the pressure, creating a tension between the real Essex of the rural towns and villages and the interloper, the scene-stealer, in the form of the urbanisation of the county emanating from London. Such bleeding of the metropolitan into bucolic Essex provoked horror when places such as Dagenham and Canvey Island grew as suburbs during the nineteenth and twentieth centuries, and there is part of the painfully sluggish, wilfully obstructive, British mindset that still doesn't fully acknowledge these places as part of its own.

There is a pervasive myth of the lost Essex idyll, corrupted by the leaking of housing for aspirational or desperate Londoners. Essex culture is tied up with modernisation: much of it would be under water were it not for reinforced concrete walls, or the draining techniques such as practised by the Dutch on Canvey Island, for example, centuries ago. Subsequent modernisations brought with them street after street of comfortable housing – but of course this created a feeling that something sacred was lost in the triumph of functional living.

The writer S.L. Bensusan used visits to the Dengie to document how the Essex countryman received the influx of London writers and artists in his book *Back of Beyond: A Countryman's Pre-War Commonplace Book* (1946): 'Now the countryman has his village and nothing else; those who

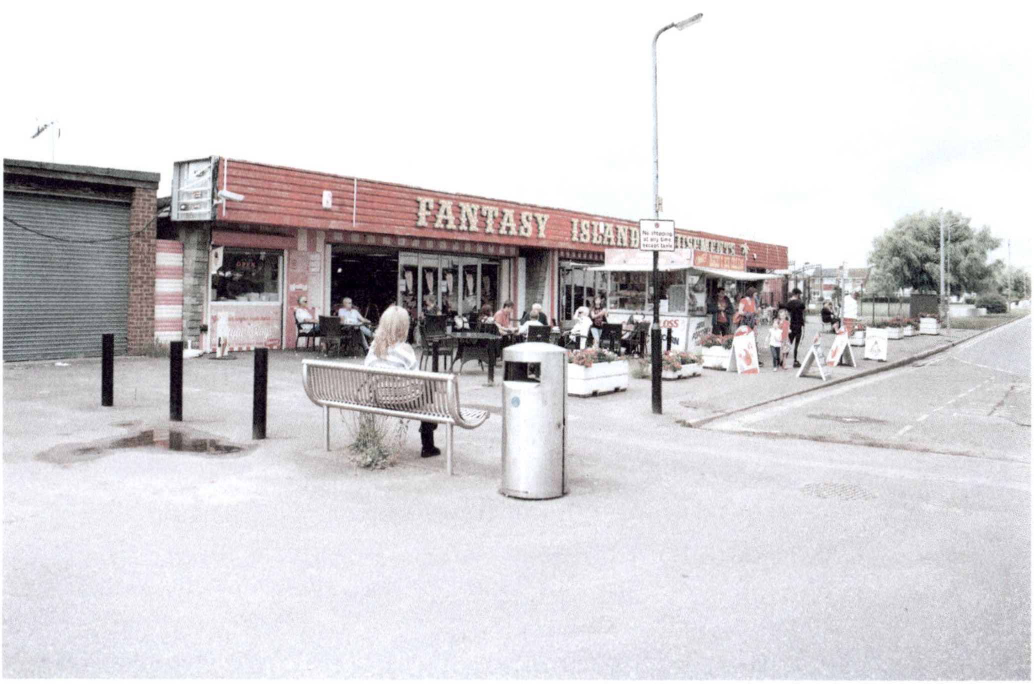

Fantasy Island Amusements, Canvey Island

were here when he could first take notice are in a sense his brethren; those who came a little later may be taken on sufferance; late arrivals are intruders upon his privacy, aliens, suspects, "furriners".'

A London-born writer with bylines in *Vanity Fair* and *Illustrated London News*, Bensusan settled in Essex for a time, using the remoteness of country life as inspiration for his *Marshland* series. Bensusan's encounter with a villager was instructive to the way he saw trade-off between rural Essex and London. '"We don't go where other folk belong", said one candid old countryman to me in the early days of my sojourn in his village, when I protested mildly against his suggestions that I had come down from "Lunnon" to get away from the policeman on duty there. "An' we don't want that other folk should come where we belong", he went on. "Tain't seemly."'

Bensusan had previously written a book about Morocco, and compared the countryman's desire for privacy to the Moroccan need for sacred ceremony. 'In parts of Morocco before the French occupation no white man could venture, there were towns in the Atlas and even in more accessible parts that were called sacred. There are in other lands ceremonies that no stranger may witness. Our country men have no sacred cities, no secret ceremonies but they will keep very quiet indeed about certain customs; the stranger within their gates may have no part in them.'

Bensusan's idea of the sacred is an important one when looking at the changing face of Essex. A century's increase in communications and transportation extracts context from land and in its place imbues locality with a sense of deferring to the elsewhere. Much of Essex is ambiguous, in-between. Townies in exile in the not-quite countryside. Suburbanites with roots in the East End. Old Essex farming families whose businesses petered out after the kids got jobs in 'The City' and moved into a gated community in a zhuzhed up Essex village, half lives haunting suburban-marshland collisions.

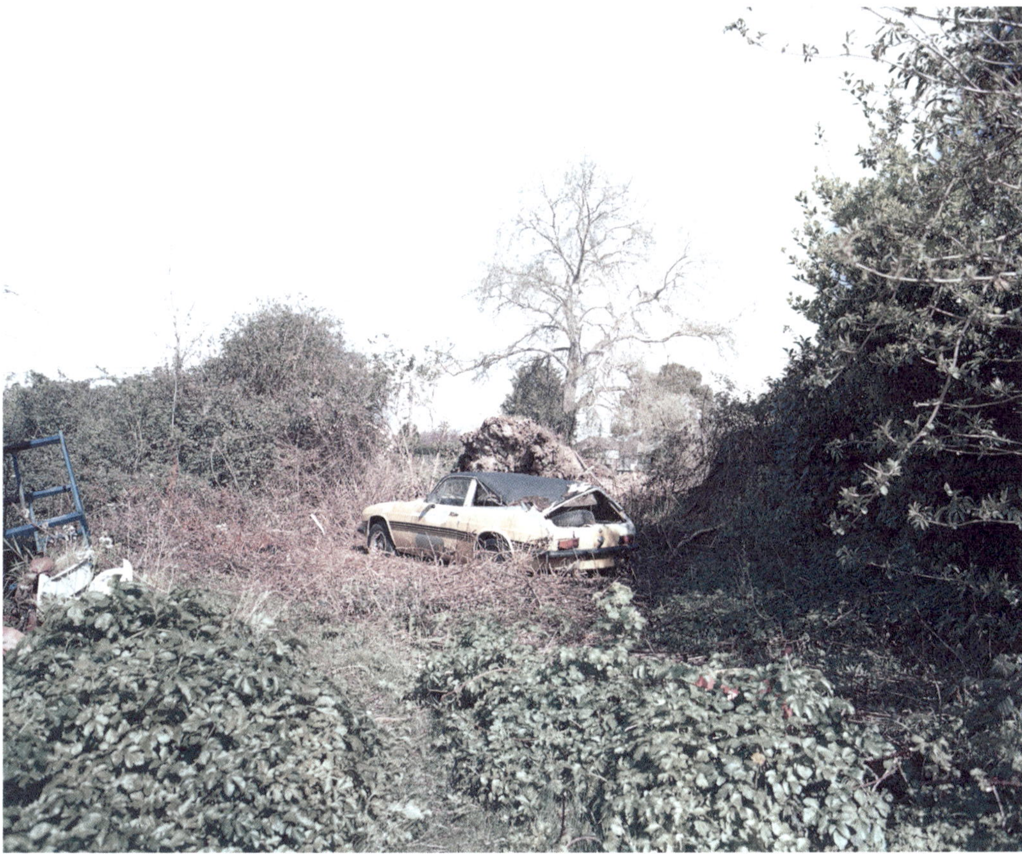

An Essex Roadside

After the Radical Writing Retreat dinner in Bradwell had finished, Joe Hill, Director of Southend's Focal Point Gallery, offered me a lift to South Woodham Ferrers, where I was staying that evening. As we drove through the darkness of the Dengie, at a bend alongside a hedge, we passed an overturned car. It was just left there, as if its owner had parked it like that and left for a night's kip.

The rural car wreckage is as much an Essexian site as the meticulously shambling vistas of 'Constable country'. Joyrides that were only ever going to end one way: abandoned boy-racer miscalculations. I have read in recent months that the number of arson attacks on cars in Essex rose by thirty-four per cent from 2015 to 2016, a figure more than twice the national average.

'To invent the sailing ship or the steamer is to invent the shipwreck', wrote Paul Virilio. 'To invent the train is to invent the rail accident of derailment. To invent the family automobile is to produce the pile-up on the highway.' Or to invent the solitary Essex country lane is to invent the automobile wreckage that will inevitably inhabit it. It reverses the once sacred myth of the filthy city. It is said that modern London, with its gleaming financial sectors and privatised public space, has been cleansed of its grime and grit, its danger and deviance. But here in the out of the way, forgotten places of Essex, a wantonness still exhales.

TIM BURROWS writes about culture and place for publications including the *Guardian*, *Somesuch Stories* and the *Quietus*. A recurring subject in his work is Essex. His short story *Broadgate*, set between the county's marshland and the City of London, is included in the anthology *An Unreliable Guide to London* (2016), published by Influx Press, which also published his long-form essay on the Essex Thames Estuary, *Going Back Home* (2014). He is currently working on a non-fiction book about the county.

FURTHER READING

Christopher Barker, 'Life at Tilty Mill', *Granta 80: The Group*, 1 January 2003

Edward Bawden, *Life in an English Village* (Penguin 1949)

S.L. Bensusan and H. Cranmer-Byng, *Essex Plays* (Benham 1933)

S.L. Bensusan, *Back of Beyond, A Countryman's Pre-War Commonplace Book* (Blandford 1945)

Walter Besant, *East London* (Chatto & Windus 1901)

Gillian Darley, 'Essex, 1951', *London Review of Books*, 18 July 2017

Imogen Holst, *Gustav Holst: A Biography* (Oxford University Press 1958)

Kaz Janowski, 'Memories of a Happy Childhood in Kelvedon Camp', www.polishresettlementcampsintheuk.co.uk, accessed 16 December 2017

Todd Kuchta, *Semi-Detached Empire: Suburbia and the Colonization of Britain* (The University of Virginia Press 2010)

Rachel Lichtenstein, *Estuary: Out From London to the Sea* (Hamish Hamilton 2016)

Henry Mayhew, *London Labour and the London Poor*, 1849–50 (Penguin 1985)

Jonathan Raban, *Coasting* (The Harvill Press 1986)

Jonathan Raban, *Soft City* (The Harvill Press 1974)

B.A. Stait, *Rivenhall: The History of an Essex Airfield* (Alan Sutton Publishing 1984)

Francis Wheen, *Tom Driberg: His Life and Indiscretions* (Chatto & Windus 1990)

Ken Worpole and Jason Orton, *The New English Landscape* (Field Station 2013)

Rob Young, *Electric Eden: Unearthing Britain's Visionary Music* (Faber 2010)

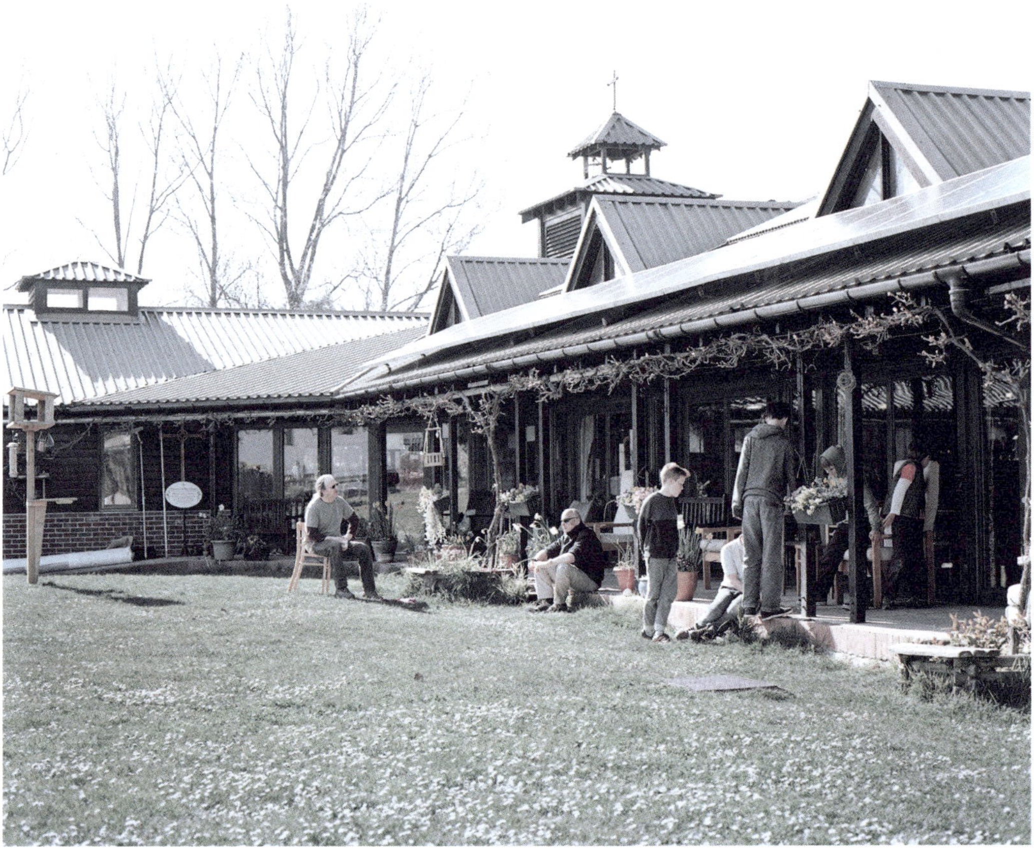

Oth◇na C◇mmunity, Bradwell-on-Sea

The Road to Othona

Communitarian Settlements in Essex 1880–2018

Ken Worpole

NOTHING GOES TO WASTE

The Othona Community, a seemingly improvised settlement hidden in a small woodland copse on the flat arable Dengie Peninsula in Essex, shelters on reclaimed land close to where the Blackwater Estuary meets the North Sea. Established by RAF padre, Norman Motley, in 1946 as a religious retreat – a place where British and German Christians could meet in a spirit of reconciliation following the horrors of the Second World War – early members occupied a couple of redundant wartime Nissen huts tucked behind the sea wall. The settlement has grown substantially since then.

The first time I visited Othona some years ago – the name is taken from that of the former Roman fort that once occupied the site – it was a wintry day of cold, blustery rain. Driving the last two miles on a straight single-track road bisecting endless windswept fields, I imagined myself hurrying towards the edge of the known world. The peninsula is notoriously isolated, fringed by vast expanses of estuarian sea and sky; Defoe found the territory intolerable.

How the weather changes everything. For two days in April 2017, organisers of the Essex Book Festival collaborated with staff at Southend's Focal Point Gallery to run a short residential writers' workshop at Othona devoted to the subject of landscape writing. On this occasion, outstanding Easter weather brought high blue skies, dazzling marine light, and a profusion of hawthorn blossom and birdsong. The Othona staff provided space, accommodation and wonderful food, but also offered an inspiring model of an off-grid, ecologically self-sufficient settlement as environmentally ambitious as it is religiously unobtrusive and comfortable in its own skin. The story of this and other communitarian 'experiments in living' is the subject of this chapter.

Othona didn't start out with high-minded environmental principles, though its founder was notoriously intolerant of waste, and keen on practicalities: the recurring text for many of his sermons was 'faith without works is barren'. Since its inception, however, Othona has increasingly combined religious principles with those of ecological self-sufficiency. Motley's background intriguingly follows the formative experiences of a number of other religious and political activists who shaped the Essex communitarian tradition. Born into a large working-class family in East London, he was member of the choir at St John of Jerusalem Church in Hackney, an avid student of religion and music, and by the age of sixteen was teaching a WEA (Workers' Educational Association) evening class on the music of Beethoven.

As a military chaplain during the war, Motley organised a series of discussion groups that grew to become the 'Answer-Back' movement, encouraging men and women of all ranks to 'debate such matters as the evils of war and the existence of a living God'. In later life he described himself as 'one who has been left-wing all his life in the Keynes, Temple, Attlee, Lansbury tradition'. In the Othona newsletter in summer 2016, his son-in-law, Richard Marshall, recalled that, 'He always seemed a very human and well-read person, who grew out of East End socialism.' Motley wrote in one of his published letters that, 'We can begin to *incarnate* our concern for intelligent conservation by using more land to produce food – fruit and vegetables and flowers.' He further added that 'Self-sufficiency is encouraged, bringing out latent qualities and helping achieve unity.'

There is little aesthetic unity however in the eclectic collection of buildings that occupies the site, but it matters not a whit. No architectural determinism here. The campus consists of a miscellany of old Nissen huts, barns and sheds, a demountable former NatWest Bank, yurts, a timber-framed pavilion administration block, a weatherboard bungalow, and, most recently the Solar Building constructed from rammed earth, straw bales, and timber, and raised high off the ground to provide additional flood protection. Like much of the surrounding territory, the site lies close to sea level.

Nevertheless, the eccentric collection of buildings is interconnected – one might even say incarnated – in other ways, principally by an intricate energy and waste disposal system, now tried and tested over years of extensive improvement and use. One medium-sized wind turbine, together with a series of photo-voltaic panels, provides all the electricity needed for a residential campus that can accommodate up to 70 people at any one time – lighting, heating, cooking, hot water, along with a variety of other needs. All 'grey water' and sewage is collected, broken down and pumped into a series of reed beds where it is filtered naturally in stages, before returning to the soil and water table.

Utility services and energy distribution networks are hidden in plain sight. In the washrooms all the plumbing is on show, supported by pressurised tanks and pumps whirring on and off, while sensors switch lights and heating on and off as required by human activity, all of the switchgear, fuse boxes, openly accessible to view and mounted on plywood casings for immediate access. The buildings and plant rooms quietly hum with the noise of pumps, electrical re-sets and feedback systems, adding to the sense of human and environmental integration. Nothing goes to waste.

The original encampment was chosen for its proximity to the adjacent isolated Chapel of St Peter-on-the-Wall, a solitary four-square building exercising a profound presence in empty landscape, one of only a handful of seventh-century churches still extant in England. Dating from around 653, during the bishopric of St Cedd, the chapel is constructed in rough-cut masonry along with bricks and tiles rescued from the remains of the former Roman fort. The modest building with its steep pitched roof nevertheless stands tall on the horizon, especially when viewed from across the estuary. Badgers work ceaselessly on the remaining ruins of the old Roman fort close by, throwing up earth and rubble into an unfinished jigsaw of broken parts.

In his history of the Othona Community, *Much Ado About Something* (1985), Motley vividly recalled the day in March 1946 when he and his wife and two others drove to Bradwell to see the site that was to become the location of their great experiment:

> On that vivid afternoon we came under the spell of that ancient building and of the whole area of the Blackwater Estuary. St Peter's is situated a few hundred yards from the south shores of the river at the point where it enters the North Sea. There, one can breathe. The land on which we stood is almost a peninsula, with the mile-wide estuary to the north and Bradwell Bay behind – and all round, and curving to the south, the North Sea. The cry of the curlew was heard, and a variety of maritime flora and many sea birds were evident on the saltings; and withal, a great silence.

The 'community' of Othona is a moveable feast. There is a small group of paid workers who run the settlement, supported by volunteer helpers, but at any one time visitors are coming and going, either in groups or as individuals, staying perhaps for a few days or sometimes several weeks. Thus the community is re-constituted on a daily basis, avoiding any danger of becoming sectarian or inward-looking. In the course of a single year up to 1,500 people come to Othona. Whether religious or not, most find that the marshland setting, the wide skies and the tidal foreshore combine to contribute to a sense not just of retreat from the world but of emotional renewal.

This sense of the renewal to be found at the water's edge is now shared by others, particularly members of religious groups based in the ethnic minority communities of London and Essex. When in 2010 I accompanied the environmentalist and academic Jules Pretty on his epic coastal walk from London to Norfolk – subsequently published as *This Luminous Coast* – we found ourselves on a very hot August Bank Holiday Sunday striding along the promenade which runs from Leigh-on-Sea to Shoeburyness. On a number of beaches there were large gatherings of the religious faithful, sometimes singing hymns, sometimes at prayer, but also, one assumes, enjoying the light on the sea, the bright sky, and, for the children, large expanses of shingle and sand where they could roam and play at will. I was later told that more than 14,000 Hindus had gathered on Shoebury beach the previous August Bank Holiday to celebrate the birthday of the Hindu god, Ganesha.

Whether we choose to call Othona a retreat, an elective community, or an alternative way of living – and Norman Motley himself spoke of the need for 'cells of good living' – all such terms suggest a requirement for spaces that act as a counterpoint to the daily demands of mainstream society. Essex has a strong tradition of such places, as we shall see.

TOLSTOY IN ESSEX

'Back to the land' sentiments have been a key ingredient in English social and religious movements as far back as the Diggers and the Levellers in the seventeenth century. Utopian visions have invariably been based on a mythical place – an as yet undiscovered island, or a faraway country – where the land is cultivated easily and freely, its fruits shared equally by all. As such aspirations became more formalised, a word that captured both the spatial qualities of such ideal settlements, as well as their relationship to the mainstream society, came into use: the colony. From the Latin word, *colonia*, meaning farm, the term came to mean a purposeful settlement, frequently isolated from the rest of society. Initially a form of voluntary separation, in the age of imperial expansion, the process of 'colonialisation' came to be associated with the often forcible expropriation of other people's lands for land-grabbing settlement.

Nevertheless, in its early iteration, the idea of the colony possessed radical possibilities. In 1827, Quaker William Allen, a follower of cooperator Robert Owen, published a pamphlet called *Colonies at Home*, arguing for villages of small farmers living and working cooperatively. In his study *Principles of Political Economy* (1848), one of the most influential works of nineteenth-century philosophy, John Stuart Mill called for the establishment of land colonies where people might live and work more sociably away from the temptations and harshness of the city. In *On Liberty*, published in 1859 and equally seminal, he further argued for 'experiments in living' as a means of developing new ideas in human and social relations. But why did Essex become such fertile ground for such experiments?

The anarchist planner and writer Colin Ward was an early exponent of the view that Essex had more than its share of model communities due to its close proximity to London. As such it was an ideal location for communitarian and therapeutic settlements instigated by social reformers concerned with the multiple social problems caused by the widespread poverty and slum conditions of the capital's East End. Furthermore, Ward argued, land prices were relatively cheap following the agricultural depression of the 1880s, especially in south-east Essex where soil quality was considered poor.

To these reasons should be added the relatively inaccessible nature – and therefore greater privacy – of the extensive coastal landscape. Much of this lies away from the county's principal road network, including as it does isolated marshes, creeks and inlets, lonely farmsteads and, perhaps most significantly of all, several islands. Thus for the conscience-stricken brewing family member, the social reformer Frederick Charrington, Osea Island on the River Blackwater, seemed an ideal setting to establish a temperance retreat in 1903, while Mersea Island was home to a variety of camping and chalet colonies (some religious, some political), and Canvey Island to such idealistic establishments as Hotel Ozonia, The Settlement and The Girls Bungalow.

Foulness Island likewise has been singularly isolated, strictly off-limits to the public since the Second World War and under the control of the Ministry of Defence. Despite this, it has a civilian population of more than 200, some working for the island's defence establishment, some farming on the island, but others travelling off the island to work in and around Southend. Meanwhile Horsey Island, Skippers Island and Two Tree Island, the first in private hands, the latter two under the management of Essex Wildlife Trust, are important bird sanctuaries. Furthermore, Mersea Island is home to a small population of red squirrels, protected from the incursion of grey squirrels by its tidal separation from the mainland. Island ecologies are different from mainland ecologies, whether for squirrels or humans, as Darwin famously realised.

If Othona remains the most successful communitarian settlement in Essex, the Salvation Army Land and Industrial Colony, at Hadleigh, overlooking the Thames close to the estuary, has lasted longest. Opened in 1890, the colony still thrives, though its aims and members have changed considerably. 'Encouragement without coercion' was the motto of the early colony, which was designed to rehabilitate men from the East End slums suffering from destitution, homelessness, alcohol addiction and other afflictions, through a regime of hard outdoor work, prayer and abstinence. Thanks to an impressive programme of fund-raising, General Booth, founder of the Salvation Army, whose idea the Hadleigh colony had been, was able to buy 1,500 acres of drained marshes, meadows, arable and pasture lands close to Hadleigh Castle. Early colonists worked the land, cultivated an extensive market garden, bred Shire horses, and maintained a dairy herd and a large piggery. They also operated a brickfield on the site, producing up to two million bricks each year.

In the 1950s my family moved to Hadleigh, and although the colony was declared firmly out of bounds by my own and the parents of other children in the area, we nevertheless wandered around and sometimes through it during the school holidays, and bought soft drinks from the colony shop. By this time it was no longer impoverished men who made up the colonists, but rather younger men who had been in trouble of some kind, which was exactly why our parents wanted us to stay well away. Today it is run as an organic farm and petting centre, operating a successful public restaurant and visitors' centre, providing training and work opportunities in farming and catering services for young people with learning disabilities.

The farm colony has now been in continuing operation for more than 120 years. Between the wars the Salvation Army was sadly compromised – along with a number of other child-care agencies – by its involvement in schemes to send children and young people either orphaned or in care to populate and work the land in the colonies, particularly to Canada, Australia and New Zealand, where many of them suffered hardship and unhappiness. This was an unsupportable episode in what otherwise had been a long and largely commendable exercise in rehabilitation.

A quite different exercise in the rehabilitation of young offenders occurred in Great Bardfield in Essex rather later, and one that still enjoys considerable esteem in the history of therapeutic communities. Early in 1935, the Quaker David Wills – the first person in England to train as a psychiatric social worker – wrote an article in *The Friend* (A Quaker weekly) suggesting it was time for a bolder experiment in the treatment of young offenders. And at this time Miss Cicely Craven of the Howard League for Penal Reform put him in touch with psychiatrist, Marjorie Franklin, who had just formed the Q Camps Committee with the same aim in mind.

The purpose of Q Camps was to provide for the rehabilitation of young men in exceptional personal difficulties – some also in trouble with the law – in a therapeutic community away from the temptations of the city. In the summer of 1936 Q Camps Committee bought a twenty-six-acre field near Great Bardfield in Essex. Wills, his team of helpers and the young men lived in tents while they set themselves about the task of cultivating the land and building themselves living quarters that they began to occupy by November. In his account of this camp, *Hawkspur Experiment* (1941), Wills describes in great detail the trials and tribulations of working with disaffected adolescents, many of them described in extremely detailed but anonymous case studies. In the Preface to the second edition published in 1967, Wills recounted what happened to many of them during and after the war to which most were conscripted in 1939. Happily some survived and flourished, though others died in the war or disappeared from the records. The influence of Wills and his experience at Great Bardfield, is still discussed and valued in the treatment of disturbed young people today.

While the Salvation Army colony in Hadleigh was the first land colony in Essex, the same decade produced others. It was a fertile era for 'New Life' experiments, a number of which can directly trace their origins to the widespread influence of Russian novelist, Leo Tolstoy, whose Christian pacifism and ascetic pietism won admirers across the world. Three such pioneer communities in Essex were established in Purleigh (1896), Ashingdon (1897) and Wickford (1898).

What we first knew about these places is owed to the early research of Colin Ward and his colleague, Dennis Hardy, to whose work we are all indebted. According to Hardy, when he visited The Chase in Ashingdon in the 1970s to view the remains of the Ashingdon Colony, it was still an unmade road made up of small-holdings, including cottages named 'Brotherhood Cottage' and 'Walden'.

The four-acre plot in which the Brotherhood Cottage stood was purchased by James Evans in 1897; Evans, having been a member of the Brotherhood Church in Southgate Road, Hackney, a Christian Socialist sect, was much influenced by Tolstoy. This constituted the origins of the colony, and here Evans kept goats and grew vegetables in the spirit of practical self-sufficiency. Hardy also tells of another local radical in this small constellation, Frederick M. von Browne, who lived nearby in a cottage called Anarchae Keep. In 1940 Brotherhood Cottage passed into the hands of his son, and eventually it fell into disrepair.

Rather late in the day, in 1941 in fact, the Tolstoyan publisher C.W. Daniel also arrived at The Chase and set up a printing press there in a house renamed Oprodan. C.W. Daniel – along with his wife, Florence Worland – were among the principal figures in the spread of Tolstoyan ideas in England in the early years of the twentieth century. Charles Daniel was the organiser of the London Tolstoyan Society from 1900 onwards and its most active speaker, and in 1902 set up his own publishing company, C.W. Daniel Company Ltd., which he ran for the rest of his life, first in London but latterly in Ashingdon. The firm concentrated on spreading the ideas of political economist Henry George, on social reform, pacifism and many 'New Life' preoccupations.

In addition to books, Charles and Florence edited and published a number of journals including *Healthy Life,* which was later renamed *The Crank,* and *Open Road,* to which Tolstoy himself contributed. But they also published work by D.H. Lawrence, as well as being the first English-language publisher of European philosophers Søren Kierkegaard and José Ortega y Gasset. Florence died in 1927, but Charles lived on, dying at Ashingdon in January 1955, in his later years keenly promoting the ideas of Maximillian Bircher-Benner (inventor of muesli), and Edward Bach (pioneer of flower remedies). Thus, in the development of postwar New Age philosophies and therapies, Essex communitarians were once again in the vanguard.

As a young man Daniel had got to know Vladimir Grigoryevich Chertkov, an ardent admirer and translator of Tolstoy who came to live in London in 1897 to promote the work of the Russian novelist, by now an influential figure across the world. Chertkov soon moved to a small Tolstoyan/anarchist settlement at Cock Clarks, near Purleigh, where he set up the Free Word Press and the Free Age Press with his wife, Anna Konstantinovna, publishing Tolstoy in translation, and for whom Daniel acted as an agent. Other Russians came to Purleigh too, including a small group of Doukhobors (Spirit Warriors of Christ), fleeing from persecution in the mother country.

According to one of the colonists, Hubert Hammond, life was, however briefly, harmonious, healthy and happy. Fruit trees were planted, glasshouses established, tool sheds, workshops and animal houses erected, and more than 7,000 bricks made in the first year. In the evening, tea was taken, songs sung, and discussions ensued. There was also dancing. The Purleigh Colony was abandoned however in 1900, with the Chertkovs and some of their followers moving to Bournemouth, while others went to the Whiteway Colony in Gloucestershire, which still survives today.

Midway between Purleigh and Ashingdon, but closer to London, Henry Power, formerly of the Croydon Brotherhood Church, along with other enthusiasts purchased twenty-nine acres of land and three cottages to the south of Downham Church, in Wickford, Essex, in the summer of 1898.

Alas little more is known of the Wickford Colony other than that it petered out early in its development, leaving little trace, though for other reasons dealt with later, the small rather makeshift town, which had an extensive network of plotland developments and small-holdings, re-emerged as a pioneer in another area of 'New Life' philosophy, notably as the birthplace of English naturism.

One of the heroic figures of the 'back to the land' movement – not only in Essex but far beyond – was Thomas Smith, who by the end of his life had garnered an international reputation for his pioneering work in horticulture. This eventually earned him a Fellowship of the Royal Horticultural Society (RHS), and a RHS Gold Medal in 1950. Under the spell of Robert Blatchford's 1894 manifesto, *Merrie England*, Smith settled with his family in Mayland on the River Blackwater the following year, determined to create a new arcadia. The initial venture soon attracted the attention of Fabian Society enthusiasts such as George Lansbury, Joseph Rowntree and Joseph Fels. Fels was an American, the scion of former Eastern European immigrants, who had inherited a fortune from the manufacture of soap and had come to England to embrace the Fabian cause. He was also a devoted follower of the land economist Henry George. Arriving in England in 1901, Fels was soon persuaded that rural depopulation was a growing problem, and according to his wife Mary, in her biography of her husband, *Joseph Fels: His Life & Work* (1920), 'hoped for England to become an agricultural country again'. It was Fels who underwrote the expansion of the Mayland Colony after meeting Smith, subsequently buying 600 acres of farmland, which he divided up into twenty-one separate small-holdings. These were all to be made available to families wishing to start a new life away from the poverty of the city, and in some cases, from failed attempts to farm in the colonies, particularly Australia.

2022

MUM:

don't enter (or read on).

OAP:

hide cake please

it was too hot last night!

Fels made Smith the estate manager, and his home, The Homestead in Grange Avenue, became the administrative centre for the whole scheme. We are told that 'he also cycled to Old Heath, Southminster, and South Woodham Ferrers to oversee new colonies that were forming there.' It is possible that the South Woodham Ferrers Colony referred to is what became known as the Salthaven Colony, on the site of which a thriving community orchard now stands, which author Gillian Darley and I visited in the summer of 2016.

Within a few years the Mayland experiment was growing its own food, producing its own meat and dairy products, and providing homes and a school, along with other social amenities for the colonists. Moreover, it was able to export produce to other parts of the region through the establishment of a short rail link to a river jetty, where boats could moor at high tide and from there set sail around the coast. The railway consisted of a small number of wooden trucks on bogies, pulled by horses – and at times by the workers themselves – carrying goods from The Homestead to the dock jetty. Visitors to the colony included Peter Kropotkin, H. Rider Haggard, Sidney and Beatrice Webb, Keir Hardie and the indefatigable George Lansbury.

In 1909 Fels published Smith's book, *French Gardening*, under the imprint of the Utopia Press, with an introduction by the Russian anarchist, Peter Kropotkin. This became one of the most influential works on market gardening ever written. It was followed by the publication in 1913 of *The Profitable Culture of Vegetables*, the dedication of which read, 'This Book is Dedicated By The Author to His Friend Joseph Fels in Admiration of The Gallant Fight He is Making Throughout the World To Break Down The Monopoly in Land'. Smith's work and publications eventually earned him widespread admiration and praise; his RHS Gold Medal being awarded 'in recognition of the work you have done for horticulture and in particular as the author of that magnificent book *The Profitable Culture of Vegetables.'* Smith died in 1955, and is buried in Mayland church.

The early death of Fels in 1914, and the outbreak of the First World War, ended the experiment in its original form, though the community survived and a number of the plot-holders managed to buy their small-holdings and continue to make a living there. Some of the walnut trees still survive as do many of the hawthorn hedges marking out the lanes and boundaries. The former railway track is now a straight dark tunnel of trees leading to the skeletal remains of the original jetty at the head of the narrow Mayland Creek, also known as Pigeon Dock.

Further south at Stanford-le-Hope close to the River Thames, a former army officer known as Captain Petavel formed a limited company in 1909 with friends to purchase Moore Place, a seventeenth-century farmhouse with outbuildings and fifteen acres of land. He wished to establish a workers' cooperative for the unemployed, with the enthusiastic support of Swedenborgian church minister, the Reverend A. Ryland. The farm was re-opened as a Simple Life Guest House and Vegetarian Colony, where visitors and residents could enjoy fresh air and locally produced food. Tented accommodation was also provided, with the Essex Weekly News reporting 'quite a number of canvas erections on the greensward in front of the old homestead.'

Petavel had served as an officer in the Royal Engineers in India and on his return to England in 1895 had developed an interest in town planning and land matters, corresponding with the eminent geographer and planner Patrick Geddes. Petavel held strong Christian views, publishing in 1911 *The Coming Triumph of Christian Civilisation.* Alas the colony at Moore Place did not attract the numbers expected, and within a few years its founder concentrated on writing about the need for new kinds of productive education. In 1915 he returned to India at the invitation of the poet Rabindranath Tagore – who had become an admirer of Petavel's ideas on education – and Petavel was made Principal of the Maharaja Cossimbazar's Polytechnic Institute, and remained in India until his death in 1945, working on education colonies there. In 1930 Moore Place was purchased by the Wayfarers Benevolent Association and opened as a hostel dedicated to rescuing young men from vagrancy. The building was finally demolished in the early 1960s.

WELCOME TO THE HOTEL OZONIA

Tuberculosis (usually abbreviated to TB and often termed 'consumption') was a disease that caused the death of millions across the world well into the twentieth century. In Britain it was the cause of one in eight deaths at this time, and the single most common cause of death amongst men. Robert Louis Stevenson and D.H. Lawrence were among its better-known victims. Until the development of appropriate drugs, and mass vaccination programmes, the recommended treatment was fresh air, sunshine and rest. Europeans wealthy enough to afford it could take themselves off to a sanatorium, many of which were located in high altitude settlements in the Swiss, German or Austrian mountains. Those less fortunate might attend an open-air school – and these were found all over Europe in the early twentieth century – or spend time convalescing close to the sea. In time new ideas in town planning and architecture caught up with the idea of designing for healthier populations, soon to become a signature motif of the Modern Movement.

One element of this new preoccupation with public health was the cult of naturism, already well-established in northern Europe. Britain's first nudist (or naturist) colony was opened in Essex, at Wickford in 1924, under the name of Moonella. Thanks to the work of the South East Essex Community Archive, the site has been almost certainly identified as belonging to a bungalow called 'Sunbeam' at 133 Castledon

Road, Wickford (long since demolished). Older Wickford residents recall there being a sign on the large gate to the side of the bungalow leading to small field enclosed by a high hedge, which read: 'Private – For Sunbeam Users Only'.

In its first incarnation, Moonella was the brainchild of members of the English Gymnosophical Society, formed in 1922 by Harold Clare Booth, Mark Harold Sorensen and Rex Wellbye. This society held its London meetings at the Minerva Café, High Holborn, also the home of the Women's Freedom League. All Moonella members adopted club names to preserve their anonymity, such as Chong, Lorelli, Thwang and Zex, and were encouraged to wear sandals and headwear 'in the Greek style'. Harold Clare Booth was a committee member of the British Society for the Study of Sex Psychology, founded in 1914, and one of the more influential organisations advocating greater understanding of the diverse range of human sexual behaviour. Booth took his place on the committee as a representative of the National Physical Laboratory, one of the UK's oldest research bodies, still extant. Wellbye later became the unofficial historian of British naturism, writing regularly for the Sunbathing Association newsletter, sunbathing being the more acceptable name into which naturism had mutated. Without doubt the most august member of Moonella was the novelist, Ursula Bloom, the daughter of an Essex vicar and at one time one of the world's best-selling authors. Bloom kept this aspect of her life under close wraps, though on several occasions she did publish articles about English naturism as if from the perspective of an inquisitive but detached journalist.

Elsewhere in Essex a recuperative culture blossomed too. In the first decades of the twentieth century Canvey Island began to be promoted as an ideal health resort: easily reached from London by train, surrounded by sea, and conspicuously flat and easy for walking, cycling and swimming. Cheap accommodation could also be found, either in caravan parks or in small hotels and guesthouses.

One such holiday home was The Girls Bungalow Holiday Home established in 1909 by a Clara Grace James, for working girls from East London: this was a philanthropic venture rather than a commercial one. James had had an eventful life. London-born but orphaned at a young age, she joined the Women's Trade Union Association at the age of twenty-three and for a while was the only women member of the London Trades Council. She trained as a gymnastic teacher and devoted much of her life to setting up clubs and activities for young working-class women, sometimes under the rubric of an organisation called Working Girls at Play. Having established The Girls Bungalow on Canvey, she spent the rest of her life on the island, a founder member of the Labour Party and The Women's Institute there, eventually becoming a district councillor and a Justice of the Peace.

In 1937 a temperance hotel opened on Canvey Island's Seaview Road called 'Ozonia', and its somewhat bizarre appearance is still remembered by many, including myself. The architect was Ernest George Trobridge, an adherent of the Swedenborgian faith, and an architect of eclectic originality. The building was a rather dramatic confection, consisting of an irregular thatched roof, eyebrow eves, dormer windows, shingled balconies, all combining to produce an extensive corner building, part gingerbread house, part mock-Tudor mansion. It is said to have contained some 60 rooms. The Canvey Community Archive contains a fascinating account of its fabrication by Harry Russell, a man who worked on its original construction. Even more bizarre than its external appearance was the hotel's interior decoration, undertaken by a 'down on his luck artist', according to Russell, with each guest room decorated with fantasy murals, some of them dream landscapes, others Hieronymus Bosch-style portraits of hell (possibly to deter any would-be drinkers). Alas the outbreak of war in 1939 put an end to this and many other 'New Life' projects of the 1930s, though the building was not finally demolished until the 1960s.

One name recurs again and again in the story of these pioneer communities: George Lansbury. Trade unionist, Mayor of Poplar Council, Labour MP and, near the end of his life, Leader of the Labour Party, Lansbury embodied many of the interests and aspirations of the 'New Life' era. He was a staunch Christian, a pacifist, a teetotaller, and a modest man who refused to wear mayoral or parliamentary robes. He also represented something more powerful and pervasive at this time. This was the ethical force of East London's unique blend of Christian socialism, which permeated, and for a while shaped, the political and religious world of communitarian Essex. When Norman Motley was described by his son-in-law as a person 'who grew out of East End socialism', this was precisely the milieu which formed him.

Lansbury was a close friend of Joseph Fels from 1903 onwards, and a key supporter of the Mayland community and the Laindon plotlands, both of which Fels part-financed. Both had links to Patrick Geddes (as had Captain Petavel), as well as close friendships with the remarkable McMillan sisters: Rachel McMillan and Margaret McMillan. It was the McMillans who pioneered nursery education and health provision for children in Britain, opening the first school clinic in Bow in 1908. They went on to promote free nursery provision (and open-air schooling) in 1910 in Deptford, and for decades afterwards pioneered public provision for children and young mothers across Britain. In 1906 it was principally Lansbury who set up the Christian Socialist League, through which he met people such as Conrad Noel, later to become notorious as the red vicar of Thaxted in north Essex. Towards the end of his life it was once again Lansbury who converted writer and pacifist Vera Brittain to ethical socialism, and who in turn helped fund Frating Hall Farm near Colchester.

Lansbury's strong support for socialist and activist Annie Besant during the match girls' strike, and his relationship to the early trade union and feminist upheavals in East London is well documented by the historian Seth Koven in *The Match Girl and the Heiress* (2014). Koven's wonderful book traces the crossfertilisation of nonconformist religious movements with those of the early socialist, pacifist and suffragette elements of East London's political radicalism. These came together in notions of a 'New Life' to come, giving lie to the widely held belief amongst late Victorian and early Edwardian reformers that the East End was, in the words of one, a 'moral Sahara'.

The impoverished district of Bow in London's East End became the epicentre of this new moral crusade, one largely inspired by the ideals of Christian socialism. One of the two principal subjects of Koven's book was Muriel Lester who, with her lifelong friend, match girl Nellie Dowell, ultimately established Kingsley Hall in Bow in 1915, named after Muriel's brother Kingsley Lester, who had died young. Lester and Dowell were convinced Christians, feminists and socialists, choosing to live austerely in a small terraced house in Bow; although Lester herself had come from a wealthy Loughton family. They devoted their lives to serving the poor.

Kingsley Hall was a gathering place for many different kinds of organisations and idealists, and became a conduit for ideas from a variety of Eastern philosophies, greatly influencing the cult of Theosophy, to which Annie Besant, George Lansbury, and other East London political activists were attracted. Already by 1890, the London Theosophical Society had established Bow Lodge at 193 Bow Road, as a club for the match girls and subsequently as a 'Brotherhood for Boys'. Koven describes George Lansbury as 'the Lester sisters' chief guide and political patron in Bow and Poplar.' In the 1960s Kingsley Hall became a home for R.D. Laing's anti-psychiatry movement.

From the 1890s onwards London's East End churches witnessed a procession of radical appointments. The most famous of these was Stewart Headlam, a member of the

Christian Socialist League, and strong advocate of the land reforms advocated by Henry George. He was another close friend of Annie Besant and Lansbury, and a supporter of the Women's Trade Union League, in which Clara Grace James was active. Sometimes called 'the slum priest', Headlam was an enthusiastic devotee of the Music Hall culture of East London, which didn't endear him to the Anglican hierarchy. Novels of the East End by writers such as Arthur Morrison and Simon Blumenfeld, always have a radical priest stirring things up at key moments of the action.

The resurgence of radical politics in the 1930s witnessed a new wave of idealistic settlements, some with a Christian ethos, the best known of which was the Adelphi Centre at Langham in Essex. A large mansion and grounds previously known as Langham Oaks had been purchased in 1934 by the Peace Pledge Union, a pacifist movement then growing in popularity under the leadership of the charismatic Anglican priest, Dick Sheppard. The centre was intended to become both a religious retreat but also a study centre for new social principles, with two energetic idealists at the helm – poet Max Plowman and writer John Middleton Murry. At the outset it operated as a rural commune, farming the adjacent land, though by 1937 the mansion was used as a home for Basque refugee children fleeing the Spanish Civil War. The highlight of the Adelphi study programme was a summer school organised in 1936, whose participants included – along with Plowman and Murry – George Orwell, Herbert Read, Karl Polanyi, Reinhold Niebuhr and almost certainly Vera Brittain.

Alas Murry came with a reputation for being good at starting things but not very good at keeping them running, and also had a reputation for pursuing a complicated love life, which invariably created tensions close to home. In 2012 Gillian Darley and I interviewed Enid Howard, Peter Wells and Gillian Wells, two of whom had been a part of the Adelphi project shortly before the outbreak of the Second World War. As Christians and pacifists they then went on to establish the

370 acre Frating Hall Farm near Colchester, a working farm where conscientious objectors could properly claim to be in 'reserved occupations' as agricultural workers. Capital to buy the farm had partly come from another one of Lansbury's protégés, writer and member of the Anglican Pacifist Fellowship, Vera Brittain. Her memoir of the First World War, *Testament of Youth* (1933), had made her famous. Brittain's daughter – later to become the politician Shirley Williams – spent some time there as a child. Luckily several of the key people at Frating Hall, including those we interviewed, had farming experience – though additional support came from nearby Quaker farmers – yet despite proven farming competence, local villagers still disapproved of their pacifist views.

Murry meanwhile moved over the border to Suffolk where he tried – and failed again – to run a successful farm on progressive lines, a story he tells without too much bitterness in his fascinating book, *Community Farm* (1952). To the end he retained a strong belief in the redemptive power of work on the land. 'Work on the land is necessary to the life of man in a way that no other work can be', he had written, and in his later years he remained unwavering in his own 'back to the land' sentiments: 'I believe service to the land is an unconditional good.'

IN SPITE OF THEIR DEFEAT?

Reflecting on the fragility of political hopes and ideals, William Morris, another Essex radical, once wrote that:

> I pondered all these things, and how men fight and lose the battle, and the thing that they fought for comes about in spite of their defeat, and when it comes turns out not to be what they meant, and other men have to fight for what they meant under another name.

Many of the changes that the idealists of the early twentieth century wished to see eventually came to pass: the eradication of insanitary slum housing, an end to long-term unemployment and dependence on charity (or long hours in harsh and dangerous factory conditions), the disappearance of widespread malnutrition and chronic, avoidable diseases. Today most people also enjoy paid holidays, better educational opportunities and greater leisure time. Yet the communitarians wanted something more. They wanted these things to come about in the name of human fellowship, and for people to participate in the management and making of their own lives in communities of equals, through cooperation and mutual assent.

None of those involved ever combined to form a mass movement, let alone wished to seize political power to achieve their ideals. Instead they nurtured ideas and different ways of doing things. In time many of these ideas began to be emulated by others, and even legislated upon to support what subsequently came to be regarded as the norms of civilised living. Without the Mayland pioneers, the Salvation Army colonists, the Q Camp therapists, the Captain Petavels, the dedication of women such as Clara Grace James, Nellie Dowell, Muriel Lester and the McMillan sisters, the sexual radicals of the Moonella colony, the unpretentious humanity of Labour politicians such as George Lansbury, or the religious devotionalism of people like Stewart Headlam and Norman Motley, we may have had to wait longer for the social revolution which produced child-centred nursery education, the therapeutic rehabilitation of young offenders and the chronically addicted, women's rights at work and in the home, the development of the self-build tradition of the plotland communities (which helped inspire the New Towns), unadulterated food, more healthy lifestyles, greater sexual awareness, and even the conviviality of rambling and cycling in groups in open countryside. This was no small achievement.

What is also evident is that the exuberance and optimism of late Victorian social radicalism derived from a powerful admixture of a redemptive socialist politics with a strong element of nonconformist Christian humility, allied to a belief in service to others. Today's political culture seems threadbare by comparison. There has always been a strong tension between politics as the achievement of managerial power, and politics as active engagement in day-to-day change on the ground. That same tension emerges most urgently today in arguments about the relative merits of representative democracy and direct democracy.

The 'do-it-yourself' culture of the land colonists, plotlanders and religious pioneers at least addressed the practicalities – as well as the impracticalities – of new ideas for living. The Essex communitarians were remarkably far-sighted (or 'prefigurative' to use a more grandiose expression) in what kinds of values and ways of life might come about in the future – and to a large degree their beliefs have been vindicated. The slums of East London are gone. The political ideals that dispelled them were often first formulated and put into practice by the utopians and visionaries out there on the margins and the marshes. The weather brightened from the east.

KEN WORPOLE is the author of many books on architecture, landscape and public policy, including two collaborations with photographer Jason Orton on the social history and landscape of coastal Essex: *350 Miles: An Essex Journey* (2005) and *The New English Landscape* (2013). His most recent book is *New Jerusalem: The Good City and the Good Society* (2015). A founder member of the think-tank Demos, Ken was described by *The Independent* as 'one of the shrewdest and sharpest observers of the English social landscape'.

FURTHER READING

Below is a bibliography of the key books and printed sources used in writing this essay. There is also the world of online information, though I am particularly grateful to the Canvey Community Archive at www.canveyisland.org, and to Wickford History at www.wickfordhistory.org.uk (accessed 26 September 2017).

In addition I would like to thank Enid Howard, Shawn Kholucy, Peter Wells and Gillian Wells for telling the story of Frating Hall Farm; Kevin Bruce for recounting the early days of the Othona Community; Simon Brinkley of Thurrock Museum; the staff at Othona for their warmth and generosity during the Radical ESSEX residential writing workshop; Jo Nancarrow and Ros Green of the Essex Book Festival; Dennis Hardy for helpful correspondence and lifelong inspiration. Special thanks also to all at Focal Point Gallery in Southend for setting the whole Radical ESSEX project in motion, which now enjoys a life of its own.

Barbara Bates, *Bargaining for Life: A Social History of Tuberculosis 1876–1938* (University of Pennsylvania Press 1992)

T.J. Carney, 'The Simple Life at Stanford-le-Hope 1909–1914', *Panorama*, vol.27, 1985

Alain Corbin, *The Lure of the Sea* (Penguin Books 1995)

Gillian Darley, *Villages of Vision: A Study of Strange Utopias* (Five Leaves Publications 2007)

Gareth Evans & Di Robson, *Towards Re-enchantment: Place and It's Meanings* (Artevents 2010)

Eileen Everitt, *The Development of Lower Mayland and Maylandsea During the 20th Century* (Maylandsea 2007)

Mary Fels, *Joseph Fels: His Life-Work* (Allen & Unwin 1920)

John Field, *Working Men's Bodies: Work Camps in Britain, 1880–1940* (Manchester University Press 2013)

Hilda Grieve, *The Great Tide: The Story of the 1953 Flood Disaster in Essex* (Essex Record Office 1959)

Dennis Hardy, *Alternative Communities in Nineteenth Century England* (Longman 1979)

Dennis Hardy, *Utopian England: Community Experiments 1900–1945* (E. & F.N. Spon 2000)

Dennis Hardy and Colin Ward, *Arcadia for All: The Legacy of a Makeshift Landscape* (Five Leaves Publications 2003)

Bob Holman, *Good Old George: The Life of George Lansbury* (Lion Publishing 1990)

Seth Koven, *The Match Girl and the Heiress* (Princeton University Press 2014)

Janet Marshall, *Norman Motley: Portrait of a Man of Vision* (Malador 2016)

Fred McCave, *A History of Canvey Island* (Ian Henry Publishers 1985)

Norman Motley, *Letters to a Community 1970–1980* (The Othona Community 1986)

Norman Motley, *Much Ado About Something: A History of the Othona Community* (The Othona Community 1985)

John Middleton Murry, *Community Farm* (Peter Nevill Ltd 1952)

Jules Pretty, *This Luminous Coast* (Full Circle Editions 2011)

Marina O'Connell, 'Land Settlements in East Anglia', *Managed Retreat*, no.1, 2013

Raphael Samuel, *The Lost World of British Communism* (Verso 2006)

Alexandra Walsham, *The Reformation of the Landscape: Religion, Identity and Memory in Early Modern Britain and Ireland* (Oxford University Press 2011)

Nicolas Walter, 'C.W. Daniel: The Odd Man', *The Raven: Anarchist Quarterly*, no.9, 1990

Colin Ward, 'A Century of Land Settlement in Essex' in *Talking Green* (Five Leaves Publications 2012)

Sylvia Townsend Warner, *The True Heart* (1929) (Virago 1981)

Sylvia Townsend Warner, 'The Essex Marshes' in *With the Hunted: Selected Writings* (Black Dog Books 2012)

W. David Wills, *The Hawkspur Experiment* (Allen & Unwin 1967)

Ken Worpole, *Here Comes the Sun: Architecture and Public Space in Twentieth-Century European Culture* (Reaktion Books 2000)

Ken Worpole, *New Jerusalem: The Good City and the Good Society* (Swedenborg Society 2015)

Ken Worpole and Jason Orton, *350 Miles: An Essex Journey* (Essex County Council 2005)

Ken Worpole and Jason Orton, *The New English Landscape* (Field Station 2013)

Ian Yearsley, *Islands of Essex* (Ian Henry Publications 2000)

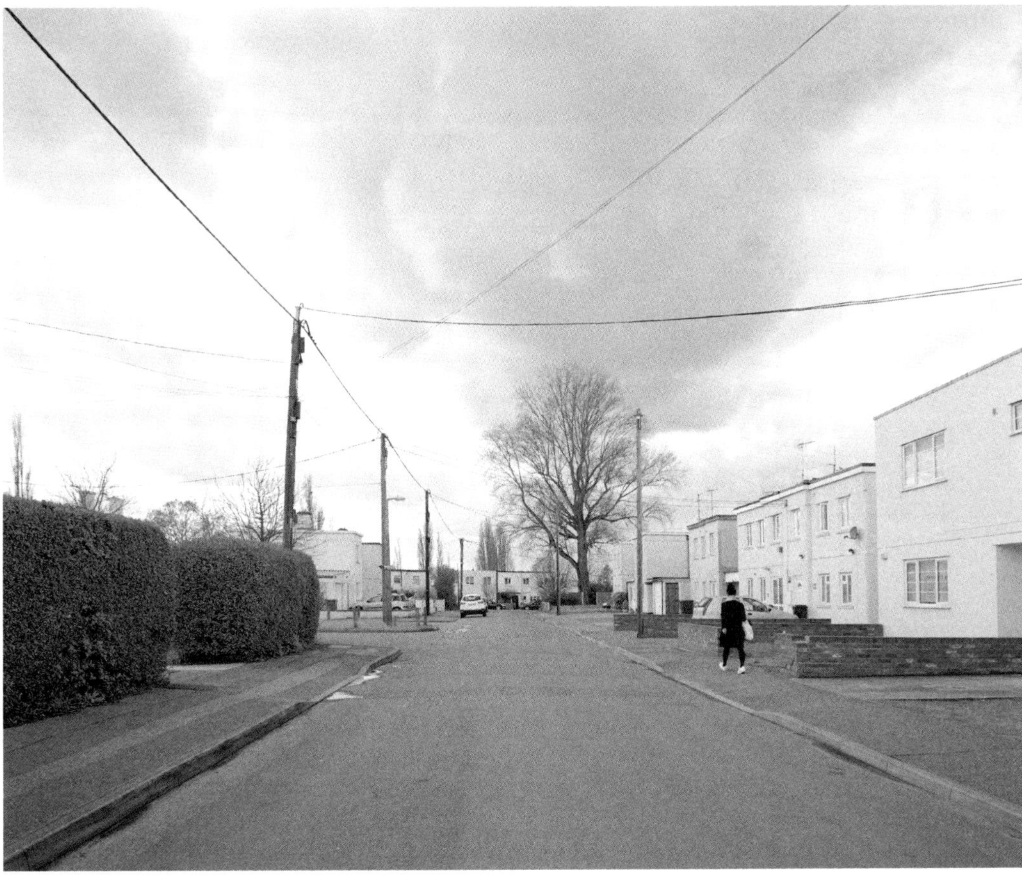

Clockh◇use Way, Braintree

The Rise and Fall

Charles Holland

THE BEGINNING

Modernism began in Essex. Modern architecture has many antecedents, buildings that have influenced or anticipated aspects of it. But the first clearly modernist houses in the UK, the ones that made the most decisive break with the past, were built on Clockhouse Way in Braintree in 1919.

They were designed by Charles H.B. Quennell and built by the Unit Construction Company to demonstrate the possibilities of mass-produced house building. Uncompromisingly industrial in their aesthetic, they employed precast concrete floors and flat roofs and their blockwork walls were left fair-faced and unadorned. In the context of the early twentieth century this was boldly innovative stuff, a rigorous attempt to apply manufacturing logic to the 'problem' of housing.

The Unit Construction Company was an offshoot of Francis Henry Crittall's Window Manufacturing Company and the houses were intended for workers of his nearby factory. So as well as offering improved levels of accommodation, they boasted the company's own steel-framed windows. Walking around Clockhouse Way today, the houses have inevitably lost some of their modernity, their starkness buried under layers of pastel-coloured render, porches, foliage and even decorative pargetting. They have become anglicised, Essexised even, and no two are the same, not even the pair that have been listed Grade 2 by Historic England. No doubt the flat roofs and lack of traditional house signifiers still mark them out as a little odd, not quite ‘proper’ houses. Certainly the homes around them that were constructed later look more traditional and ‘familiar’.

The industrialised modernity that these houses represented has not been embraced in this country as an aesthetic. We may be the beneficiaries of its road networks, mass-produced goods and infrastructure, we may even live in houses that are the products of mass production themselves, but we don’t like this to be expressed or made evident in the architecture.

Despite this the houses on Clockhouse Way were a precursor to a number of other housing projects across the county, settlements which include philanthropic workers villages, holiday parks and ultimately the postwar New Towns.For this reason, Essex is a good place to start to trace our relationship to modernism, not just its aesthetic but its ambitious social programme too.

Crittall themselves developed a more ambitious settlement a few miles to the south of Clockhouse Way. Silver End was originally a hamlet for farm labourers that Crittall extended in the late 1920s to house workers for its new factory. Silver End’s garden-suburb-influenced layout was master planned by C. Murray Hennell (who had also worked on Welwyn Garden City) and with houses designed by different architects in a variety of styles. Hennell contributed a series of simple, stripped-Georgian terraces and semi-detached units that actually form the bulk of the village. But Silver End is better known for the houses designed by Thomas S. Tait and Frederick MacManus of Sir John Burnet and Partners in a more experimental modernist style. Tait and MacManus’s houses comprise two streets of terraces for workers, and a number of more ambitious detached houses for factory managers. They are all flat-roofed and white-rendered with triangular-plan oriel windows and art deco detailing. In this they closely resemble New Ways, the Northamptonshire house designed by the pioneering German architect Peter Behrens in 1926. But from an urban perspective the houses

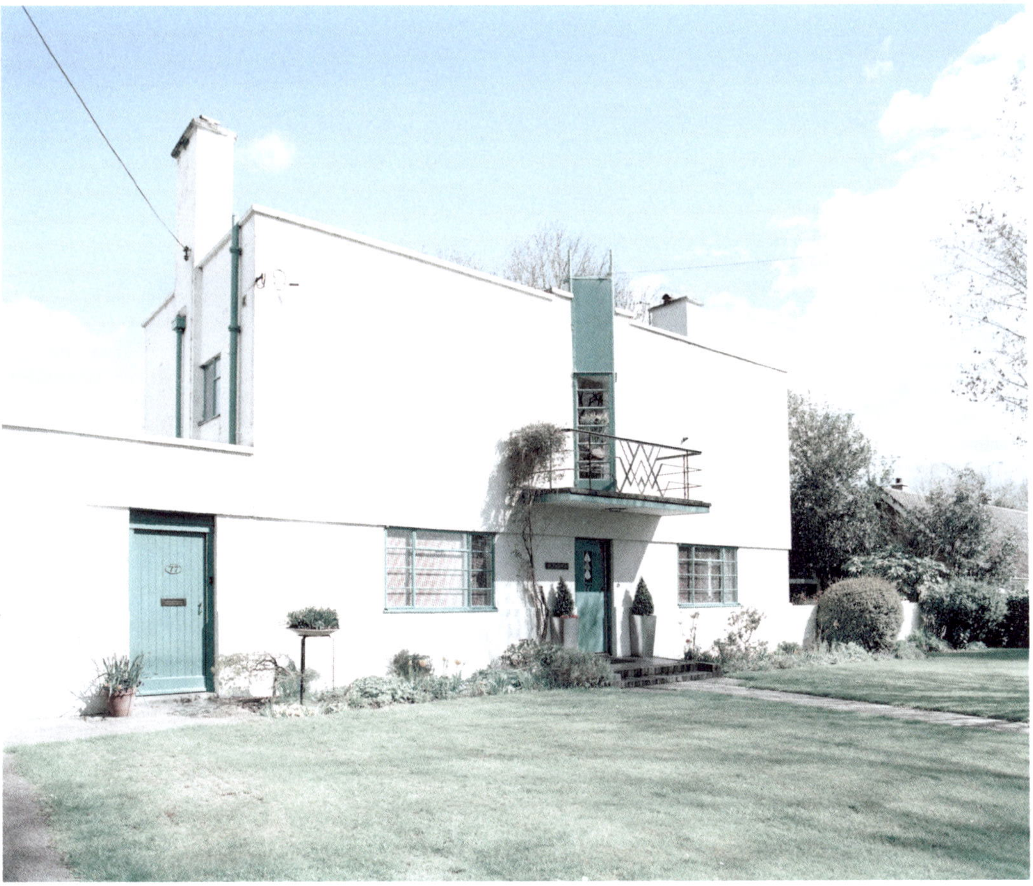

Wolverton, Silver End

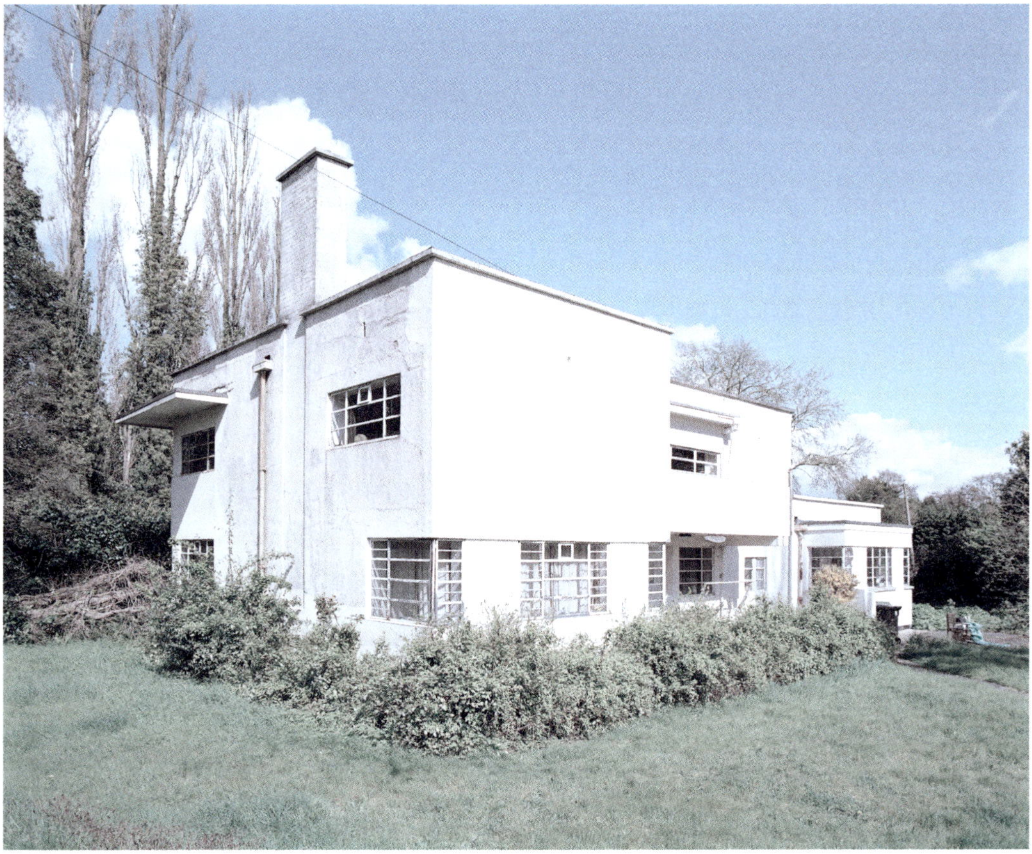

Le Chateau, Silver End

at Silver End are more important, an ambitious attempt to develop a modernist village typology.

Like Clockhouse Way, Silver End was as much advertisement as community, a built flagship intended to display the versatility of the Crittall product in action. This relationship between architecture and an emerging consumer and leisure culture found another Essex manifestation in Frinton-on-Sea. Frinton is a notoriously conservative resort town on the north Essex coast that until relatively recently resisted the vulgarity of either a pub or a fish and chip shop. Men are still banned from removing their shirts on the headland and there is a strong air of 'retired colonel' about the place. Frinton boasts a golf course, a large number of teashops and wide avenues lined with big, baggy Edwardian houses including one bona-fide masterpiece in architect and interior designer Charles Voysey's, The Homestead.

None of this prepares you for Frinton Park Estate, the modernist development planned on the edge of the town by Oliver Hill in 1934 for the South Coast Property Investment Company. Hill was an intriguing character, something of a party animal and an early proselytiser for modernism, along with the benefits of sunbathing, sea swimming and naturism. He designed the spectacular Midland Hotel, Morecambe Bay and a delightful modernist public house on the Isle of Thanet called The Prospect Inn, but Frinton Park Estate was his most ambitious pre-war project.

It wasn't a success, partly because the flat-roofed, art-deco-influenced houses designed by Hill – along with others including Serge Chermayeff, Wells Coates and Maxwell Fry – proved hard to sell. Mortgage lenders were suspicious of their innovative construction methods and buyers were put off by the austere aesthetic. Only a handful of genuinely modernist designs were completed – mostly by Hill or his later replacement R.G. Page – and these are now pepper-potted between later, more traditional-looking fare.

Visit Frinton-on-Sea today and you can read the recent history of British housing in the bizarre juxtapositions of decorated bungalows and abstract white cubes. Rising sun motifs recur in the railings, gates and coloured-glass windows of the Oliver Hill houses, creating a particularly English kind of suburban modernism. Palm trees suggest a sense of continental glamour and the houses themselves, with their angular balconies and ship-like handrails, appear considerably more sophisticated than anything that came after.

The most striking house is Hill's own design. Built as the show home, The Round House contains a floor mosaic depicting the plan for the whole estate. It is like a diorama of a future that never quite arrived. Hill also designed a large, sweeping hotel on the beachfront that was never realised. This design was a development of his majestic Midland Hotel built in Morecambe. The drawings for the Frinton hotel seem to anticipate a chic Mediterranean lifestyle of sunbathing and elegant evening dinners watching the sun go down, a vision hard to imagine on a grey day with the muddy North Sea churning away in the distance. But it was part of modernism's project to reinvent the everyday and to stimulate an almost completely new way of life.

Today, the concrete roads of the estate are cracked and some of the houses, like those at Silver End, languish sadly in the undergrowth. The fate of Frinton Park Court, the estate's planned shopping centre – is symptomatic. It never quite got off the ground to start with and in recent years was used as a Masonic hall before being demolished in 2015.

Despite this, there is a sense that the houses of Frinton Park Estate are being re-appraised and inevitably bought up by design enthusiasts. Some have been enthusiastically refurbished and there is even a recent new arrival that attempts, somewhat crudely, to ape the style of the early houses.

Oliver Hill was a proselytiser for the new style, but as architectural historian Alan Powers notes in his biography

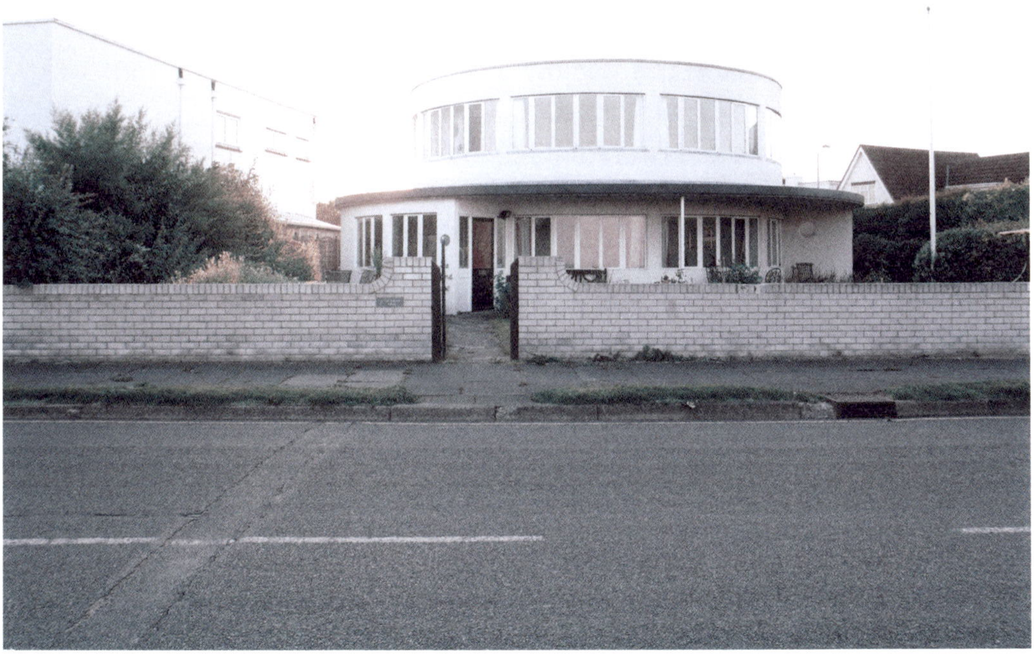

The R◇und House, Frint◇n-on-Sea

of Hill, he was more concerned with the hedonistic potential of modernism than its revolutionary impulses. His interest in both modernist aesthetics and nudity may have put him doubly at odds with the genteel conservatism of Frinton, but once again Essex seemed to offer a place where such experiments could at least take place.

There is another ambitious pre-war modernist settlement to visit, this time on the banks of the River Thames Estuary. This is where in 1932 the Czech industrialist Tomas Bata chose to build one of his shoe factories and a small town in which to house its workers. East Tilbury's modernist housing and factory buildings loom incongruously out of the Essex marshes. They are an early example of both modernism and globalisation, a twin to the original Bata town of Zlín in the Czech Republic and the progenitor of other factories in the worldwide Bata empire.

Bata-Ville – as it was known – was designed by the company's in-house architects František Lydie Gahura, and Vladimír Karfík. Like Silver End, it was laid out according to Garden City principles with roads of semi-detached worker housing fanning out from a radial centre occupied by larger, managers' houses. These latter houses have spacious open verandas that stand in defiance to the kind of exposure to wind and rain likely for residents of the Thames flood plain.

The worker houses employed an innovative concrete wall construction system with integrated services, while the factory buildings themselves had equally pioneering arc-welded steel frames clad externally with brick and continuous rows of vast Crittall-framed windows. More explicitly than Silver End, the factory announced itself with large supergraphic signage visible for miles around and a bronze statue of Bata himself was erected in the mid 1950s.

Alongside the factory and housing there were a number of social and civic buildings including a cinema, hotel and a shopping centre. The hotel is a large, ocean-liner of a building, its scale and logic almost completely unexpected after negotiating the small roads approaching the town. Like the cinema and social club, it is no longer operational. The village hall, painted (perhaps originally) in two shades of brown is still going. The shoe factory itself closed in 2005 and the parts that still seem to be in any kind of use are employed for that growth industry of the UK, self-storage.

Two public buildings from this period, both sited on Essex's estuarine coast, are worthy of mention. The Royal Corinthian Yacht Club at Burnham-on-Crouch was designed by Joseph Emberton in 1931. Emberton was also the architect of Simpsons of Piccadilly and the casino on Blackpool's seafront, and his buildings give expression to a glamorous and hedonistic form of modernism.

His yacht club at Burnham was included in the *Modern Architecture: International Exhibition* curated by Henry-Russell Hitchcock and Philip Johnson at the Museum of Modern Art, New York, in 1932 and has a spectacular quality that is still striking today. Like a beautiful ocean liner temporarily anchored off the muddy banks of the River Crouch, its cantilevered terraces lean over the river frontage in a cascade of glass and concrete.

Less spectacular but still striking is the Labworth Café that overlooks the Thames Estuary in Canvey Island. Built in 1932, the café is actually the only building by the celebrated engineer Ove Arup who designed it whilst working for the contracting company Christiani & Nielsen.

The Labworth was built during Canvey's brief heyday as a holiday resort. Originally consisting of a cantilevered glazed drum hovering over two wings, much of its sculptural dynamism has been lost due to changes in its relationship to the sea defences. The wings – originally supported on slender columns – have also been filled in and the delicate 1930s typeface of its parapet signage has been replaced with cruder metal text.

The building remains an important Essex landmark though and one that has figured in much of its cultural iconography.

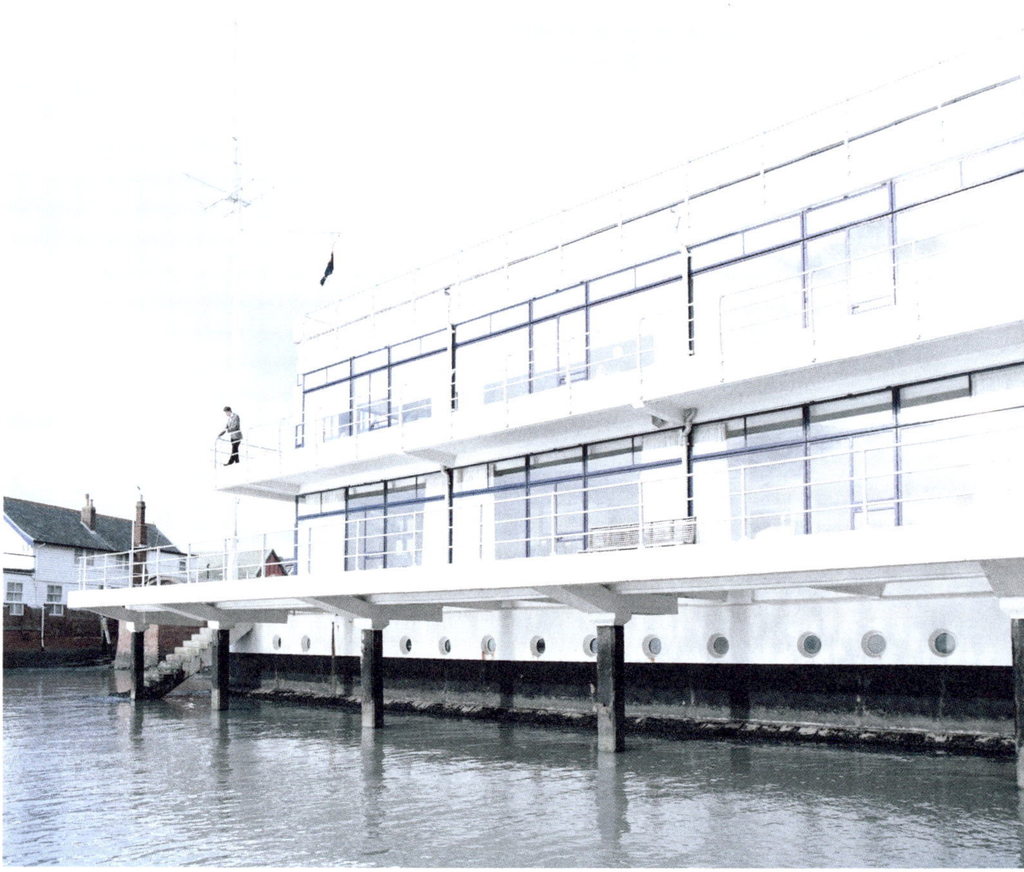

Royal Corinthian Yacht Club, Burnham-on-Crouch

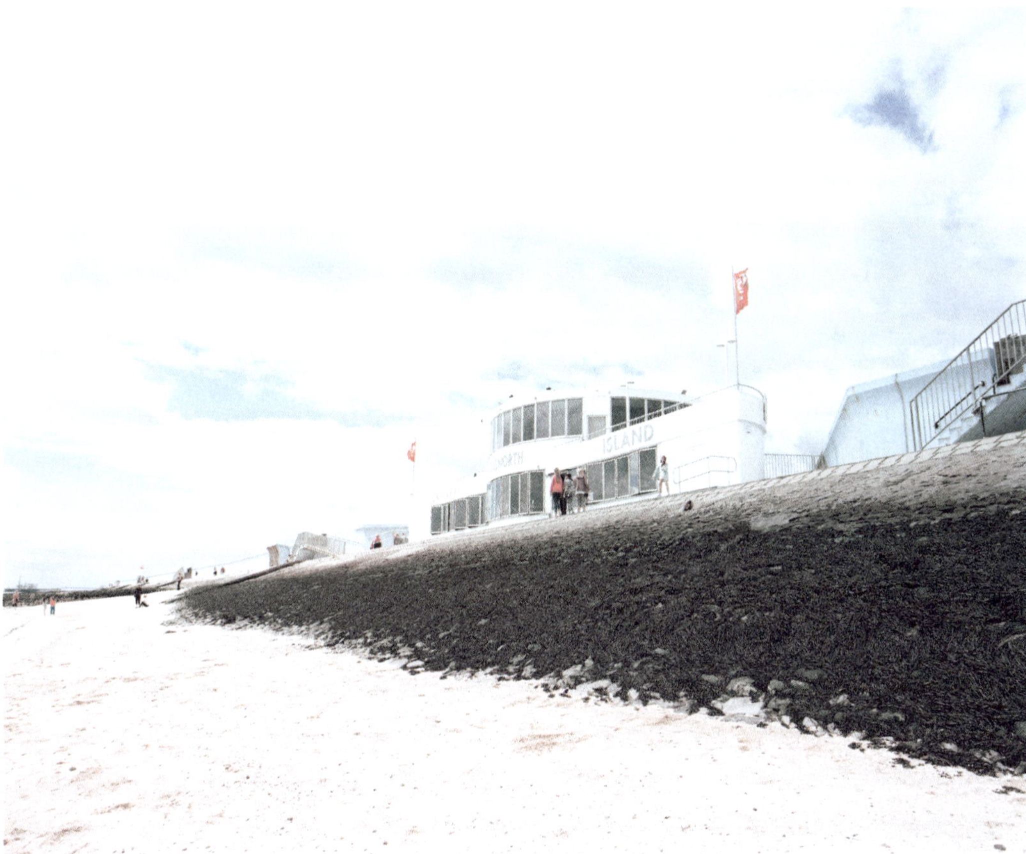

Labworth Café, Canvey Island

Most notably it was used in photoshoots for the Canvey Island-based pub-rock band Dr Feelgood, who heroically re-imagined this stretch of muddy Essex estuary as the 'Thames Delta' in the late 1970s. Early modernism had a particular affinity with the seaside in the UK, but the Labworth Café is a very specifically Essex variant, situated not exactly on the sea but on an island on the banks of the Thames.

The boundary between Essex and London was amended in 1965 and its fringe towns, including Romford, Ilford and Barking, became part of Greater London. Despite this administrative change of status, they remain defiantly Essex in spirit and popular with East Enders moving out to the leafier(ish) suburbs. There are notable examples of postwar transport architecture to be found, including Gants Hill and Redbridge Underground stations by Charles Holden and the remarkably elegant Newbury Bus Station by Oliver Hill.

An even more interesting architectural story can be found in Romford and Gidea Park. Romford Garden Suburb was the product of two architectural competitions intended to drum up buyers for the area's expansion in the early twentieth century. Liberal MP and landowner Sir Herbert Raphael organised an international exhibition of homes in 1910, commissioning 140 designs including a pair of cottages by prominent Arts and Crafts architect M.H. Baillie Scott and a wonderfully taut little detached house by Richard Parker and Raymond Unwin, the designers of Letchworth Garden City. A second phase of housing was commissioned in 1934 and included 64 Heath Drive, a still startling exercise in white-walled abstraction designed by Francis Skinner of Berthold Lubetkin's Tecton group.

Today, Romford Garden Suburb is obviously well-off and smart. There are 'jags and rollers' in the driveways and an air of comfortable affluence pervades the place. The earlier Arts and Crafts influenced houses lend

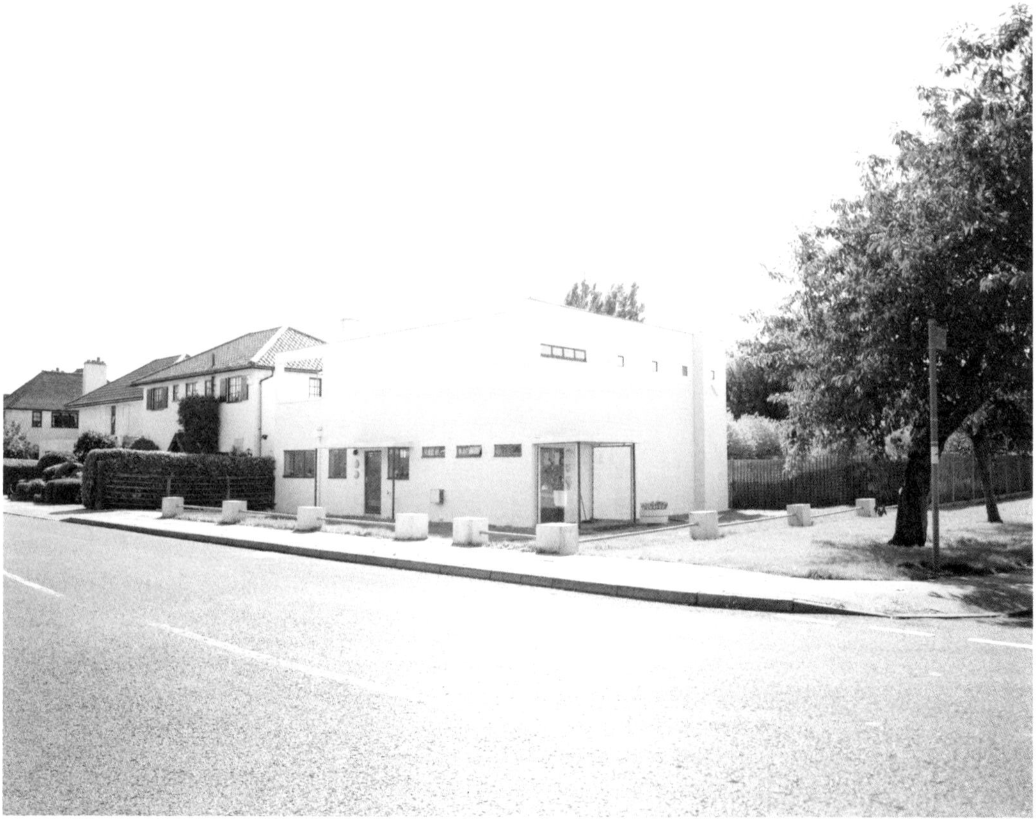

64 Heath Drive, Gidea Park

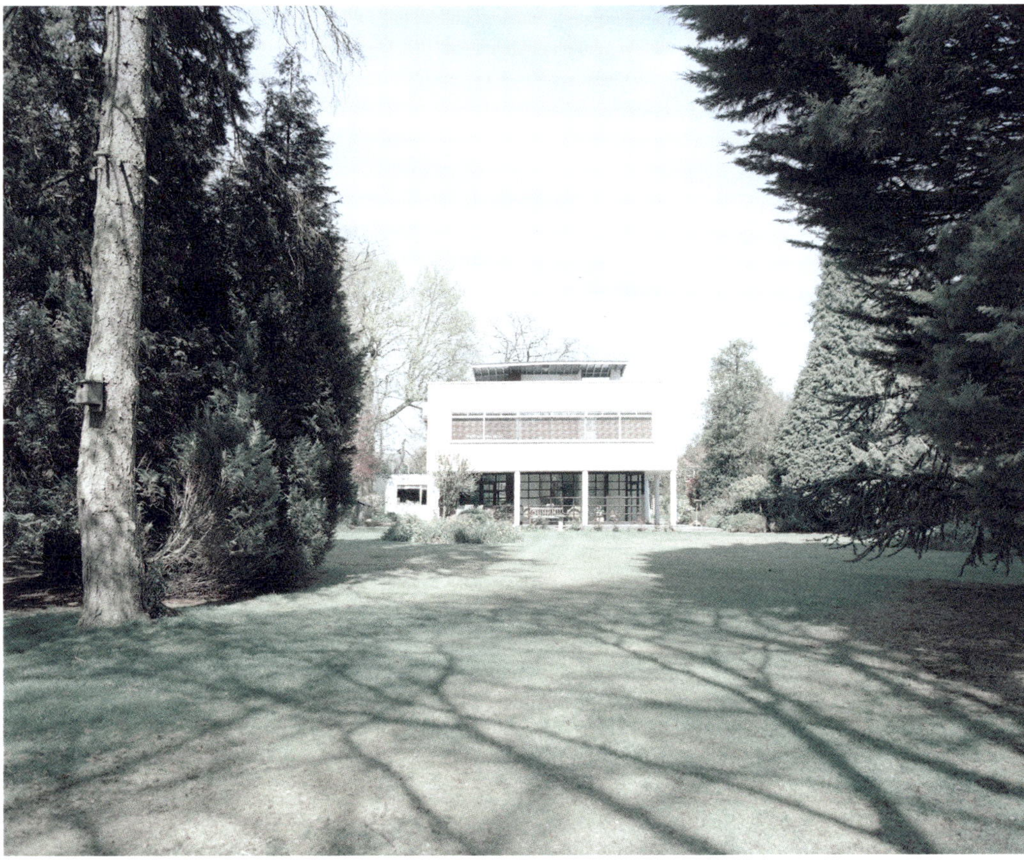

Shipwrights, Benfleet

themselves well to these current aspirations with their exaggerated signifiers of home, richly decorative brickwork and leaded-light windows. The Tecton-designed house has no such signs of upward mobility; instead it sits inscrutable and aloof like a soberly dressed aesthete at an ostentatious neighbour's party.

It is not the only modernist-influenced house in the area, but it is the most extreme. Internally, it opens on to a courtyard and a shallow pool, sheltered by delicate awnings held aloft by thin circular-section columns. The richness of this Corbusian-influenced interior world only serves to intensify the sense that the house belongs to a different vision of Romford's future than the one that surrounds it today.

64 Heath Drive owes its existence to the phenomena of Jewish artists and intellectuals fleeing Nazi Germany in the 1930s. Berthold Lubetkin left Paris in 1931 and emigrated to London where he set up the Tecton group of architects. Responsible for such renowned buildings as the Highpoint I and II flats in Highgate and London Zoo's Penguin Pool, Lubetkin was one of the most influential and inventive architects of the era. Not the least of his contributions was the nurturing of younger talent, and along with Skinner a number of important British architects passed through the Tecton office, including Denys Lasdun.

Ernö Goldfinger, another émigré, this time from Hungary via Paris, designed Hill Pasture in Broxted in 1938 for the garden designer Humphrey Waterfield. Waterfield had in fact commissioned Gerald Flower to design the house, but Goldfinger worked in Flower's office at the time and took the project on. Relatively unknown and much altered at a later date, the house was nonetheless highly regarded by Goldfinger himself and was refurbished by the modernist architect John Winter in the 1990s.

The Swiss architect Douglas Niel Martin-Kaye settled for a few years in the Southend area in the 1920s, where he designed a handful of white-walled, early modernist houses, and Wells Coates, architect of the Lawn Road flats in Hampstead, designed Shipwrights in Benfleet in 1937. Other examples by similarly well-known architects that might have happened – such as Tecton and Chermayeff's planned involvement in Frinton Park Estate – never came to fruition.

THE MIDDLE

To a large extent, Essex's postwar relationship with modernism is bound up with the new towns of Harlow and Basildon. Here the civic modernism that emerged after the Second World War came to fruition in the ambitious social and urban project of the new towns. A full account of these two towns is beyond the scope of this essay (see Gillian Darley's chapter referring to new town development) but a brief account of their most notable architects is important in an analysis of the county's modernist history.

While the early experiments of the 1920s and 1930s were essentially the products of private speculation, the new towns were a state-sponsored architectural programme. This was the period when modernism prevailed and when its tenets were in synch with the social democratic political programme of the day. No longer the preserve of left-field experiments or ambitious philanthropists, modernism was genuinely helping to build a new world.

Essex is unusual in having two new towns, a reflection of both its proximity to London and its postwar ambitions. Of the two, Harlow – on the boundary between Essex and Hertfordshire – is the more architecturally ambitious. Planned in 1947 by Frederick Gibberd for a population of 60,000 people, it was one of the first generation of new towns. Gibberd enlisted an impressive roll call of postwar architects including H.T. Cadbury Brown, Michael Neylan, Clifford Culpin and Leonard Manesseh.

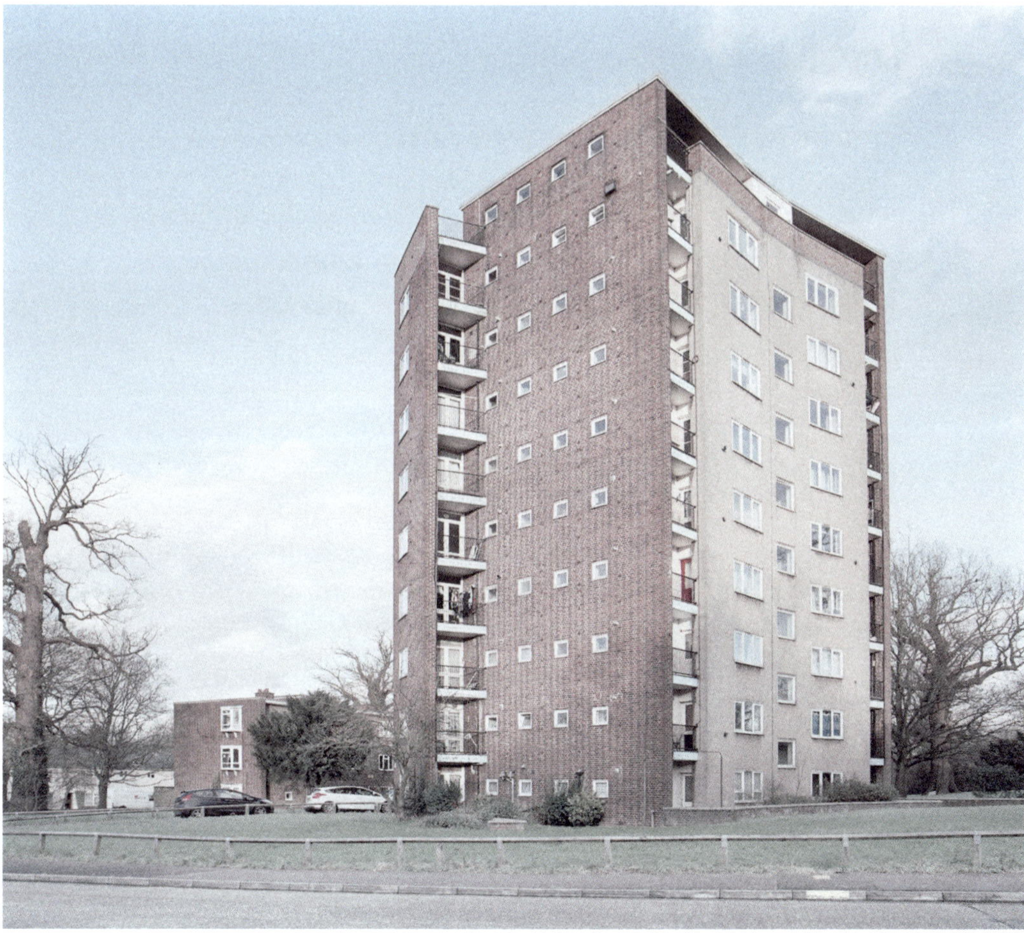

The Lawn, Harlow

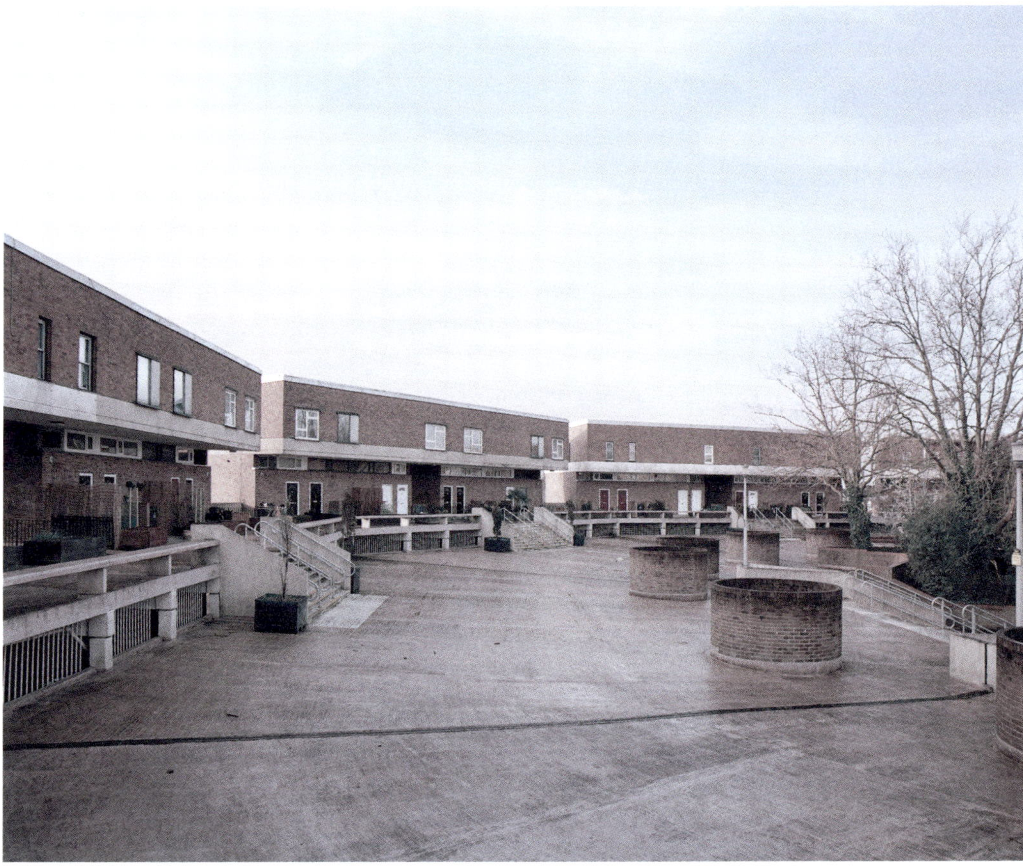

Bishopsfield Estate, Harlow

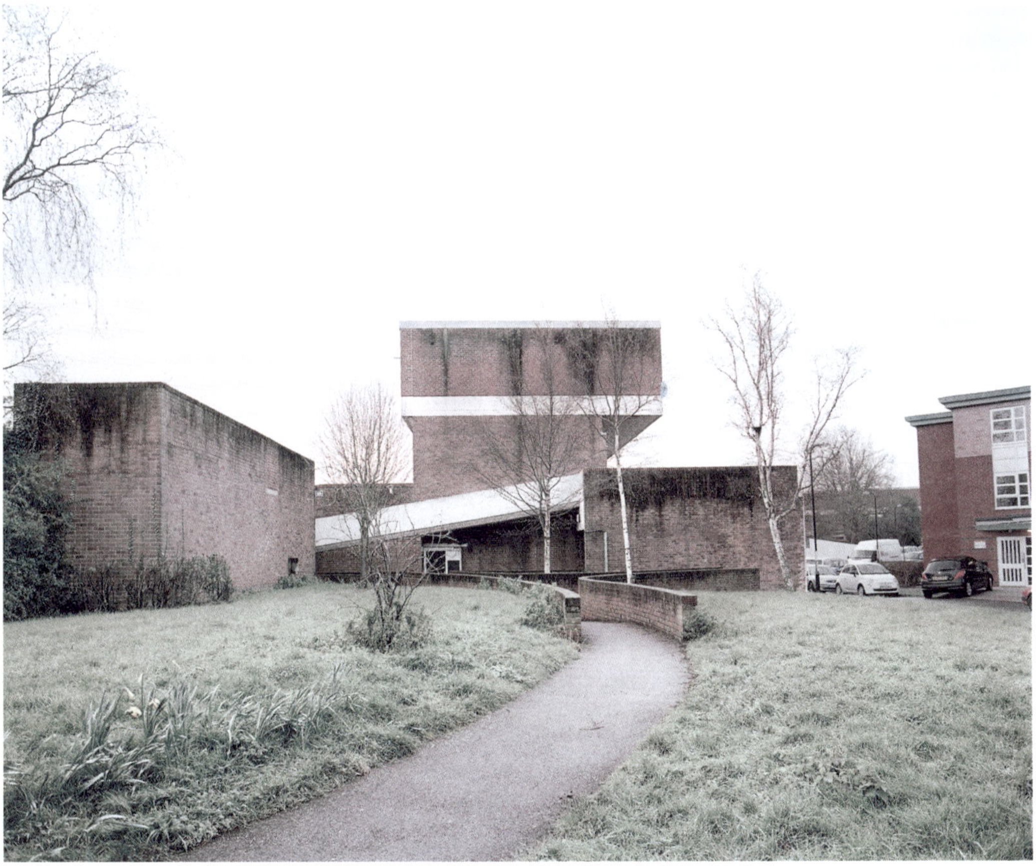

Bishopsfield Estate, Harlow

Gibberd designed the town centre and market place with its picturesque clock tower along a number of housing schemes, but the most striking development was undoubtedly the Bishopsfield Estate by Michael Neylan. While much of Harlow employed a polite 'festival of Britain' form of modernism, Bishopsfield has a forceful, sculptural quality that has proved predictably divisive. Strongly urban and very dense groups of flats span out from a raised piazza that attempts to echo – in the vein of a number of postwar Brutalist estates – a medieval Italian hill town.

Harlow was distinguished over other new towns by the consistency of Gibberd's control and overall vision. He was retained by Harlow Development Corporation until it was wound up in 1980. The quality and number of public sculptures in the town – including work by Barbara Hepworth, Elisabeth Frink and William Mitchell – was the consequence of the Harlow Arts Trust in which Gibberd's wife Patricia Fox-Edwards was highly instrumental.

The Gibberds actually moved to the outskirts of Harlow, refurbishing and extending an existing house there in 1957. Between them the Gibberds created an extraordinary garden, a sort of modernist picturesque landscape filled with contemporary sculptures, along with fragments of historic buildings and architectural ornament, including a set of classical columns 'salvaged' from Coutts Bank in London. Contemporaneous photographs of Gibberd in his garden, flamboyantly dressed and with abundant moustache and long silver hair are strongly redolent of another era when his patrician vision was in tune with the political times.

Basildon boasted a less spectacular roll call of architects although there are notable housing estates by Leonard Manesseh and Ahrends Burton and Koralek. Much of the housing was designed by the development corporation's own architects in a more vernacular-inflected modernist mode that nonetheless pursued important innovations in timber frame technology and sustainable design.

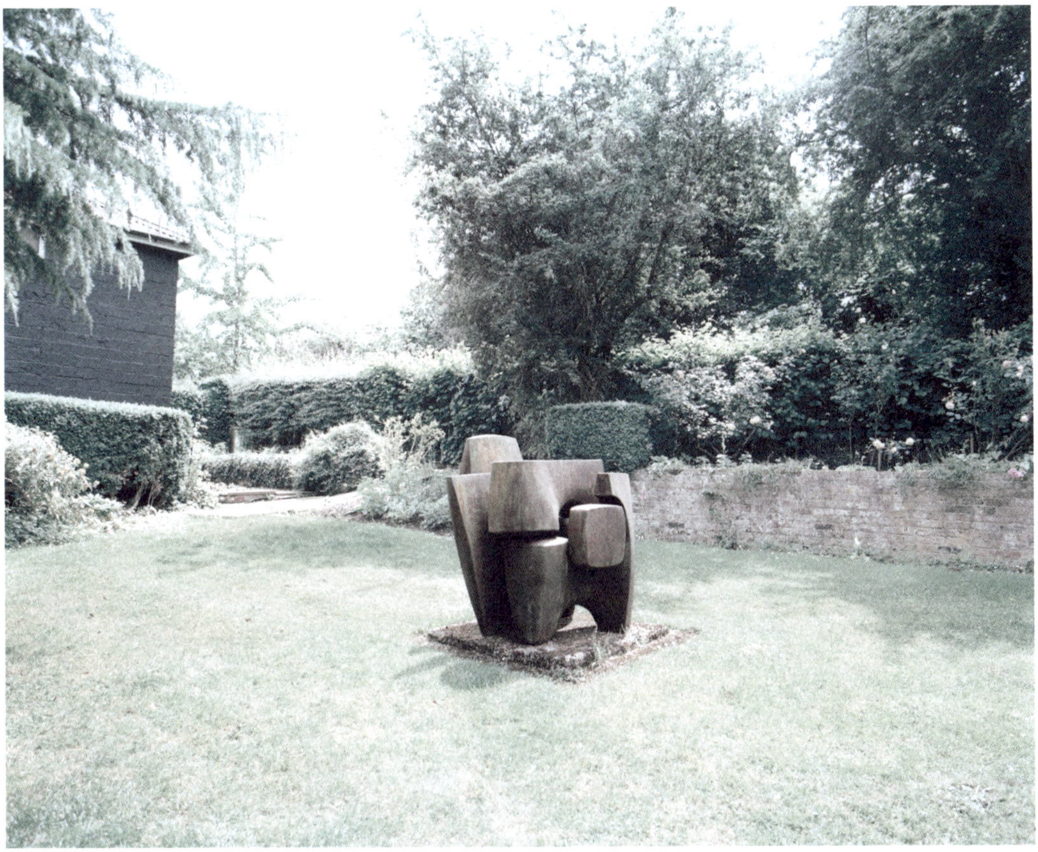

The Gibberd Garden, Harlow

Several members of the corporation's Architecture Department built their own homes in Essex, including group leaders Clive Plumb and David Brewster. These houses continued the same themes at the scale of the individual, one-off house. Plumb's house – located at the end of a cul-de-sac in the village of Great Leighs – is small in scale and retreats from view. It is a single storey L-shape in plan and almost single aspect towards a garden enclosed on two sides. Built by Plumb himself in 1976, it employed pioneering solar collector panels and allowed for future re-organisation and adaptation.

David Brewster's house in the nearby village of Writtle is tucked away down a pedestrian walkway behind the picturesque village green. Like Plumb's house it was self-built by the architect and employs timber-frame construction. In this case, the frame forms a large, pyramidal structure enclosing an open-planned tent-like space with a bedroom perched up in the apex. Next door is another slightly smaller house also designed and built by Webster and employing the same geometry and palette of timber, fair-faced brick and tiles.

The architectural language of all three houses is familiar from Basildon, a vernacular-inflected but still modernist aesthetic of mono-pitch roofs, neo-Brutalist brickwork and open planning. If this work retreated from the more obviously heroic architecture of Silver End or East Tilbury, it still pursued a faith in technology and innovative spatial organisation drawn from earlier modernist experimentation.

Another branch of late-modernist planning can be found in East Hanningfield where several streets of new houses were designed by James Gowan for Chelmsford District Council in 1978. Gowan had previously been in partnership with James Stirling with whom he had designed the iconoclastic Engineering Building at Leicester University in 1963. Gowan's solo career may have been less flamboyant than Stirling's (and less dogged by high-profile technical failings) but in many ways their post-Leicester trajectory was similar.

East Hanningfield can be seen as Gowan's version of Stirling's swing towards architectural postmodernism. Both moved on from modernism, embracing, in Gowan's case, elements of vernacular housing, neo-Brutalism and a gentler Scandinavian influence. In their exaggerated mono-pitch roofs, decorative brickwork and interlocking ground plans, there are traces of Alvar Aalto, Gunnar Asplund and Jorn Utzon in the East Hanningfield houses. In this there are strong visual similarities to the group of houses designed by Clifford Culpin in Great Waltham, near Chelmsford, which also employ mono-pitched roofs, but combined with white-washed brick that increases the debt to Aalto.

The abstracted but still recognisable 'houseness' of Gowan's East Hanningfield scheme can be seen as a belated reaction to the flat-roofed modernism begun several decades before at Clockhouse Way. Their decorative brickwork and arts and crafts inflections are subtly postmodernist and pay as much attention to vernacular sources as they do modernist ones. Gowan even included a Stirling-esque joke: the surrounds of the numerous porthole window are formed from standard precast concrete sewer pipes. Whether this was a sardonic comment or an act of pragmatic expediency is not recorded.

Perhaps because Essex is not a county of second-home owners or the wealthy bourgeoisie, it does not abound in architecturally ambitious one-off houses. There *are* one or two interesting postwar houses but you have to hunt them down. One remarkable example can be found in Ulting, a tiny village tucked away down a winding lane on the outskirts of Maldon, which is lined with pink-plastered houses. There is a tiny but handsome brick schoolhouse and a church that overlooks a particularly serene stretch of the River Chelmer. Somewhere amongst all this, lurking in the undergrowth, is one of Richard and Su Rogers's earliest buildings, a bright yellow steel-framed tribute to the Los Angeles Case Study houses.

The house at Ulting was commissioned by Humphrey Spender, brother of poet Stephen, photographer, painter, textile designer and all-round modernist polymath. Built in 1968, it consists of two rectangular sheds, one containing the house and the other Spender's studio. Both have externally expressed steel portal frames in-filled with floor-to-ceiling single glazing or crinkly metal cladding. They look like a pair of miniature industrial buildings parked in a mature garden.

Although he died in 2005, it is still full of Spender's remarkably diverse output: paintings, prints, fabrics and found objects are scattered around, preserved as if he has just popped over to the house for a cup of tea. The house itself is wonderful, un-refurbished and almost completely original. The plan is a compact rectangle, neatly organised and extremely logical if you ignore the alarming structural details which possibly work better under the Californian sun than an Essex winter. But the joy is in the visual connections to the garden and the vivid, practically psychedelic colour scheme. The JCB-yellow roof trusses are augmented by purple doors and striped curtains that run through a rainbow of shades of orange. Sadly the original bright red carpet has been replaced by a more subdued tone, but the interior still has the capacity to shock; its late-1960s grooviness sitting incongruously in the bucolic countryside.

For all its visual rhetoric of mass production, the Spender House is not in itself an ambitious social experiment. Its late 1960s take on the industrial aesthetic links it conceptually rather than programmatically to places like Silver End or East Tilbury. But it still points to a radical idea of what rural architecture could be. The Spender House is a techno-hymn to Arcadianism, appropriately enough set within an Edenic orchard. Wandering around its beautiful garden, flowers curling around the tension wires that brace the structure, an alternative history of postwar housing comes to mind.

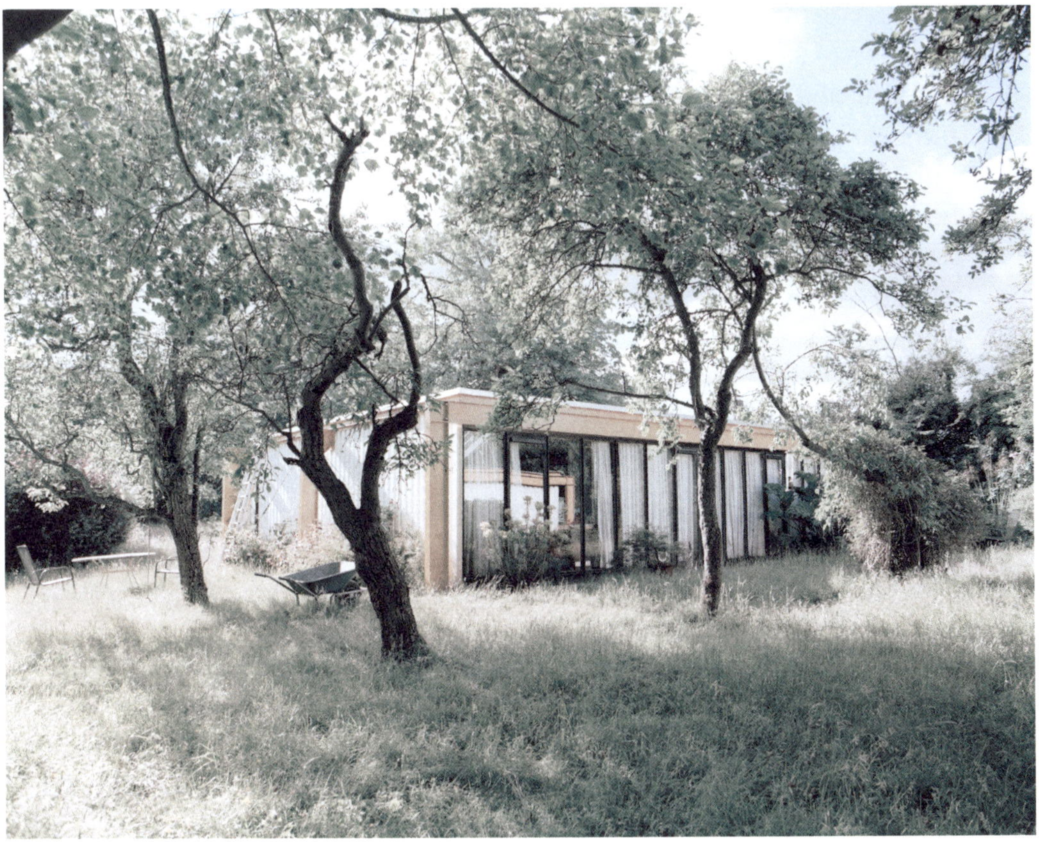

Spender House, Ulting

Researching this essay I came across a black-and-white photograph from the early 1980s. It is a fairly typical 'band photo' of the period, five hopeful aspirants with the bouffant hair and tight T-shirts of a certain kind of pop wannabe.

The band were called Right Hand Man and they were the winners of a competition in 1981 to write a song about South Woodham Ferrers (SWF), a new town planned by Essex County Council. Both the song and the promotional video that it accompanied celebrated SWF as a comfortably familiar and traditional looking Essex town. The song's jaunty lyrics explicitly embrace a retrospective aesthetic of neo-vernacular houses and faux-medieval spatial planning, accompanied by the requisite smiling children and majorettes.

SWF is in many ways the antithesis of the new town modernism of Harlow and Basildon. It was a product of the Residential Design Guide, an influential document published by Essex County Council in 1973. The Essex Design Guide, as it became known, can be seen as a rejection of modernism enshrined in statutory planning guidance. It became one of the most influential planning documents ever produced in the UK, ushering in a form of neo-vernacular architecture that has become ubiquitous for new developments across the country. It favoured loose groupings of houses in arrangements that evoked village settlement patterns. It also encouraged the use of traditional Essex building materials such as weatherboarding, brick and plaster.

South Woodham Ferrers was the Essex Design Guide's first significant manifestation. Before it no one had ever thought to disguise a supermarket as an agricultural barn or a new street of houses as medieval farm cottages. The street names in SWF provide a literary underpinning for this merry mythmaking, many of them culled from the work of J.R.R. Tolkien including Gandalf's Ride and Elrond's Rest.

While this conceit might feel just about plausible gazing out of your window across the mudflats of the River Crouch estuary, it becomes trickier when confronting the commercial reality of the town centre.

This is predicated around a vast Asda superstore whose car park effectively forms the town's market square. Meanwhile, the 'actual' square – complete with bandstand – is squeezed behind the Asda with the store's service entrances facing on to it. Asda in fact owns much of the town centre having bought large chunks of it from Essex County Council. Their dominance is not so much an unfortunate by-product as a fundamental part of SWF's DNA.

SWF was opened by the Queen in 1981, a year and a half after Margaret Thatcher's first election victory. Her government ushered in a rejection of the social-democratic project of the postwar era. This radical break from consensus included – perhaps as a compensatory move – a strain of cultural nostalgia for pre-modern social conventions. SWF could be viewed as the spatial corollary of this particular combination of social conservatism and economic liberalism. And it continued to grow throughout the 1980s, expanding like an urban manifestation of her core demographic. Today it is both busy and slightly desolate in the manner of many small towns. The awkward compromises of fitting contemporary commercial activities into vernacular forms means that there are dead ends and bleak alleyways as problematic as the ones that the Essex Design Guide was meant to design out.

The architect Raymond Erith moved to Dedham in north Essex in 1936 and practised there until his death in 1973. Against the tide of postwar modernism, Erith's architecture was classical in spirit and Georgian in inspiration. His office was a throwback in every sense. Occupying a group of cottages on Dedham High Street, drawings were produced on ancient boards to antiquated paper sizes, all according to Erith's strict rules of architectural draughtsmanship. In her account of Erith's practice, his daughter Lucy Archer describes a daily routine of intense drawing followed by sherry in the study and of weekends spent polishing the Bentley.

Ploughing an almost solitary furrow, Erith designed a number of classical houses and public projects – including the refurbishment of numbers 10, 11 and 12 Downing Street – but the majority of his projects were in north Essex and Suffolk. The resulting buildings are austere and elegant yet playful. They re-combine elements of classical architecture in a way that suggests the idea of progressive classicism – a phrase coined by Erith to describe the work of his architectural hero Sir John Soane – is not an oxymoron.

Great House in Dedham itself typifies his style: a plain, flat-fronted neo-Georgian facade with a curious two-thirds scale doorway and windows placed close to the edge of walls in an almost modernist manner. It is on one level a pretty convincing piece of pastiche and on another an innovative example of classicism evolving into something else.

At the other end of Dedham High Street, Erith designed a series of detached houses known collectively as Frog Meadow. Each one takes a classical or vernacular archetype – Georgian farmhouse, classical villa etc. – and subtly adapts it to the setting. Sited informally around a curving country road and set back behind a narrow brook, the houses are surprisingly successful and undoubtedly elegantly done.

They were built over a number of years beginning in 1967 and ending in 1980. They show the slow evolution of Erith's practice and the arrival in it of another classical architect, Quinlan Terry. Terry would eventually take over the small, rambling office in Dedham High Street turning it into, first, Quinlan Terry and Partners and then later Quinlan and Francis Terry when he was joined by his architect son. The work continued Erith's classical trajectory though perhaps without quite the same subtlety or grace. But more significantly, the times had changed. While Erith ran counter to the prevailing orthodoxy of modernism, representing a gently itinerant strain of his own, Terry's work became championed by Prince Charles and associated with a wider rejection of modern architecture by society.

Quinlan Terry was a key figure in this 1980s period, claiming a link between classicism and Christianity and re-associating traditional architecture with the political and royal establishment. What does this mean in the context of Radical ESSEX and a chapter intended to explore the county's undoubtedly remarkable modernist legacy? To return to the opening paragraph of this essay, I think it is possible to trace both the beginning and the end of modernism in Essex.

If Clockhouse Way is the start of modernism then the combination of the Essex Design Guide and Quinlan Terry look suspiciously like its end. Not in the literal sense of course: contemporary buildings continue to be designed and built, here as elsewhere. And in many respects the quality and ambition of these has improved in recent decades. But something has also undoubtedly been lost. The sense of forward trajectory, of the ability of modern architecture and technology to solve society's problems has evaporated. If in 1926, Francis Crittall and his architects were re-imagining what a village could be, by the late 1970s Erith and the Essex Design Guide were reaching back to past archetypes.

CODA

Perhaps because it was unburdened by the desirability of more conventionally picturesque counties, for a few fleeting decades Essex embraced a vision of the future that seems lost to us today. Nostalgia, traditionalism and the contradictory impulses of late-twentieth century neo-liberalism came to reject that future but not before it produced a remarkable legacy of modernist experimentation.

Modernism left its mark on Essex it's true. But Essex left its mark on modernism too. The particular character and colour of the county, from its industrial ex-urban London fringe to its agricultural north, produced a vision of architecture that was both international and highly particular, a genuinely home-grown modernism. And it is all still there for the most part, very much lived-in and sometimes almost lost under decades of resident adaptations or domestic makeovers.

This chapter describes the modernist architecture of Essex as it is today, the legacy of a remarkable period in the history of housing. But although that period came to an end, the housing still stands as a potent symbol of how we could retrieve that pioneering spirit and start to build optimistically again for the future.

CHARLES HOLLAND is an architect, teacher and writer. He is the principal of Charles Holland Architects (CHA), a design and research practice whose current work includes residential, civic and public art projects. Charles is a Professor of Architecture at the University of Brighton where his research focuses on housing and new settlements, particularly in suburban and 'ruburban' settings. He writes and lectures about architecture and the work of his practice regularly and contributes a monthly column to the *RIBA Journal* on the subject of utopias.

FURTHER READING

A Design Guide for Residential Areas (Essex County Council 1973)

Lucy Archer, *Raymond Erith, Architect* (The Cygnet Press 1985)

James Bettley and Nikolaus Pevsner (eds.), *The Buildings of England: Essex* (Yale University Press 2007)

David J. Blake, *Window Vision* (Crittall Windows 1989)

Charles McKean, *Architectural Guide to Cambridge and East Anglia* (RIBA Publications Ltd 1982)

Alan Powers, *Oliver Hill, Architect and Lover of Life*, 1887–1968 (Mouton Publications 1989)

Norman Scarfe, *Essex: A Shell Guide* (Faber & Faber 1968)

Note: Sections of 'The Rise and Fall' were previously published in *Icon*, no.149, 1 November 2015

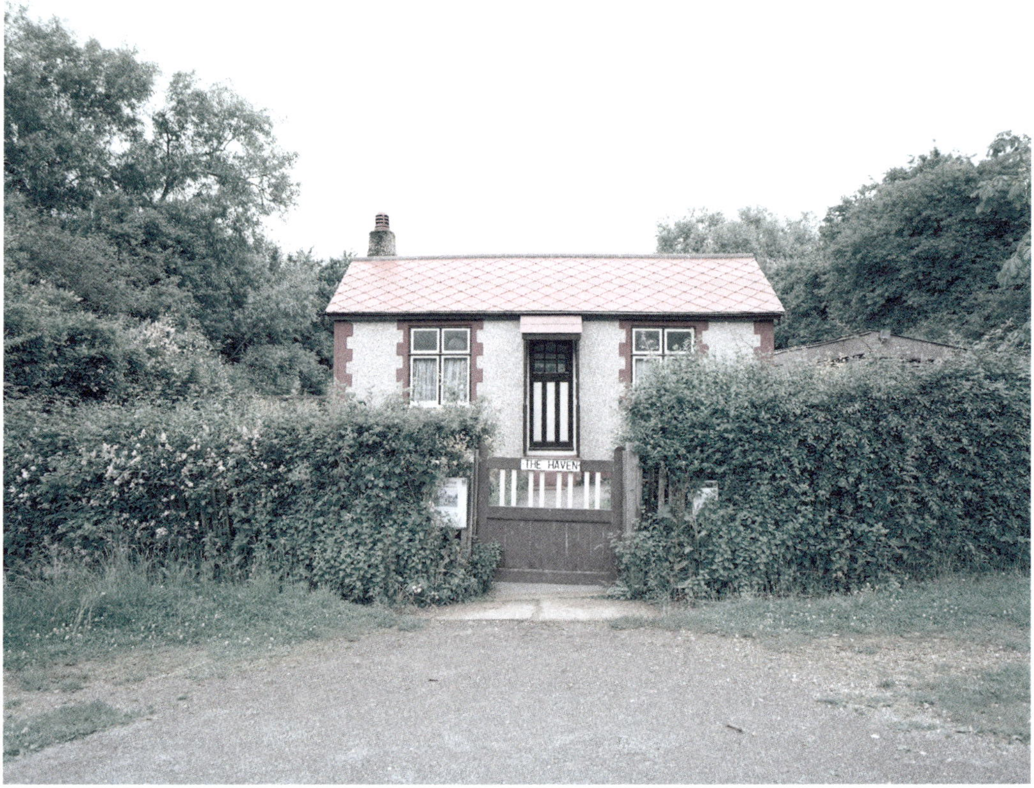

The Haven Plotlands Museum, Laindon

From Plotlands to New Towns

Gillian Darley

The push and pull between East London and Essex proved, for centuries, to be a necessary and fruitful tension, but by the late-nineteenth century it had reached crisis point. In 1888 the housing reformer Octavia Hill published an essay for the periodical *Nineteenth Century* titled 'More Air for London', in which she gave statistics, based on an area within a four-mile radius from Charing Cross, to illustrate the shocking imbalance between the eastern and western halves of the capital. In the entire east and north-east sections she estimated that 223 acres of public open space were available, while in the west and south-west, a handsome 1,701 acres. That statistic became even more telling when measured against population density, as in the east, every acre of open ground served 7,481 people, in the west, the figure fell to 682.

The housing crisis in London, about which Octavia Hill had just offered her firsthand observations and years of experience to the Royal Commission on the Housing of the Working Classes (1884–85), would have repercussions far beyond the then limits of the capital. Newly constituted local authorities for outer districts tentatively tried out, and applied, the by-laws to a tidal wave of new housing development, designed to challenge the dreadful deficiencies of old housing stock. In Leyton, then part of the county of Essex, the surveyor for the municipal borough that had been formed in 1873, was to approve some 7,000 plans in the decade between 1882 and 1892.

However Leyton, as everywhere in the outer suburbs, also offered other options. Outliers in a world of unselfconscious self-sufficiency were to be found wherever indeterminate pieces of land were available and were occupied by those with the skills to fend for themselves. The solutions were essentially ad hoc. Lea Bridge railway station, opened in 1840, had brought development in its wake, and with it the services, water and gas and, later, electricity and sewage. All required structures and land, as did the railways themselves, occupying extensive freight yards. A wedge of ground running alongside the railway track close to Lea Bridge station may have been surplus land or had fallen into disuse by the 1880s. As such it provided a handy site for almost 70 'shacks', later dignified by the name 'Bungalow Town' (although this generic, but pejorative, term was widely applied to irregular settlements). Whatever the explanation, and whoever the residents were (quite possibly those displaced by new and orthodox developments), they had access to wells and earth closets, and were watched over by a timber mission church. They lived there undisturbed until the 1920s, when the site was cleared to provide a dirt track for football and speedway, possibly the initiative of the new landlord of The Greyhound public house, Jack Noseworthy.

The residents were largely self-supporting, rearing ducks and growing vegetables, reflecting the long-established economy of the Lea Valley with its nursery gardens and smallholdings. An image, dating from around 1920, shows a couple of cottages elaborated with trelliswork and overlooking prize-winning gardens; an earlier photograph shows a shack or two with, as yet, no sign of cultivation on the rough ground. Perhaps the average condition of the rudimentary cottages in the diminutive trackside hamlet lay somewhere between the two.

Unmarked, little noticed and scarcely recorded, Bungalow Town, Lea Bridge represented the same spirit and initiative that drove those who became known as 'plotlanders' in the next generation. Marginal homeowners rather than squatters, they were caught between the exigencies of providing themselves with decent, weatherproof shelter, but also creating homes. Despite being no more than basic single-storey structures, these often flourished as individualistic expressions of domestic *bricolage*. A photograph of a pair of early shacks on Canvey Island shows them encrusted with turrets, bound by verandas and trelliswork and topped by weathervanes.

As the railway lines running eastwards proliferated, access to workmen's fares under the Cheap Trains Act 1883 had driven the development of London's eastern suburbs but also offered the tempting prospect of access, by train or charabanc, to the coast and countryside. At much the same time, a seismic shift in the pattern of land ownership was taking place, largely due to the catastrophe in agriculture. In Essex, as elsewhere, farm bankruptcies rose dramatically, driven by the combined effects of low crop prices (due to cheap American grain imports), the difficulties and cost of working the rock-solid, heavy clay known locally as 'three-horse land' and a prolonged run of poor weather and lost harvests. A Royal Commission in 1893 surveyed the scene. Rowland Prothero, the historian of agriculture writing just before the First World War, noted that 'thousands of acres which had formerly yielded great crops and paid high rent, had passed out of cultivation into ranches for cattle or temporary sheep-runs.' Added to these difficulties was an acute shortage of labour, during and after the war.

The eventual state of almost all the former farmland in south-east Essex, the area between the Blackwater and the Thames, to the east of Billericay, was a wasteland of rough scrub, the default setting for untended, little grazed ground. As farmers failed, estate agents, small-time entrepreneurs and opportunistic developers intervened, parcelling up the land. Some of it went into large-scale conventional development around the nodal points of the railway stations, the rest into more and more, ever smaller, plots. The railway company shareholders and those now disposing of redundant farmland were often in cahoots and a suggestible, working-class market was ready for their inducements.

Access to some of the most remote areas of south-east Essex had come with the opening of a new station at Laindon in 1888 serving a line that ran directly from Barking to Pitsea, on the London Tilbury and Southend route. Pitsea was also the junction for two different lines and another firm, the Great Eastern Railway company, also ran to Southend. There was, happily for impoverished passengers, stiff competition on ticket prices.

In the early 1920s the pre-war trickle became a flood. Potential purchasers, lured out of London to attend the auctions with free rail tickets and a lavish meal, possibly alerted by no more than a notice on the back of a London tram ticket or by a poster in the pub, might need to buy two or three adjacent plots in order to secure enough ground. Once in the auctioneers' tent, the transaction usually required the deposit of a pound to secure the title deeds and thereafter a succession of modest monthly payments. The promises that the vendors offered, such as metalled roads and mains drainage, were rarely worth the paper on which they were written.

To begin with the Londoners were looking for holiday homes, easily accessible by train or bus, the kind of basic summerhouses within allotment gardens to be found all over northern Europe. Many families began their forays into country life from the shelter of tents or rudimentary sheds, in due season and with an area of ground marginally larger than the average allotment, enough for some fruit trees. Even temporarily, the summer escape from the East End, and the independence it heralded, was a huge relief and signalled the beginning of an incremental shift in style of life and work. Dennis Hardy and Colin Ward interviewed some of the last generation of plotland children for their book *Arcadia for All* (2003) and revealed lives as varied as their houses.

Exemplifying what might draw a family from Limehouse, Poplar or East Ham to the area was the auction of the first portion of the Dunton Hills Estate. It was held at 4pm on 3 July 1924, with 183 freehold plots offered in long thin fingers, typically 7 × 53 metres in length. Hyperbole tinged the details; the estate was pleasantly situated on the south-west slope of the 'celebrated' Laindon Hills, and commercial options were offered too, such as plots with frontages on to the main road – locations that might support a shop. There is 'every possibility' of a station being added to the line between the existing halts at East Horndon and Laindon. There was mains water on the road, although that was more than a mile away, as those who came from London on the bus soon discovered.

A modest single-storey house type developed, easily denigrated as a 'shack' but in reality these were weather-tight structures, on occasion disguising a disused railway carriage or incorporating a caravan. Usually, they were built of lapped timber, with two rooms. Builders often brought the materials with them on the train. Later modernisation and extension might add a couple of extra rooms, as at The Haven, Dunton (now the Plotlands Museum), or even a skin of pebbledash and an outhouse or two. It took a considerable time for the authorities to realise the enormous scale of what had grown up, in effect these were ad hoc settlements that they were now trying to regularise. In 1931, Stanley Adshead's South Essex planning survey compared the rate of new settlement to that of industrialising Lancashire during the entire nineteenth century. This modern version, Professor Adshead suggested, was a benevolent form of colonisation, an admirably enterprising endeavour in an area of non-viable farmland. Whether this was what George Lansbury, by then leader of the Labour Party, had in mind when he called for 'reclaiming, recreating rural England' must remain a moot point, but it was far more progressive than his well-intentioned 1904 scheme to provide practical relief for Poplar men through a farm settlement at Laindon, to be devalued, with time, into little more than a 'workhouse out-station'.

The Haven, which tells the history of plotlands to an engaged public, is, ironically enough, set amidst a naturalised landscape overseen by Essex Wildlife Trust, a solitary 'shack'. The many others that once stood on the Dunton site are marked by, at most, their foundations in the undergrowth of a recently wooded area, grown up since 1989. Visitors are reminded of the practical difficulties of plotland life; until 1937 residents got their water from standpipes, petrol- or paraffin-driven generators provided the only power until gas came in the 1940s, while the tracks were often impassable in winter.

Only the layout of the earth lanes around the area remains, reinforced by the immediacy of firsthand accounts from the volunteers who run the museum. Roy's mother was from Poplar and came out for summer weeks in the 1930s. She stayed, marrying a Dunton man whose family had been local farm workers for generations. His parents were offered cash for their plot, or a house in Basildon New Town. They realised, he told me, that their rent on the new house would be neatly met by the interest from the cash settlement. His father was quite happy to move into town, in his old age enjoying watching the cars pass by his windows.

During and immediately after the Second World War, with the intensive bombing of the docks and adjacent boroughs, the attitude to what constituted decent housing moved down a gear, yet a settled population, albeit largely outside the remit of local bureaucracies and frequently without services, was to be a considerable, prolonged, headache for the authorities. At worst it threatened a public health nightmare at a period when the epidemics of urban poverty were still in the grandparental memory.

Norman Scarfe's contribution to the Land Utilisation Survey (1942) for L. Dudley Stamp was on Essex. After describing the well-hedged, rolling agricultural acres of the south of the county he changed tone; at Laindon, he reported: 'Into this poor bramble-covered region has penetrated a vast array of tiny bungalows, corrugated-iron shanties with dreadful rutted roads, reminiscent of the backwoods. Mankind seems to have sought relief from the rush and roar of London in the wilderness of wild nature with a few poultry, goats, rabbits and perhaps cows.' Scarfe, not to be confused with his namesake the author of *Essex: A Shell Guide* (1968), had sympathetically caught the motivation of the urban escapees as well as their dire conditions.

With the passing of the Housing Act 1944 (Temporary Accommodation), a range of random existing structures were pressed into service. Outside Halstead, for example, on the Sudbury road at Ashford Lodge, a Prisoner of War camp had been built, called HQ 129 Italian Labour Battalion. Some 500 Italians (and later a smaller number of Germans) were housed there before repatriation. The camp consisted of a series of redoubtable Nissen huts, served by mains water and provided with a chapel and a medical centre. Arguably the standard of housing here was higher than much of the local rural stock, unimproved since the nineteenth century. The first impulse of the local authority had been to prevent squatters claiming these huts, but they then realised that the huts offered utilitarian emergency housing stock, which was more quickly available than prefabs, and a stopgap prior to the setting up of a local authority house-building programme.

With the driving force of the New Towns Act 1946, the compulsory purchase of 7,800 acres of land, stretching from Laindon to Pitsea, to enable the establishment of Basildon New Town in 1949 (only two years after Harlow) appeared to be a seamless planning solution – at least to planners. On the ground, the compulsory purchase mechanism, and the levels of compensation offered, led to furious disputes and labyrinthine legal confusion. Without mortgages, title to a particular plot was frequently unclear, lost in the years of fly-by-night auctions and pressured transactions. Yet the value of the freeholds would prove to be a way of dealing with, and defusing, much of the initial strong opposition from the plotlanders.

Basildon was the only self-selected new town site in the south. Essex County Council and Billericay District Council had joined forces to petition the Minister, Lewis Silkin, for designation. Even the County Boroughs of East Ham and West Ham had supported it, as an area where many of their former residents already lived and to which others might move, a logical overspill zone. The Development Corporation was appointed in 1949, but even then the process was taking place in, if not the dark, then the dusk. At the time of the 1951 census Bernard Braine, Conservative MP for Billericay, pointed out that the number of people living on the acres in question was not, as had been estimated, 17,000 but almost 11,000 more. The informality of the entire process, reaching back several decades, and the way in which the plotlanders had been scarcely noticed, let alone their number estimated correctly, is in utter contrast to the establishment of the new towns by the ministry, tending to be bureaucratic to a fault. A political divide opened. Labour councillors lost their seats in drifts and, as Colin Ward wrote, the debate over compensation became 'a controversy between two opposing conceptions of social and individual rights in land'.

Basildon, like Harlow, was planned around the neighbourhood unit, rooted in planner and sociologist Clarence Perry's 1920s ideas from the United States. Although the notion was continually criticised in Britain, the theoretical basis of planning residential areas in concert with their amenities, an attempt to offer something of the social and functional complexity of a small town, was eagerly adopted. In the so-called 'Live Architecture' exhibition at Poplar, the Lansbury estate built for the Festival of Britain in 1951, a reduced version was rolled out. Churches, schools, market, old people's housing and residential provision in various configurations were the glue in the integrated mix, offering urbanity within the greater urban area. Several of the professionals involved there, in particular Frederick Gibberd, Geoffrey Jellicoe and Judith Ledeboer, were to be stalwarts in the planning and design of the early new towns.

It was easier to design and build the signature buildings of a new town than to layout and construct, against a pressing schedule, the much-needed housing. Car ownership had been estimated at twenty-five per cent in the original Basildon masterplan and was cut back even further. By 1968 the provision was 200 per cent, two spaces per household. Hence the planning of vehicle routes and parking strategies had to be entirely reconsidered and the status of the highway engineer soared. Lionel Brett, (to be Lord Esher) who with his partner Kenneth Boyd designed the Ghyllgrove Estate in Basildon, wrote in 1953 that new town architects found themselves frustrated by a vile cocktail of obstacles and impediments which he listed as 'Red tape, lack of funds, engineering restrictions, consumer's conservatism, inefficient organization.'

The consensus was that housing schemes generated by the London County Council were rather less burdened, although the pre-war dispersal of Londoners to immense estates such as Becontree, and postwar to the numerous 'out-country' estates was heavily criticised, particularly by sociologists. For their part, the architectural profession had its knives out for the new towns. J.M. Richards and Gordon Cullen in their lacerating *Architectural Review* article 'Failure of the New Towns', referred to 'prairie planning', and considered that 'what should have been a great adventure has come to nothing.' Loosely applied Garden City principles had led to suburbanisation, the loss of those civilising qualities of urbanity. However Nikolaus Pevsner in his 1954 Essex volume in the *Buildings of England* series disagreed, suggesting that 'under the skilful hands of Frederick Gibberd' something completely unprecedented in Britain was appearing at Harlow, 'a taste of what a completely modern, if not a completely urban community, can provide in the way of visual pleasures.'

From the very beginning, and in stark contrast to the seeming invisibility of the old self-built settlements, all eyes were on the bold and expensive new town programme. As a social and physical revolution by central government, these towns were the face of the Welfare State and the enlightened democracy of which Britain saw itself as champion. From the beginning, the burgeoning towns were reported on intensively, in newspapers at home and abroad, published in critical detail in the professional journals and discussed in the pages of leading periodicals; they were the subject of radio programmes, Pathé News features and, with television, soon prodded and examined in front of an expanding and eager new audience.

But first, came public relations. *Charley in New Town* (1948) is an eight-minute Halas and Batchelor animation, one of a brilliant Central Office of Information series selling all the variant aspects of new welfare provision and measures to the postwar public, to be seen on cinema screens everywhere. Charley, a gangling youth with a cowlick, is bicycling down an empty parkway road, past a row of semi-detached Garden City type cottages liberally interspersed with mature trees. 'My, this is a grand way to start the day' he enthuses, 'a bit different from what it used to be, I can tell you!' Cut to belching smoke, an overcrowded bus, swarming crowds on pavements, while the commentator intones, 'drab-looking houses and ugly factories'. A figure in striped trousers and bow tie (a planner or a 'Man from the Ministry', the viewers are left to draw their own conclusions), presents a history of the small town and the vicissitudes of industrialisation: 'Our town has turned into a monster'. It could only be contained by a green belt. Best of all would be to make a fresh start. Cities might have to be built upwards ('Don't be silly, what about my pram?'; 'What about my garden'), a solution quickly ruled out ('Alright, no skyscrapers').

So the preferred solution is the 'New Town', favoured by road and rail links, fresh water and countryside. Zoning would keep manufacturing downwind, while parks and playing fields, good shops, a 'posh theatre' and civic centre concert hall would complete the picture. 'It works out fine, just you try it.'

In fact, Basildon was an afterthought. Patrick Abercrombie's Greater London Plan of 1944, published the following year, suggested Ongar as the second Essex New Town. The modest village of Chipping Ongar, its antiquity in its name, with a pre-war population well below 3,000, was to be expanded into six neighbourhoods, each accommodating 10,000 people. In Peter Shepheard's delightful sun-washed renderings in the report, Greensted, a village a little to the west, was envisaged as a traffic-free centre, with a handsome Ritz cinema as the focal feature. In the accompanying aerial rendering, its tiny ancient church, St Andrews, the only surviving log-built church in the country, is shown preserved nearby, a fly in aspic. A cordon sanitaire of mature trees and parkland separates it from the pedestrian shopping area and, beyond, the immense spread of generic low-rise housing, laced together by an ambitious road system, reaching to the horizon.

The site was quietly dropped when it became clear that the costs of upgrading Ongar's antediluvian railway links, work that would require the building of an eight-mile long connection to Brentwood as well as electrification of all train services, would have been prohibitive. The Treasury must have been enormously relieved when Basildon, itself no more than a small village set within a number of other similar-sized settlements, was suggested as an alternative possibility, a highly unusual new town since the site was enthusiastically promoted by the local authority itself. In 1949 Basildon was inserted alongside Harlow, designated in 1947 and on which work, masterminded by Frederick Gibberd and the landscape architect Sylvia Crowe, had already begun. Crowe held the same role at Basildon but found the team there 'less than

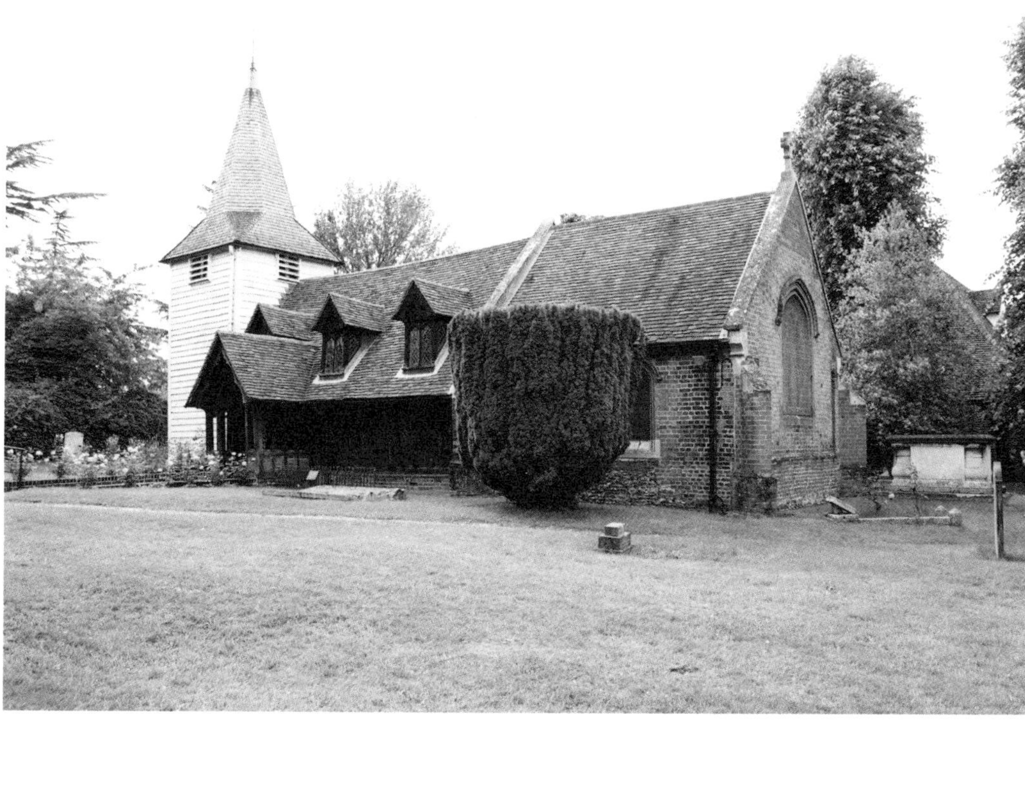

St Andrews Church, Greensted

sympathetic towards landscape'. Looking back, she described the site as 'dismal', marred by its 'solid, horrible clay' as opposed to Harlow, 'a lovely, very humanised landscape'.

Unknown until now, in the mid 1950s architect and town planner Geoffrey Jellicoe had been commissioned to intervene. He was asked, he recalled in 1984, 'to see if it were possible for "Motopia" to be built at Basildon new town. It wasn't but it suggests fun in the landscape.' Jellicoe wrote the explanation when presenting the little notebook of sketches to landscape architect Todd Longstaffe-Gowan, now in the archive of Niall Hobhouse's Drawing Matter in Somerset. Fun was in desperately short supply on the beleaguered site and it was not surprising that the Development Corporation approached Jellicoe (who was already designing some housing there) for his characteristically light touch. Motopia (published as a book in 1961) was an exercise carried out, over more than two decades, for the Glass Age Development Committee of Pilkingtons of St Helens, his fellow members being Ove Arup, engineer, and Edward Mills, architect. Jellicoe wrote that it was 'the diagram of an idea only and should not be taken literally, but the separation of traffic and the thorough greening of the new town (all features illustrated by Gordon Cullen in the book) were appealing and feasible concepts that may have played some part in the early planning of Basildon.

An insight into the development of Basildon, built over the sites of the plotland retreats that many thousands of Londoners had come to call home, comes from a 1967 interview with General Manager, Charles Boniface. He had joined the Development Corporation as Chief Solicitor in late 1949, some months after the body was set up. A solicitor in private practice before the war, he served as a commando and was still suffering from the effects of a severe spinal injury. He decided to take up a temporary legal post within Essex County Council and there became interested in town and country planning, which he sensed was proceeding on the wrong lines, overwhelmingly negative when 'we needed a positive approach'. Interested in Harlow, he saw creative possibilities ahead.

Recruitment, consultation and planning took up to two years. The major task for the legal team was to proceed through a succession of Public Enquiries. The first, dealing with the Master Plan for 80,000 was held in June 1951. It was peremptory ('over in a day') but Boniface was eager to open up a democratic process, even if modern public participation was far in the future. 'Now people are almost encouraged to make their objections, and this is a good thing.' If grievances were aired in a public arena the major misapprehensions could be dealt with, he hoped. Looking back, he said nothing of the furious compensation disputes or the political fallout, nor did his deferential interviewer press these points. But implicit throughout was that the Development Corporation must work hard to make citizens out of the plotlanders and their neighbours, whether Essex villagers or the new influx from East London.

In 1954 Boniface was appointed General Manager, in succession to a Brigadier. The town was rising neither on a virgin site 'nor even around a nice neat nucleus of an old town'. Put bluntly: 'We were building on what was a rural slum, with 5,600 properties, many of them substandard, in the way of our development.' They had to be acquired; 'I don't like using compulsory powers against people' was Boniface's line, and the challenge was winning them over. Arguing that the Development Corporation's powers and actions were for the good of the majority, Boniface's aim was to 'woo' them. He demonstrated the difficulties: two widows appeared together in his office with identical sets of deeds for the same piece of land. Each document represented clear title to the freehold in question. With his guidance, they settled on 'a Judgement of Solomon', half each. At the other extreme were those who argued for squatters' rights, which the legal team had to persuade them was, here, not the case.

The scale of Boniface's task was clear in the figures he cited. By 1967, the Development Corporation had pursued some 8,000 separate acquisitions, amounting to a mere 4,000 acres. Often a resident was allowed to stay on, pending redevelopment, but with the site valuation fixed. (The Haven was valued in March 1959 but the Mills family, who built their house in 1934, stayed there until 1975). The infrastructure was a large part of the cost; initially the Development Corporation faced 78 miles of dirt track, some remained. The cost of installing mains drainage, to be discharged into the Thames rather than the more convenient river Crouch, was enormous. Meanwhile the new town grew, to 70,000 at the time of this interview with Boniface. They planned for building 1,100 houses a year until 1971, before settling into a natural pattern of expansion. 'Otherwise it runs the risk of becoming an overspill problem' and therefore being as problematic as London itself. For Boniface, 'a Development Corporation must build a self-sufficient town'. On this he had found himself strongly disagreeing with Essex County Council, whose view was laissez faire.

In the 1967 interview, Boniface felt vindicated, proud of what he termed the 'social success of the town', of which he had once despaired. The families who had settled there, with everything around them new, had begun to participate and to become engaged in civic life. New schools, a regional hospital, libraries and more had helped give a Charley-style buoyancy to it all. The lengthy and complex process, as seen through Boniface's eyes, had been painful and tortuous, but had finally begun to bring rewards as the new town emerged from its chrysalis.

By the publication of a second edition of Pevsner's *Essex* in 1965, the target population of Basildon had been adjusted to well over 100,000. Pevsner remarks on the growing architectural urbanity of the town, the grouping, massing and style that suggested a sense of self, as opposed – as is implied – to growth in and around the various straggling villages in the designated area. In his *Essex Shell Guide* Norman Scarfe concurred. He included a photograph of Brooke House, the fourteen-storey block of flats that determinedly brought a residential strand to the town centre, standing over 'the best new central piazza in England' – all under the guidance of Sir Basil Spence who was consultant adviser on the town centre. The town was, in architectural as well as social terms, beginning to define itself.

Perceptively, Housing and Health Minister Aneurin Bevan, quoted by Lynsey Hanley, author of *Estates: An Intimate History* (2007) had seen the pre-war problems of single-tenure, single-class mass estates, referring to them as 'castrated communities' and arguing for 'the living tapestry of a mixed community'. The inference was that council housing should not be only for the working classes and Bevan had ensured the term was not used in housing legislation. But the tenure and employment basis of the new towns went against high hopes of social balance, also shared by Lewis Silkin. In the early years Basildon Development Corporation built over 15,000 properties for rent and just 286 for sale. Private developers and housing associations, as well as Basildon Council itself (since 1994 responsible for all social housing in the town) added small numbers to the total. In 1992, electoral analysts considered Basildon 'the capital of the C2s' (referring to the skilled working class) and 'Basildon Man' was born.

The major employer in Basildon in its early years was Ford, building an immense tractor factory which was completed in 1964 and generating large numbers of manual jobs as well as a flying visit from Henry Ford Jr. Another American visitor was the developer James Rouse who toured British new towns in 1963 while he was building two unusual planned communities in the US – Cross Keys village and the new town of Columbia, both in Maryland – market-led counter-arguments to American suburban sprawl. He judged Basildon's housing 'dull, but adequate' and noted that rent collection was falling behind at Brooke House. But most of their discussion was around the nature of a new neighbourhood, its size and the amenities that were needed to anchor it. Boniface told Rouse he preferred much smaller developments, which 'make more noise' and 'have more spirit' than the existing neigbourhoods. The knotty problem of social cohesion remained a worry.

In 1959, Christopher Chataway visited Harlow for the BBC current affairs series *Panorama.* He wanted to investigate its attempt to be, and to build, a classless society; the Olympic hero and future Conservative MP particularly liked the 'one class sort of atmosphere', so suggestive of North America. But then it all unravelled. On camera, one woman disagreed, she didn't think 'management and workers should live closely together', as it would be 'embarrassing for both sides'. Her husband wouldn't want to be living next to work colleagues (inferring that they would be his subordinates). A prim-looking girl in a school uniform, living in Harlow but educated privately, did not know her neighbours since, she replied in cut-glass tones, 'Mummy doesn't think they are right for us.'

Such characters, or characterisations, emerge blinking into the light in Angus Wilson's surprisingly astute new town novel, *Late Call* (1964). Although he claimed a location in the West Midlands it is likely that Carshall New Town was Harlow, with which Wilson would have been familiar. With its public art and water features, varied housing types to mix up the social strata (much as Henrietta Barnett had attempted to do, unsuccessfully, in Hampstead Garden Suburb) and its stew of aspirations and views all set down on a *tabula rasa*, the similarities with Harlow were difficult to disguise. Wilson captures detail – from the clash between pre-war furnishings imported into a sub-modernist interior, to the responses of the individuals in a particularly ill-assorted family who were a little too middle class for their new home and a little too politically left of centre for the prevailing local mood. Neatly, it is the character Sylvia Calvert, the grandmother who comes, unwillingly, to live in Carshall New Town with her son's family but who emerges as its most eloquent advocate, becoming inordinately proud of the architecture and buildings such as the 'Oyster', the civic centre built of glass with black panels and red cedar ceilings. 'People from all over the world come to see it – architects and that, you know.'

As the new towns took shape they also became ideal field stations for sociologists. If the idiosyncrasies of the plotlands have tended to emerge afterwards in memory and reminiscence, the new towns were under the microscope, the microphone or the camera from the start. Norman MacKenzie, later to be a founder of the Open University – jewel in the crown of next generation new town, Milton Keynes – looked at their difficulties in a Home Service broadcast in 1953, when several thousand of the early houses in the London area towns were already occupied, and with many more coming on stream. The amenities lagged far behind. But this brought ingenuity. A cinema operated from a factory out of hours, while a prefab hut served a different purpose each day of the week – church, scout hut, community hall, youth club, venue for whist-drives and dance hall – a loose-fit solution replacing the buildings and resources developed over generations in a usual town or village. Encouraged, people were taking the initiative – an allotment association, music or photography club, pigeon fanciers or political party groups all soon developed. Newcomers could meet the existing residents. Social interaction came about through interest groups, just as Frederic Osborn, arch-proponent of new towns, had said it would.

The early new town attitude towards providing amenities remained 'make do and mend', much closer to the plotlanders self-help ethos than the architecturally deterministic neighbourhood unit environment. In 1967 Ray Gosling made a BBC radio programme about a Basildon youth club, one of two programmes called *Gang Enterprise*. He reported on a group of bored young people spurred into action in 1961 by an off-the-cuff suggestion by a local doctor who told them, 'If you find a want – fill it yourself.' The masterstroke of the Riverside Club was to coerce the leader of the Rogues, a local gang, to chair the club committee. The general manager was an enthusiastic supporter of the initiative, which gained generous funds from the Carnegie Foundation, and claimed that it became known as 'Boniface's Brothel' as a result. It was, as intended, to be a stopgap solution since over time, Basildon began to have more alternatives to offer its disaffected youth (a Mecca dance hall, youth services, a bowling alley and a Wimpy) and the club changed its nature with success. But, as Gosling wrote in *The Listener* afterwards, it had all begun as, 'an extension of street-corner friendships, a close but not a closed community ... they made their own rules' and, as a result, an amenity was born, on the basis of self-help rather than officialdom.

The conflict at the heart of the innocent self-expression of the plotlanders and the political drive towards a physically planned and manageable environment, returning rates and taxes to local and national exchequers, sharing in, and paying for, public amenities in an equable fashion, was an enduring open sore. Once again, now in the early 1970s, Essex County Council earmarked another spread of plotlands with potential to become a second generation new town, the council's own South Woodham Ferrers. Here, round the inconspicuous village of Woodham Ferrers, there had been some two hundred plots, largely concentrated on the site of two failed farms, Champions and Eyotts, sold strenuously to Londoners with the usual inducements. A riverside location made it particularly appealing. Fifty years later, a compulsory purchase programme swept away a tangle of unmade roads and 'handmade' houses, though a single cleared plot was retained as a memorial (a pleasant community orchard). The town now has a population of just over 16,000. It is, in many ways, the loudest possible retort to Harlow and

Basildon, where the car was delegated to a rear garage yard and the architecture looked determinedly ahead.

In *Riverside Country Town* (1981), the promotional film for South Woodham Ferrers made by the council's education unit, the message is saccharine: 'When you feel you need to start a whole new lifestyle but you think you'll never lose those downtown blues ...' South Woodham Ferrers is 'a whole new place to be'. Here, 'where the old world meets the new', in a town 'where nothing is as old as it seems', the vernacular revival took hold. Back in 1949, in *Life in an English Village*, a celebration of Great Bardfield – one of the three Festival of Britain Essex villages – the editor Noel Carrington observed, 'as the life of the village changes, so must its physical appearance... Not all the new houses can be replicas of the old for the sake of conformity', and, quoting the authoritative planner Thomas Sharp who argued that, 'there never was a rural style of architecture'.

In 1981 no simple Charley peddled through a dreamscape but owner-occupier nuclear families shopped in chilled aisles under the weather-boarded supermarket clock tower that rose over the retail core, wandered down to the water's edge or watched their daughters step out as drum majorettes. The purposeful civic modernism represented by central Basildon or Harlow had long since ceded to tiled retail barns, designer double garages, all couched in a kind of italicised 'Essex Design Guide' architecture, and of course, jobs within easy reach on the motorway system. It was just the beginning of a state of mind, and a reality, from which we are about to take our leave.

GILLIAN DARLEY is a widely published writer and broadcaster. Her first book, *Villages of Vision* (1975) was revised, with an extended gazetteer, in 2007. Other publications include *John Soane* (1999), *Octavia Hill* (2010), *John Evelyn* (2006) and *Ian Nairn, Words in Place* (2013, with David McKie). She is president of the Twentieth Century Society. Darley's absorption and interest in Essex is both personal and professional and her next book, due to be published in 2018 by Old Street Publishing, is titled *Excellent Essex*.

FURTHER READING

Octavia Hill's essay 'More Air for London' was published in the periodical *Nineteenth Century*, February 1888. I quoted extensively from her evidence to the Royal Commission on the Housing for the Working Classes in the revised edition of Gillian Darley, *Octavia Hill: Social Reformer and Founder of the National Trust* (Francis Boutle Publishers 2010) pp.213–17.

For a (frustratingly) brief mention of the Lea Bridge 'Bungalow Town' see W.R. Powell (ed.), *The History of the County of Essex* (Victoria County History 1973), p.182; a local history blog provides maps and images http://leabridge.org.uk/gazetteer/archaeology/shanty-town.html. The story of the plotlands has been told, in countless different forms, by Colin Ward, a lifelong advocate for self-build and cooperative housing, and above all in Dennis Hardy and Colin Ward, *Arcadia for All: The Legacy of a Makeshift Landscape* (Five Leaves Publications 2003), especially chapter 1, Property and Freedom, and chapter 6, Arcadia in the Countryside. The Haven Plotlands Museum at Langdon is run by Essex Wildlife Trust and their website will give details of access. They have a number of informative information boards, from which I have taken information. For blogs and online references to plotlands, see http://www.benfleethistory.org.uk/page/the_story_of_surene and http://www.basildon.com/history/basildon/basildon-new-town-2.html. Norman Scarfe's description of plotlands in L. Dudley Stamp's *Land Utilisation Survey* is quoted in John Hunter, *The Essex Landscape: A Study of Its Form and History* (Essex Record Office Publications 1999), pp.168–69. The short afterlife of the Halstead POW camp is told at http://www.halsteadhistory.org.uk/pow.html and features in a pamphlet from Halstead Museum. Frank Schaffer, *The New Town Story* (MacGibbon and Kee 1970) gives nuts and bolts information on Basildon, pp.290–92; plotland clearance is discussed on pp.82–83. Colin Ward, *New Town, Home Town: The Lessons of Experience* (Calouste Gulbenkian Foundation 1993) tells the wider story in the light of experience. The references to Lionel Brett are from Otto Saumarez-Smith's 'Planning Politics and Central Area Redevelopment, circa 1963' (PhD, Cambridge 2015). The Central Office of Information film *Charley in New Town* (1948) can be viewed at https://www.youtube.com/watch?v=Ta_n1wLARKM.

Essex Record Office (ERO) is an invaluable source, with online material and relevant blogs. For early images and text see ERO D/DS 4/20; http://www.essexrecordofficeblog.co.uk/the-passing-of-the-plotlands/ includes archive images, before and after maps and photographs http://www.essexrecordofficeblog.co.uk/tag/new-town/.

Sylvia Crowe's comments are quoted in Geoffrey Collens and Wendy Powell (eds.), *Sylvia Crowe* (Landscape Design Trust Monographs 1999) p.56.

Charles Boniface was interviewed (badly) in 1967 and the tape is available at ERO, SA 20/2/7/1. The response of James Rouse to the new towns, here Basildon, is cited in Mark Clapson, *Anglo-American Crossroads: Urban Planning and Research in Britain, 1940–2010* (Bloomsbury 2013), pp.102–03.

One of many BBC broadcasts and articles on the new town programmes is Norman MacKenzie, 'Creating New Towns for Old' *The Listener*, 9 April 1953. Again for the BBC, a later view on social provision in Basildon, Ray Gosling 'A World of their Own Making', *The Listener*, 13 June 1968. The in-house promotional film for South Woodham Ferrers can be found at https://www.youtube.com/watch?v=JzkbZCOXUoQ.

All online references accessed 22 September 2017.

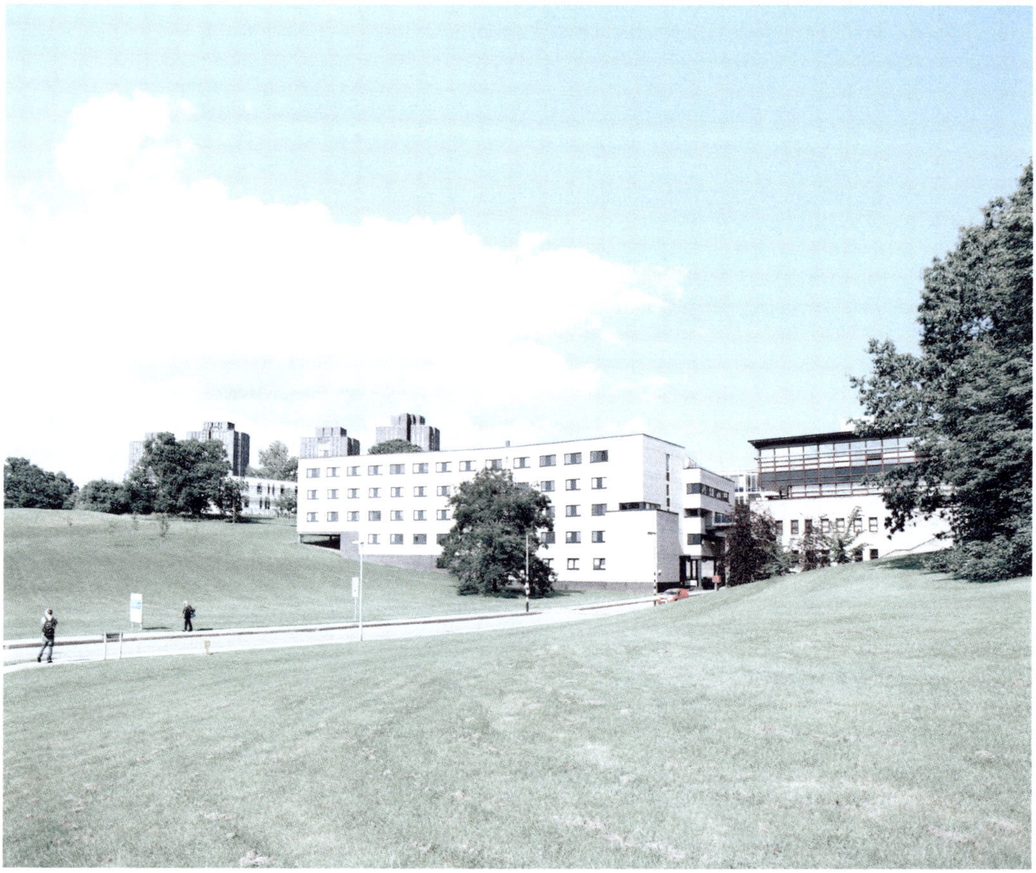

University of Essex, Colchester

University Radicalism

Planning the University of Essex, 1960–68

Jules Lubbock

THE 1950S AND THE SCIENTIFIC REVOLUTION

Plate glass and concrete, politically radical, the very spirit of '68 – nowadays the University of Essex is perceived as the archetypal 1960s university. When it was mooted in the 1950s however, its agenda was far from politically radical; it aimed to produce technocrats for British industry.

The 1950s are now considered dull compared to the Swinging Sixties. Unfairly – there was great creativity in the arts and sciences, as well as major political and social change: Pop art, Elvis, DNA, espresso bars, American civil rights, the Campaign for Nuclear Disarmament, jet airliners and much more. The University of Essex, one of the 'Shakespearean Seven' New Universities was a product of this ferment. Its story, problems and development are those of a university planned to address the era's problems that came into being in the Swinging Sixties.

Sputnik, the first orbital satellite, symbolises a key moment. Launched on 4 October 1957 by the Soviet Union, it overtook the West at a bound. Sir Winston Churchill, by then in his mid 80s, voiced widespread anxiety about Britain's diminishing status, particularly after the 1956 Suez fiasco: 'We have fallen hopelessly behind in technical education. This is the mechanised age and where are we?' Since the war he had championed a British equivalent to MIT, the Massachusetts Institute of Technology, but this was obstructed by highly conservative university scientists. A book, *The Stagnant Society* (1961), summed up the general malaise.

To stir up debate C.P. Snow, novelist and scientist, published *The Two Cultures* (1959). He deplored the divide between science and the humanities. More important, he pinpointed a rift within science itself, between pure and applied. Britain must train technologists.

There were broader concerns and debates within postwar government and academic circles about higher education policy, in which two remarkable Scottish academics played leading roles. The first was Keith, later Lord, Murray, an economist and Rector of Lincoln College, Oxford, who in 1952 was appointed chairman of the University Grants Committee (UGC) a section of the Treasury responsible for financing universities. The Chancellor of the Exchequer was the liberal Conservative Essex MP, R.A. Butler, architect of the great Education Act 1944 and subsequently first Chancellor of Essex University. The Butler Act had greatly increased the number of sixth formers qualified for higher education, but there were insufficient university places, only 50,000 in 1950 compared to one million today. Murray's brief was to meet the demand. He increased spending fifteenfold, founded the New Universities and commissioned the 1963 Robbins Report which established the expansionary policy still in operation today.

Lord Lindsay, on the other hand, was a Christian Socialist, educational visionary, an eminent philosopher and Master of Balliol who became the founding Principal of Keele University upon his retirement from Oxford in 1949; at Keele, Lindsay experimented with many features by which the New Universities would become known.

On the 1947 Committee for the Denazification of German Universities, Lindsay condemned German research-centred, elitist, technical universities as 'evil and sinful', deemed a factor in the rise of the Nazism. Technical education should be combined with student democracy and self-government, as well as a broad liberal education.

The county of Essex had much industry, including Ford and Marconi, a fast-growing population with many eighteen year olds frustrated by the shortage of university places. In 1960 Essex County Council presented their *Proposal* for a new university to the UGC. They got the go-ahead in 1961.

The UGC appointed an Academic Planning Board to determine Essex's character and choose a Vice-Chancellor. The chairman was Noel, later Lord Annan, the young modernising Provost of King's College, Cambridge, once described in a phrase of C.P. Snow as 'a man with the future in his bones'. He had tried, but failed, to introduce Sociology at Cambridge.

Annan's *Report* of February 1962 raised Essex's ambitions from the local to the national. Essex, more than the other New Universities, would stop Britain falling further behind by specialising narrowly in the production of a technocratic elite in advanced technology and scientific management. To achieve this, it would focus on the applied sciences and the social sciences, particularly Sociology, then little taught in Britain. The humanities took a back seat. Churchill's campaign for a British MIT would be realised at Essex.

Annan envisaged Essex as a 'New Cambridge' for modernisers of his own ilk. By the standards of the time it would be very big, with 10,000 students compared to the British average of 3,000. By limiting the science and social science departments initially to six, those departments could be very large, providing critical mass and economies of scale. Each year Essex would turn out more than 3,000 recruits for the 'officer class' of Snow's 'Scientific Revolution'. I arrived in 1971 as a new lecturer in Art History, but had no inkling of any of this; to this day few people do.

Academic policy

The founding Vice-Chancellor started work in September 1962. Albert Sloman was only forty-one years old and Professor of Spanish at Liverpool University. Asked about his qualifications to lead a technological university, he replied: 'There are not many academics who can assemble an aircraft engine, put it in the plane and fly it.' He had been a wartime fighter pilot and had a strong interest in mathematics and economics. Joining him as architect and master planner was Kenneth Capon of Architects' Co-Partnership, AC-P, a radical firm specialising in educational buildings. Capon had caught the eye of Annan, who commissioned a development plan for King's College. Capon proposed four high rise towers opposite the famous Chapel. The fellows rejected it, but Annan secured Capon's appointment at Essex.

After Christmas 1962 Capon presented Sloman with a draft layout made with his son's Lego. He recycled elements of the King's scheme, including eighteen high rise residential towers and twenty courtyards around a pedestrian street descending the valley of Wivenhoe Park, outside Colchester. It was urban and highly concentrated so as to preserve the eighteenth-century landscaped gardens, painted by John Constable, as well as to create a unified community. Spaces for living and teaching were close together, as were buildings for different subjects.

At the London launch on 22 October 1963 Sloman expressed urgency about the need to train modern leaders, specialists, not amateur all-rounders, but with a breadth of understanding. He reiterated that Essex had 'down-to-earth practical plans intended to meet the needs of the country and in particular of industry and commerce'. Two months earlier, at the March on Washington, Martin Luther King Jr had delivered his speech – 'I Have a Dream.' The Sixties had arrived. In November 1963 Sloman gave the prestigious Reith Lectures on BBC radio, published as *A University in the Making.* While adhering to Annan's technocratic blueprint, Sloman introduced important modifications in academic policy, student life and community.

Research, the humanities and the unity of knowledge

Research became a top priority. Essex County Council and Annan envisaged a teaching-only university, but Sloman believed teaching 'cannot be divorced from research'. This was revolutionary; few university staff in Britain did much research, then considered somewhat Germanic and ungentlemanly. Sloman also wanted to collaborate with industry. He beefed up the Humanities, albeit in a modernised form called Comparative Studies. There would be no separate departments of History, Philosophy or Modern Languages but a single department of Literature, collaborating with Government to study the cultures of the modern world comparatively: the United States, Soviet Russia, Latin America and Britain. Like Lindsay, Sloman regarded human knowledge as a unity within an undivided continuum; subject boundaries were artificial and intellectually damaging. Whereas the traditional university was a federation of separate departments, Essex would be a federation of overlapping Schools – Science, Social Science and Comparative Studies. Departmental empire-building, which had killed off the British MIT, was discouraged. Sloman also hoped to heal the rift between Snow's 'Two Cultures'.

Student independence, self-education and recreation

While existing universities still acted legally *in loco parentis* – in the role of parents – through single-sex colleges and halls of residence, Essex would treat its students as adults, respecting their demand for independence. However, the rationale for 'no rules' was not liberalism as an end in itself, but as a means of preparing the future technocrats for corporate life. Sloman's 'new man' would be a social animal, an 'outward-looking expert' nurtured in self-governing flats in the towers where men and women lived together. The Essex technocrat would not be a socially maladroit boffin or geek. Again, Sloman was emulating Lindsay's Keele Experiment.

Self-education was as important as formal teaching. In the university library, with books on open access, students could study their own subject and serendipitously discover related topics shelved nearby. After teaching, students would explore the arts and culture as well as engaging in sports, creating a 24/7 university.

Community

Sloman doubled Annan's target size to 20,000, to allow for even larger departments where scientists could afford cutting-edge equipment such as cyclotrons. This bigness, unparalleled in Britain, would be reconciled with intimacy through small groups for teaching and living and through the architecture. Essex could be big, but also a community; it could train technocrats, who would also be cultivated and sociable; one could have both the arts and the sciences and thereby reconcile the Two Cultures. It was possible to have 'both-and' rather than 'either-or'. Essex would be a social and academic experiment yet executed with military elan: 'Attack on a narrow front, and where there is a breakthrough go hell bent ahead', as Sloman forthrightly put it.

Fostering community

The final master plan was unveiled at the launch in October 1963. It expressed Sloman's lofty ambitions and catered for his academic and social requirements. A campus of 20,000 must be big. Since the earlier concept of the Lego model, a key innovation was that the high street now consisted of five linked pedestrian squares with teaching courtyards behind them. More courtyards could be added as student numbers grew. The twenty-eight fourteen-storey accommodation towers resembled an Italian hill town like Montepulciano. Everything was close together, no more than a five-minute walk from the centre.

Unifying knowledge

To prevent departmental empire-building there were no freestanding buildings. Departments and Schools were distributed along corridors zigzagging around the five squares. Thus literary critics would encounter sociologists who would encounter mathematicians and physicists.

Accommodating students

There was one flat on each floor of the towers with a dozen bedsits for students who shared a kitchen and common room to create a social group from different subjects. Even with 20,000 students no one need feel isolated. The towers were clustered close to squares and seminar rooms. Around the squares are shops, restaurants, rooms for student societies and indoor sport. There was no Senior Common Room nor a Students' Union; staff and students would mingle. The importance of the library as a symbol of research and self-education is emphasised by its dominant position at the head of the valley beside the highest square overlooking a new lake. Newspapers called Essex a 'space age' university. Capon summed up its character: 'The English love making things shaggy and softening everything up. We decided to do something fierce to let them work within.'

New Brutalism: Modern architecture in the 1950s

As well as introducing new concepts of higher education, the University of Essex was influenced by New Brutalism, a major shift in contemporary architecture. Initiated by young British architects in the early 1950s, Brutalists used powerful sculptural forms, often in raw concrete, unlike the steel and glass graph-paper grids of classic modernism. They favoured the compact layouts of traditional cities with streets and squares rather than modernist towers dotted around parkland. Brutalism aimed to create powerful and memorable places rather than beautiful ones.

Le Corbusier, the most influential architect of the twentieth century, was the inspiration. A pioneer of the rationalist modern style in the 1920s, postwar he built the massive Unité d'habitation in Marseilles and a priory, La Tourette, near Lyon. There is no mistaking the source of the pattern of windows in the Essex teaching buildings. Writers also contributed. Jane Jacobs's 1961 polemic against modernist comprehensive redevelopment, *The Death and Life of Great American Cities,* has influenced city planning ever since. She too favoured traditional cities, their communities and the theatre of street life, portrayed by English photographers, Nigel Henderson and Roger Mayne. The squares at Essex were intended to foster a similar kind of everyday theatricality.

Architects' Co-Partnership in the 1950s

The firm which Kenneth Capon helped to found just before the Second World War was based on the conviction that architecture should serve a social purpose and change society instead of merely looking beautiful. Nonetheless Capon believed that aesthetics were central to that objective. He was the boldest architect in AC-P as indicated by his proposal for twelve-storey towers in the heart of Cambridge.

THE BUILDINGS

As well as the ingenuity of their layout, the buildings at Essex are notable for their powerful and memorable image. I shall describe the first stage of construction, completed in 1967, a microcosm of the whole, consisting of a north-south pedestrian route connecting the Physics Courtyard, which was the first teaching building, Square 4, the first square, the Hexagon restaurant and the first two residential towers. The library was on the adjacent Square 5.

The Physics Courtyard and Square 4

These buildings are constructed with a standardised system of smoothly surfaced concrete posts and lintels, or beams. Repetitiveness is relieved by a random pattern of mullions, the vertical divisions between windows, borrowed from Le Corbusier's La Tourette. Dramatic spiral staircases, sadly demolished, led down to the Physics Courtyard, stepped in grass to form an outdoor theatre with a stage and loggia behind. The loggia has since been enclosed for offices. The courtyard was also intended as a refuge from the bustle of Square 4. Capon's intention was 'to create something analogous to the repose and absence of straining after incident' of eighteenth-century London squares. But within this understated urban fabric, Capon allowed room for some monuments which could be 'individual and nonconformist', as he put it; 'if they can be jewels, so much the better'.

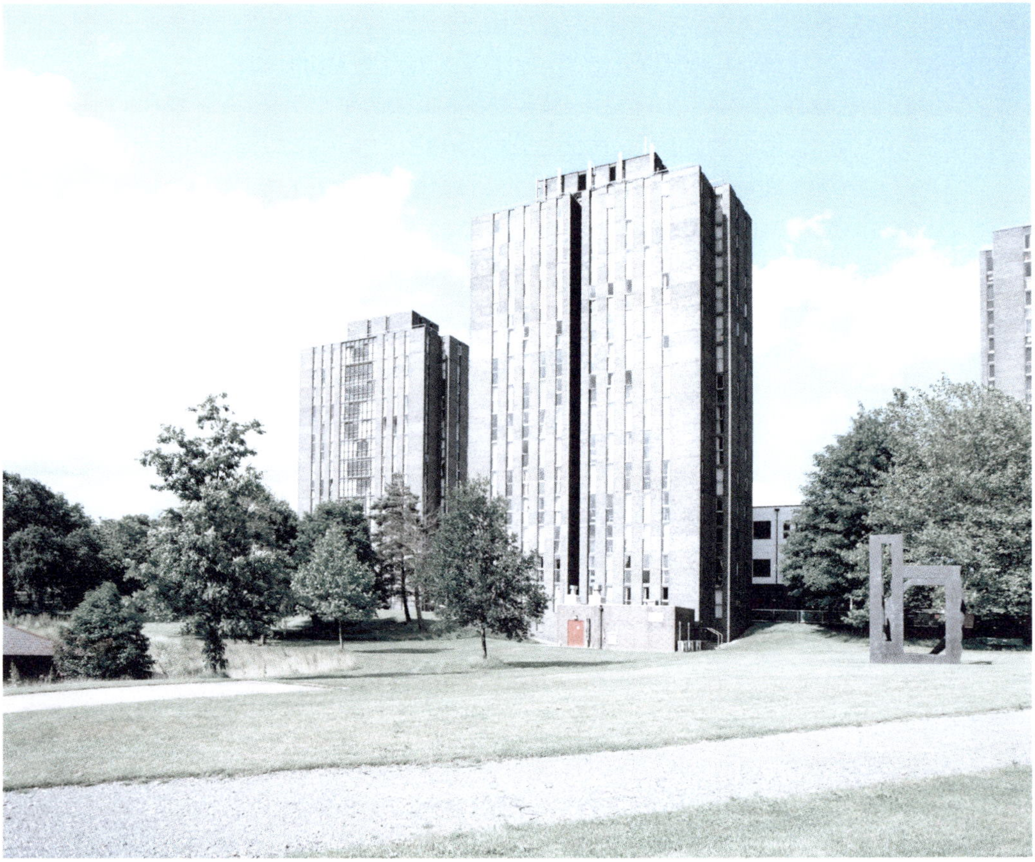

University of Essex, Colchester

The first monument was the Hexagon restaurant. On the outside it looks like a spaceship raised upon fin-like concrete piers. A glorious undivided space lies within, twenty-four metres wide and eight metres high it resembles a medieval baptistery. Daylight comes largely from a central skylight, as in the Roman Pantheon, providing enclosure and dramatic illumination. A magnificent dome, a shallow hexagonal pyramid, encompasses all. The Hexagon is the shape of a quartz crystal. It is a jewel, quite literally.

North Towers

The Towers anchor the university to the skyline. They are brick without an internal frame, almost unique at that time. Grey-blue engineering brick was strong and created a powerful silhouette. From different viewpoints, they present an infinite variety of groupings; sometimes they cluster together like a castle, they line up in futuristic skyscraper canyons, they mass together like cliffs, from some angles they even look like spires. They are majestic rather than beautiful, possessing a severe and mysterious majesty. They may have been intended to convey the solemnity of a war memorial, for which towers and obelisks have traditionally been used. Capon wanted them to proclaim, 'this is the University of Essex and it is important.'

The library was the only free-standing building, set beside a new lake. Capon explained that 'architecturally, its position is as significant as that of Magdalen Tower in the curving High Street of Oxford. It symbolises what the university stands for – the conservation and discovery of knowledge, the importance of self-education, and the inter-relationship of subjects'. The overall impression is one of power in its unadorned post and lintel construction, its massive concrete piers with their chipped concrete fluting supporting cantilevered beams, which carry the four storeys of book stacks and reading space. A temple of scholarship, it resembles an English country house in its command of the view of park and lakes. Sadly this relationship was destroyed by a 2014 office building separating lake from library.

Originally one entered under the imposing colonnade of overhanging beams and was channelled through a small architectural gem, an entrance vestibule, the jewel in the crown both of the library and the campus. There were three sections: a ground-floor corridor; this led up to a top-lit hexagonal staircase; and one finally entered the library through a top-lit upper corridor. Staircases enable an architect to control the user's experience. The ground-floor passageway was lit on both sides by narrow floor-to-ceiling windows separated by wide mullions, creating a penumbra while providing glimpses of the park. The stripes of light and shade in the windows and in the patterns they threw upon floor and ceiling suggested steps, framing the staircase itself. Because the stairwell was windowless, apart from the skylight, one gradually left behind the outside world of sensory experience and was drawn through the austere chapel-like enclosure, into a domain of thought and reflection; Sloman's haven for self-education. Capon explained his intention 'to create a cloistral feeling that would put the reader in the right emotional frame of mind' for entering the library. The librarians always called it 'The Cloisters'. It was demolished in 2012.

CONCLUSION

Employing the heroic style and planning concepts of New Brutalism, the massive buildings of the University of Essex embody the ambitions of its founders to create a British MIT, serving the 'military-industrial-political complex'. Those ambitions, however, were rapidly derailed. In May 1968, as Jess Twyman explains in the following pages, students prevented a government scientist, involved in research into chemical and biological weapons, from lecturing to the Chemistry Society. Sloman, urged on by his founding science professors against more cautious advice from the social scientists, summarily suspended three student leaders. It was a disastrous overreaction. The students rebelled. Essex became the national symbol of student unrest. Headteachers refused to provide references for applicants to Essex, the consequent slump in student demand led eventually to the closure of Physics and Chemistry. Maths narrowly escaped. Government funding fell off, closure was threatened and student numbers did not rise above 3,000 until well into the new millennium. There was little need for new buildings. What was built was timid rather than fierce. Brutalism had fallen out of fashion and Capon's buildings were little respected. The Cloisters and the spiral stairs were demolished; internal light wells and external loggias were filled in, offices were built beside the lake, some of the carefully crafted concrete surfaces were painted. The austere interior of the Hexagon was disguised by garish postmodern decor.

The deeper causes of the debacle were the unintended consequences of some naïve early decisions. Annan's insistence upon Sociology, which supplied many of the student leaders of the 1968 uprising and staff sympathisers, was inconsistent with his technocratic goal of a British MIT. In his Reith Lectures, Sloman tied himself in knots trying to reconcile Annan's blueprint with Lindsay's vision of a liberal education. Consequently those lectures are highly ambiguous. Depending upon who you were, they could be read either as a plan to revitalise the British economy or as a manifesto for radicalism in education and society. The latter interpretation attracted left-wing students who were speedily disillusioned by the authoritarianism they found on arrival. With hindsight Sloman should probably not have delivered them, certainly not published them as a book. But he had been a fighter pilot.

Essex's social sciences and humanities are now the basis of its reputation. Far from training an elite of scientific managers, the Business School is notable for its Marxist Professor of Accounting. This epitomises Essex's radical ethos, which Anthony Forster, the present Vice-Chancellor, unlike his predecessors, has fully embraced, alongside the forcefulness of the 1960s architecture, to rebrand and market the university.

JULES LUBBOCK is Emeritus Professor of Art History at the University of Essex. He has divided his time between studying the early Renaissance in Italy and commenting upon contemporary architecture and planning. In the early 1980s he was the architecture and design critic of the *New Statesman* and he also wrote speeches for the Prince of Wales. Since about 1990 he has been trying, with mixed success, to persuade his colleagues at the University of Essex of the merits of the 1960s campus and to conserve it.

FURTHER READING

Noel Annan, *The First Report of the Academic Planning Board* (Privately printed, 1962. Available through the Albert Sloman Library)

Elain Harwood, *Space, Hope and Brutalism: English Architecture 1945–1975* (Yale University Press 2015)

Stefan Muthesius, *The Post-War University: Utopianist Campus and College* (Yale University Press 2001)

David Phillips, 'Lindsay and the German Universities: An Oxford Contribution to the Post-War Reform Debate', *Oxford Review of Education*, vol.6, no.1, 1980

[The Robbins Report], *Higher Education Report*, HMSO, 1963

Albert Sloman, *A University in the Making*, BBC, London, 1964

University Radicalism

Student Uprising at University of Essex

Jess Twyman

East Essex Gazette, 25 October 1963

'UNIVERSITY OF A SPACE AGE:
TOWERS AND TERRACES IN THE AIR
A space age cultural city with a Manhattan Island silhouette, designed to reach far into the architectural and academic realms of the 21st century, is the revolutionary concept of the new University of Essex.'

Albert Sloman, founding Vice-Chancellor and Architects' Co-Partnership's Kenneth Capon might have provided the blueprint for the University of Essex, but it was the students who shaped it and made it their own. Newly opened in 1964, from the start Essex was known as a 'liberal' university, where students were encouraged to think for themselves. Young men and women who wanted to be part of a forward-thinking institution applied to study the latest approaches to science, technology and the humanities, alongside new subjects such as Sociology and Latin American Studies. But most of all, the students wanted the freedom Albert Sloman promised.

The Sun, 3 October 1964

'NO RULES VARSITY OPENS ITS DOORS – AND THE NEW STUDENTS STEP UP TO KNOCK DOWN TRADITION!'

Albert Sloman insisted on breaking with tradition: Essex would be the most progressive, the most ambitious and the most international university in the UK. It would also be the most democratic. As envisaged in his Reith Lectures in 1963, Sloman wanted to create a university where 'apart from its formal teaching, we ought to give students the chance to think and argue about the fundamental problems of life, and stand on their own two feet'. There would be no hierarchies and no empire-building. To this end, students and academics were to share the same social spaces – with no separate restaurants, bars or common rooms. This was to thwart any possibility of academics having an artificially inflated status or an unwillingness to explain themselves outside the classroom. Rather, staff and students would constantly mix together, engendering conversations that would ignite minds and advance academia. As Kenneth Capon explained romantically, 'the Students' Union of Paris is the Boulevard St Michel'.

Albert Sloman also refused traditional halls of residence, with their clear division of the sexes and curfews set firmly in place. Instead, students were free to make their own decisions about how they lived their lives. Neither academic nor physical structures would get in the way of this. The iconic high-rise accommodation towers at Essex offered a far more cosmopolitan way of life, with students sharing large communal apartments where they cooked and socialised. Male and female students mixed freely in the Towers – something that was considered scandalous at the time, with the *Times Educational Supplement* pointedly commenting that they represented 'the new permissiveness in society'. However, Sloman had taught at Berkeley, University of California and insisted that apartment living was the new way forward.

What surprised everyone was the direction in which this kindling of young minds would take the University, as in less than five years it was to be defined by sit-ins, blockades and riots. How much of this is down to its Brutalist architecture continues to be contested. For decades, Essex was vilified for its high-rise living and harsh urban landscape, but this has settled into a begrudging respect, recognising that the campus architecture has created a global, critically engaged community.

The Observer, 12 May 1968

'CRISIS DAY AT DREAM UNIVERSITY'

Essex students had always protested – 'from day one', was how Albert Sloman's wife Marie later recalled events – as the postwar generation came of age. It began with demonstrations against fox hunting and escalated at high-profile occasions, including when Prime Minister Harold Wilson received an honorary degree in 1967. As campus was still being built, the ceremony took place in Colchester, with anti-Vietnam War protests outside in the streets. With a long history as a garrison town, Colchester's military police were quickly dispatched to bring the students under control and the ceremony proceeded without interruption. However, it was in February 1968 that student demonstrations received their first national publicity. Enoch Powell was invited to speak on campus by the Conservative Association; students began heckling before he gave what was widely viewed as a prequel to his infamous 'Rivers of Blood' speech. As the MP drove away, his car was attacked. Six students were summoned to disciplinary hearings, but sit-ins prevented them from taking place. A week later, the local Conservative MP Antony Buck stood up in the House of Commons, complaining, 'It is insufferable that a man with the record of Mr Enoch Powell should be called a fascist by undergraduates.' Albert Sloman was later to say with pride that 'our chaps discovered Powell a year before anyone else', but at the time, the incident left the University feeling that they would have to act more decisively in future.

A few weeks after Powell's visit, on 17 March, University of Essex students went on the anti-Vietnam War demonstration in London, where mounted police charged the crowds as thousands of protesters clashed with the police outside the US Embassy in Grosvenor Square, leading to over 200 arrests. Internationally, tensions continued to rise: Martin Luther King Jr was shot on 4 April, and in France students from the universities of Nanterre and Sorbonne began to protest in Paris, joining forces with thousands of workers to bring the country to its knees. In Czechoslovakia (now the Czech Republic) the Prague Spring continued to rumble towards an imminent Soviet invasion. Essex student Mike Gonzalez was to recall of the time that his university 'was not a bubble, it was reflecting the changes, transformations and shifts that were going on in Higher Education, but also more broadly and globally'.

If Enoch Powell's racism had lit the touch paper at Essex, it was the visit of Dr Thomas Inch that was to prove incendiary. On 7 May 1968, Dr Inch from the Ministry of Defence's biological and chemical research facility in Porton Down was invited by the Chemistry Society to speak on campus. It was during a time when Agent Orange chemical spray was deployed in the Vietnam War and, as the Grosvenor Square demonstration two months earlier had proven, students were hugely concerned. Moreover, they believed that Porton Down wanted to recruit Essex students for their chemical weapon research. In a carefully planned protest, an indictment was read out interrupting Dr Inch's lecture as he attempted to speak, citing chemical and biological warfare activities at Porton Down. The protest led to the abandonment of Dr Inch's lecture and the police were brought in, this time with dogs – probably for the first time at an English university. Students outnumbered police and managed to prevent arrests.

A few days later, three students – Pete Archard, Raphael Halberstadt and David Triesman – were suspended and summarily ordered off campus. While criticised for standing in the way of freedom of speech, they were not notified of any official charges and had no opportunity to present their defence. The University fell into uproar, with staff now joining students in their outrage at the injustice of the suspended students not being able to give their side of events.

The next week, a meeting was called that brought together students, staff and Vice-Chancellor Albert Sloman, who until this point had been conspicuous by his absence. As the *Spectator* reported, there was the 'incongruous spectacle of Dr Albert Sloman, the slight, immaculately dressed Vice-Chancellor, addressing bearded and pink-cheeked students' who voted overwhelmingly to support the suspended students. Founding Professor of Sociology Peter Townsend was to recall, 'I remember whole days when almost the entire complement of the university, including its cleaners, porters and gardeners as well as secretarial staff, teachers and students, were gathered to debate the merits, causes and outcomes of different forms of action.' The students went on to declare the University closed and created their own 'Free University'. Their newly formed university had its own timetable, which included lectures on 'Freedom of Speech' and the 'Social Psychology of Conflict' during the day, while in the evening students hung out in squares, singing along to the likes of the *Vietnam Song* by Country Joe & the Fish.

The Observer, 19 May 1968

'SOVIETS ON CAMPUS'

The protests at Essex were deliberately publicised by newspapers and politicians concerned to crush left-wing movements. Incidents in the older universities attracted less than their fair share of publicity. Lord Butler, the University's chancellor, alongside Lord Alport, a member of the University's council, accused communist agitators of infiltrating campus, with Lord Alport stating in the *Daily Telegraph* that 'the Communists are by no means fools and realise this is the best nursery for the propagation of their political and disruptive views.' Students interviewed by the BBC thought this was absurd, saying that 'it is a presumption that people aren't capable of wanting to change their situation without being motivated by communist agitators ... To blame communism is a failure to understand the real problems that are facing Britain as a democratic society.' The threat of communist infiltrators at Essex was never substantiated. Rather, it was a group of highly articulate, politically engaged students who were able to galvanise campus into action.

Soon after, the University agreed to an inquiry, when all students and staff present were exhaustively interviewed and a detailed – albeit confusing – picture of what had happened was recorded. A reconciliatory mood prevailed, with the suspended students reinstated and allowed to continue their studies. End-of-year exams were coming up and campus calmed down as the reality of sitting exams had a sobering effect.

The Daily Telegraph, 26 November 1970

'CAMPUS FREEDOM PLAN CRASHES IN WAVE OF VIOLENCE'

Essex continued to protest throughout the late 1960s and 1970s, often followed by damning headlines in the press. In 1970 the *Daily Telegraph* accused Essex of allowing students too much freedom, while laying much of the blame on its alienating Brutalist architecture and high-rise flats. Student recruitment suffered as parents steered their children clear of Essex, while many head teachers refused to sign pupil's applications to this challenging institution. Yet through their numerous demonstrations, pickets and sit-ins, students supported striking miners, women's rights and IRA campaigns at home, while focusing on inequalities in Latin America and the Middle East with equal fervour. Away from the newspaper headlines, it was actually a time of great intellectual growth and creativity at Essex. Many students were stimulated to consider social as well as political issues seriously for the first time. The standard of intellectual debate rose sharply as this analytical engagement was applied across all areas of academic life. Sociologist Émile Durkheim coined a term for these highly charged moments, calling them 'moments of collective effervescence', when new ideas are born. Students practised this critical involvement in their spare time as well, with their own initiatives, such as the student newspaper *Wyvern*, revealing their depth of knowledge and creativity. Annual festivals also created platforms for conversation and debate, with the Revolutionary Festival of 1969 bringing together theatre, film cooperatives, agitprop and music – although much of this was upstaged by a car being set alight in a campus square!

An example of the University's academic inventiveness is the Department of Sociology's founding professor, Peter Townsend. He was concerned with issues of structural inequality and the treatment of the most vulnerable in society, including the elderly, children and the disabled. Through his work, Townsend revealed the extent of social inequality in the UK. The publication of his major survey, *Poverty in the United Kingdom* (1979), revolutionised thinking about poverty. He also demonstrated the importance of getting involved in the community by creating platforms for support, such as his work for the Child Poverty Action Group and the Disability Alliance. This adamant refusal to abide by the narrow norms of academia helped cement Townsend's legacy as one of the great pioneers of sociological research in Britain. It was also this breadth of thinking that allowed him to bring together a distinctive interdisciplinary department that included academics with backgrounds in social policy, anthropology, social history, social psychology, geography and the natural sciences.

Vulture, 2 May 1987

'THE END OF AN ERA FOR ESSEX V-C'

Perhaps not surprisingly, Prime Minister Margaret Thatcher cut funding for UK universities. In an interview in the student newspaper *Vulture*, on his retirement in 1987, Albert Sloman called this decision 'profoundly mistaken and highly damaging'. This led to the University of Essex staying at a 3,000-student intake for another decade, although it was recognised for its academic achievements by entering the Top 20 in the country for research a year later.

By the 1990s, campus had settled down to the business of studying, and student numbers started to grow steadily. International students had always been an important part of the University's global outlook and it became the UK's most international university in 1986, with overseas students forming twenty-three per cent of its population. By 2007, the University had expanded its numbers to 10,000 students. This is the figure Albert Sloman always hoped to reach in the campus's first phase, with a critical mass of students large enough to dominate the sometimes foreboding architecture. When it was first built and people saw the raw, shuttered concrete, Kenneth Capon was asked, 'Where is the decoration?' He retorted, 'The students will be the decoration'. This had finally come true.

The University of Essex's architecture continues to grow to accommodate increasing student numbers – there are now also new campuses in the south of the county, at Southend and Loughton. In Colchester the new buildings are, for the most part, additions to the platform of five interconnecting squares that make up the central spine laid down by Albert Sloman and Kenneth Capon more than fifty years ago, thereby securing the basis of their master plan. The squares – eerily bleak in the early days as 1,000–2,000 students moved around campus – are now bustling with life as over 12,000 students criss-cross campus to get to their classes.

This is significant, as many past complaints about the architecture can be explained by the necessity of greater numbers to create the 24/7 metropolis envisaged by Sloman and Capon. The squares and other original large-scale buildings – such as the library, the Hexagon restaurant and the accommodation Towers – remain the architectural success stories, while the small-scale labyrinth of corridors, seminar rooms and offices often confuse. Nonetheless, the integration of the corridors – with one academic department being seamlessly connected to another – does contribute to Essex's strong sense of community.

The Guardian, 10 November 2010

'STUDENT PROTEST OVER FEES TURNS VIOLENT'

In 2010, students defied expectations, with an estimated 50,000 turning out to vent their anger in a national protest in London against government plans to raise tuition fees to £9,000 per year. The 2017 UK general election result has shown the power students have to make a difference, while public opinion is shifting in support of a generation of students that will be significantly more in debt than their parents. For the moment, however, student unrest at Essex is a thing of the past. Today there are many channels through which students can be heard. They have representation on the main committees of campus and the Vice-Chancellor meets with the president of the Students' Union on a weekly basis. The Students' Union has recently made the decision to leave the National Union of Students, stating that it does not provide value for money and is 'too political'. At Essex, the Students' Union tell us, they would rather sit down and discuss an issue than go on a demonstration. While this readiness to engage with authority is a far cry from the approach of previous generations, it can be effective. For example, students recently convinced the University to create fee-waiving bursaries for Syrian refugees.

Today, questions about the influence of the University's architecture on student behaviour are rarely raised, as Brutalism's sculptural forms and soaring lines finally gain the admiration they deserve. Perhaps in our more cynical age, there is a nostalgia for the hope that propelled this postwar generation, with their steadfast belief that they could change the world and build a better future. Albert Sloman's own utopian vision was born out of abhorrence for the atrocities of fascism he had witnessed in the Second World War. This might also go some way to explaining his heavy handedness with the May '68 riots. Freedom of speech had been worth fighting for and when he saw students standing in the way of it, Sloman felt compelled to act. It backfired. Sloman's authoritarian reaction was not consistent with the liberal campus envisaged in his Reith Lectures, leaving students and staff both angry and confused. Essex took years to recover from the protests, blockades and sit-ins that continued until the 1980s; funding was withdrawn, recruitment suffered and building work slowed to a trickle. Nonetheless, what remains clear is that Sloman had created a critically engaged community that was able to think for itself. The intellectual growth and creativity that he encouraged helped to spark the 'moments of collective effervescence' – when new ideas are born – that marked out Essex as one of the most exciting places to study in the UK. While things have clearly settled down in Colchester, each generation of students continues to be met by an academic community that demands that they think for themselves – and that come what may – you always question authority and hold it to account.

JESS TWYMAN is Director at Art Exchange, University of Essex. She is curator of numerous exhibitions, including *Fallen* (2017), *Movement of the People* (2016) and *Something Fierce* (2014, co-curated with Jules Lubbock). Her research interests include contemporary art from the margins, early Soviet art and Latin American art.

FURTHER READING

Film footage from BBC interviews with University of Essex students and staff, May 1968, East Anglian Film Archive, University of East Anglia

John Haynes (dir.), *Mustard*, documentary film, University of Essex, 2014

John Maule McKean, 'University of Essex: A Case Study', *The Architects' Journal*, 20 September 1972

May '68 Essex website http://www.essex68.org.uk/, accessed 30 October 2017

Ken Plummer (ed.), *Imaginations: Fifty Years of Essex Sociology* (Wivenbooks 2014)

Albert Sloman, *A University in the Making*, BBC, London, 1964

University of Essex May 1968 Inquiry transcript, Albert Sloman Library, University of Essex

University of Essex Press Cuttings Archive, Albert Sloman Library, University of Essex

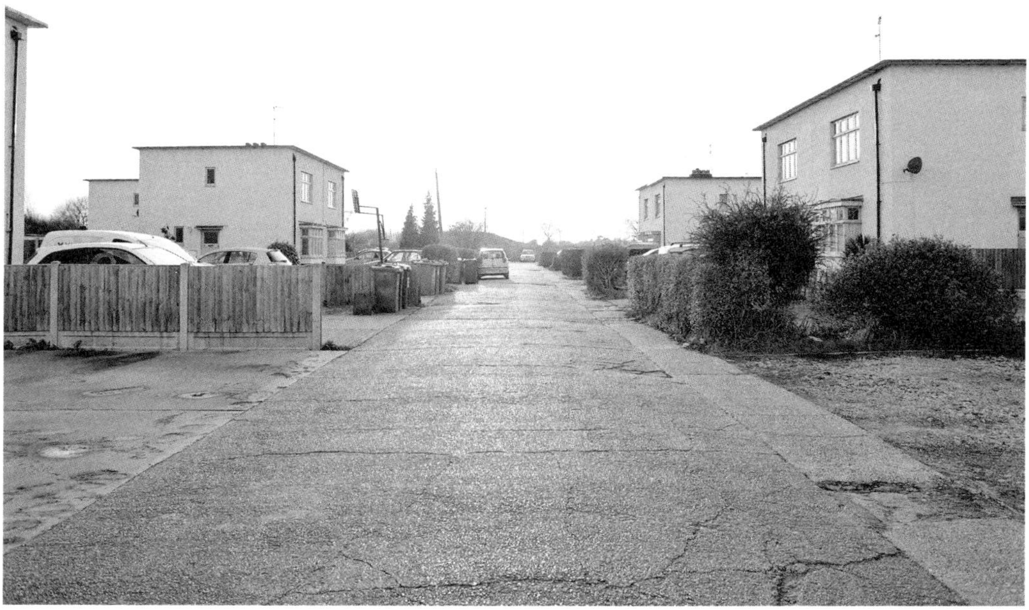

Bata Estate, East Tilbury

Bata-Ville

Rachel Lichtenstein

Beyond Tilbury town, with all its connections to the Gravesend border crossing that looks both out to the North Sea and the wider world then upriver to London, is the other end of the story, East Tilbury, with the famous Czech Bata Shoe factory now largely abandoned. The writer Iain Sinclair first visited the site whilst writing *Downriver* (1991) then later with Chris Petit when they trekked from Aldgate Pump right the length of the A13 'shadowing the river, sauntering past incredible scrapyards, wildlife habitats, landfill dumps, big container parks and the evolution of new logistic sites all of it seamlessly unravelling until we eventually tramped through the suburbs of Southend and hit the sea.'

In 2016 I hiked the seven-mile route from Tilbury Riverside to the Bata factory with Iain. He had covered the same ground so many times by then that echoes and sonar bumps kept coming back to remind him of things he half remembered from previous excursions as we walked and talked at pace. His most recent pilgrimage there had been with a woman called Carol Katz, an American designer who had come to the UK to find out more about her father who had been one of the architects on the original project. 'He was Bauhaus connected', said Iain, 'and had worked with Mies van der Rohe, he came here with this idea of merging the best of modernist architecture with a functional community, the perfect model of the Company Town.' Carol, a persistent researcher, had eventually managed to find some of her father's drawings in the library next door to the factory, which fed into a lifelong obsessive quest for her to resolve the history of her background and the way that her family, with lots of traces, had vanished. 'They had this mysterious house in Chepstow Place in Notting Hill', said Iain, 'which was the address of Robert Louis Stevenson's *Suicide Club* story, and it turned out the one book her mother had when she fled Austria on the last train was Stevenson's book. So there were all these weird coincidences that kept recurring, which she wrote about in *London: City of Disappearances* (2006). She discovered that two underground rivers also passed beneath this house, which had a very strange history and was currently occupied by the widow of Donald McWhinnie on the ground floor, who was the producer of a lot of Samuel Beckett plays for radio. I had a job there when I first knew her, painting and decorating, and I used to see Donald McWhinnie and his wife come out. It was in the snow, in winter. At one o'clock on the button every day they came outside with mufflers, long coats and woolly hats and played table tennis for exactly half an hour. You could almost set your watch. They didn't say a word to each other and then they went back inside. So it was perfectly Beckettian.'

We walked away from the dockside along a newly carved heritage trail starting at Tilbury promenade, which had been created to improve access to the historical sites along the route. By then the weather had turned. Grey menacing clouds hung overhead and a strong wind had whipped up. Shouting into the oncoming gust, whilst constantly wiping tiny particles of gritty gravel blowing up from the path on to his glasses, Iain spoke about his many journeys out on the estuary waters over the years including his recent 200-mile Swan pedalo odyssey from Hastings to the Olympic site with the artist Andrew Kötting, where they ran aground on the sands in a thunderstorm watching enormous container ships drifting close by, 'which was absolutely amazing'. He also told me about another memorable trip out to the sea forts with the musician and sound recordist Paul Burwell who he described as 'a completely anarchic spirit who regarded the river as somewhere where he had all the freedoms he couldn't get when he was on land. Every time we passed a concrete barge he would jump onto it and make recordings dangling his microphones into the water. He had been to a nautical school and knew what he was doing. We were pushing further out into deeper waters, the waves were breaking over the prow of the boat, it was a fantastic physical experience', he said enthusiastically. He talked with passion about the dramatic shifts of tide, of motoring downriver in the pitch dark, navigating along tiny channels and of the many near misses he had experienced. 'Being on the river takes you out of all the tension and weight and busyness of the city but without the remoteness of being way out on the Norfolk coast just staring out into the ferocity of the North Sea, you have the benefit on the estuary of having both things available to you. Conrad spent hours out on this river, it recharges all your batteries, all your senses.'

I had many stories of my own to share, of recent exploits undertaken whilst researching my latest book about that historic waterway. I told Iain about my extraordinary trip to Sealand, a starting point for a lot of narratives about the Thames, including Patrick Wright's BBC series *The River: The Thames in Our Time* (1999). My adventure began as dawn broke on a chilly spring morning with an exhilarating boat ride from Harwich with Prince Michael at the helm, speeding across the water on an ex-SAS military style RIB (Rigid Inflatable Boat) at 40 knots before being hauled off the boat on to the offshore naval fort (now the world's smallest independent principality) on a small wooden swing powered by the former winch from the lifeboat station on Southend Pier aptly called *Plummet*. Iain, who has known me for a long time, was amazed to hear this story. I am not a natural adventurer, rather a reluctant adrenaline junkie, who persists, mad journey after mad journey, until I get the story I am after, a desire that temporarily overrides the dangers involved.

We kept on walking, the dust whipping round our ankles, landing in our hair. The dark winding waters of the estuary ever present starboard. I shared other stories, recollections I had gathered of earlier versions of the wild, flat, semi-industrial landscape we were walking through, when the area had been absolutely jumping with life and the connection between the towns and industries alongside the riverside had still been so strong. Remnants of all that existence was still visible; the travellers' horses out on the marsh, the abandoned hulks of barges rotting in the mud, the chimneys of decommissioned power stations, the ruins of factories once vibrating with people, machinery and activity.

We soon reached the site of The World's End pub, a white weatherboard building in a depression of land, famous for its connections with Pepys and Dickens. 'Daniel Defoe did have a small brick-making factory in Tilbury', said Iain, 'but the access was so difficult, the roads were too bad, it soon shut down.' The landscape became increasingly Dutch in nature as we moved towards the seventeenth century star-shaped fort hidden into the bankside looking out onto the estuary, surrounded by watery moats on all sides, with reeds blowing in the wind. We passed a noticeboard with a potted history of the place. 'Once this begins to happen you know it's a symbol of the moment the location actually no longer has a history because the history is captured by these versions', said Iain, as he strode at speed to the next site, ignoring other information boards and the place where Queen Elizabeth I is alleged to have delivered her famous speech as the Spanish Armada prepared for invasion.

East of Tilbury Power Station we walked past Clinking Beach, the site of an untapped Victorian tip, where I had scavenged so many times before collecting rucksacks full of glass medicinal bottles, old clay pipes, tins, broken pottery, the domestic ephemera of another era. Iain told me a friend of his who had some special permission to mudlark along the whole of the Thames came there and found extraordinary

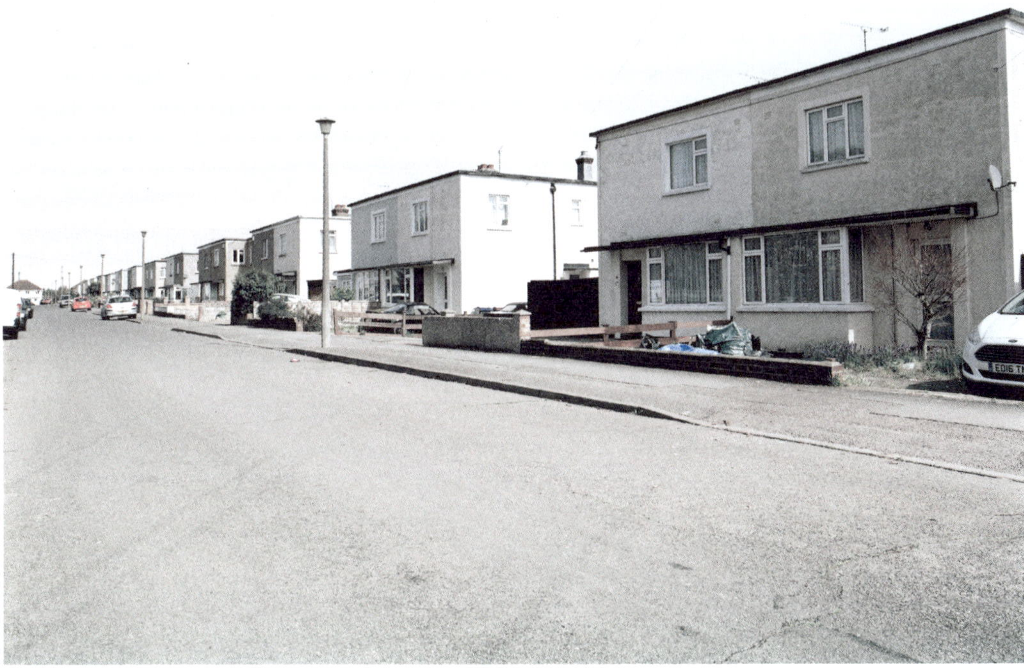

Bata Estate, East Tilbury

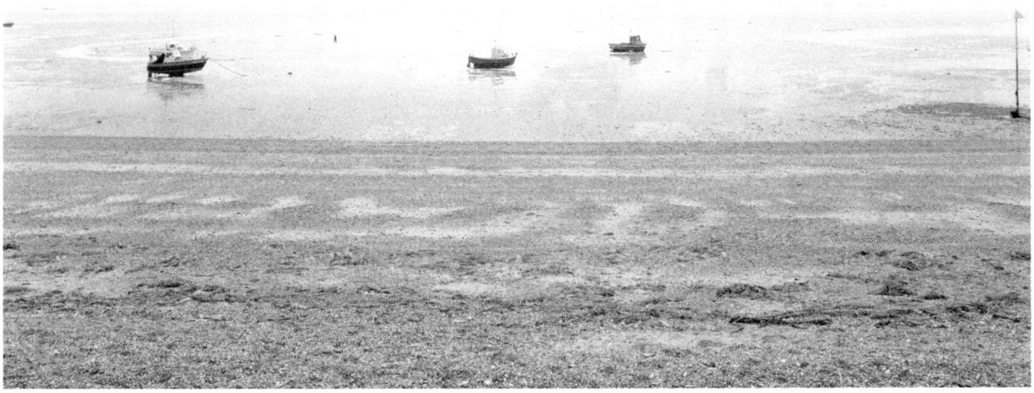

Southend-on-Sea Beach

things: Roman coins and artefacts, votive figures and medieval rings as well as pilgrims' tokens. I told him about the mudlarker from Gravesend I had interviewed for my book *Estuary* (2016), River Jim, and his nightmarish visions of drowning in the soft, deceptive, sinking mud along the coastline of the Hoo Peninsula and his story of 'straining his damn eyeballs' to find a stone head from Mesopotamia on that beach that was over 3,500 years old. We saw two people walking slowly along the shoreline in the distance with big bags over their shoulders, heads down, carefully gathering tiny objects from amongst the stones.

We seemed to leave official recorded history after then for a while, which appeared to be organised around Tilbury Fort and the history of Tilbury riverside. We entered a sort of no man's land. We walked for a long time almost along a causeway beside an enormous concrete wall covered in random graffiti. 'Here you've got a slightly foul breath of proper river air and pollution before you move up to the next heritage site and the next deep water dock', said Iain whilst inhaling deeply. We noticed how the wall had acted as a kind of buffer for endless bits of plastic; broken lighters, bottle tops, various containers, single flip-flops, which had washed up beside it when the tide had been high.
We stopped for a while and examined the miniature ecology next to the path of plastic which had merged with beautiful worn bits of driftwood, wild flowers, crisp packets, even an old shoe embedded on a thistle. We had entered a sort of hybrid zone where the plants and the plastic seemed interconnected, a place where 'people hang out because they're trying to get beyond where everything is watched on cameras'.

We passed a short concrete loading pier running out into the river in front of the power station. Two men in high-vis jackets were standing on a bit of marsh ground beside it, poking about with poles. One of them was carrying a large angle grinder over his shoulder. We stood and watched them for a while before moving on. The tall concrete wall suddenly disappeared as we moved past the power station revealing a desolate landscape of churned mud with an enormous avenue of pylons stretching into the distance where we imagined some new mega development was about to happen. A single jogger struggled past us at the same time as a small yacht sailed along the river. It was the first vessel we had seen all afternoon apart from a few iron rubbish barges moored up against a wooden platform.

The wind got stronger again as we turned a corner, creating a kind of desert storm of dust and stinging particles. 'It is bleak; it is wonderful', said Iain looking across to the shell of the Bata factory which had just about become visible in the distance along with the giant cranes of Thames Gateway. 'The super port dominates everything', said Iain. 'Everywhere we turn it's jumping around the river.'

After another mile or so we reached the approach to Coalhouse Fort, the next historic real estate. As we drew nearer the flora and fauna beside the pathway transformed from wild thistles and flowers to carefully tended hawthorn bushes covered in scented white blossom. We had entered a more domesticated landscape. The air was filled with the sound of birdsong.

The river narrowed at Coalhouse Point, just offshore sat an old radar tower. In front of it we came across a memorial bench with toys, flowers and a football attached along with a brass plaque, which told us Harry loved that spot. He had died when he was just eighteen. We headed inland off the coastal path through the landscaped gardens of Coalhouse Fort, passing another heritage board: 'Henry VIII, the new gun battery, World War Two, minefield control, essentially the reading is entirely military, history reduced to sound bites', said Iain as we briefly stopped beside the noticeboard before marching across the manicured parkland around the fort, past tepees made of old fallen trees, swings on wires and a sandpit for kids to play in. The stone circular artillery fort stood to our right, it had become obsolete almost as soon as it was constructed but remained as a poignant monument to the vulnerability of the north bank of that coastline from invaders by sea.

We exited the nicely managed landscape of the fort and came out into the town of East Tilbury. 'We're actually in a classic English village now' Iain said, as we walked through the genteel streets with a rectory, carefully mowed front lawns, the flint church and clusters of fairly strategic suburban buildings leading up to the old Bata Shoe factory which Iain described as 'a whole colony that really belongs in Czechoslovakia.'

We started walking along the main road towards the factory site. Bright yellow fields of oilseed rape swayed in the wind to our left, the grass verge beside it had become a corridor of dandelions. Cherry blossom trees covered in thick dust lined the other side of the road, behind them horses grazed in an English meadow. The cranes of Thames Gateway loomed ever larger on the coastline near Stanford-le-Hope, the village where Joseph Conrad began writing *Heart of Darkness* (1899). The novel opens with a description of the Thames Estuary as the launching place of England's great ships, where Sir Francis Drake sailed past on the *Golden Hind*, which was full of treasure, capturing the imperial ambitions of the nation of the time: 'What greatness had not floated on the ebb of that river into the mystery of an unknown earth! ... the dreams of men, the seed of commonwealths, the germs of empires.' The new super port was near completion at the time of our walk, it aimed to be the most fully automated deep-water port in Europe, able to accommodate the largest container ships in the world.

A convoy of lorries and trucks hammered past us at a remorseless speed on their way back and forth to the port. The striking central buildings of the factory stood out on the horizon, perfect examples of Middle European modernist architecture. Most of the windows had been blown out, the place looked empty. The Bata site, which included the factory and many other buildings, had been founded in 1932 by Tomas Bata, a Czech entrepreneur from a long line of shoemakers who built similar sites around the world. Bata died in a plane crash the year the factory opened in East Tilbury, but both the factory and the utopian garden community around it prospered for a further 70 years, manufacturing affordable footwear for the masses and providing jobs and homes for thousands of local people. 'If you worked there and bought into the company system you were well looked after' said Iain, as we tramped along the dusty main road. 'They had everything, social clubs, sports competitions, holidays organised, a library, their own fire service, healthcare, bars, a hotel, even their own newspaper but you had to kind of toe the line. It was a mini benevolent communist state and as long as you went along with that you were really well looked after. If you kicked against the system you could be rapidly dumped and then you lost your house as well as your job but a lot of people who lived and worked there loved it, the place was a completely self-sufficient community, Bata was family.'

We walked in silence for a while, the sound of the lorries and the choking dust made it difficult to talk. Before long we entered the Bata complex. The central factory buildings are so beautiful, predominately unused now since the site shut down in 2005. Bata-Ville, as it was once known, is a shadow of its former self. The swimming pool, tennis courts and cinema have all gone. The community who lived and worked there have been mostly dispersed. The unique modernist architecture remains, although now most buildings are in a fairly dilapidated state.

We walked at length around the Bata Estate, tall trees lined the roads, the square workers' houses behind the factory site are now predominately privately owned listed buildings visited by architecture enthusiasts and students from around the world. We stopped for a while outside a bronze statue

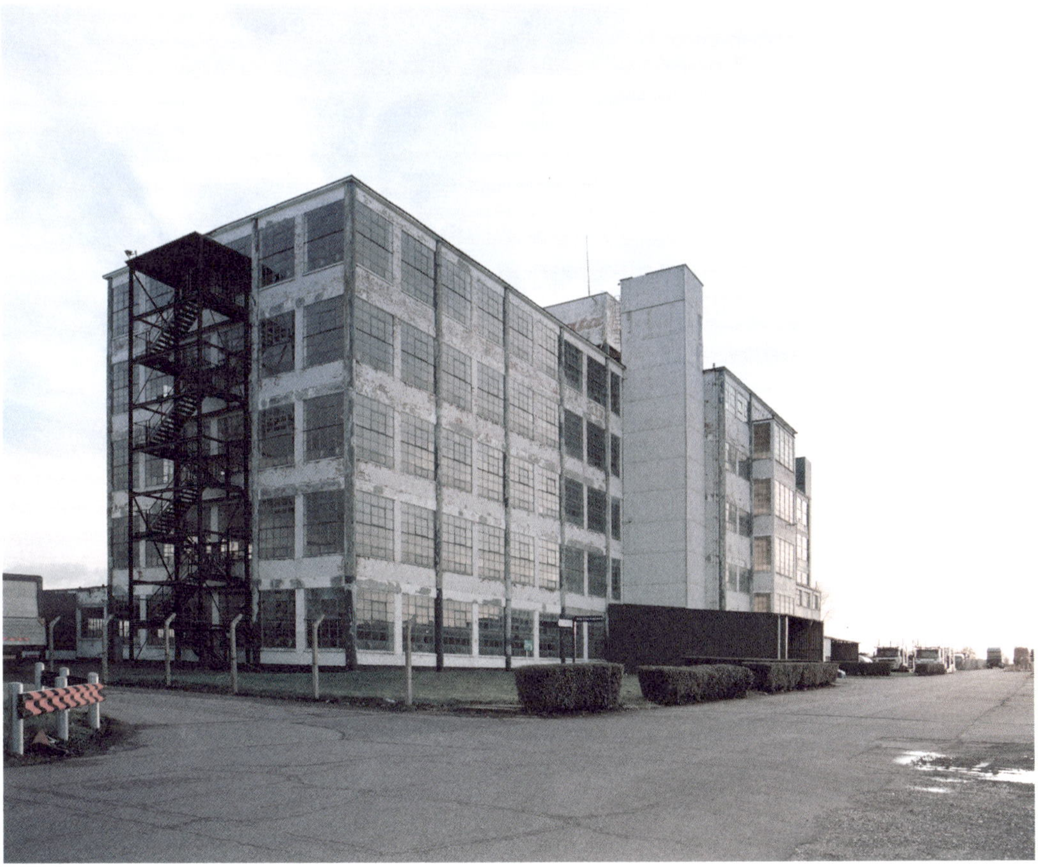

Bata Shoe Factory, East Tilbury

to Tomas Bata, which was covered in pigeon shit. Iain pointed out the social club that Mr Katz had designed nearby. We walked past a low level, single storey building with large windows at the front, which was once the leisure club for Bata. When Iain came with Carol she had photographs of what the original had looked like, it has since been broken up into King Pizza and Grill and is unrecognisable.

The library, which had also been designed by Carol's father, was shut by the time we arrived. I peered through the window, inside I could see a small display by Bata Heritage Centre, who have spent decades gathering oral testimony, photographs and other memorabilia from those who once worked and lived at the Bata Estate. I listened to some of these stories online when I got home, which had been recorded by this group of dedicated enthusiasts and heard moving tales from Bata during its heyday in the 1940s, 50s and 60s. People spoke of talent contests, dances, football tournaments and Bata-run pantomimes, they told stories of a close-knit community living in modern new houses with gardens and indoor toilets, they spoke with emotion of how grateful they were for the work, of how idyllic their childhoods had been on the estate surrounded constantly by family and friends.

A few weeks after our walk a car crashed into the entrance lobby of the East Tilbury Library and was then deliberately set alight; much of the Bata collection was seriously smoke damaged, some irreplaceable items were destroyed. The library was temporarily closed but reopened again in April 2017. The group are still in the process of applying for grants to restore the damaged collection.

RACHEL LICHTENSTEIN is a writer, curator and artist. She lives in Essex. Her publications include: *Estuary: Out From London to the Sea* (2016), *Diamond Street* (2012), *On Brick Lane* (2007), *Rodinsky's Room* (1999, with Iain Sinclair), *Keeping Pace: Older Women of the East End* (2003), *Add. 17469 A Little Dust Whispered* (2004) and *Rodinsky's Whitechapel* (1999). She has curated Shorelines: Literary Festival of the Sea for arts organisation Metal since 2011. Her artwork has been widely exhibited both in the UK and internationally, at venues including the Whitechapel Gallery, the British Library, Barbican Art Gallery, Wood Street Galleries, Pittsburgh, PA and The Jerusalem Theatre, Jerusalem.

FURTHER READING

William Addison, *Thames Estuary* (Robert Hale 1954)

Michael Bates, *Principality of Sealand: Holding the Fort* (Principality of Sealand 2015)

Joseph Conrad, *The Mirror of the Sea* (Methuen 1906)

Paul Gilson, *Sole Searching: Tales of a Thames Fisherman* (Estuary Publishing 2011)

Robert Hallmann, *Canvey Island: A History* (Phillimore 2006)

Rachel Lichtenstein, *Estuary: Out From London to the Sea* (Hamish Hamilton 2016)

Tony Moon, *Down by the Jetty: The Dr Feelgood Story* (Grand Records 2010)

Iain Sinclair, *Downriver* (Paladin 1991)

Patrick Wright, *The River: The Thames in Our Time* (BBC Books 1999)

People of Othona

Award-winning photographer Catherine Hyland has been working in residence for Radical ESSEX over the past two years, traversing the county to capture the landscapes and architecture of Essex in her unique style.

On visiting Othona Community in late 2016, she embarked on a series of portraits of residents and visitors to the site, finding it an ideal field study for her interest in researching and recording bloodlines and their related stories, particularly those subject to the external forces of territory, circumstance and religion. The Community has a long history of marital couples meeting and returning in what is essentially a ritualistic act, often starting a tradition to be passed down through the family line.

Founded in 1946, Othona Community's early pioneers created a movement that sought to pursue reconciliation and understanding between people of different faiths, cultures and nationalities for people to come together for periods of reflection, discussion, discovery and spiritual renewal. It describes itself as 'an open Christian Community, whose purpose is to provide a welcoming, accepting place with a pattern of work, worship, study and play where people of different beliefs, cultures, classes, abilities and ages can discover how to live together'.

CATHERINE HYLAND is a graduate of Chelsea College of Art and Royal College of Art, London, exhibiting most recently in the Renaissance Photography Prize and the Taylor Wessing Portrait Prize. Her practice involves extensive research, in projects guided by an interest in systems of categorisation and classification.

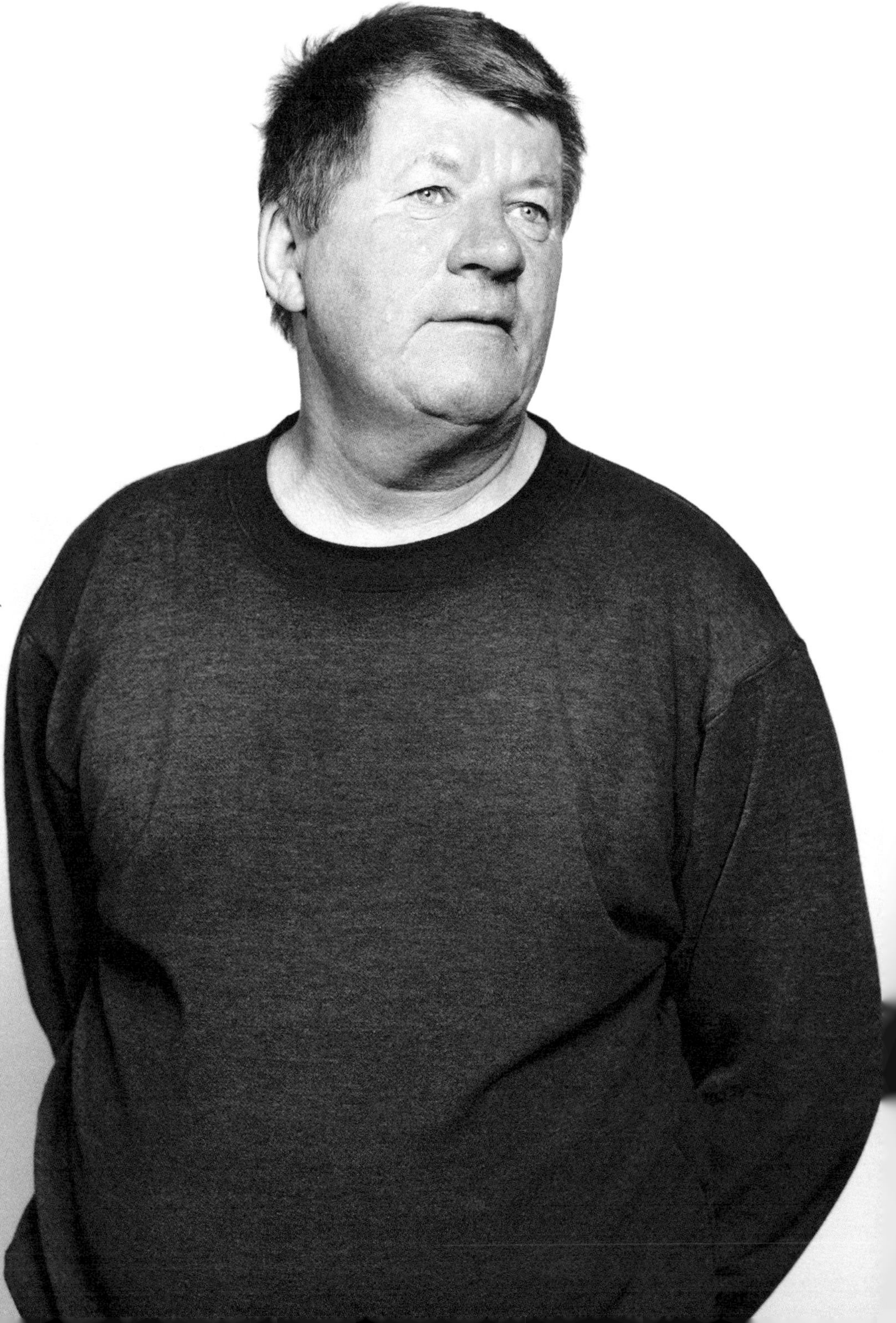

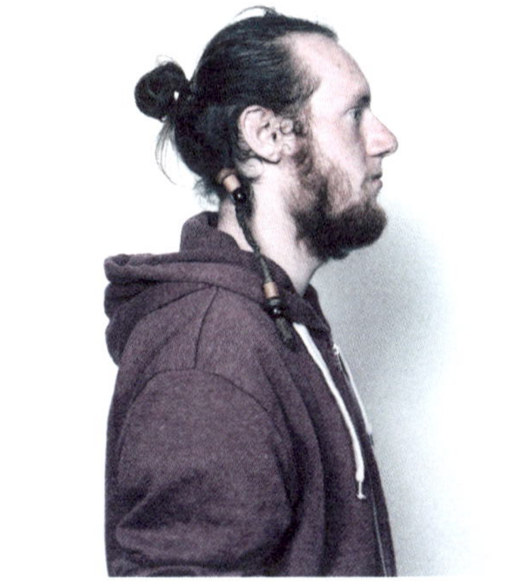

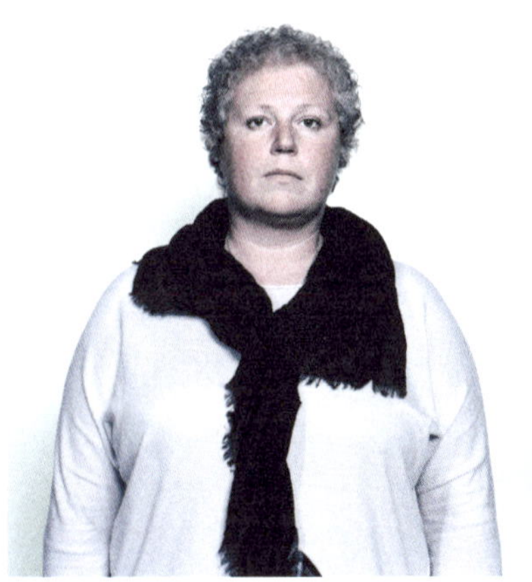

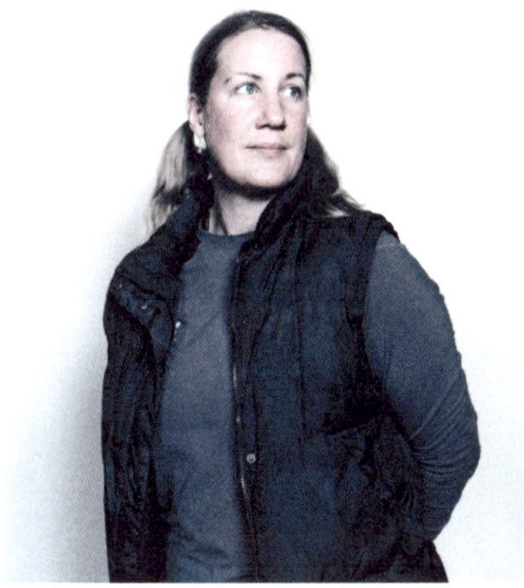

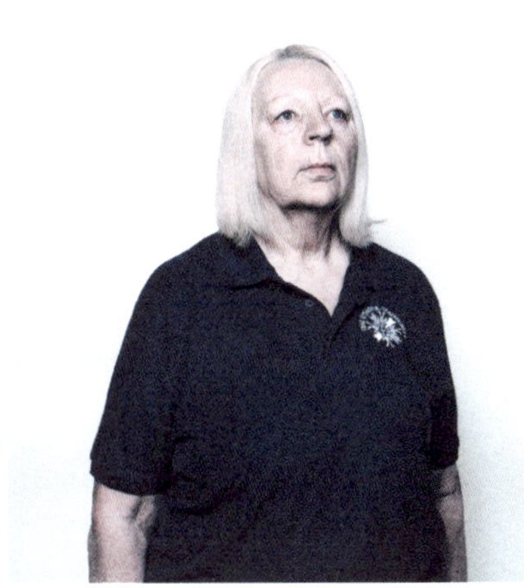

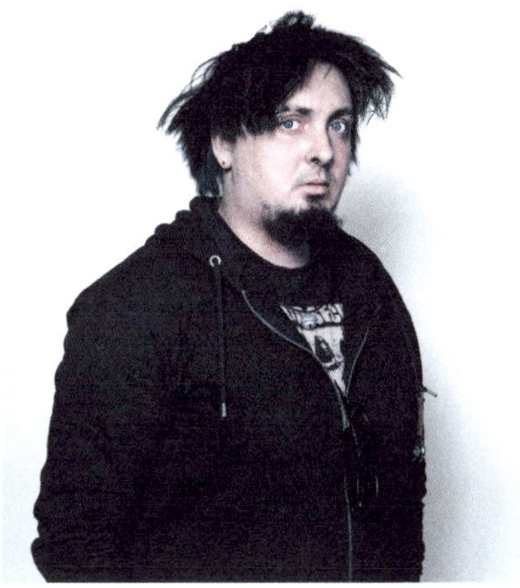

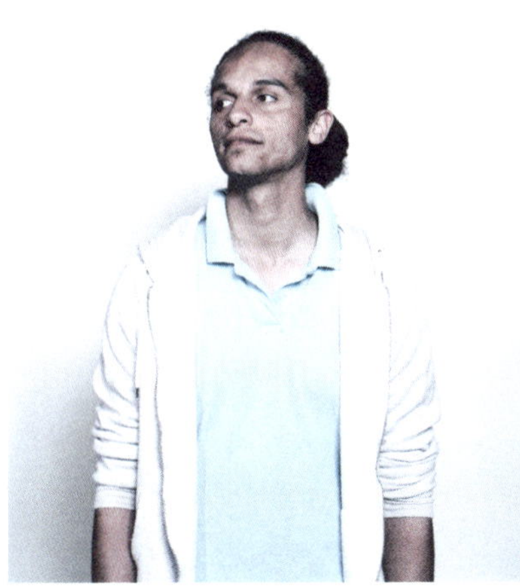

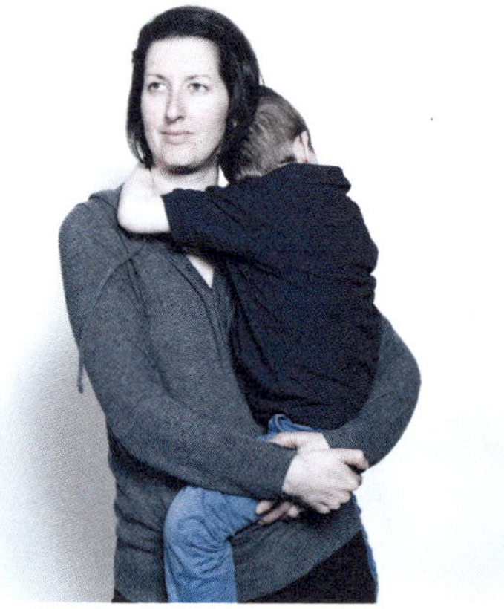

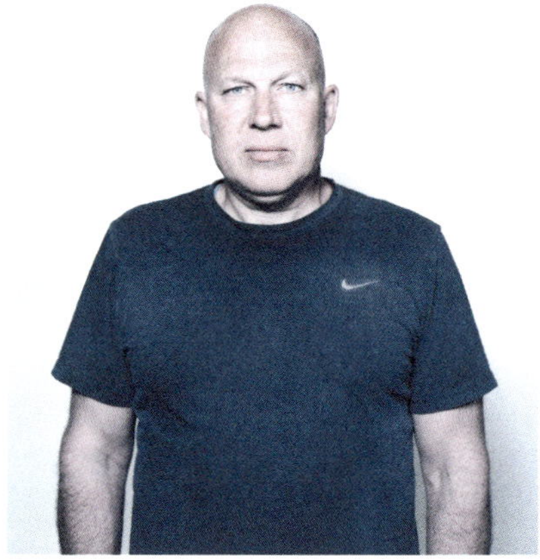

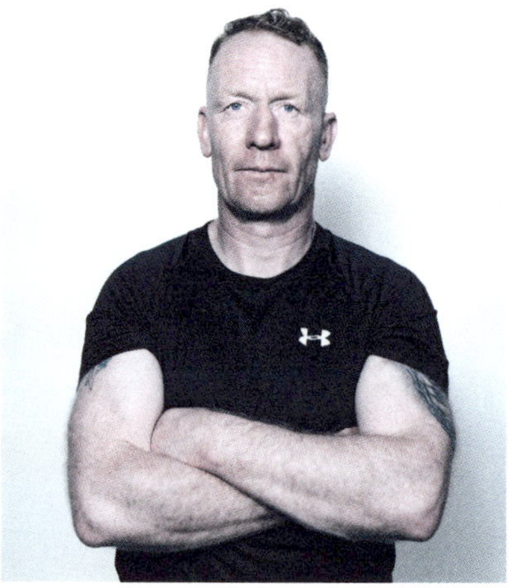

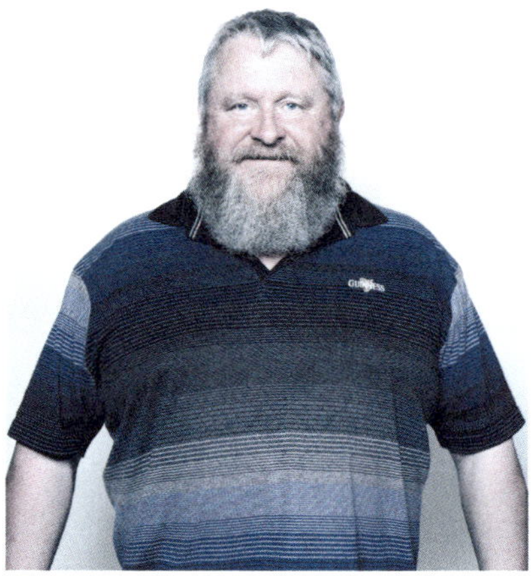

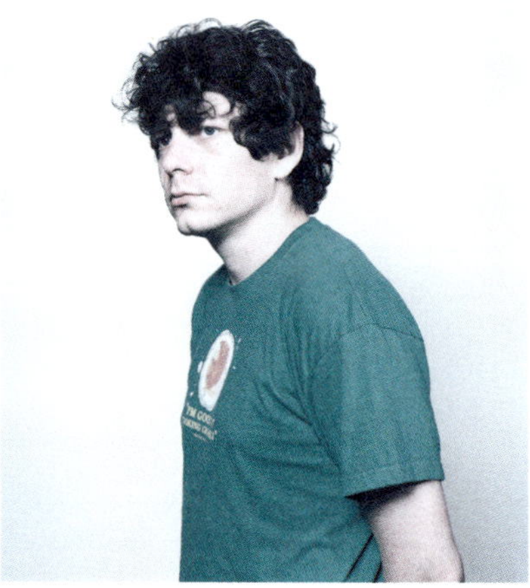

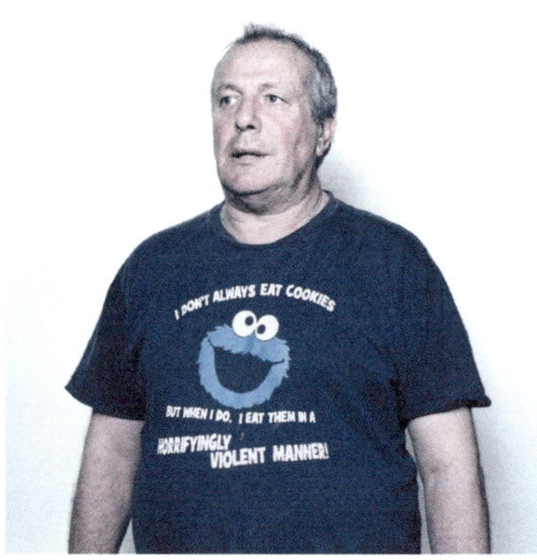
I DON'T ALWAYS EAT COOKIES
BUT WHEN I DO, I EAT THEM IN A
VIOLENT MANNER!

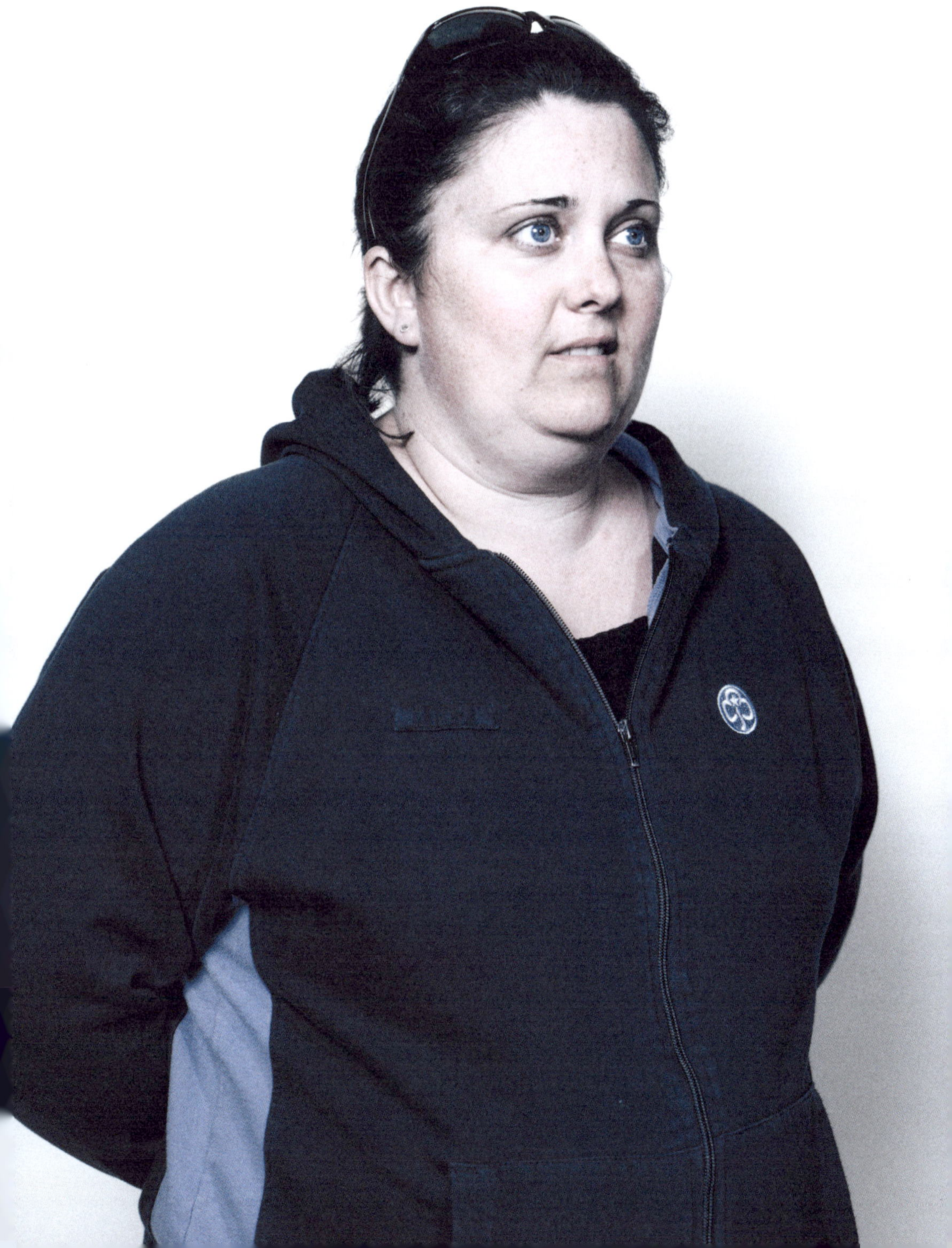

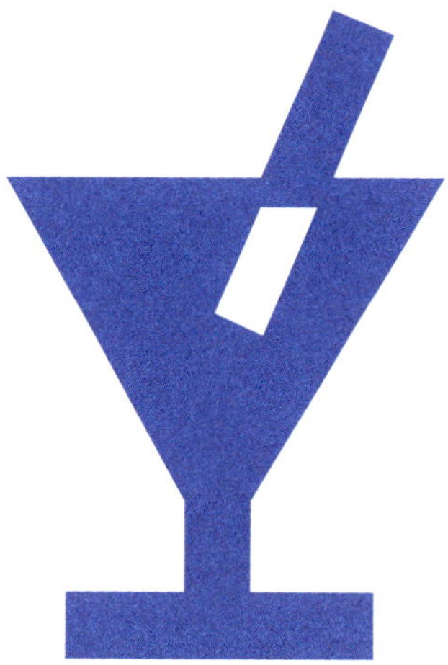

Programme

Exhibition: 'The Peculiar People' featuring new commissions by Hannah Black and Christian Nyampeta
16 April to 2 July 2016
Focal Point Gallery and Big Screen Southend

Performance: Lina Lapelyte, *Ladies,* featuring four women from the Lietuva ensemble
16 April 2016

Poetry Reading: Caspar Heinemann, *Good Health & Safety*
28 April 2016

Talk: Ken Worpole
12 May 2016

Screening: Nina Pope and Karen Guthrie, *Bata-ville: We Are Not Afraid of the Future*
21 May 2016

Talk: Penny Rimbaud, *OPEN DOOR, OPEN HEART*
26 May 2016

Talk: Christian Nyampeta
4 June 2016

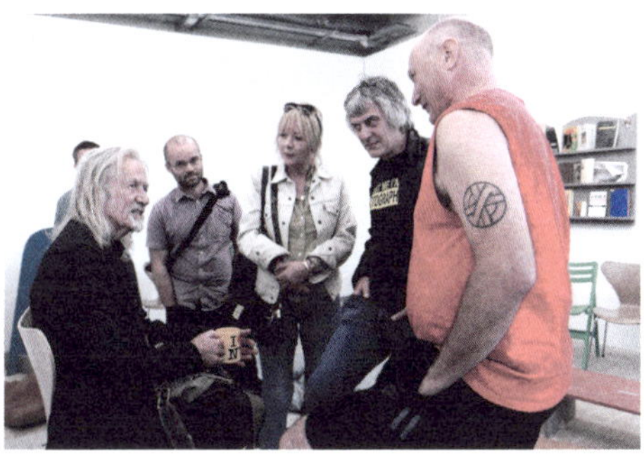

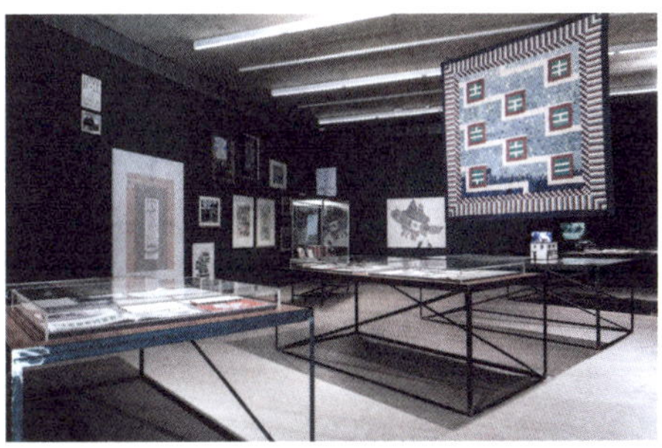

Commission: *Flood House*, a collaboration with Matthew Butcher (Bartlett School of Architecture) and curator Jes Fernie, including artwork *All Distinctions Levelled* by Ruth Ewan
16 April to 23 May 2016
Traversing the Thames Estuary

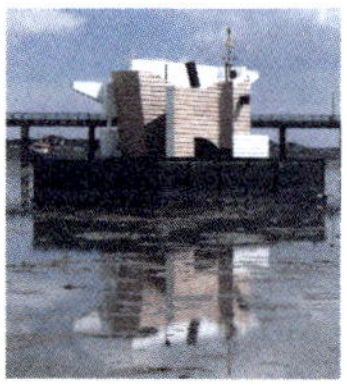

Launch Event: A conversation between Matthew Butcher and Jes Fernie at Focal Point Gallery, followed by a walk to Southend Pier for a performance of *John Ball* by Electric Belles choir
30 April 2016

Commission: Radical ESSEX Beach Hut as part of Estuary Festival, organised by Metal
12 August 2016 to 28 May 2017
Southend Pier

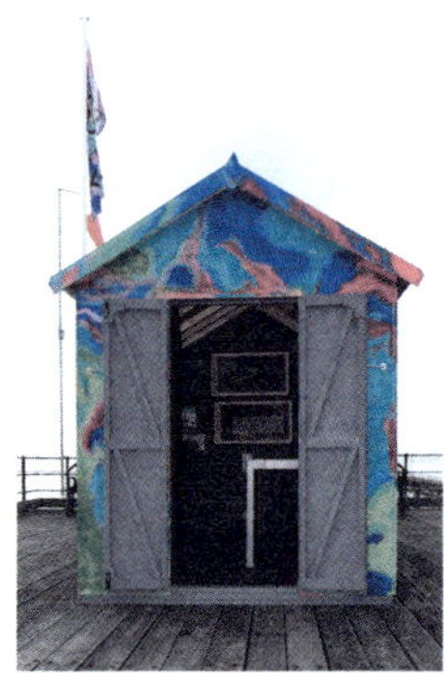

Festival: ESSEX Architecture Weekend
10 to 11 September 2016

Architectural Commission: HAT Projects
Silver End

Architectural Tours:
11 and 18 Graces Walk, Frinton Park Estate
12 Easton Way, Frinton Park Estate
18 Queen Elizabeth Avenue, Bata Estate
52 and 62 Clatterfield Gardens, Westcliff-on-Sea
64 Heath Drive, Romford
73 Vicarage Hill, Benfleet
164 Cressing Road, Braintree
180 Bishopsfield Estate, Harlow
Beecroft Art Gallery, Southend-on-Sea
Royal Corinthian Yacht Club, Burnham-on-Crouch
Tydings, Maylandsea
University of Essex, Colchester

Exhibition: 'Bata Heritage Centre'
East Tilbury Library

Exhibition: 'Frinton and Walton Heritage Trust'
Crossing Cottage, Frinton-on-Sea

Exhibition: 'Silver End Heritage Society'
Silver End Village Hall

Exhibition: 'The Haven'
Plotlands Museum, Langdon

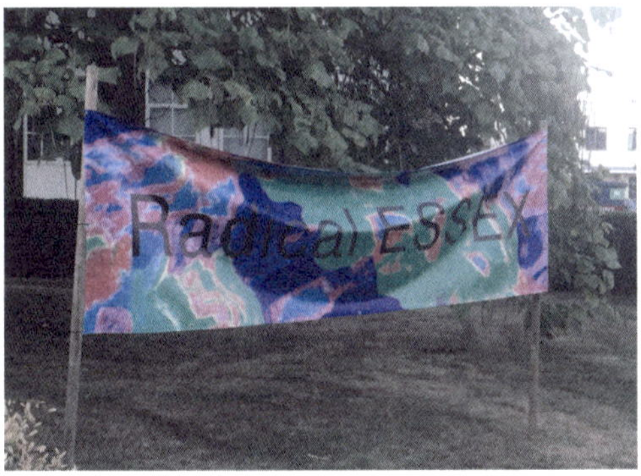

Guided Tours:
Silver End, led by Silver End Heritage Society
Bata East Tilbury, led by Bata Heritage Centre
Frinton Park Estate led by Frinton and Walton Heritage Trust

Family Workshop: *Building the Future*, organised by FPG Create with artists Florence Dwyer and Simon Worthington and India Harvey
Silver End Village Hall

Film Screening: Aerial footage of Silver End and archival films of Essex curated by Big Screen Southend, organised with Silver End Scouts
Silver End Scouts Hut

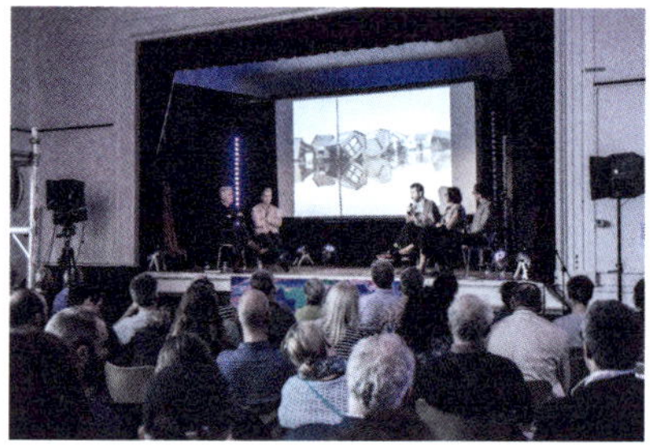

Talks Programme: curated by Warren Harper and Stephanie Sutton
Silver End Village Hall

Landscape, Identity and the London Spill with Tim Burrows, Matthew Butcher, Charles Holland, Rachel Lichtenstein and Ken Worpole

The Joy of Essex screening and in-conversation with Jonathan Meades and Gavin Haynes

The Cradle of British Modernism? Essex Architecture, the Interwar Years and Post-war Legacy with Catherine Croft, Elizabeth Darling, Alan Powers and Ellen Thorogood

Visions of Utopia with Gillian Darley, Owen Hatherley, Sam Jacob and Verity-Jane Keefe

Disco: *The Radical National Trust of South Essex*, with Depeche Mode tribute band Speak & Spell, and DJ set from Bob Stanley
Silver End Village Hall

Publication Commission: *Details* in collaboration with
Curl la Tourelle Head Architects and The Everyday Press
Published September 2016

Artist Commission: *The Radical National Trust of South Essex*
by Alan Kane
September 2016 ongoing

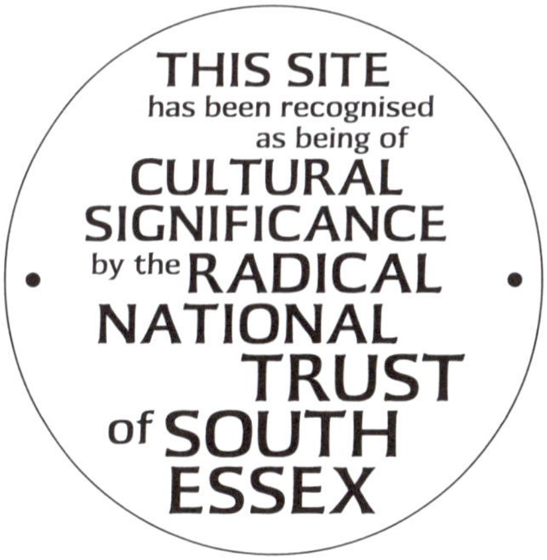

Project: *MORNING* an artwork by Shaun C. Badham
supported by Radical ESSEX
September 2016 ongoing

Walking tour in Victoria Park and archive exhibition
at King Edward Community Centre, Laindon
24 September 2016

Publication launch at Focal Point Gallery and *Moon Probe*
exhibition at Beecroft Art Gallery
12 November 2016

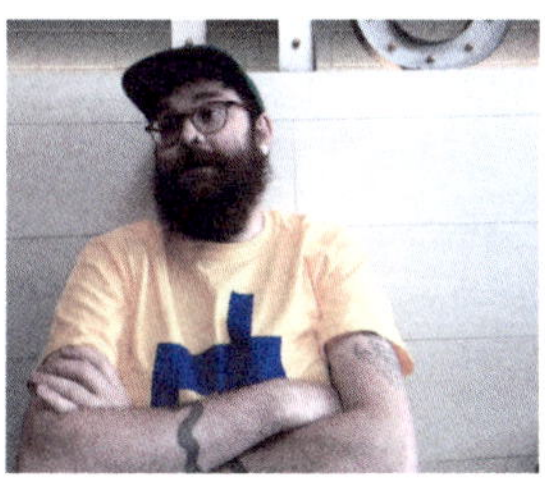

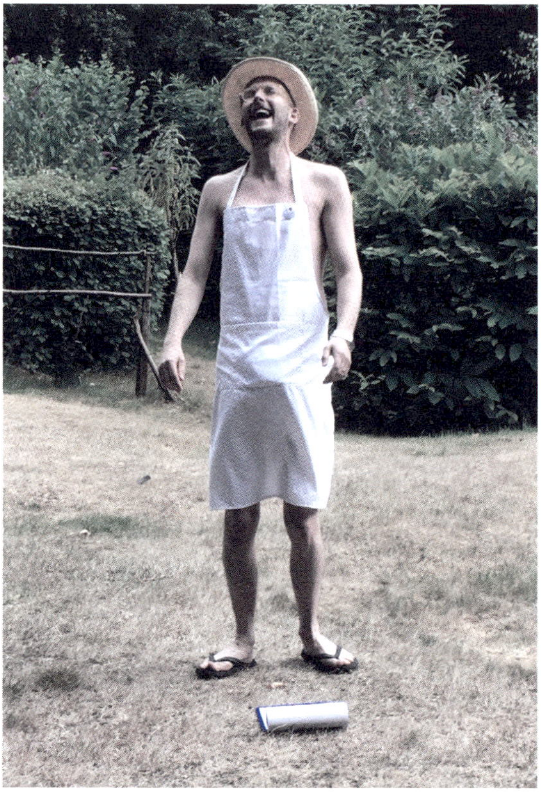

Residency: Barry Sykes
November 2016 ongoing
Oakwood Sun Club

'A CONFESSION: ANARCHY, ANONYMITY, HEALTH & EFFICIENCY' An Amateur History of Social Nudity in Modern Essex 1896–2017
10 December 2016
Focal Point Gallery

Oakwood Sun Club Open Day, including research presentation and Laughter Yoga performance
25 June 2017
Oakwood Sun Club

YouTube Playlists Programme: selections from Jennifer Lucy Allan, Shaun C. Badham, Tim Burrows, Julia Crabtree and William Evans, Jes Fernie, Verity-Jane Keefe, James Ravinet, Barry Sykes, T-Bitch and Luke Turner
November 2016 ongoing

Retreat: Radical Writing Retreat, organised in collaboration with Essex Book Festival, with readings, workshops and performances by James Canton, Ros Green, Adrian May, Glenys Newton, Philip Terry, Roma Tearne, Ken Worpole and Kate Worsley
5 to 7 April 2017
Othona Community

Performance: Scottee *From Wivenhoe, With Love*, part of Heritage Open Days Unsung Stories programme, featuring artists La John Joseph, Nando Messias and Mem Morrison
9 September 2017
Wivenhoe

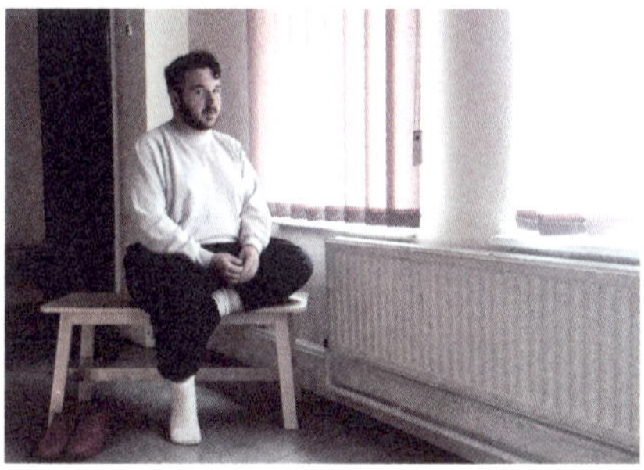

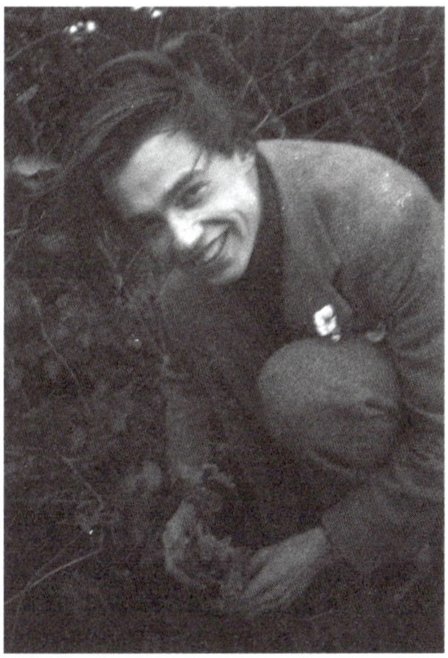

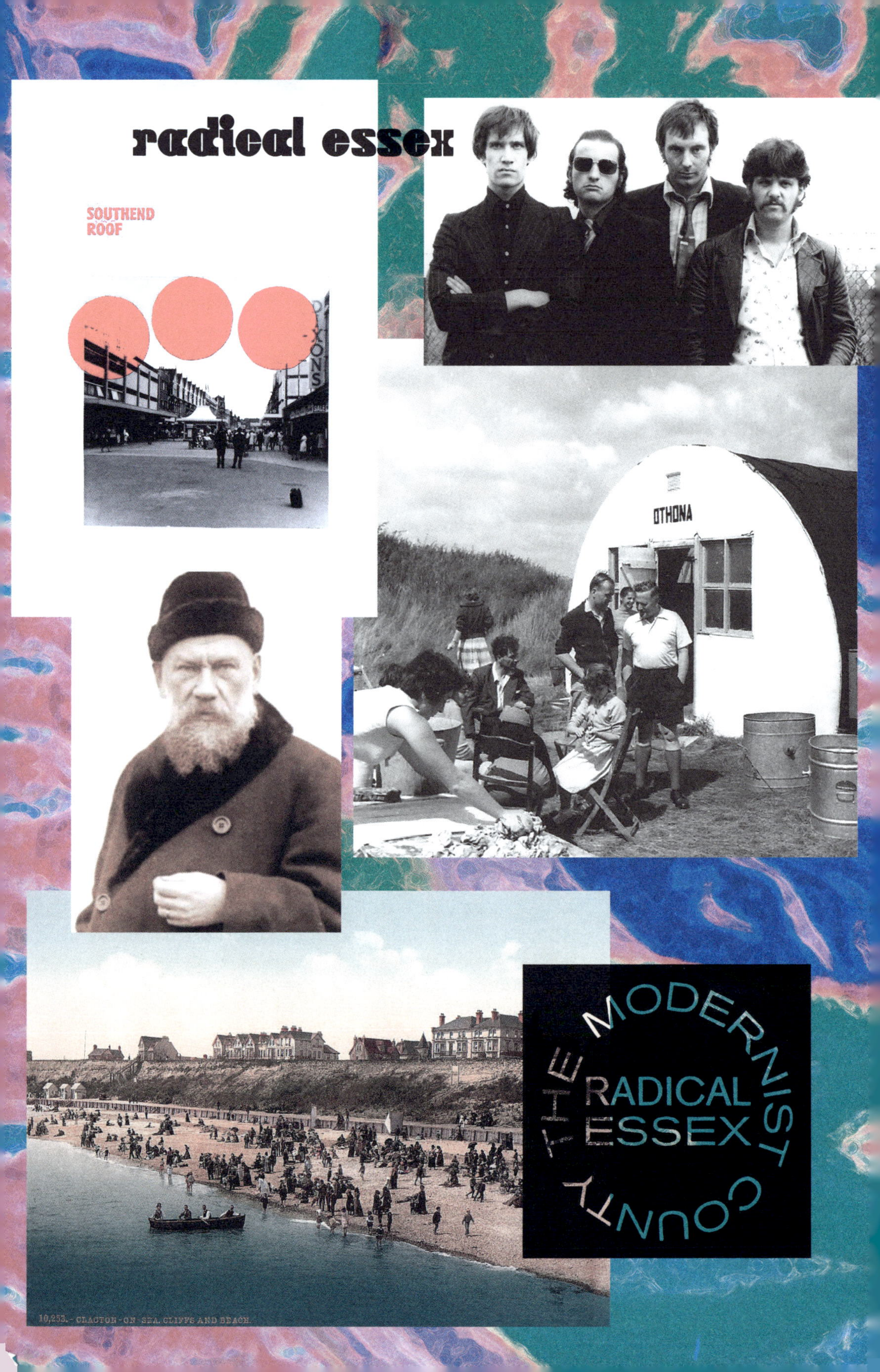
radical essex
SOUTHEND
ROOF
OTHONA
THE MODERNIST COUNTY
RADICAL
ESSEX
10,253. - CLACTON-ON-SEA. CLIFFS AND BEACH.

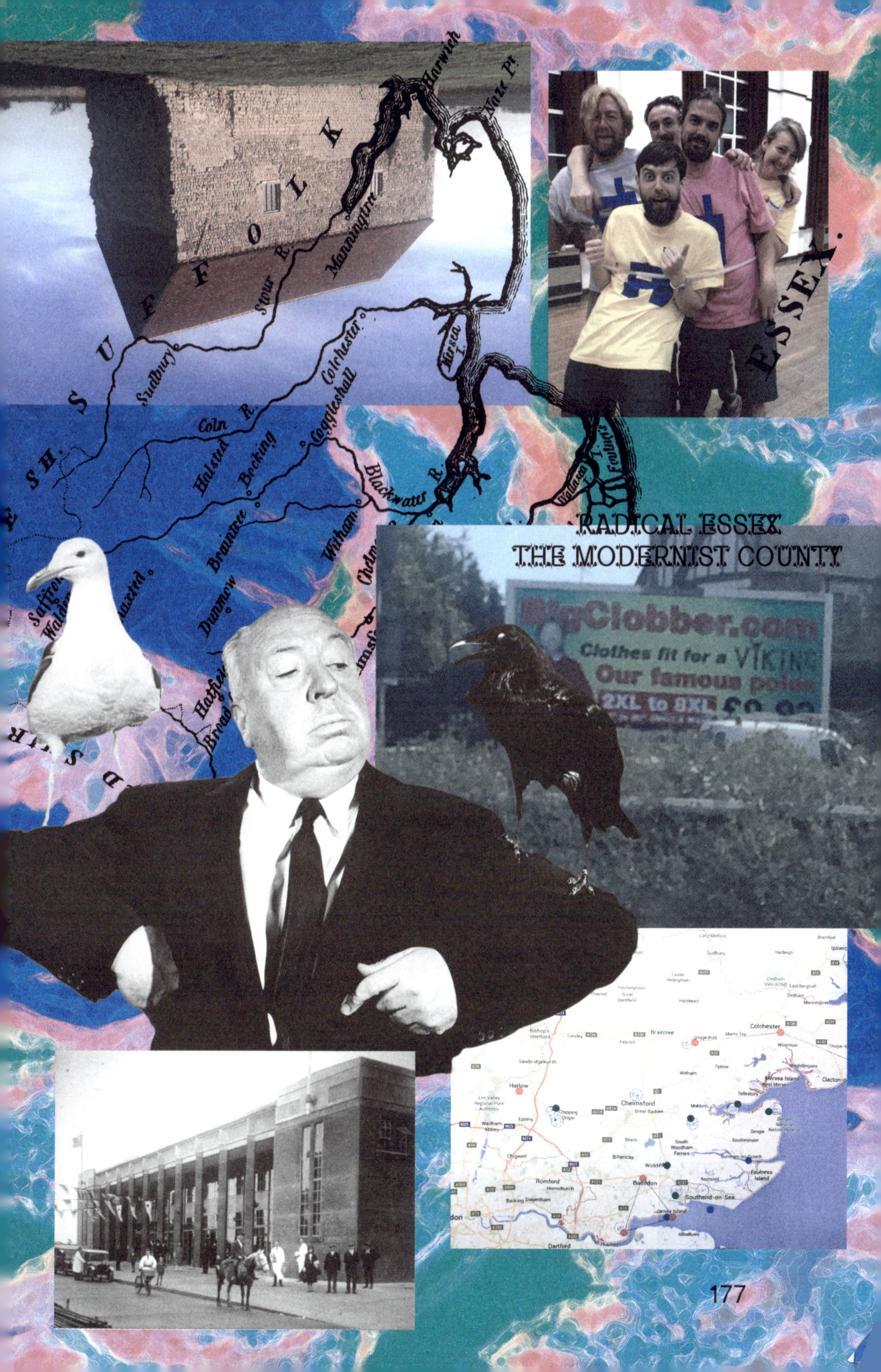
RADICAL ESSEX
THE MODERNIST COUNTY
SUFFOLK
ESSEX.
Harwich
Naze Pt.
Manningtree
Stour R.
Sudbury
Colchester
Coggleshall
Coln R.
Halsted
Bocking
Braintree
Witham
Blackwater R.
Mersea I.
Dunmow
Saffron Walden
Hatfield
BigClobber.com
Clothes fit for a VIKING
Our famous polo
2XL to 8XL
Colchester
Braintree
Chelmsford
Harlow
Romford
Basildon
Southend-on-Sea
Dartford

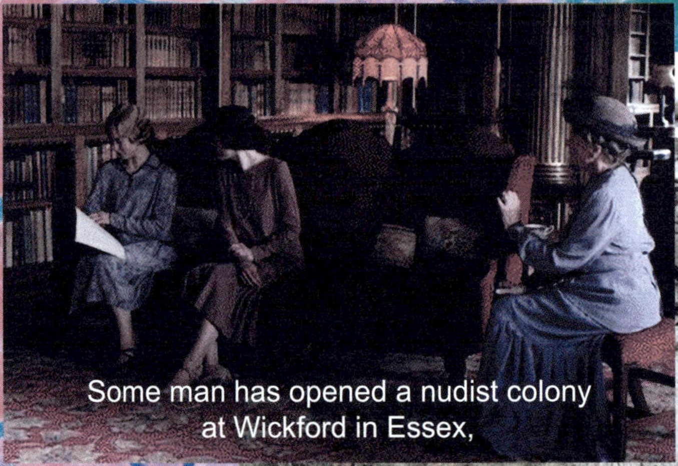

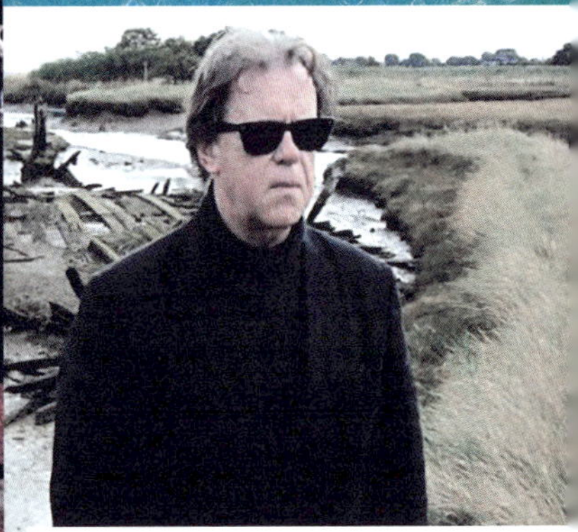

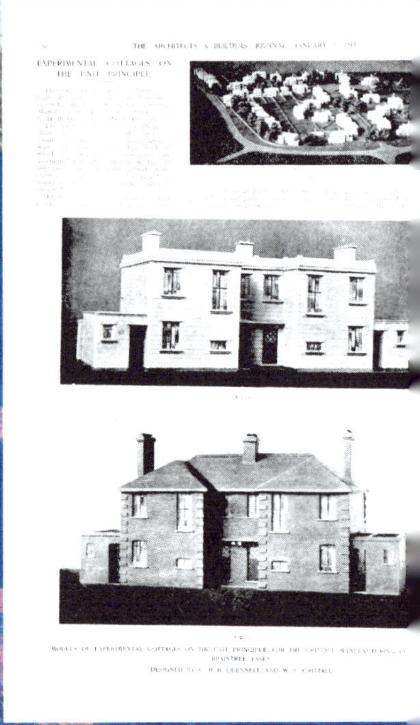
THE ARCHITECTS' & BUILDERS' JOURNAL

EXPERIMENTAL COTTAGES ON THE UNIT PRINCIPLE

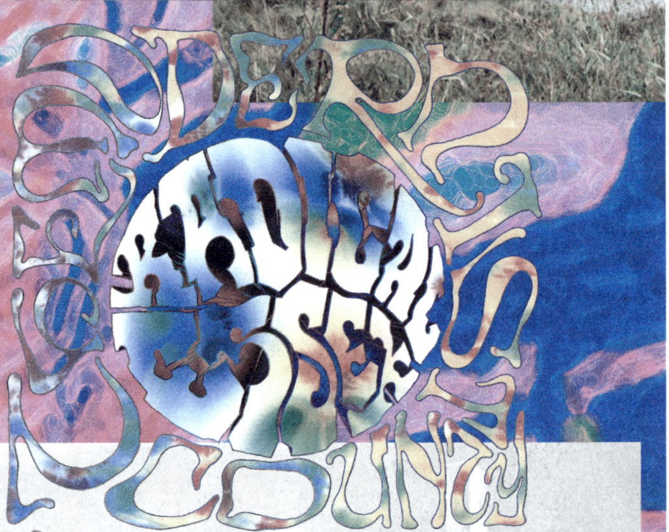

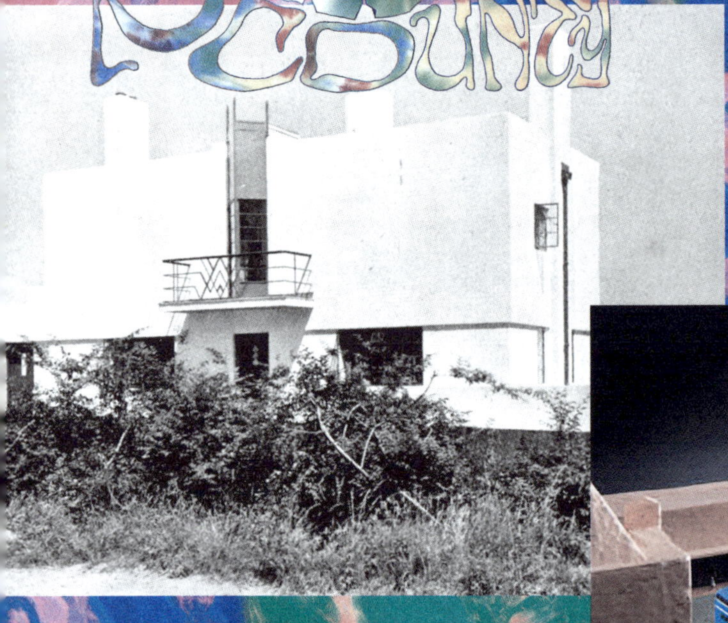

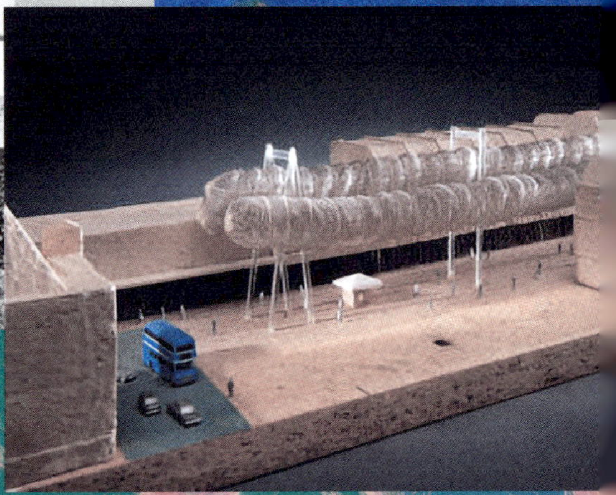

From: Joe Hill [redacted]
Subject: Amazing news for Cultural Destinations!!
Date: 16 December 2015 at 17:14
To: Riah Pryor [redacted] Hayley Dixon [redacted] Warren Harper [redacted]

JH

It must be a coincidence, but next year (2016) is exactly 500 years since Sir Thomas More wrote the first 'Utopia', and coined the term. He coined the word 'utopia' from the Greek ou-topos meaning 'no place' or 'nowhere'. But this was a pun - the almost identical Greek word eu-topos means a good place.

Best,
Joe

Joe Hill
Director
Focal Point Gallery
www.fpg.org.uk

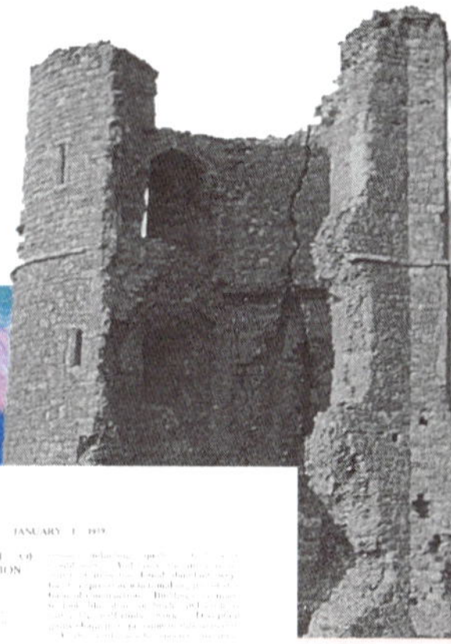

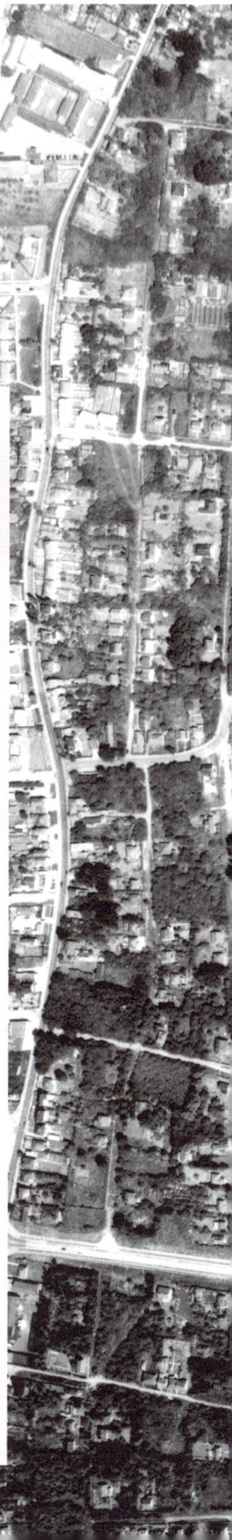

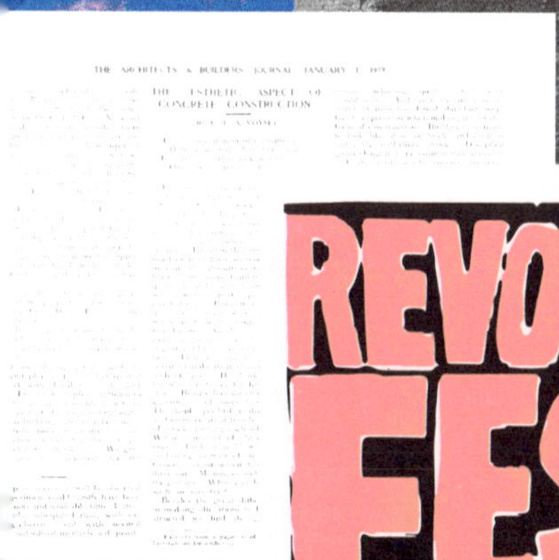

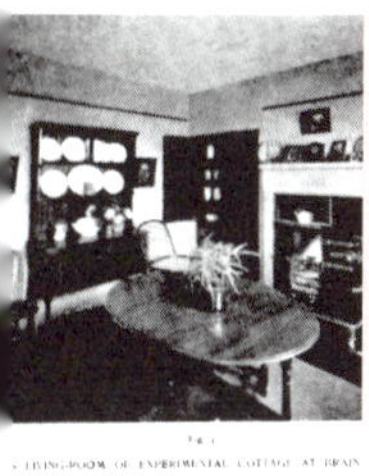

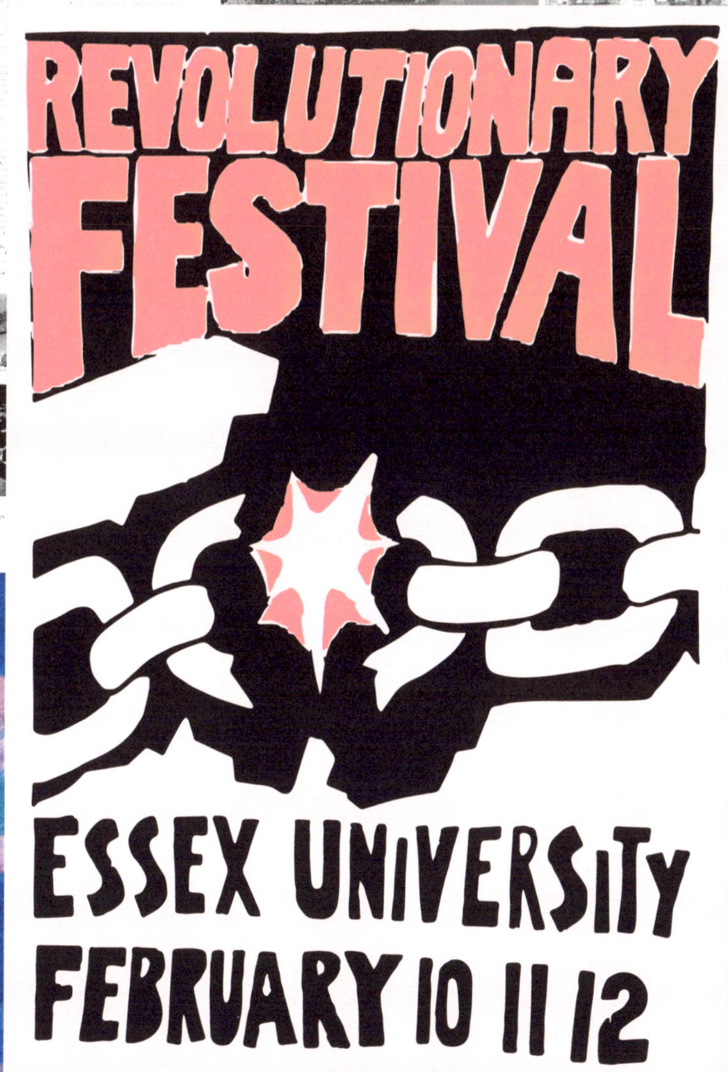

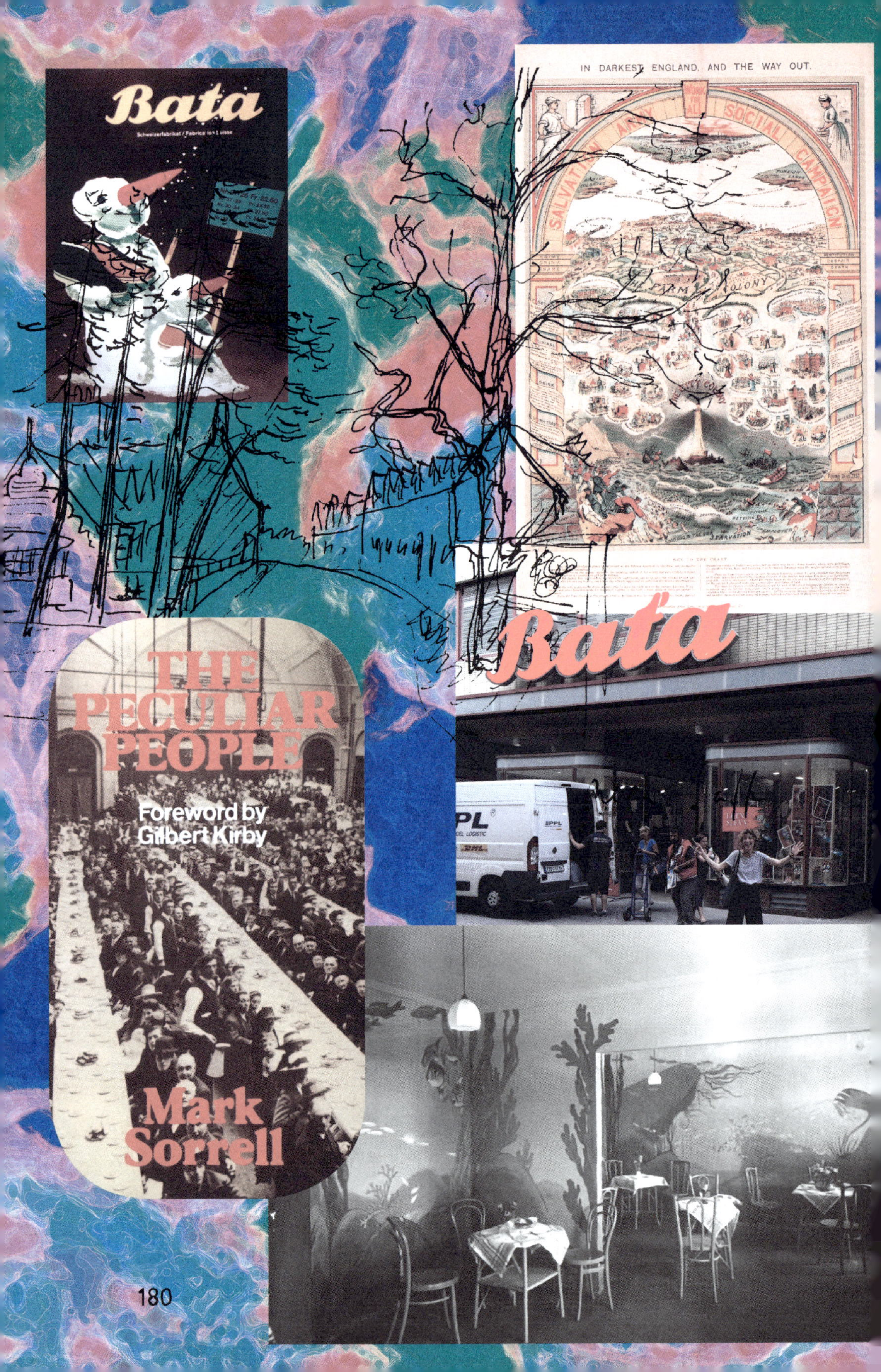
Bata
IN DARKEST ENGLAND, AND THE WAY OUT.
SALVATION ARMY SOCIAL CAMPAIGN
THE PECULIAR PEOPLE
Foreword by
Gilbert Kirby
Mark Sorrell
Bata

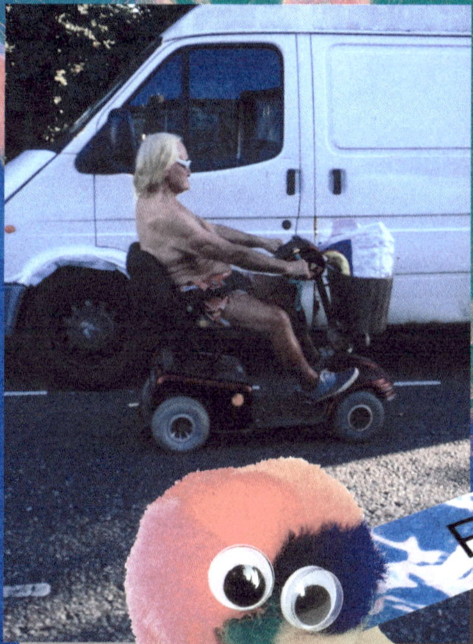

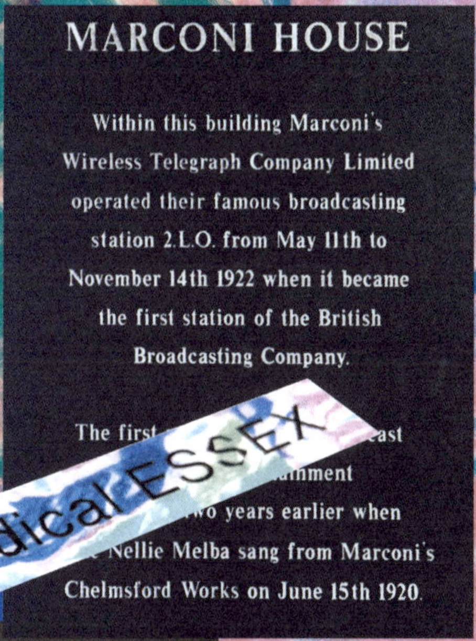
MARCONI HOUSE
Within this building Marconi's Wireless Telegraph Company Limited operated their famous broadcasting station 2.L.O. from May 11th to November 14th 1922 when it became the first station of the British Broadcasting Company.
The first
east
ainment
wo years earlier when
Nellie Melba sang from Marconi's Chelmsford Works on June 15th 1920.

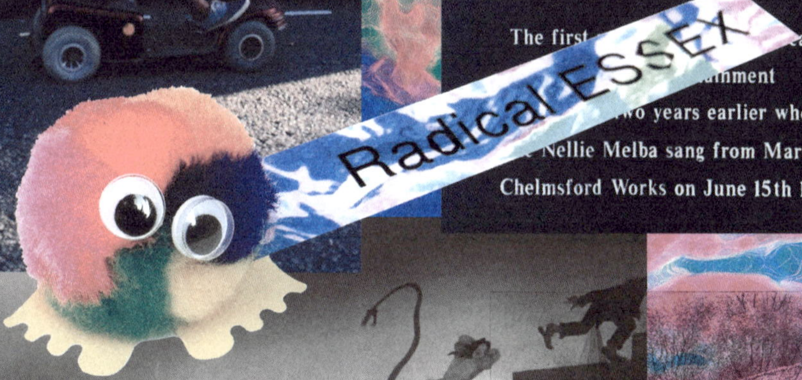
Radical ESSEX

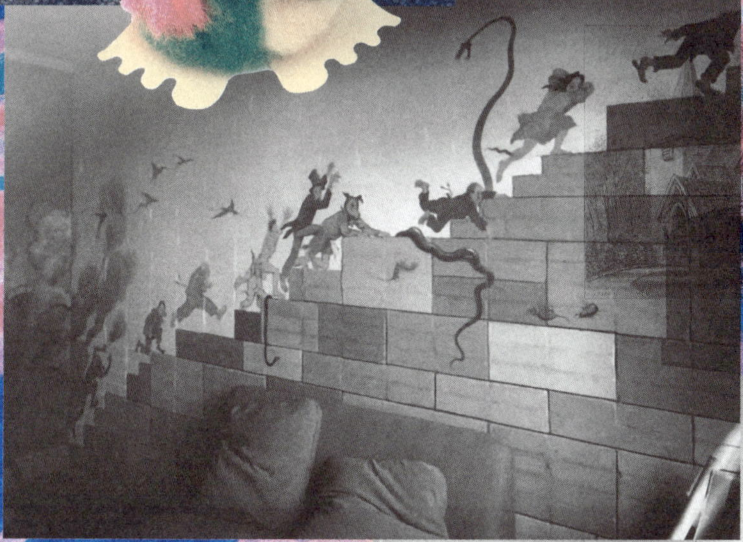

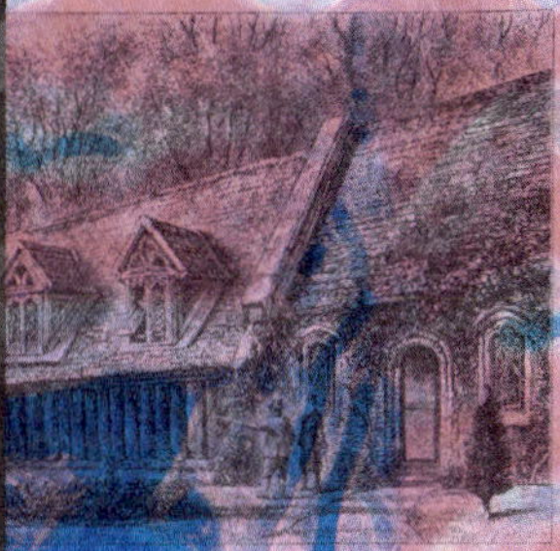

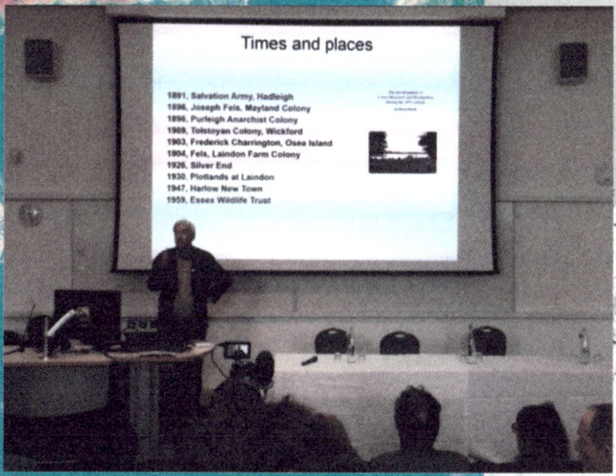
Times and places
1891, Salvation Army, Hadleigh
1896, Joseph Fels, Mayland Colony
1896, Purleigh Anarchist Colony
1989, Tolstoyan Colony, Wickford
1903, Frederick Charrington, Osea Island
1904, Fels, Laindon Farm Colony
1926, Silver End
1930, Plotlands at Laindon
1947, Harlow New Town
1959, Essex Wildlife Trust

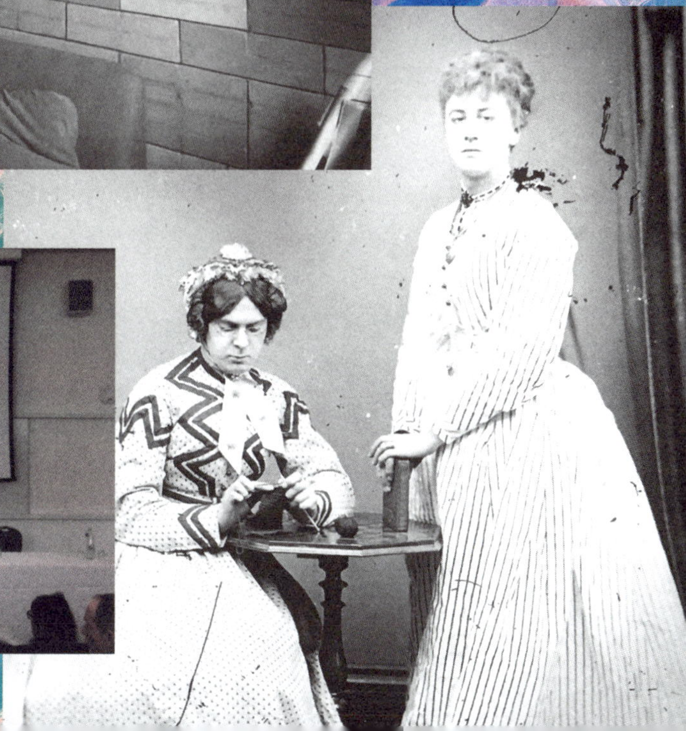

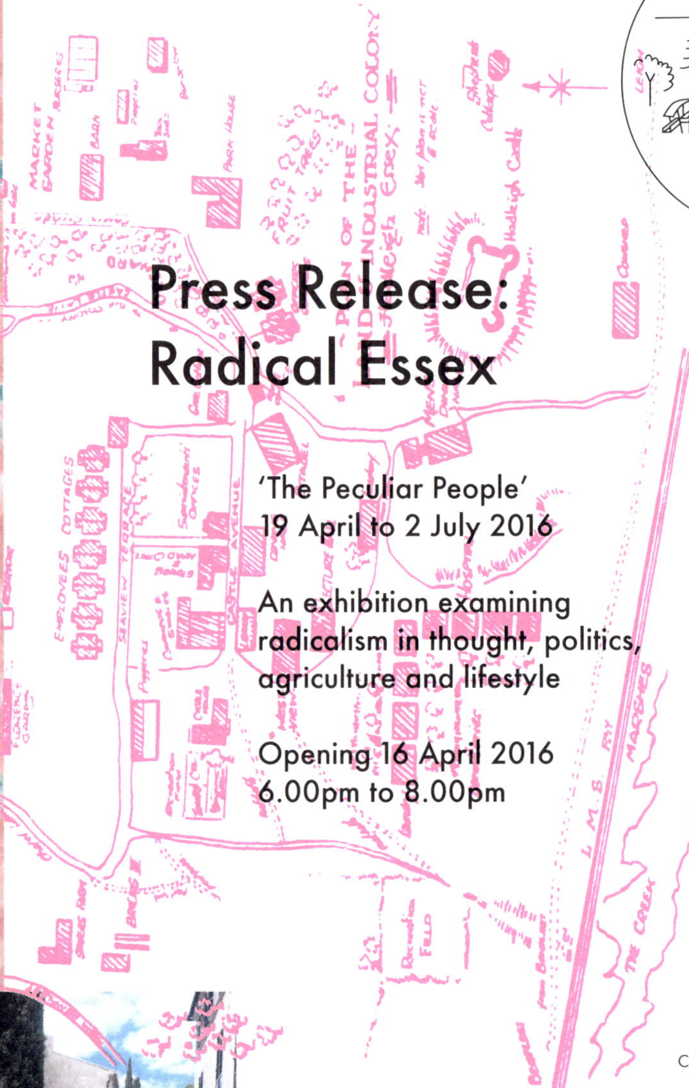

Press Release: Radical Essex

'The Peculiar People'
19 April to 2 July 2016

An exhibition examining radicalism in thought, politics, agriculture and lifestyle

Opening 16 April 2016
6.00pm to 8.00pm

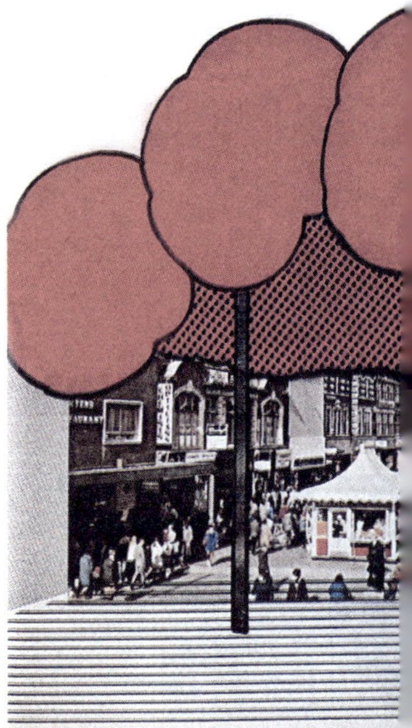

Cedric Price's proposal for Southend High Street, Archite

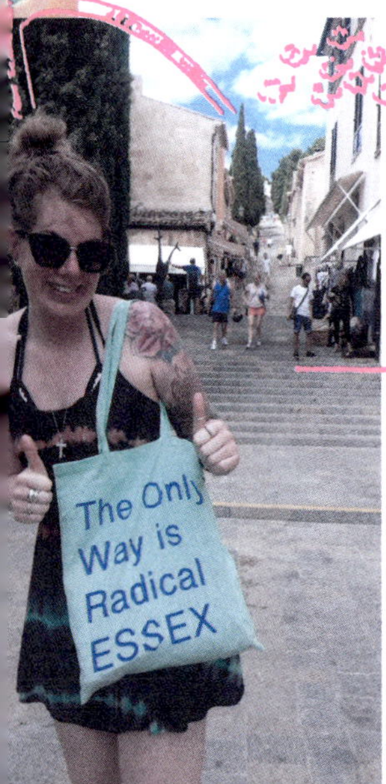

Focal Point Gallery is delighted to announce the launch of Radic project that will re-examine the history of Essex in relation to radi thought, lifestyle, politics and architecture through a programme exhibitions in 2016-2017.

The project opens with 'The Peculiar People', an exhibition and e tracing the history of ideological and social-political communal li throughout the 20th Century to the present day. These include th industrial worker estates at East Tilbury and Silver End, as well a alternative ideological communities such as the Tolstoy-inspired c colonies; each revealing Essex as a place where utopias were ir traditional ways of living were challenged and revolutionary pol architecture and literature were born and flourished.

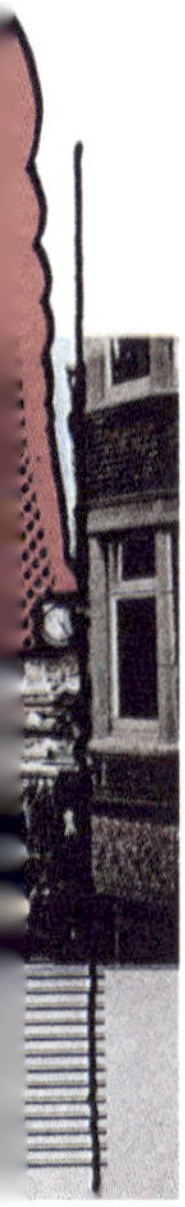

tober 1972

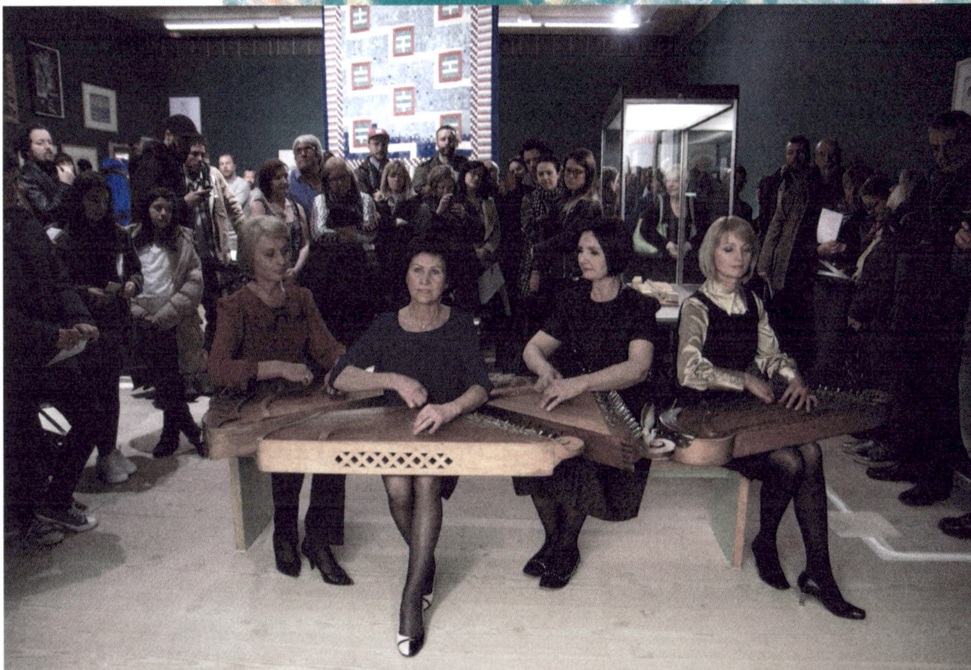

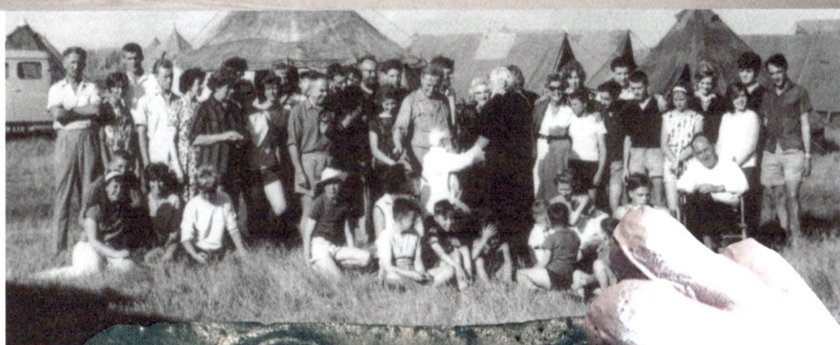

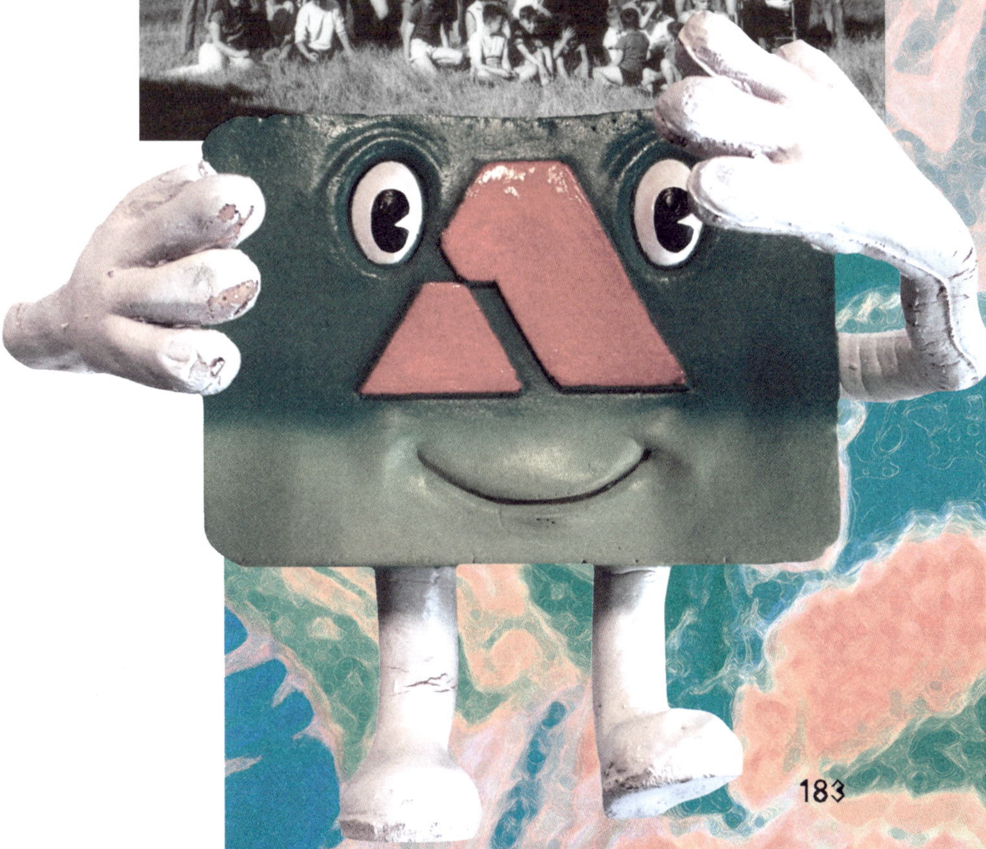

nd

iments
g

urist

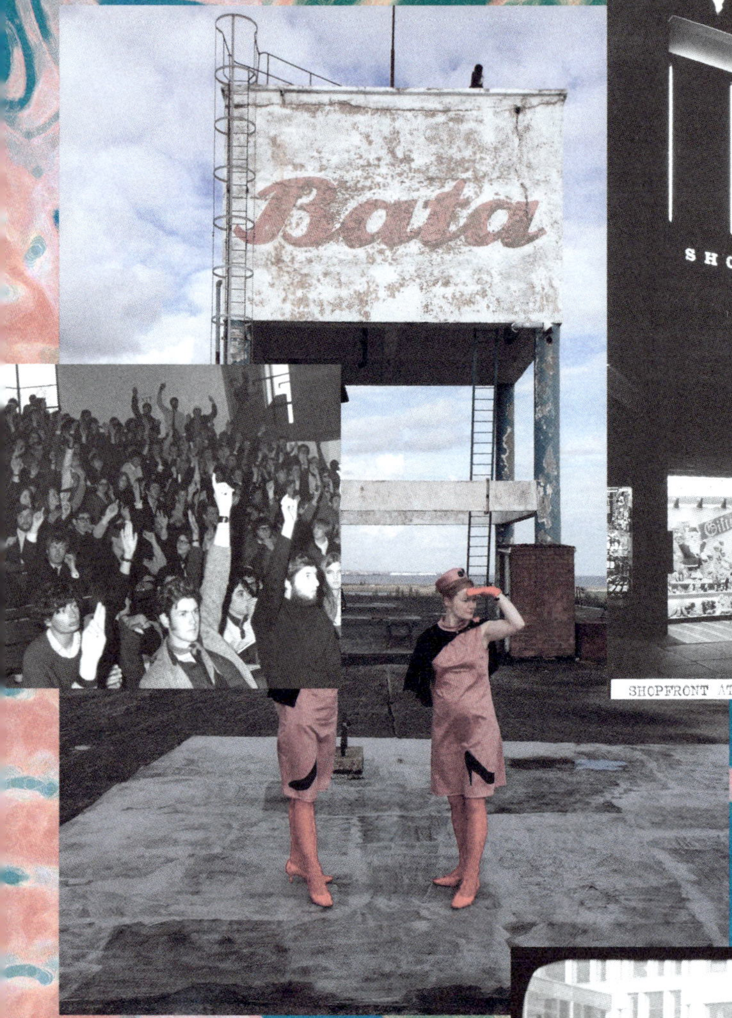

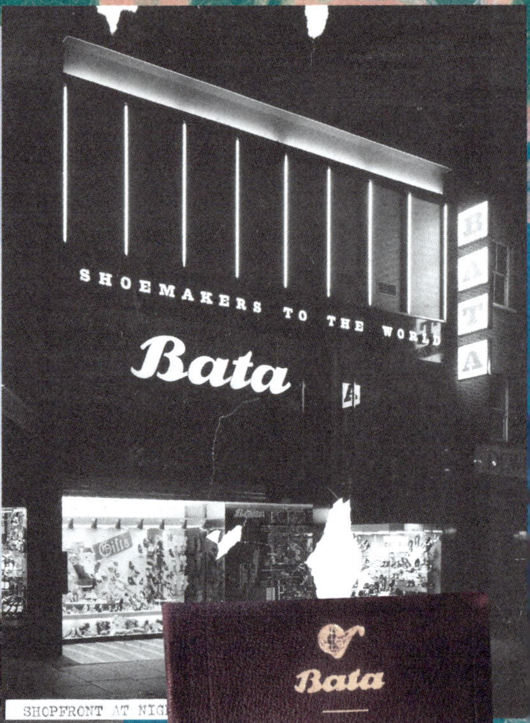

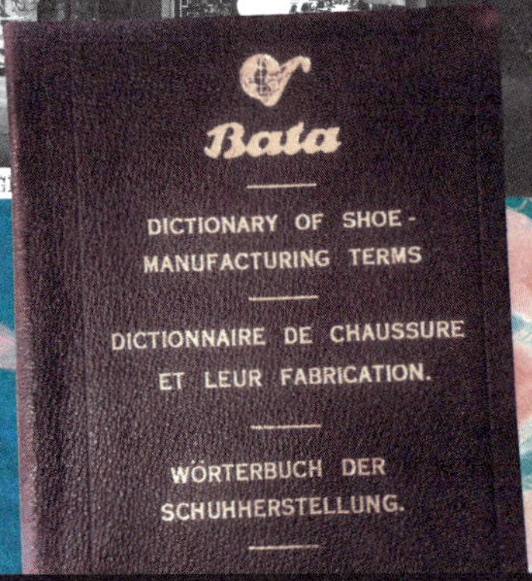

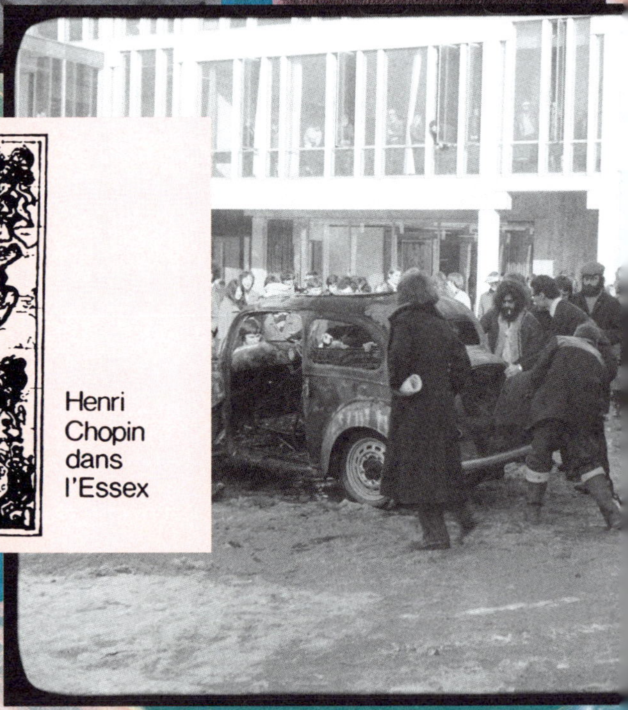

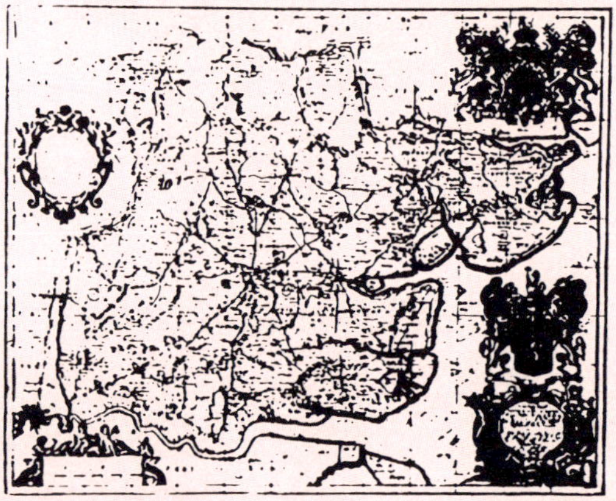

Henri Chopin dans l'Essex

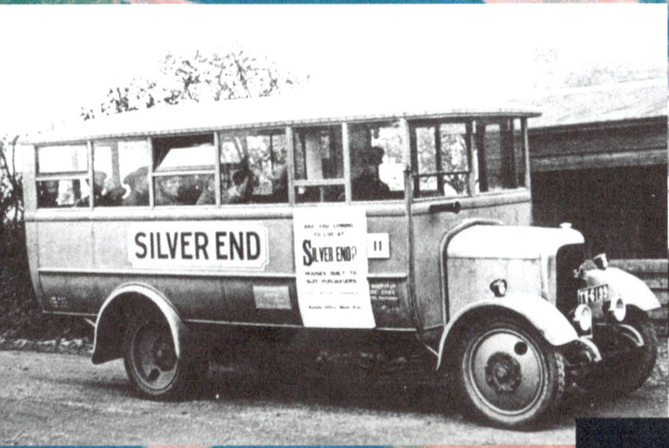
SILVER END
ARE YOU COMING
TO LIVE AT
SILVER END?
HOUSES BUILT TO
SUIT PURCHASERS
11

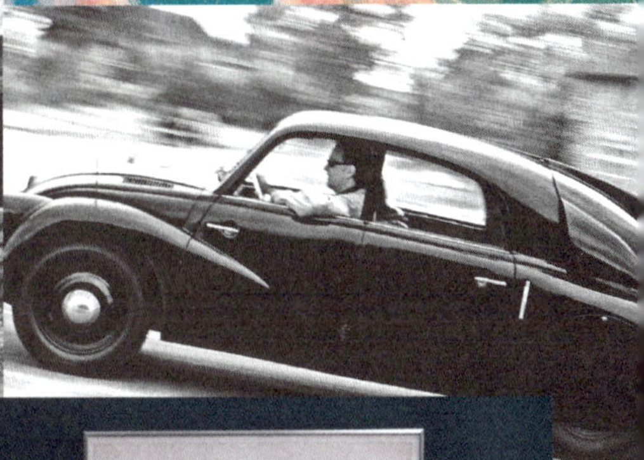

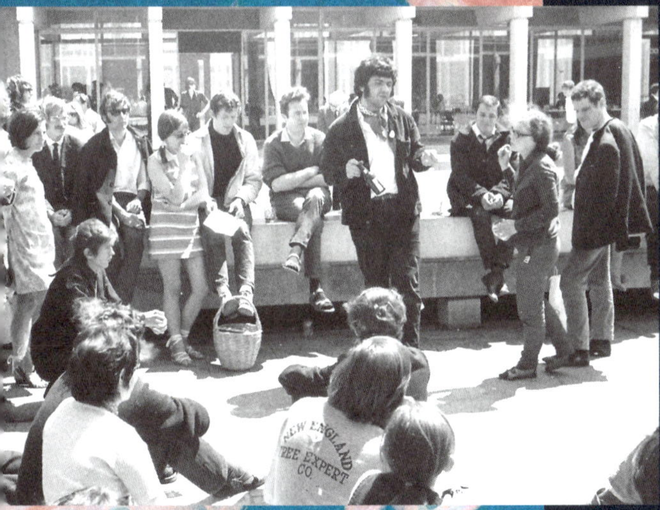
NEW ENGLAND
TREE EXPERT
CO.

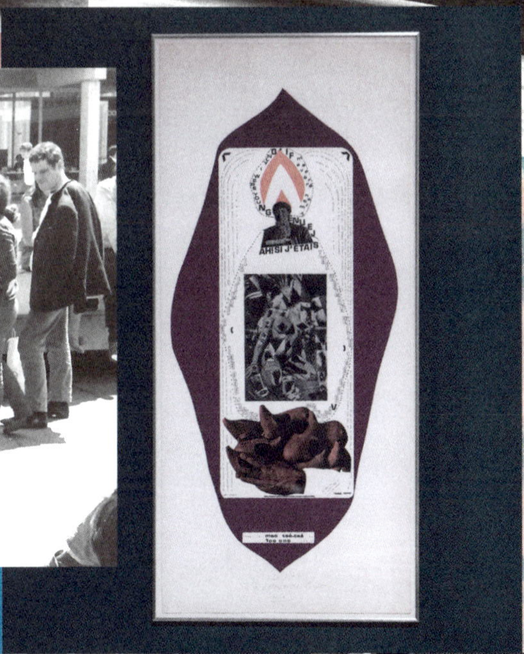
AH SI J'ETAIS

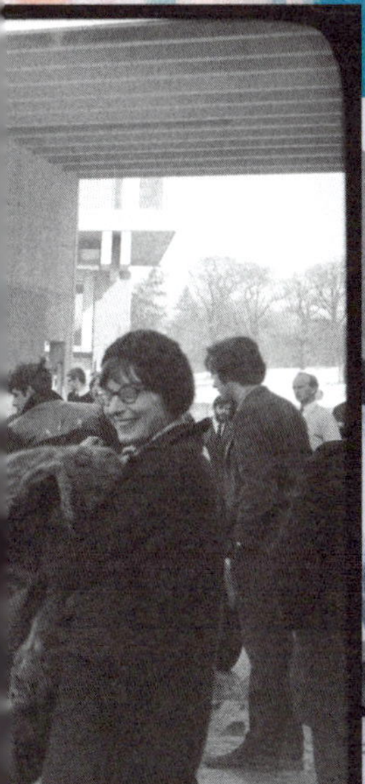

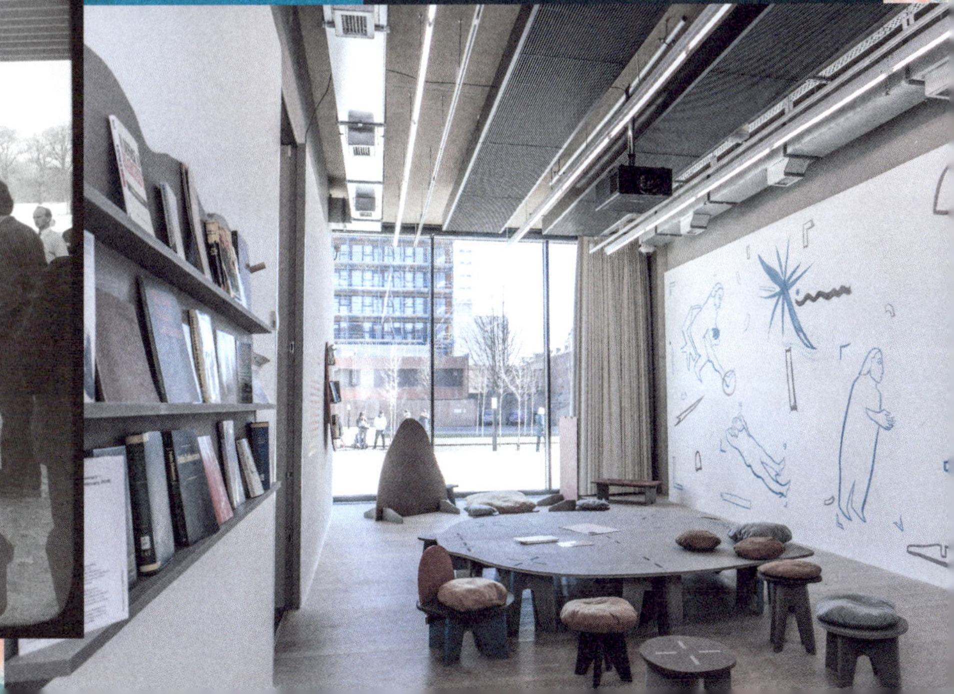

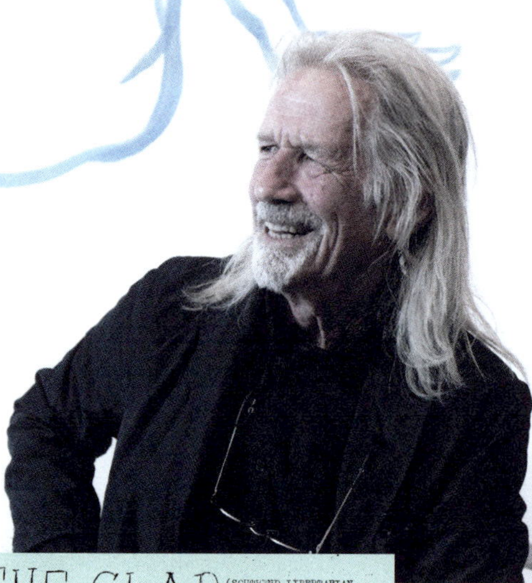

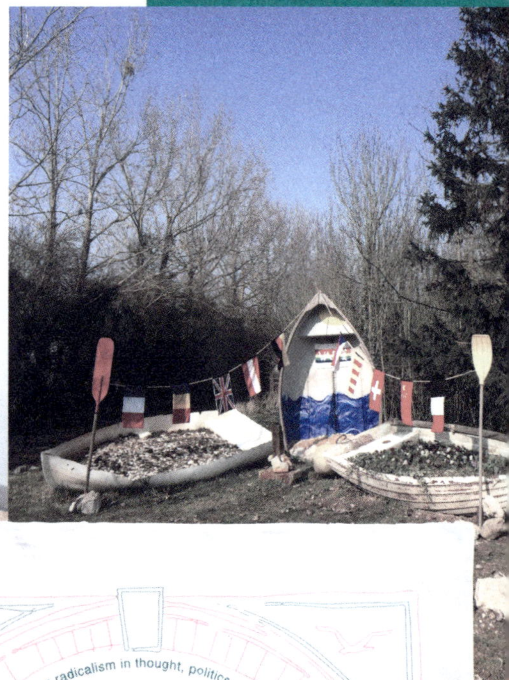

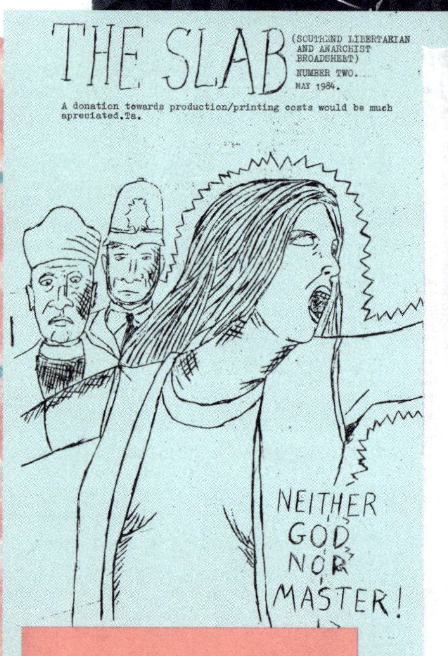
THE SLAB (SOUTHEND LIBERTARIAN AND ANARCHIST BROADSHEET)
NUMBER TWO.
MAY 1984.
A donation towards production/printing costs would be much apreciated.Ta.

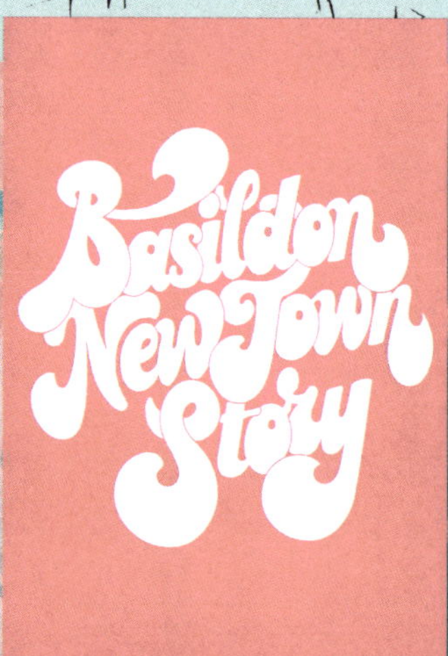

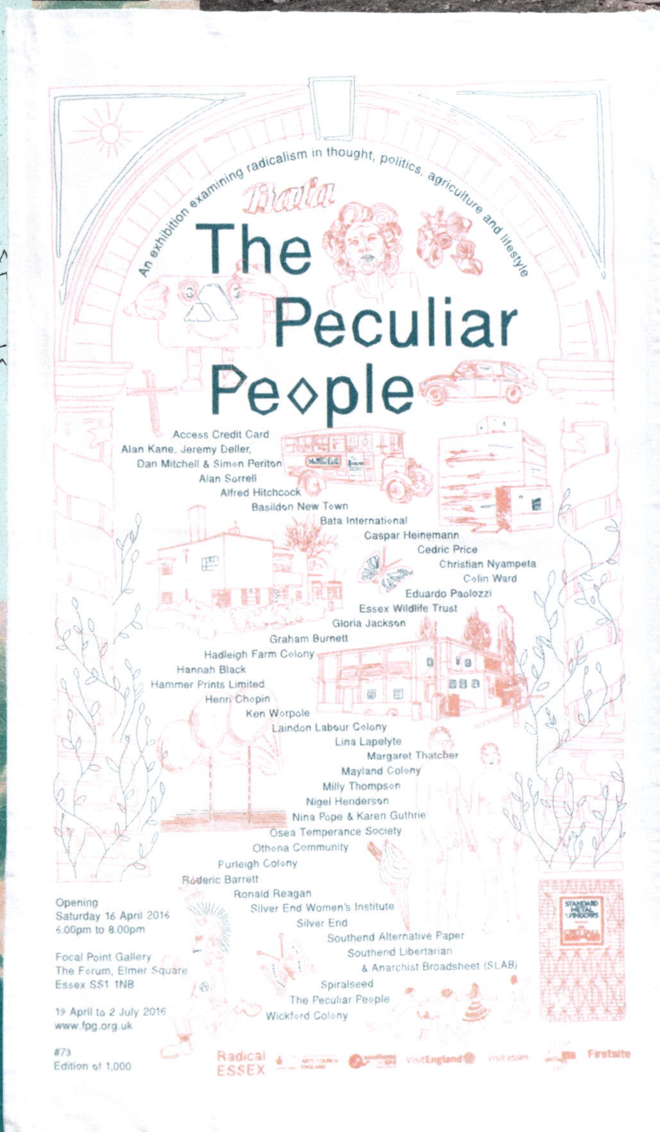

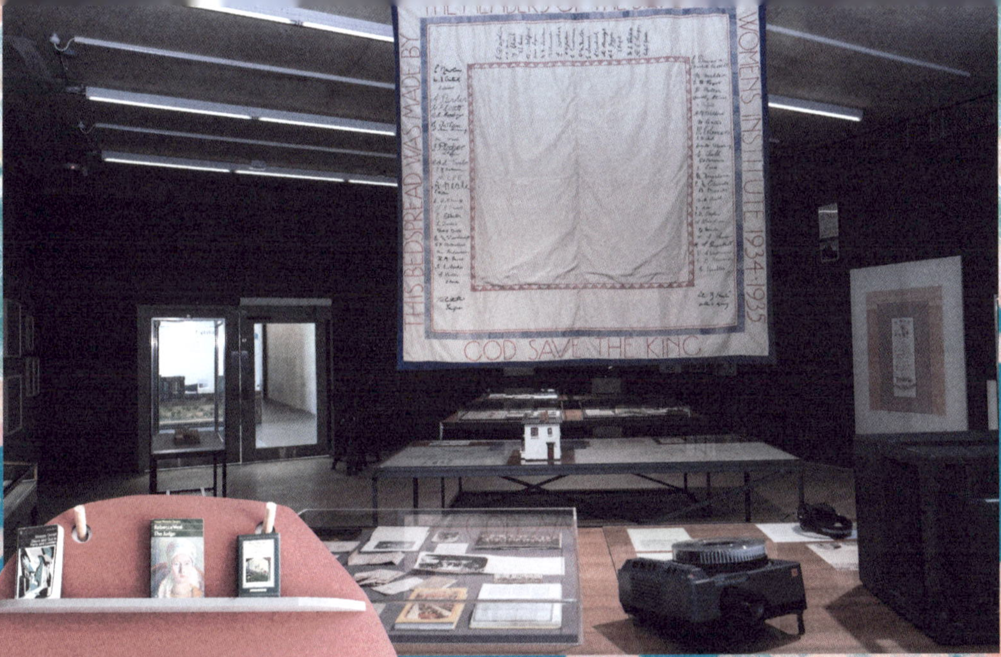

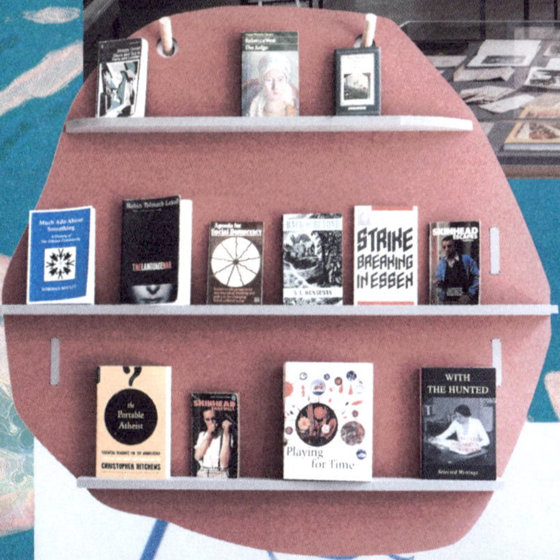

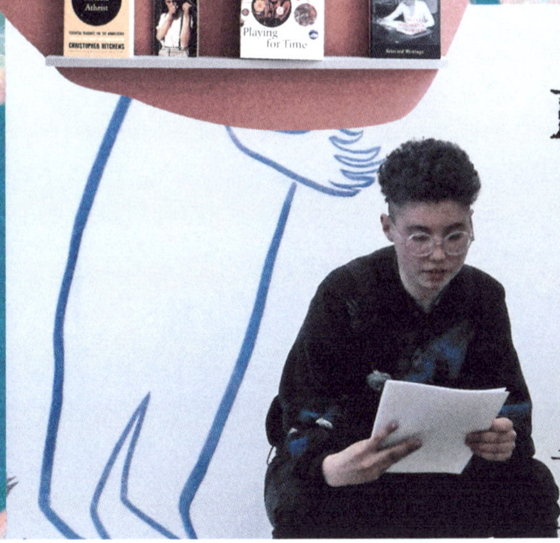

"THE PECULIAR PEOPLE"

Will (D.V.) OPEN

Castle Cottage

Near foot of CHURCH HILL,

Leigh-on-Sea,

FOR

PUBLIC WORSHIP

ON

THE LORD'S DAY,

August 8th, 1915,

at 6.30 p.m.

A Cordial Invitation to All

To Come and Hear the Gospel of the Grace of God,

How YOU may be SAVED and know your Sins forgiven.

Come and Hear. All Seats Free.

D. Reeves, Printer, 22 Victoria Avenue, Southend.

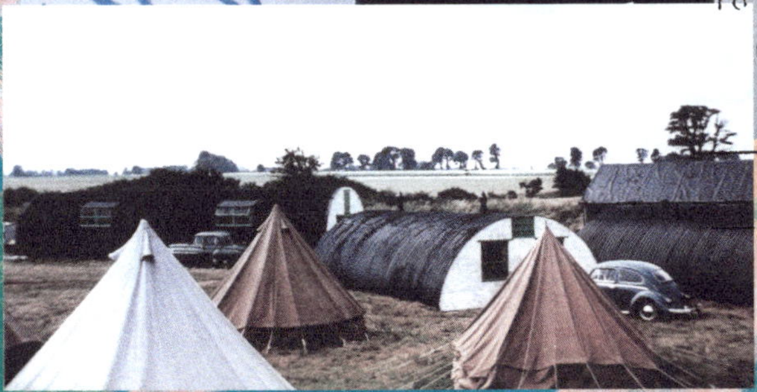

Chapel Bill, Leigh, 1915

On 23 Mar 2016, at 15:52, Ruth Ewan wrote:

Hi all

Thanks for sending the new drawing - it looks amazing!

Joe and Matthew just to fill you in since we last spoke about incorporating 'all distinctions levelled' into the weathervane. I played around with the text and rather like boiling it down to the word 'LEVEL' as if the L and E are reversed it can be read the same from both sides. See the very rough image attached. Matthew I just wanted to run this idea past you and if you are into it then I can work out something more formally.

I've just had a great conversation with a woman called Karen who was super interested in the concept and only works in copper
http://www.greensvanes.co.uk/index.html

She would in theory have the time to work on it and could also advise on the fixing etc. She said all weather vanes were copper with gold leaf pre industrial revolution and gold leaf can be seen in the moonlight… She'd need to get cracking on it this week so I said I'd get back to her tomorrow if possible for a quote.

I've also attached a bio (please edit down as required) and the extra of John Ball's speech. There is a nice bit about Ball's roving rants through Essex
here http://www.theguardian.com/tv-and-radio/2014/aug/04/melvyn-braggs-radical-lives-review

Anyway do let me know what you think as I'm aware of short timescale.

All best
Ruth

<weathervane_anatomy copy.jpg>
<Screen Shot 2016-03-23 at 14.55.15.png>
<RuthEwanBioMar16.docx>

"My good friends, things cannot go on well in England, nor ever will until everything shall be in common, when there shall be neither vassal nor lord, and all distinctions levelled; when the lords shall be no more masters than ourselves. How ill they have used us!… They have wines, spices and fine bread, when we have only rye and the refuse of fine straw; and if we drink, it must be water. They have handsome seats and manors, when we must brave the wind and rain in our labours in the field; but it is from our labour they have the wherewith to support their pomp…. Let us go to the king, who is young, and remonstrate with him on our servitude, telling him we must have it otherwise, or that we shall find a remedy for it ourselves"

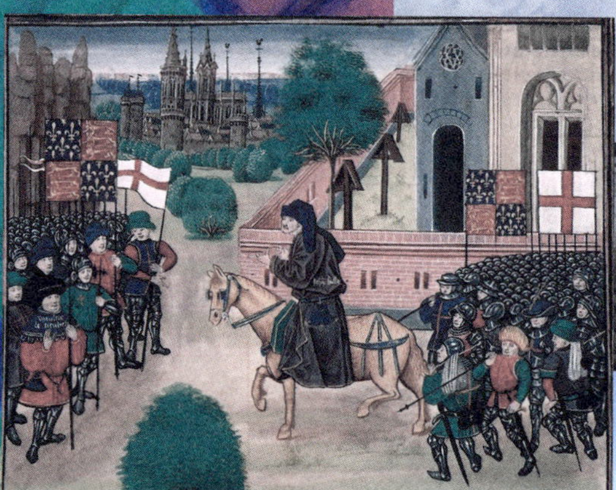

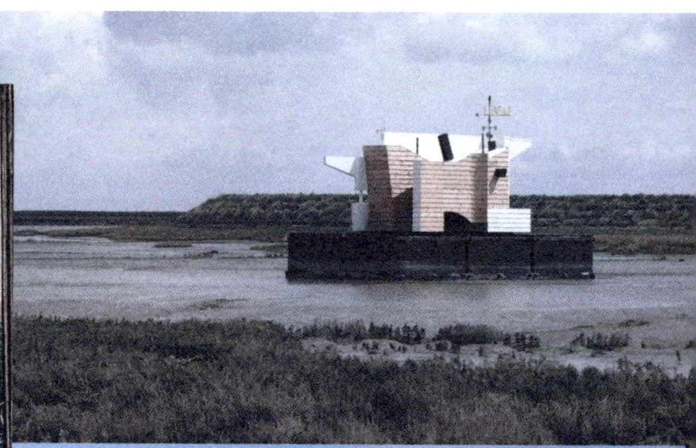

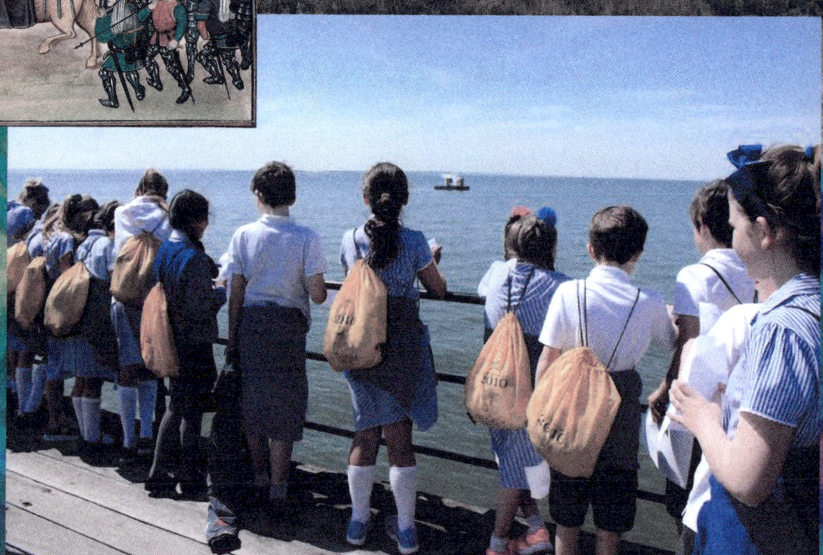

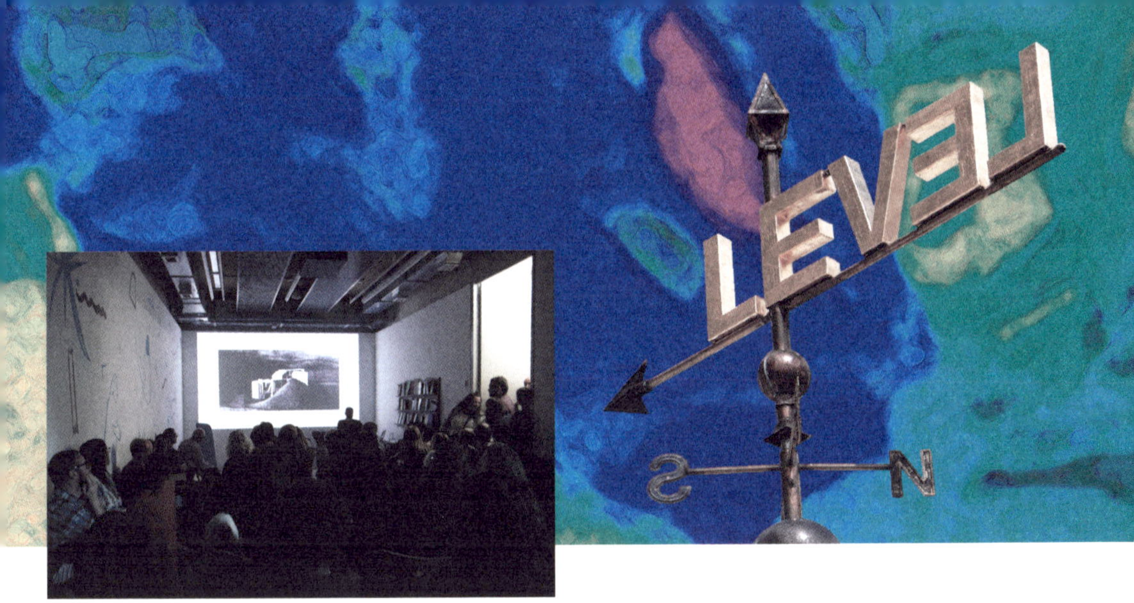

JOANNA QUINN

MUDLARK

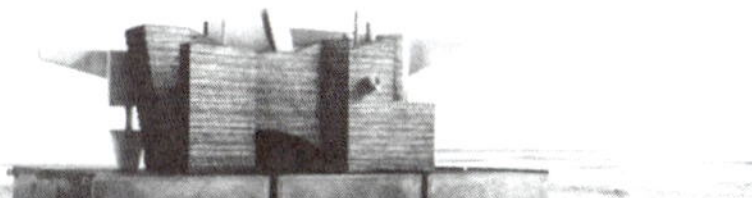

At first light, I leave my bunk. I get myself a flask of coffee, pick up my little VHF radio, my notebook, pencil and binoculars, pull the hatch open and crawl out onto the upper deck. I stay low, train my sights on a flock of ringed plovers at the edge of the estuary. They lift and fall in a chittering mass. It is low tide. We float in barely a foot of water. The sea has left the estuary, moved off on other business, exposing shining mudflats scored with the winding rivulets my daughter calls snake trails. The smell of it: salt, diesel and gloop. Something uncovered. Something very old and rich; not quite rotten but potent. The slap of shallow tea-coloured water against the sides of my swaying boat. The clinking of jars and test-tubes on the shelves inside.

Further up the estuary, past the make-shift boatyards at Leigh-on-Sea, past the rusted hulks of abandoned barges, are the bent silhouettes of winkle-pickers, out early with their buckets, grubbing in the mud for cockles. Some of them look small enough to be children. They slowly make their way round a few old fishing boats lolling on the mud, hulls exposed, waiting for the tide to return.

Beyond the winkle-pickers, where there is still deep water, the ro-ro ferries and container tankers journey back and forth. They never stop. Sailing upriver to London, past the power stations and pylons, chimneys and cranes, all the mechanised latticework of industry. Or tankers journey back and forth. They never stop. Sailing upriver to London, past the power stations and pylons, chimneys and cranes, all the mechanised latticework of industry. Or downriver, past wind farms and fog nets, following the water as it spans outwards into the North Sea. And beyond the ferries and tankers, in the hazy distance, stand the border contro rigs. Great metal structures. Square boxes balanced on single poles. They look like old-fashioned cameras, stiff and top-heavy. A line of them, miles out to sea, guarding the mouth of the estuary.

There's a creaking at the back of the boat, a hatch opening and a grunt of effort as Ajay heaves his backpack and sample kit out onto the roof. I remain where I am. It is important that I re-establish the order of command on this vessel. I need to claim back the separateness I allowed him to trespass over the first night he stayed.

"Morning, gorgeous," he says.

I look over my shoulder at him, put a finger to my lips and then gesture downwards.

"Ah," he says. "Kid's still asleep."

I nod, return to my binoculars.

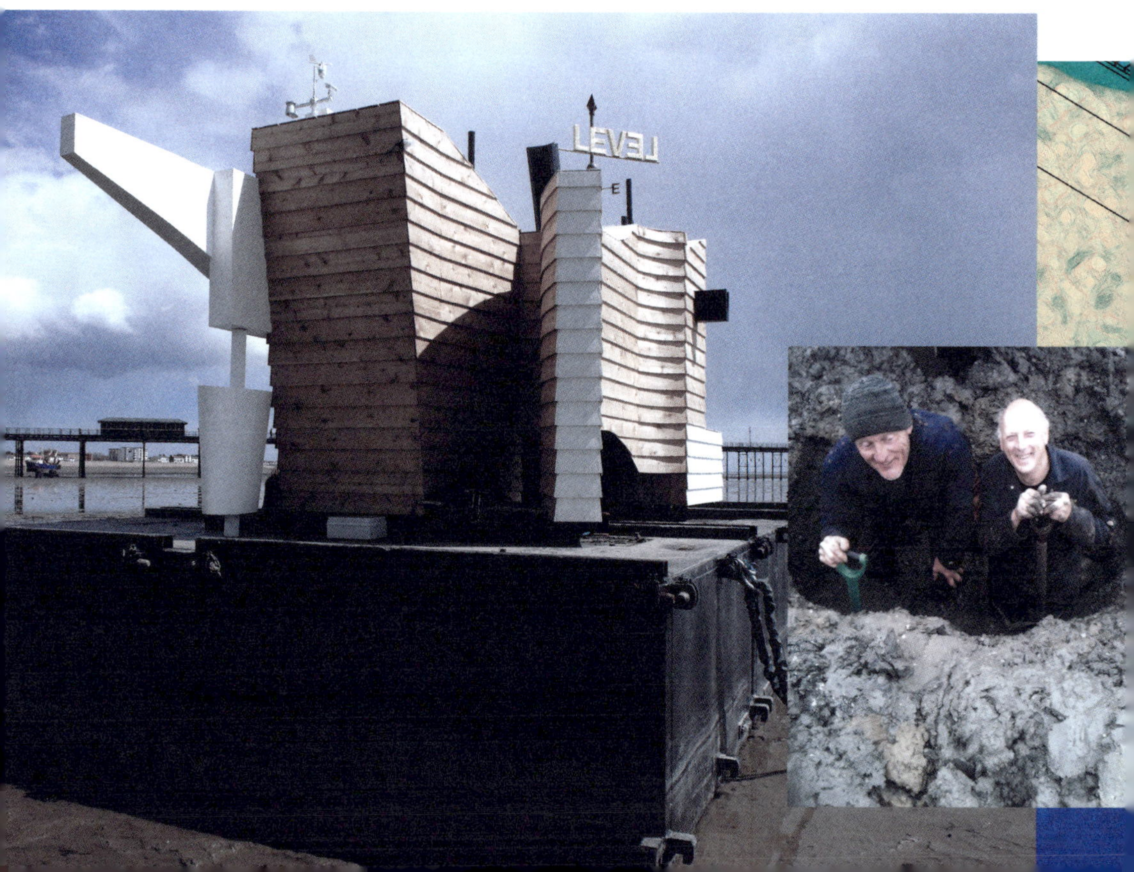

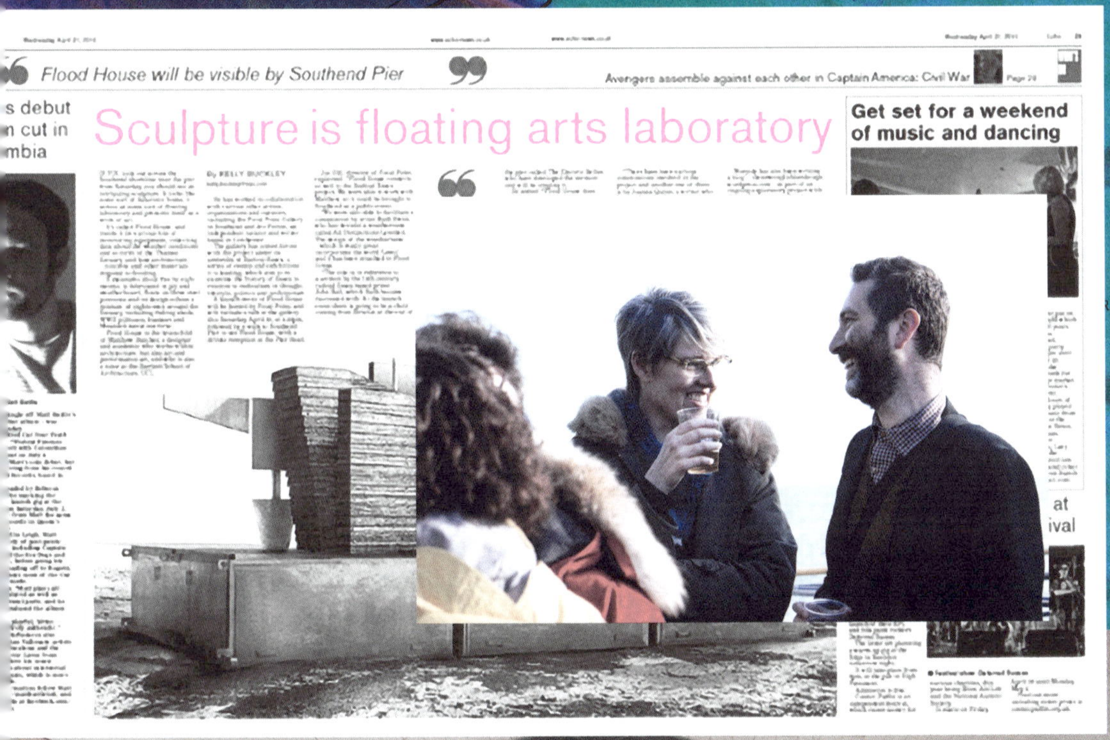

Flood House will be visible by Southend Pier

Avengers assemble against each other in Captain America: Civil War

s debut
n cut in
mbia

Sculpture is floating arts laboratory

By KELLY BUCKLEY

Get set for a weekend of music and dancing

at
ival

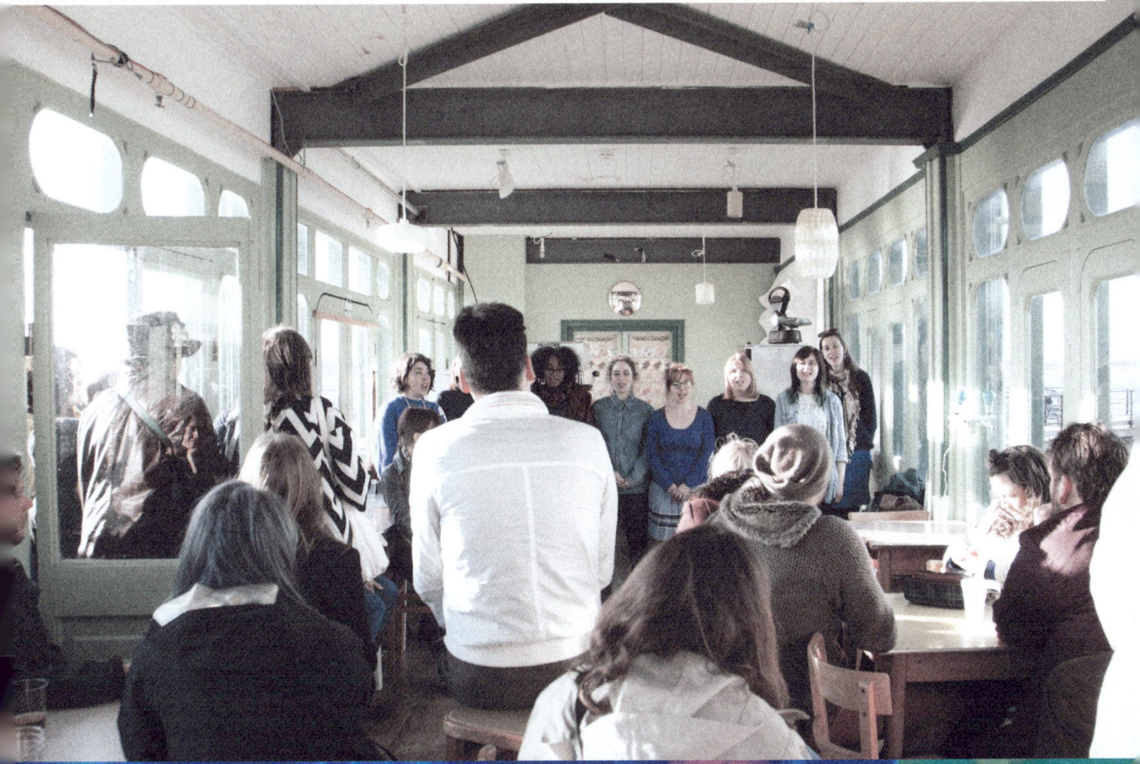

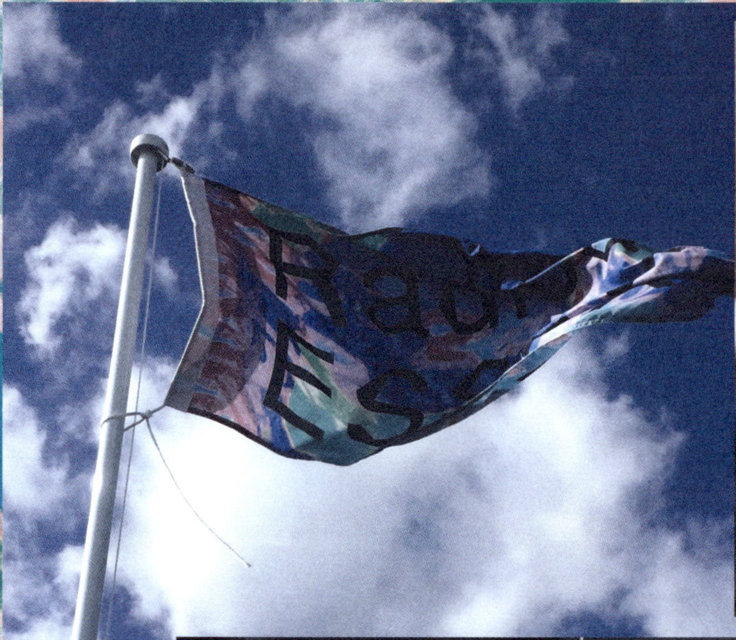

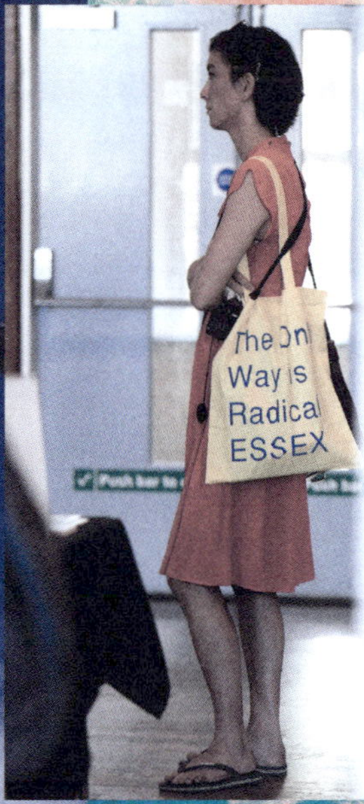
Way is
Radical
ESSEX

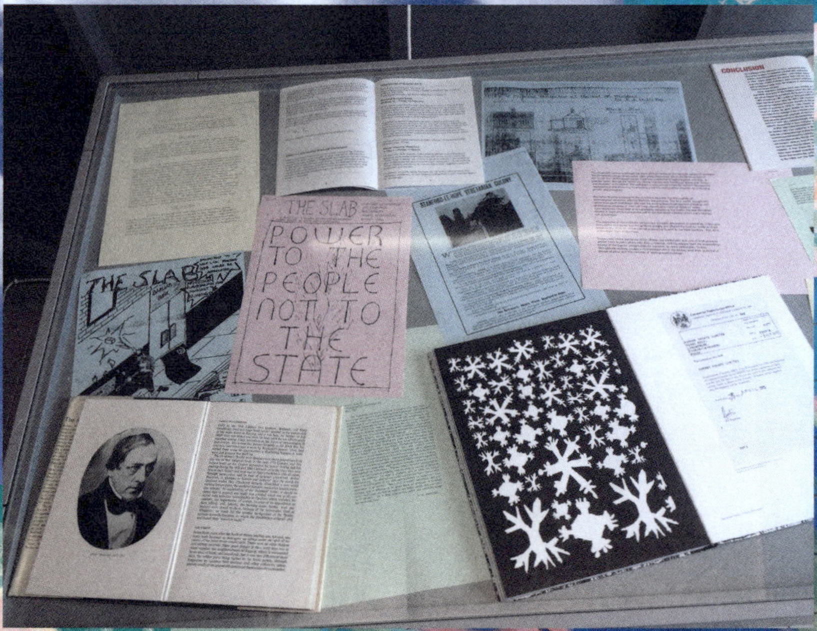
CONCLUSION
THE SLAB
POWER TO THE PEOPLE NOT TO THE STATE
THE SLAB

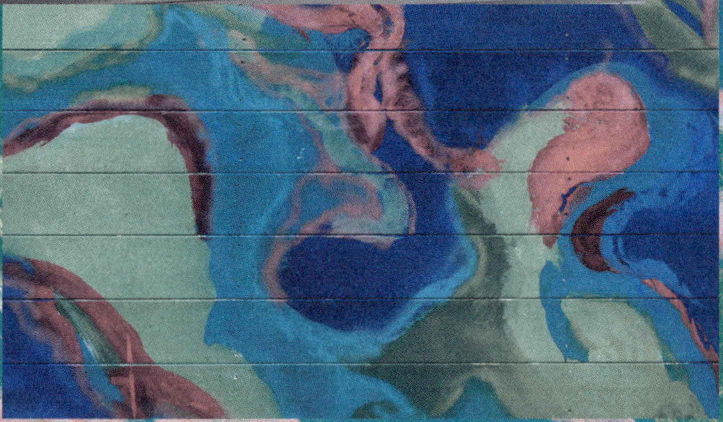

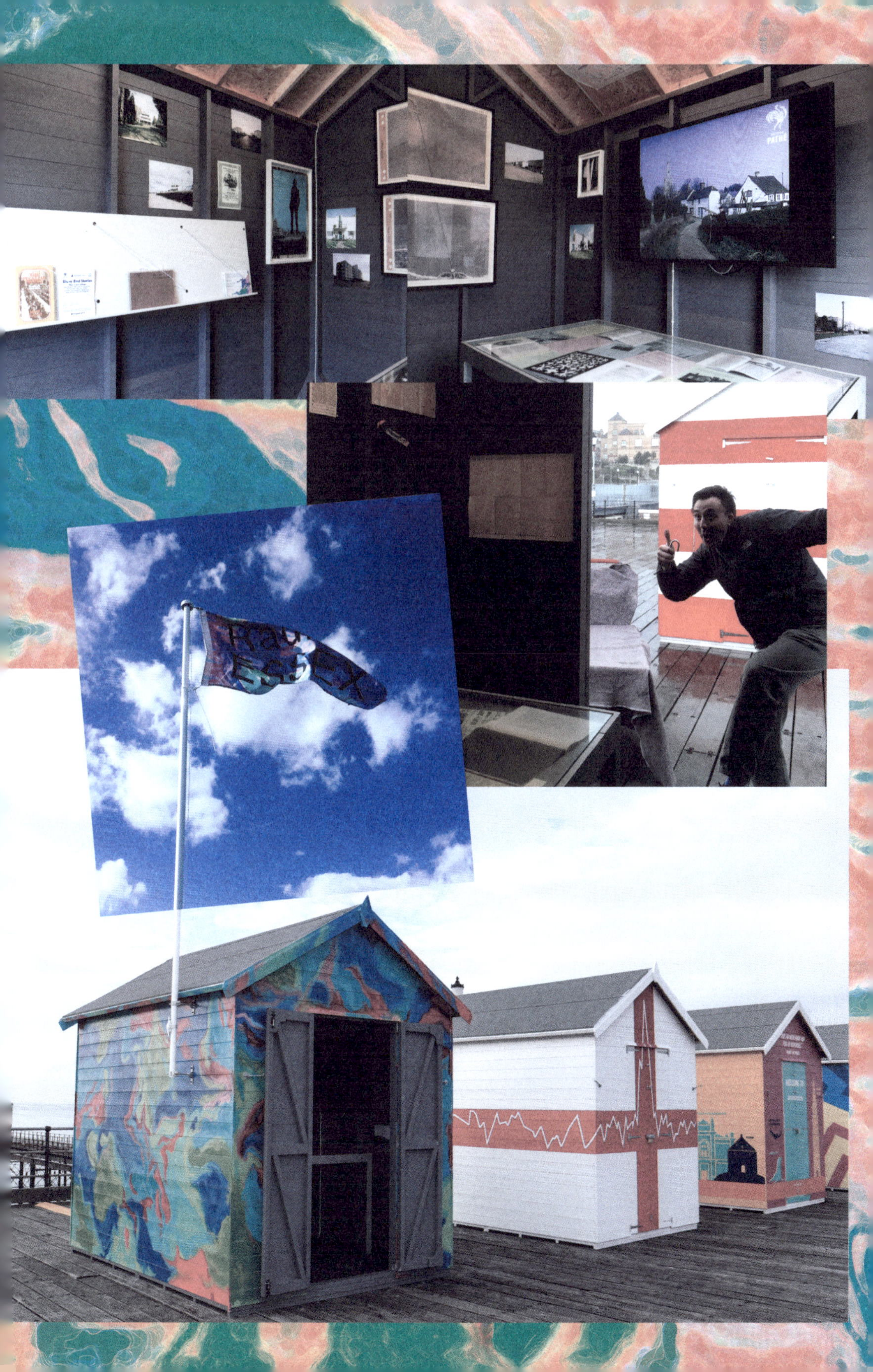

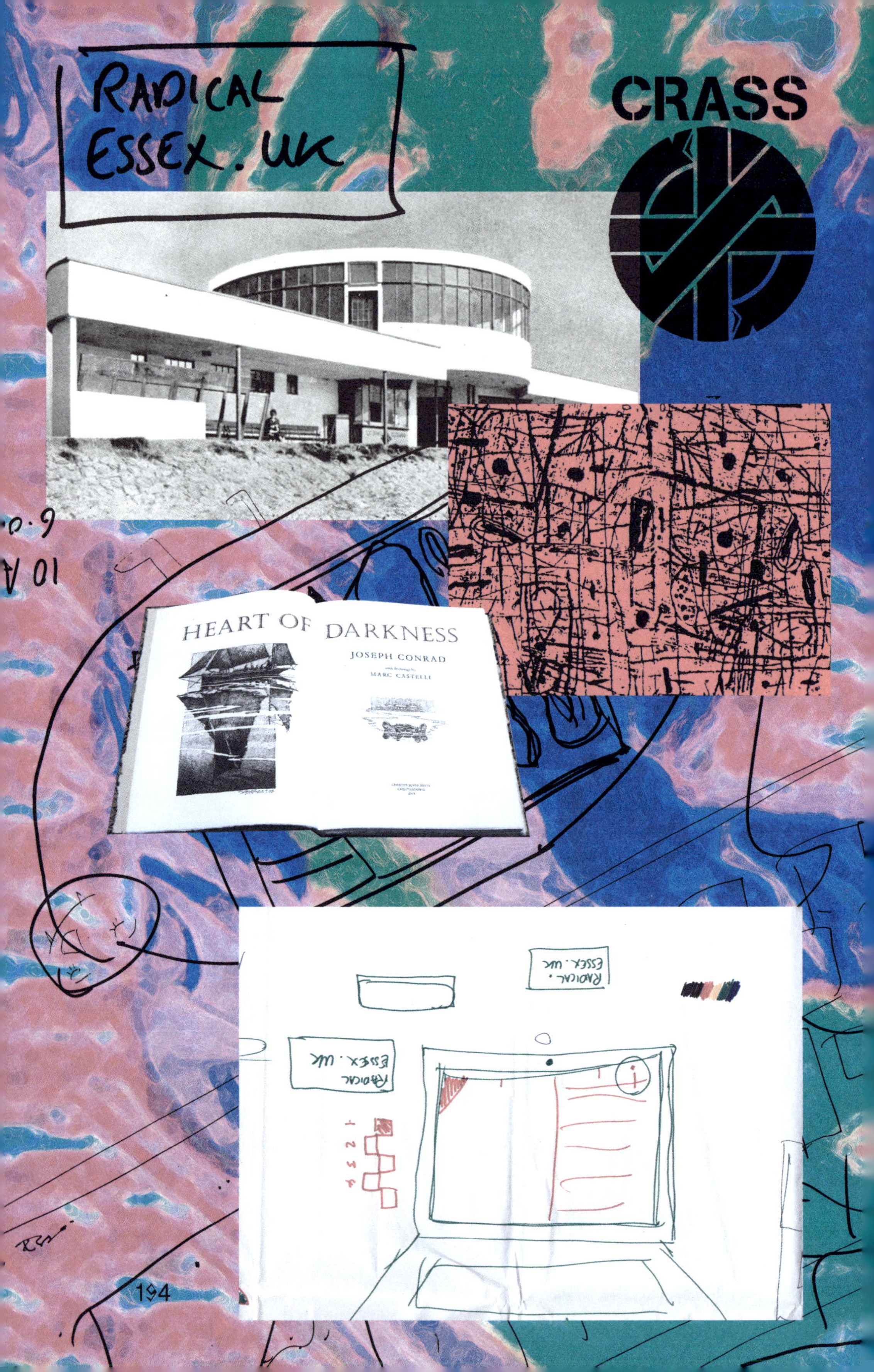
RADICAL ESSEX . UK
CRASS
HEART OF DARKNESS
JOSEPH CONRAD
MARC CASTELLI
RADICAL ESSEX . UK
RADICAL ESSEX . UK

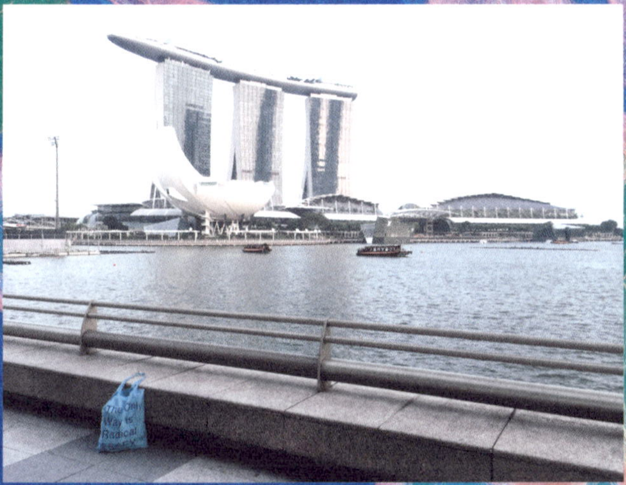

20th Century
Architecture

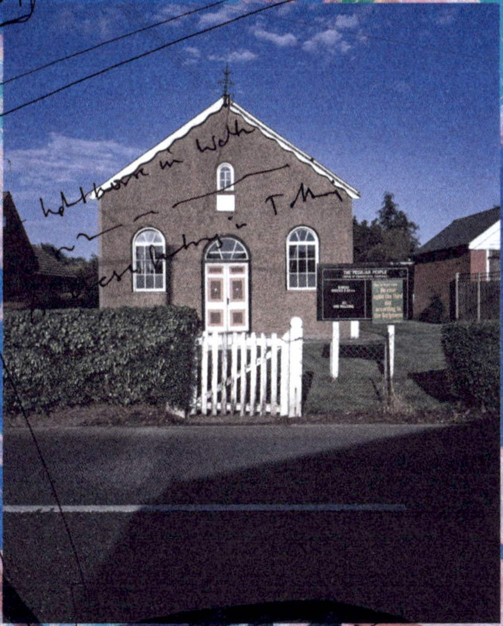

Visit, Shop,
Explore

Eat, Drink,
Stay

Radical
Commmunities

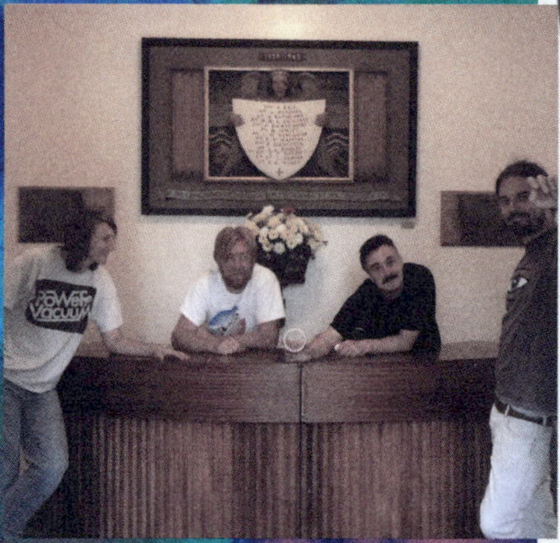

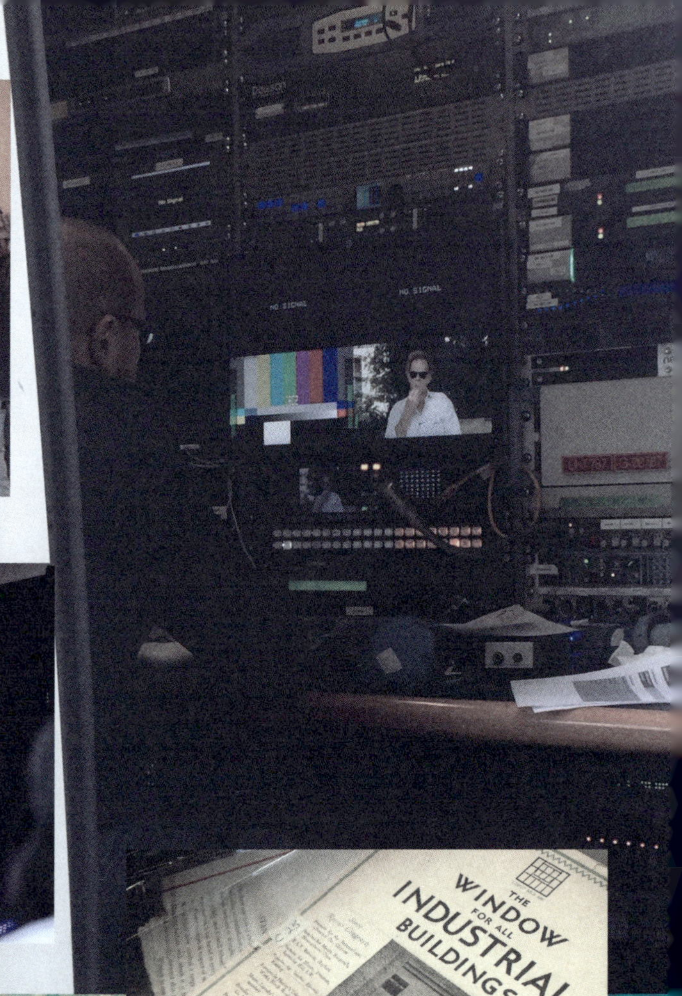

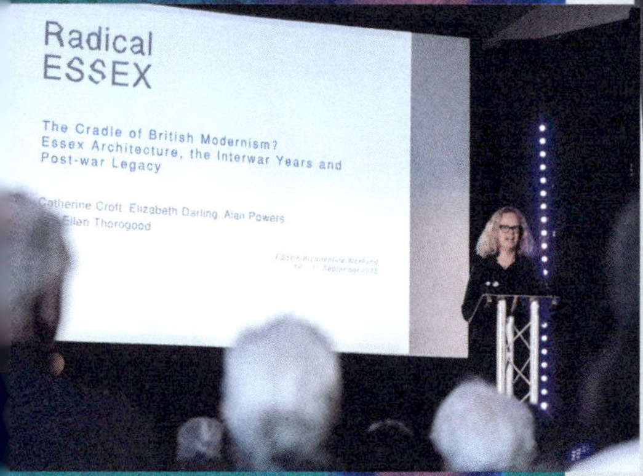
Radical
ESSEX
The Cradle of British Modernism?
Essex Architecture, the Interwar Years and
Post-war Legacy
Catherine Croft Elizabeth Darling Alan Powers
Ellen Thorogood

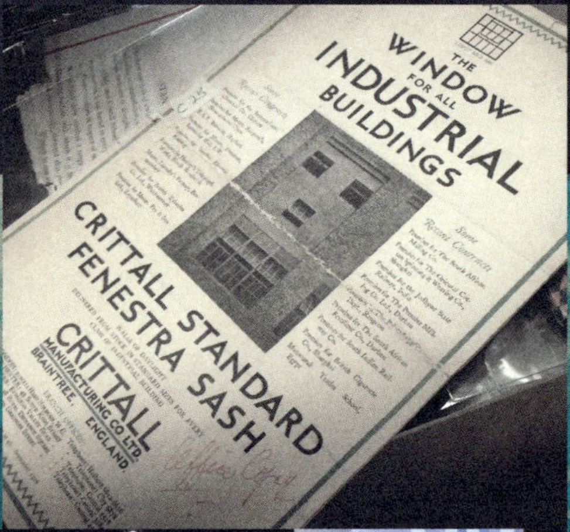
THE
WINDOW
FOR ALL
INDUSTRIAL
BUILDINGS
CRITTALL STANDARD
FENESTRA SASH
CRITTALL
MANUFACTURING CO. LTD
BRAINTREE, ENGLAND

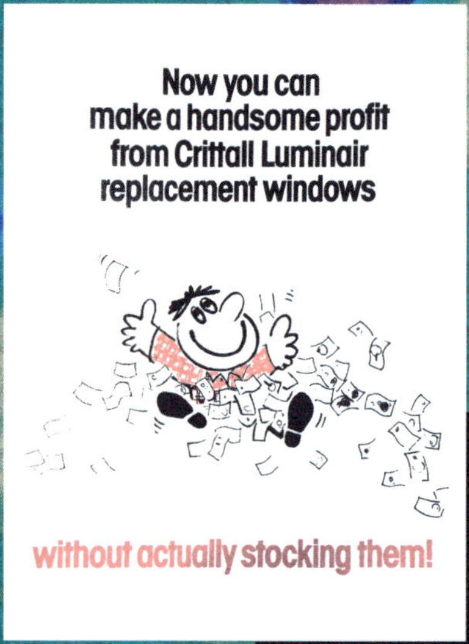
Now you can
make a handsome profit
from Crittall Luminair
replacement windows
without actually stocking them!

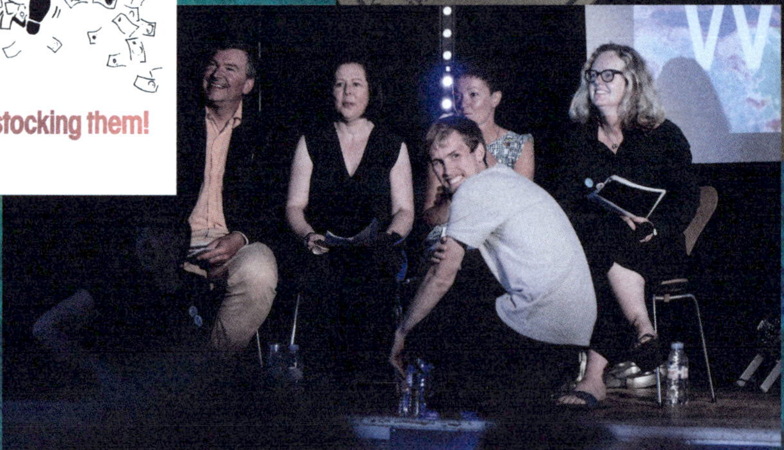

A Bumper Crop, Charles Hollanc

Vhen I think of Essex, the part of Essex I grew ıp in, I think of mud. Lots of mud. The Essex land- scape is predominantly flat and large parts of it ıre agricultural. Sugar beet, turnips and potatoes. Fields ploughed up year after year. All that makes or a lot of mud. The coast of Essex is predomi- ıantly estuarine and marshy and liable to flood ınd that makes for a lot of mud too.

This kind of landscape has its appeal for ure, but it is unlikely ground in which to grow xotic species. And yet Essex is also home to a urprising amount of artistic and architectural xperimentation, flowerings of modernist archi- ecture in the form of workers villages, holiday states and garden suburbs. This book of details aptures a number of such places: the Art Deco ouses built by the Crittall Window Company at ilver End, the white walled modernism of Oliver Hill's holiday village at Frinton-On-Sea and the ast industrial architecture of the Bata shoe fac- ory in East Tilbury.

Alongside these ambitious projects there re one-off, individual masterpieces too: Joseph mberton's Royal Corinthian Yacht Club at urnham-on-Crouch, a reinforced concrete ruise-ship permanently moored on the flood lains of the Crouch estuary. Erno Goldfinger uilt … d ube … 's ous … of ond … o cluc … d arlo … at ast … e harc … i- es… … m Ke … e e r … ly ıke … st the … d- ome … nt ome … d. otal … at cha … y pen … is ouse – a precursor to the more celebrated esign for Rogers's parents in Wimbledon – is

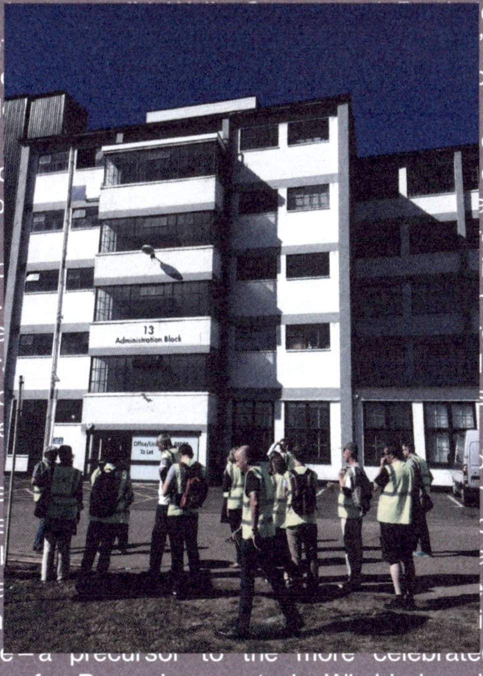

The current state of all these buildings is wort considering for what they say about our relatior ship to modernity today. Visiting Silver End, th houses appear less startling than one might thin They have mellowed with time and grown all th accoutrements of English domestic life. Bir tables, wishing wells and gnomes, as well as chi dren's toys, bicycles and trampolines fill the ga dens. Some of the houses have been repainte in Essex-friendly pastel shades while others ar hidden behind mature trees and high hedges.

Sho… ageing pro… historic sty… neering bo… ologist Ph… tions that … Corbusier … late 1920s. … shutters, fl… bare walls … decks and … nor celebra… in one of tv… ernism or … modation c…

Mod… surprisingly… of the 20t… bumper cr… Essex has … remarkable… demonstra… dream and … dream of a … life. The e… there to sh… The future can happen anywhere, even her Especially here.

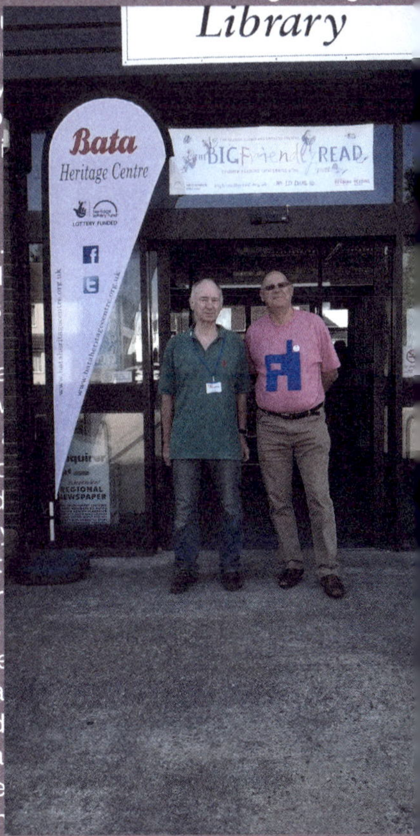

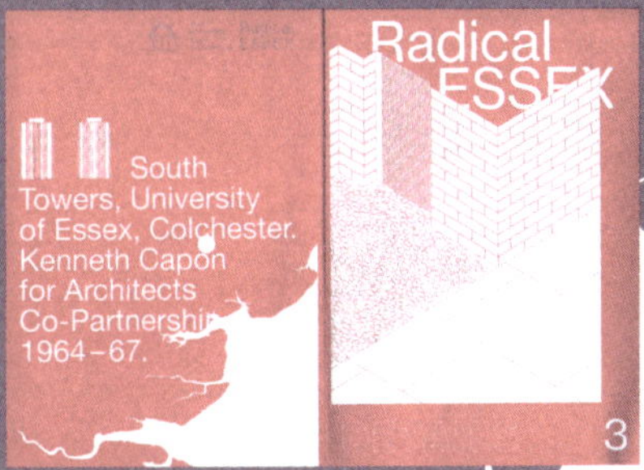

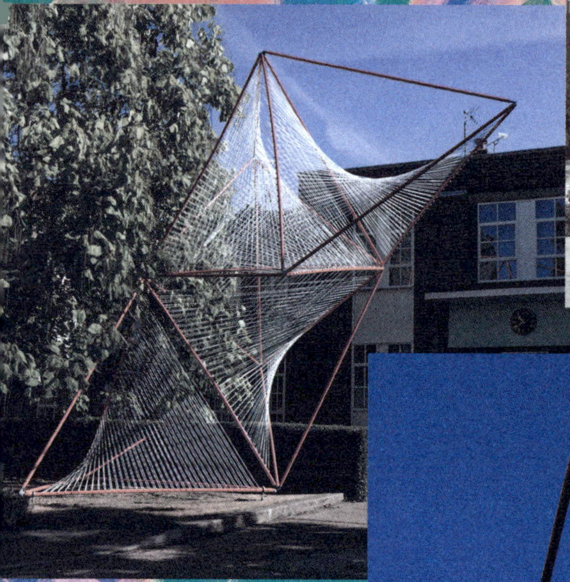

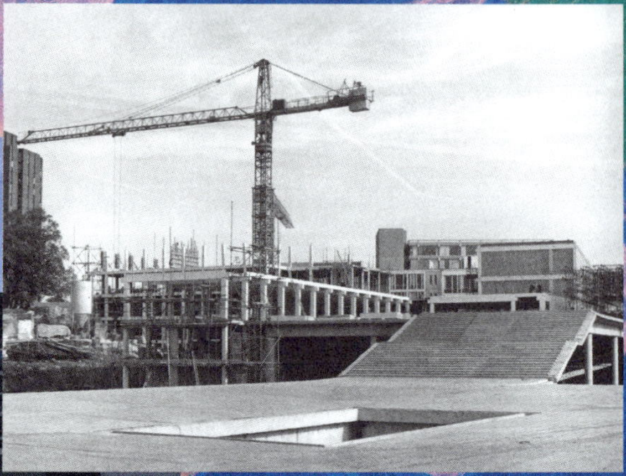

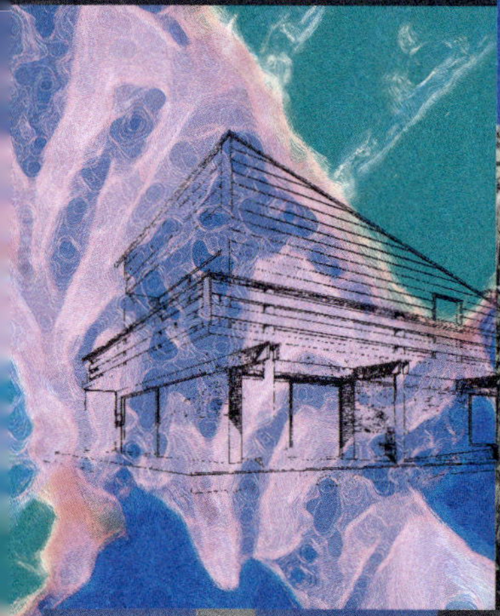

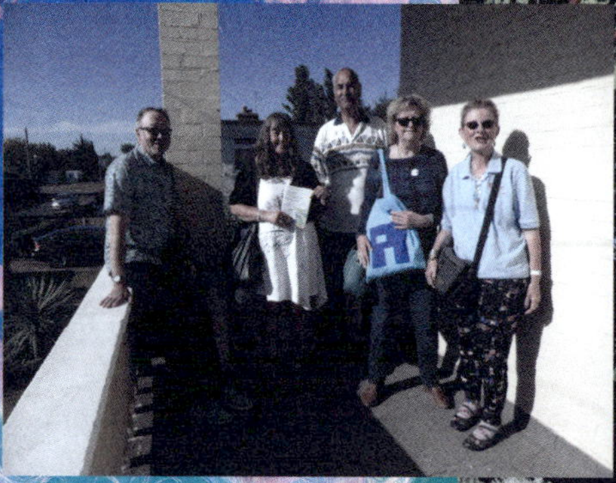

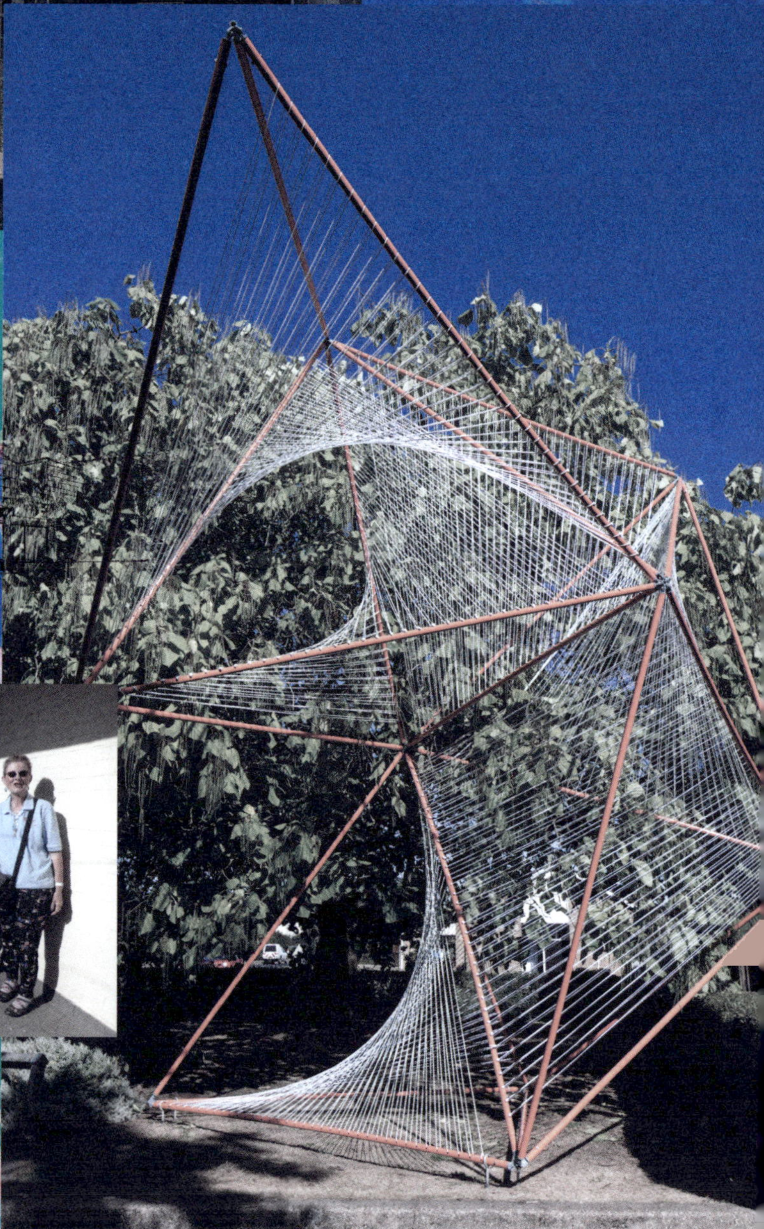

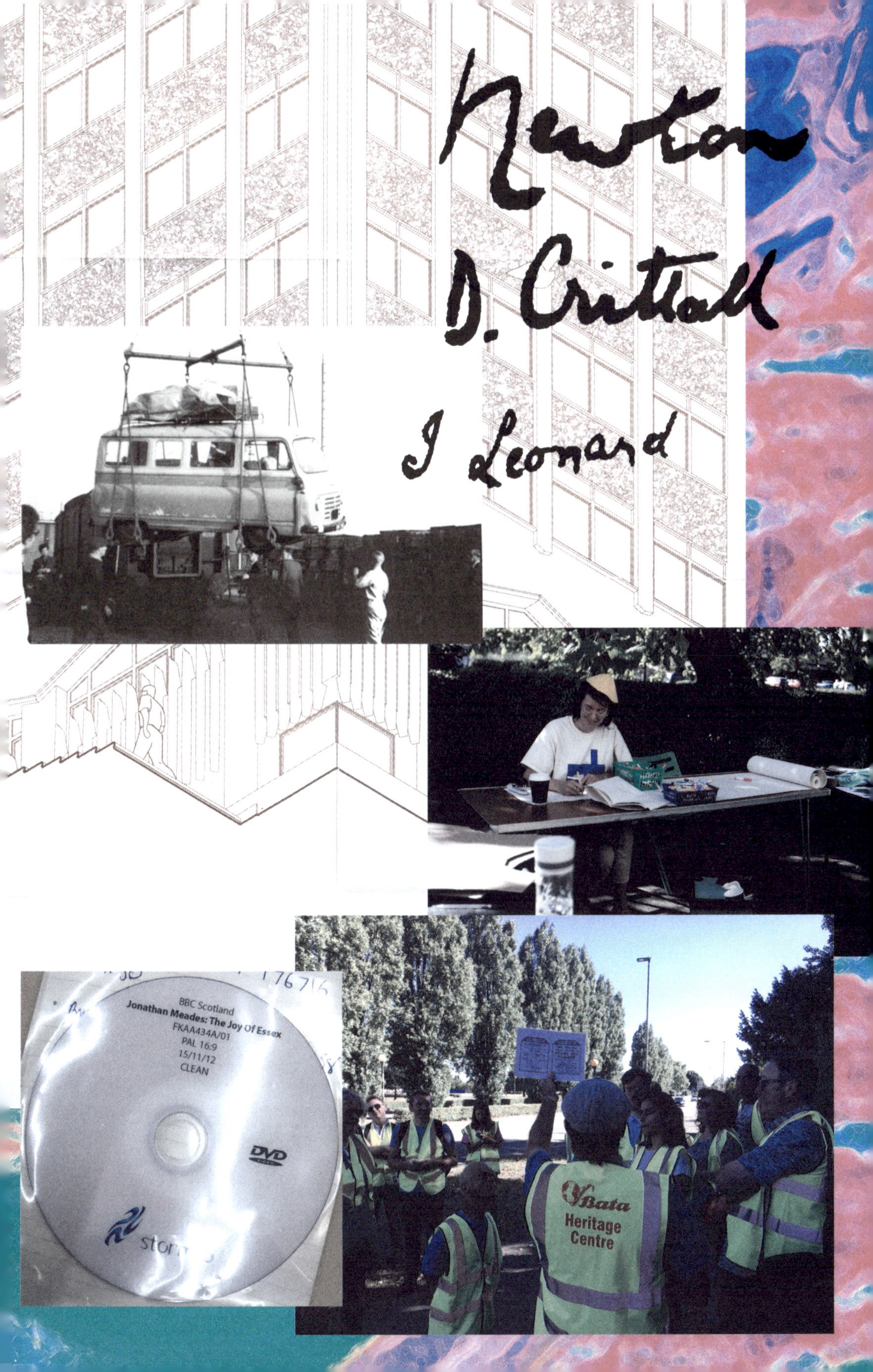
Newton
D. Crittall
I Leonard
BBC Scotland
Jonathan Meades: The Joy Of Essex
FKAA434A/01
PAL 16:9
15/11/12
CLEAN
DVD
Bata
Heritage
Centre

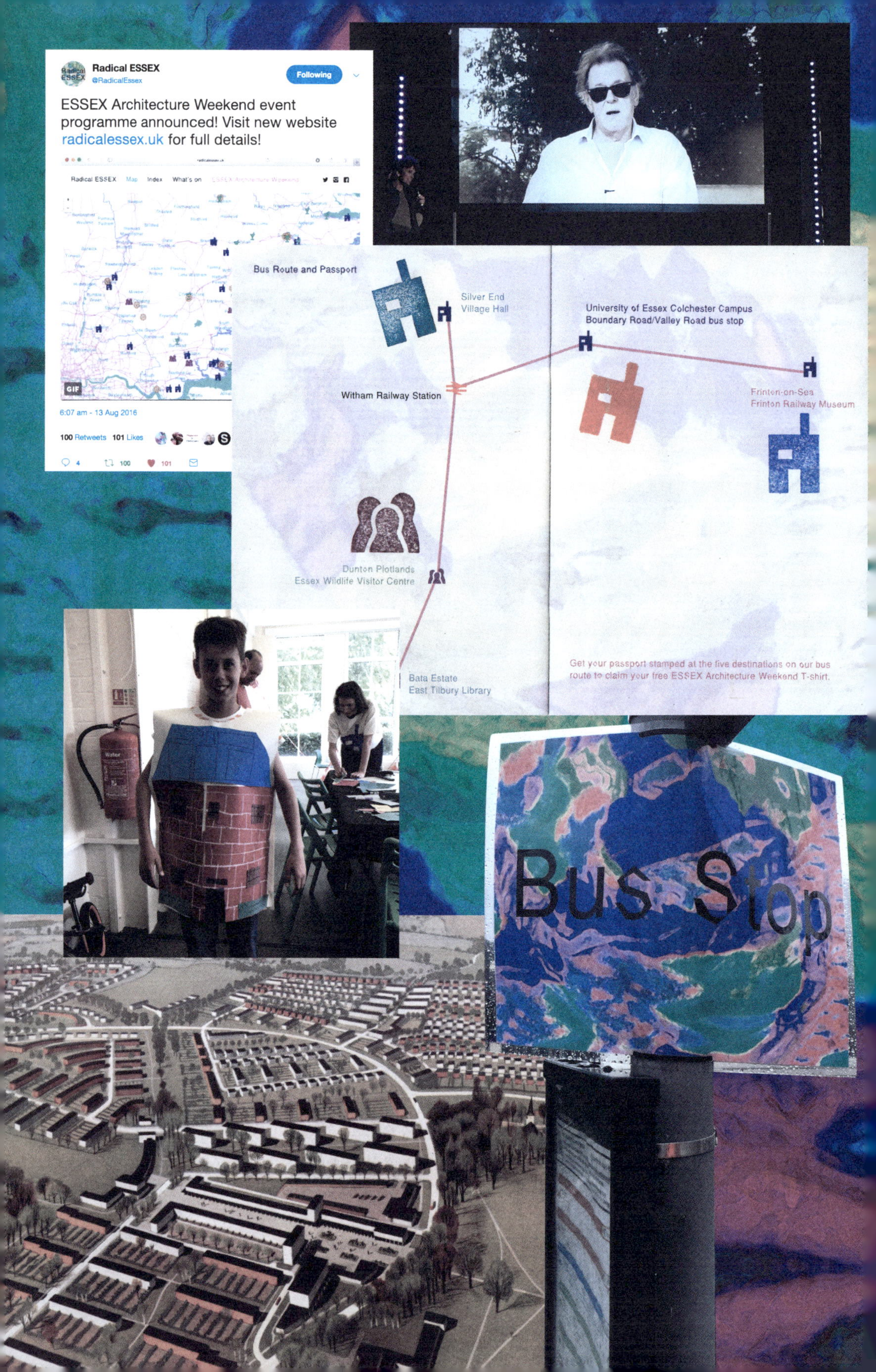
Radical ESSEX
@RadicalEssex
Following
ESSEX Architecture Weekend event programme announced! Visit new website radicalessex.uk for full details!
Radical ESSEX
Map
Index
What's on
GIF
6:07 am - 13 Aug 2016
100 Retweets 101 Likes
4
100
101
Bus Route and Passport
Silver End
Village Hall
University of Essex Colchester Campus
Boundary Road/Valley Road bus stop
Witham Railway Station
Frinton-on-Sea
Frinton Railway Museum
Dunton Plotlands
Essex Wildlife Visitor Centre
Bata Estate
East Tilbury Library
Get your passport stamped at the five destinations on our bus route to claim your free ESSEX Architecture Weekend T-shirt.
Water
Bus Stop

Frinton Park Estate Walking Tour

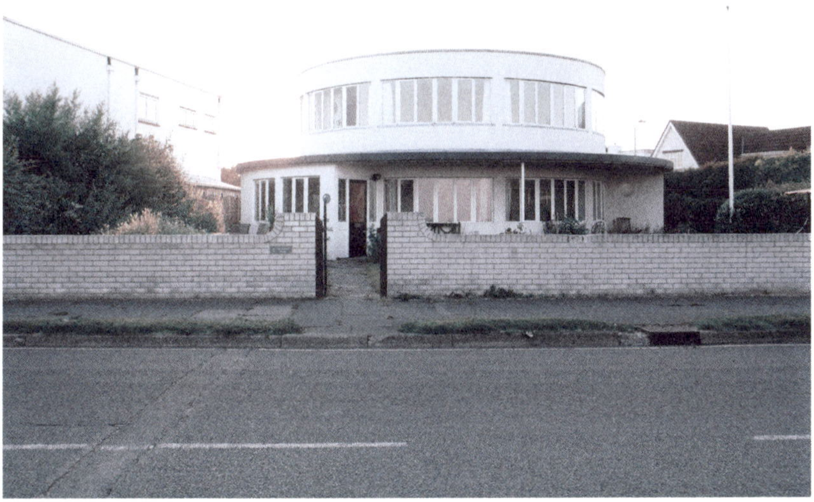

This walking tour guide was produced by Radical ESSEX in conjunction with Frinton and Walton Heritage Trust on the occasion of ESSEX Architecture Weekend, 10–11 September 2016. Radical ESSEX is a project aiming to re-examine the history of the county in relation to radicalism in thought, lifestyle, politics and architecture.

Frinton-on-Sea Area Map

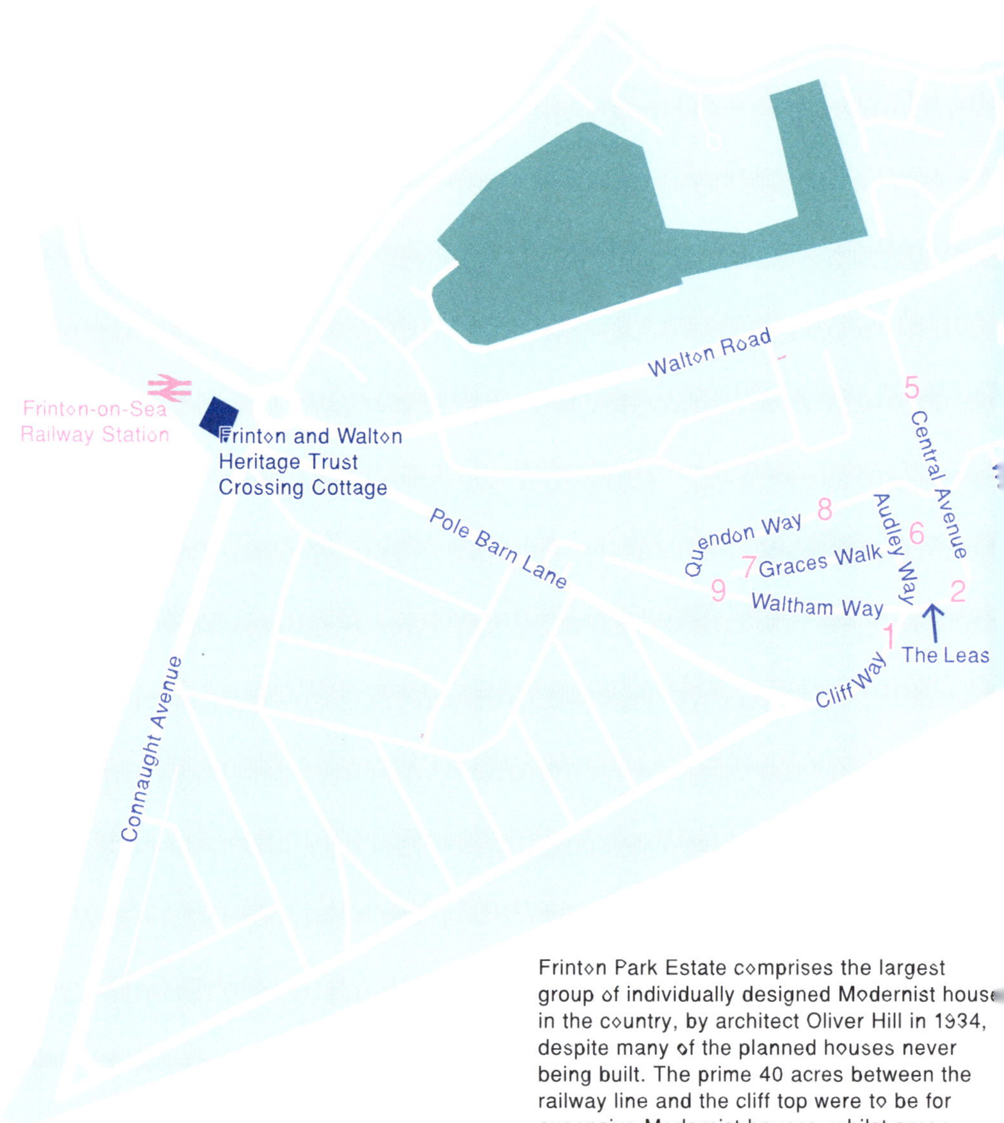

Frinton Park Estate comprises the largest group of individually designed Modernist houses in the country, by architect Oliver Hill in 1934, despite many of the planned houses never being built. The prime 40 acres between the railway line and the cliff top were to be for expensive Modernist houses, whilst areas of the rest of the Estate would be zoned for houses of high quality architectural designs called Tudor, Georgian, Elizabethan, Essex and Buckingham, and would be brick-built cottage types. Included in the scheme was a new railway station and Town Hall, churches, schools and a shopping centre designed as a circus at Walton Road.

Oliver Hill returned from a spring holiday in Palm Bay, Monte Carlo, fired with inspiration and enthusiasm for Modernist continental architecture. Hill planned the whole Estate, specifying the road names (those suffixed Ways are named after places in Essex) and designed some of the best houses including the Estate Information Bureau (now The Round House) and the proposed hotel in the undercliff, the design of which is reminiscent of The Midland Hotel at Morecombe.

Frinton & Walton Heritage Trust's headquarters, Crossing Cottage, and the Railway Museum houses an impressive selection of artefacts and archive material that tell the story of the local area. Situated in a well-maintained cottage garden, the grounds also include a wildlife area and information board. This is open for coffee mornings every Tuesday from 10am to noon, Easter to mid-October, and every third Tuesday of the month during the rest of the year. The Cottage archives and displays can be viewed during the coffee mornings, or at other times by appointment with the archivist.

The Frinton and Walton Heritage Trust have supplied the following information about the key streets to help you explore the estate.

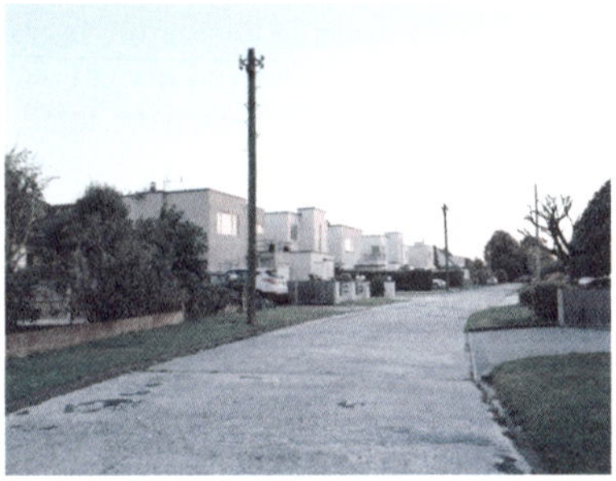

1 Cliff Way. Number 3 was designed by R. J. Page, numbers 6 and 7 by Oliver Hill, and number 4 a combination of both architects. Number 7, now known as The Round House is Grade II listed, with a mosaic floor depicting the entire community designed by Clifford and Rosemary Ellis for Carter & Co., Poole. This was illustrated in 'The Architects Journal' May 30 1935. Originally designed to be the Information Bureau with an exhibition of modern architecture by RIBA, the Office was taken over by local architects and estate agents,Tomkins, Homer and Ley in July 1935. It was converted into a house c.1947.

2 The Leas. Designed by Oliver Hill, The Leas displays monolithic, reinforced concrete cavity construction, known as the Wheeler system. The building was originally washed white with shell pink to the soffits. It was shown in F. R. S. Yorke's 'The Modern House in England' (1937 edition). The outside ladder has now been removed and a double garage has been added to the left.

3 Warley Way. Number 16 is known as Willingale, another of Oliver Hill's masterpieces. It displays render on brick/ blockwork and was a show home with five

bedrooms and a maid's room. The show home brochure indicated it to have Marion Dorn carpets and curtains and woodblock flooring in Deal or Columbian Pine.

4 Easton Way. Hill planned for plots in Easton Way to be allocated to the cream of young designers in the contemporary style such as Frederick Gibberd, Erich Mendelsohn, Serge Chermayeff, Tecton, Wells Coates, F. R. S. Yorke, Maxwell Fry, W. C. Holford & Gordon Stevenson, Raymond McGrath and Connell, Ward & Lucas. Unfortunately not many took up this opportunity. The houses built were designed by R. A. Duncan (number 10); Hall, Easton & Robertson (number 12); Frederick Etchells (numbers 14 and 19); Marshall Sisson (number 21); E. Warmley Lewis (number 23), as well as Hill himself (number 1 and Bala). Of the home Marshall Sisson designed, the Managing Director of the Frinton Park Estate said 'it has an unfortunate exterior ... (and will) be difficult to sell ... Simple square box with row of five windows in first floor at front and six on the left ... Rather neo-classical and Italian fascist'.

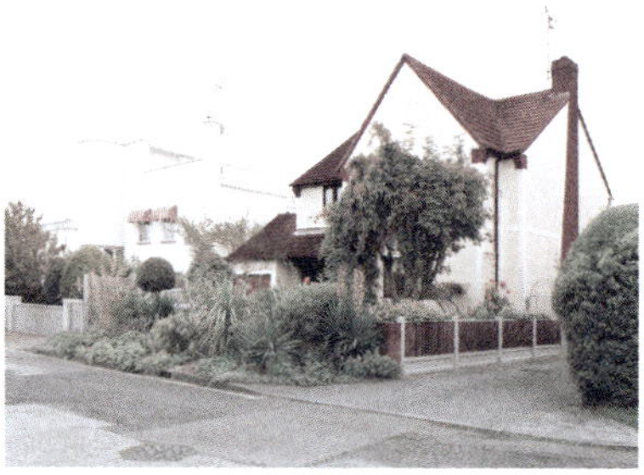

5 Central Avenue. Before 2 April 2015, if you had gone over the railway bridge you would have seen 'Frinton Park Court', the derelict remains of the intended shopping centre designed by Oliver Hill, but now unfortunately demolished. Only one bay of the circus was ever built.

6 Audley Way. Audley Way was designed by Oliver Hill. Numbers 1, 3 and 4, were featured in the original sales brochure. Number 4, Grade II listed, was built for the Rev. Robert Dobie as a seaside annex to his college at Great Chesterford, Cambridge Originally there were two ladders on the outside, now removed, with the front door repositioned and garage added to the right.

7 Graces Walk. Graces Walk was designed by J. T. Shelton, the resident architect for Tomkins, Homer & Ley with houses still showing many of the original features, for example the outside ladder at number 18. Number 10 is the only purpose built bungalow on the Estate to Hill's design.

8 Quendon Way. Numbers 55 and 57 were designed by Oliver Hill, named Dawn, Grade II listed, and Sunnyholme. Both have been sympathetically restored and extended for modern living. They were pictured in a Country Life article 'A Planned Seaside Resort' in 1935.

9 Waltham Way. Houses in Waltham Way were also designed by J. T. Shelton, based on Hill's designs. Numbers 14 and 22 both have new Crittall windows installed. Many houses have been sympathetically restored for modern living. The only pair of semi-detached houses, numbers 24 and 26, can be found here.

Frinton & Walton Heritage Trust exists to consolidate historical knowledge of the local area and provide public access to the archives artefacts and exhibits that tell the story of the community's past. For more information please visit www.fwheritage.co.uk

Photography: Catherine Hyland
Design: Fraser Muggeridge studio
Director: Joe Hill
Project Manager: Hayley Dixon
Project Assistant: Hannah Rose Whittle

www.radicalessex.uk
@RadicalEssex

Bata Estate Walking Tour

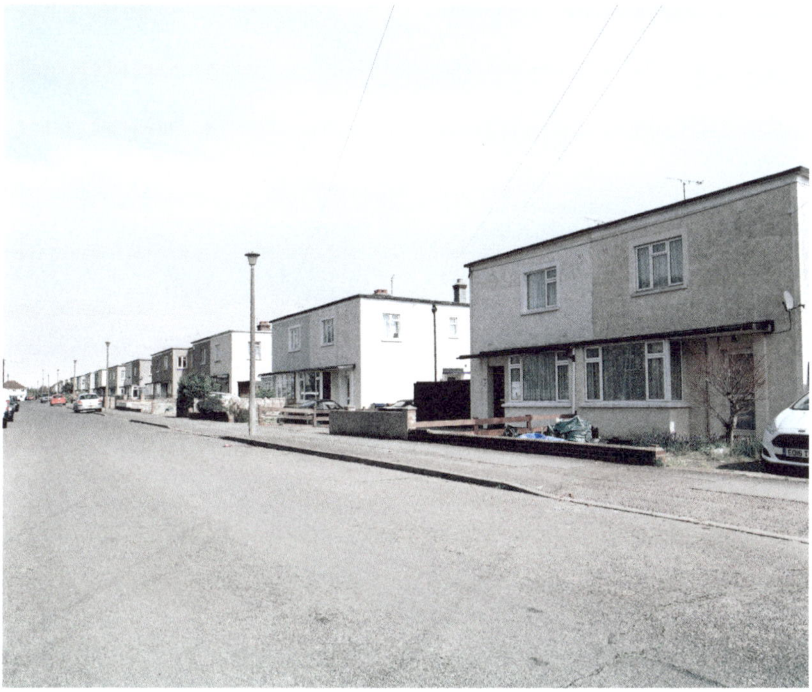

This walking tour guide was produced by Radical ESSEX in conjunction with Bata Heritage Centre on the occasion of ESSEX Architecture Weekend, 10–11 September 2016. Radical ESSEX is a project aiming to re-examine the history of the county in relation to radicalism in thought, lifestyle, politics and architecture.

East Tilbury Area Map

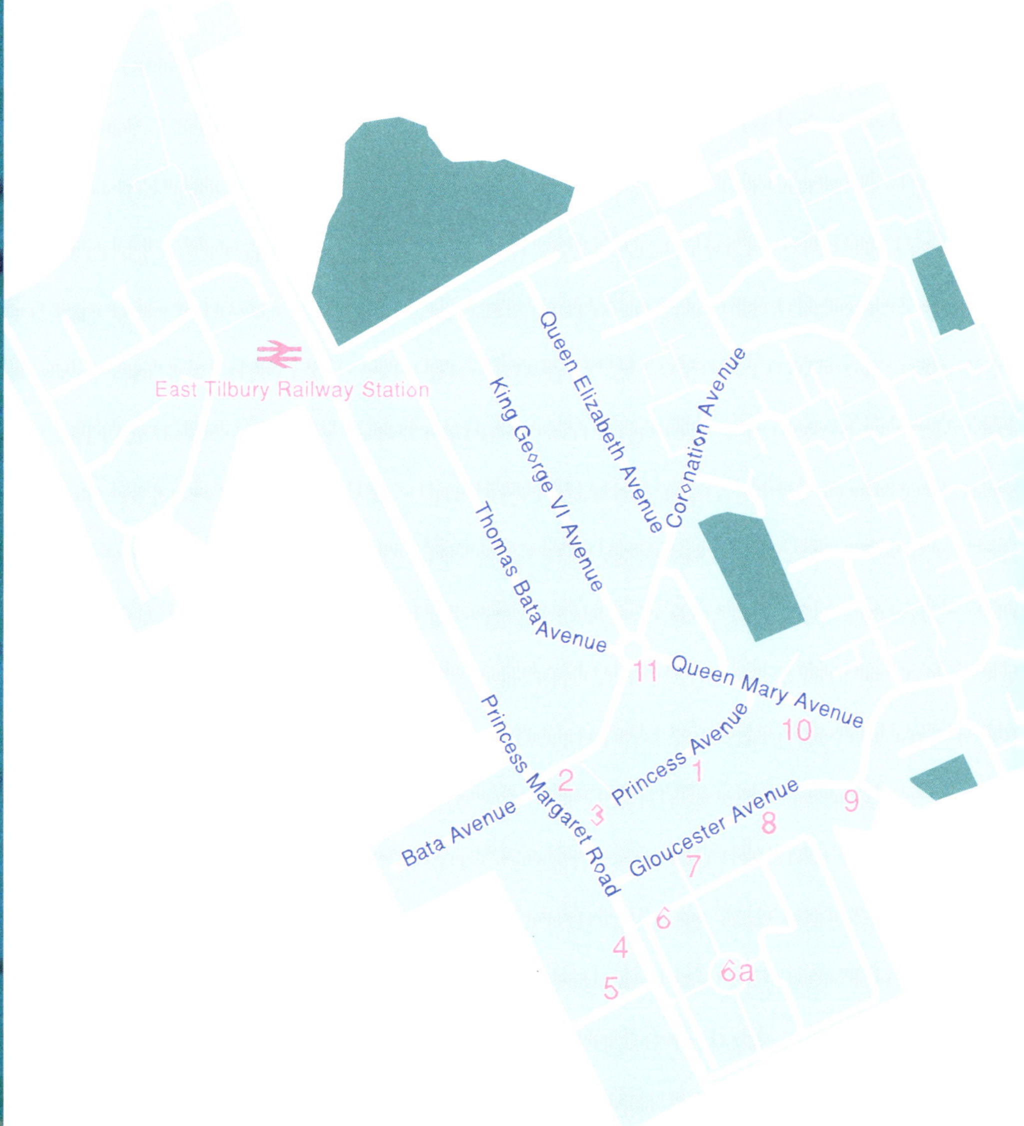

In 1933, Bata Shoe Company opened their new factory on the Essex marshes at East Tilbury. Based in Czechoslovakia, the company was founded by Tomas Bata, who was killed in 1932 in a plane crash. Over the next 70 years Bata was an important part of the local economy and an international community grew up on the Bata Estate, comprised of houses built for the workers by the company.

The best way to experience the Bata Estate is to download the Thurrock Mobile Explorer App and follow the Bata Reminiscence Trail. This is available on both iOS (search Thurrock Mobile Explorer) and Android (search Travel Thurrock) devices, best listened to on headphones.

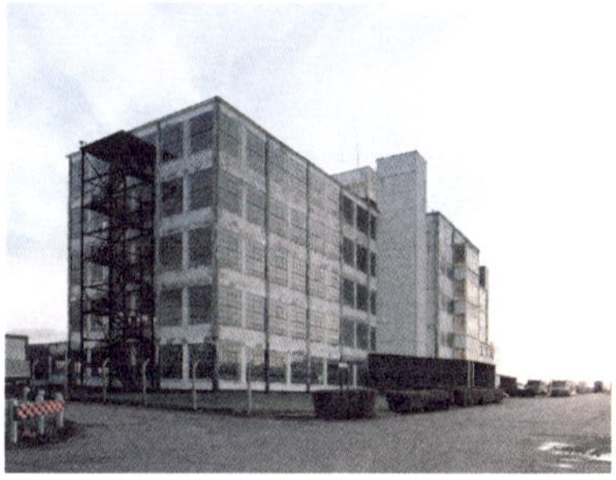

The tour is narrated by Mike Tarbard and other residents of the estate, telling stories of the site, featuring both the architecture and social history. This guide complements the audio guide, containing a reduced version of each location, which can be listened to or read in depth on the App, where you will hear tales of a time gone by, and learn about sites at each point that would have previously been seen.

The best examples of the Modernist housing can be seen on the Avenues: Bata Avenue, Thomas Bata Avenue, King George VI Avenue and Queen Elizabeth Avenue.

1 East Tilbury Library. The walk starts from the library site, currently closed due to a fire in early 2017. Make your way towards Coronation Avenue, taking note of the building on your left, the Recreation Club designed by Bronek Katz in 1960.

Turn left into Coronation Avenue and cross over Princess Margaret Road at the zebra crossing.

2 Bata Corner. Our second point of interest is Bata Avenue where the first houses were built in 1933. As you look along the Avenue the first buildings on your left and right were hostels for the young men and women who came to work for Bata, some of them as young as 14. They travelled great distances to find work, because jobs were scarce in other parts of the country and Bata provided employment and lodgings. If you look at the layout of the houses you will see that they are arranged in a chequerboard effect, this was copied from the layout of Bata houses in Zlin, Czech Republic, where Bata originated.

3 Bata Hotel and Garage. Further along on your right you will pass Production House, where the Bata garage/petrol station once stood. Stop now and look across the road to Stanford House which was the Bata Hotel, formerly called Community House. You entered by revolving doors and on the ground floor there was a ballroom, a restaurant and in the 1950s there was a Czech library later to become the residents lounge. The entire first floor was the workers canteen where hot meals were prepared for around 600 people. The other floors consisted of rooms and flats for workers. Families who worked for Bata overseas stayed in the Hotel when on leave. On the top floor was Flat number 1, which was for the use of the Bata family when they were in England.

4 Tomas Bata Statue. Continue walking towards the factory passing on your right the statue of Tomas Bata, the founder of the Bata Shoe Company.

5 Factory Gate. The building ahead of you with the revolving doors is the administration building which housed reception, retail, the managers' offices and the export department. To the left of this building you will see the gates where the workers entered. They 'clocked on' by putting a card into a machine

which stamped the time on it. The working day was from 7.30am to 4.30pm, with an hour for lunch and a short break in the morning and afternoon. If you look to your left from the gate the first building you see is number 24, the leather factory and beyond that is number 34, the rubber factory.

6 Bata Cinema. Continue to Princess Margaret Road and make your way to the crossing into the park. The cream building to your left was the cinema. It opened in 1938, closed in 1965 and is now the Village Hall. The doors are original as is some of the interior. The cinema showed films three times a week and Saturday morning films for the youngsters. The cinema occasionally hosted 'Workers Playtime'; a radio programme broadcast by the BBC featuring comedy and musical acts.

6a East Tilbury War Memorial. To your right, at the centre of the park, is the memorial dedicated to the fallen of World War II with an everlasting flame that was sculpted by Joseph Hermon Cawthra, (this is a replica as the original was stolen). The field beyond the park was the Bata Sports Ground and here is a surprise – in the 1950s and 1960s West Ham football team trained here and played charity matches against the Bata team. Afterwards there would be a Dinner Dance in the Hotel ballroom for the team, their wives and other guests.

7 Espresso Bar. As you exit the park, take a look at the building housing the takeaway shops. This building was also designed by Bronek Katz and built in 1960. Apart from the barbers, the building housed the espresso bar, which was the social hub of the Estate. You could sit with your friends with a frothy coffee freshly made from the Gaggia machine and listen to the latest sounds from the jukebox.

8 New Houses. Turn right into Gloucester Avenue passing houses built between 1939–1955 and you will come to Farm Road, which led to the Bata farm.

9 Bata Farm. The land was formerly agricultural and a large part of the farmland continued to be utilised by Bata to help keep the community more self-sufficient. The Bata farm produced milk from its own herd of dairy cattle which was delivered around the Estate in bottles embossed with the Bata name.

10 Bata College. Continue along Gloucester Avenue and turn left into Queen Mary Avenue. As you walk along, the Bata Primary School stood where the flats to your right are. Further along where Queen Mary Court stands there was the Bata Technical College which housed and trained young men for a career in the shoe trade.

11 The Avenues and Swimming Pool. Continue walking along Queen Mary Avenue, passing Princess Avenue until you reach the roundabout. To your left you will see a block of flats, this was the site of the swimming pool. You entered through a building that housed the changing facilities. The tour ends back at the library site.

Bata Heritage Centre collects the memories of the international community growing up on the Bata Estate, in order that future generations will better understand some of the social history of the 20th century. For more information please visit www.bataheritagecentre.org.uk

Photography: Catherine Hyland
Design: Fraser Muggeridge studio
Director: Joe Hill
Project Manager: Hayley Dixon
Project Assistant: Hannah Rose Whittle

www.radicalessex.uk
@RadicalEssex

FPG visit essex Firstsite Arts Council England VisitEngland southend on sea Essex County Council Colchester RIBA Architecture.com Radical ESSEX

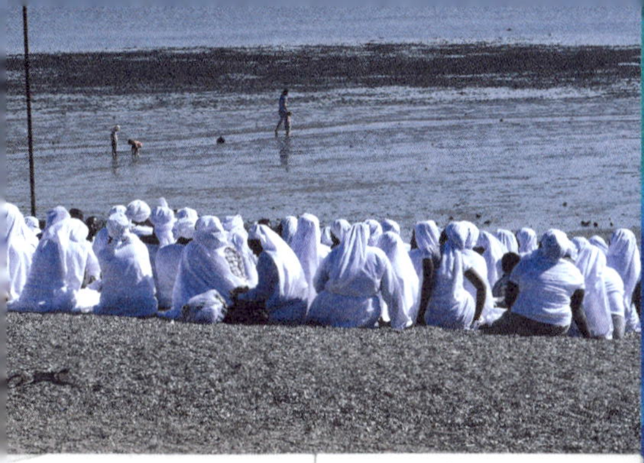

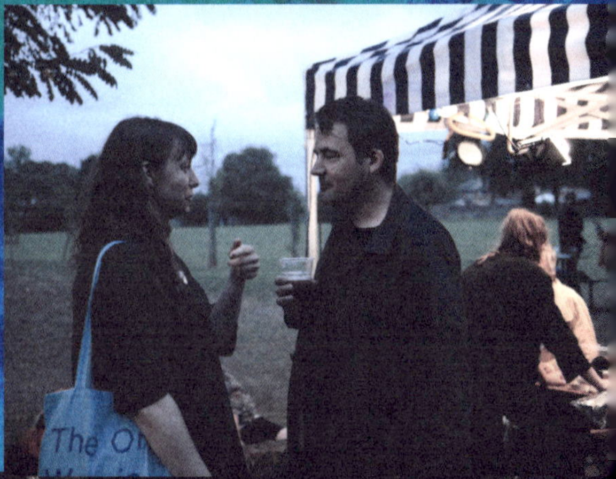

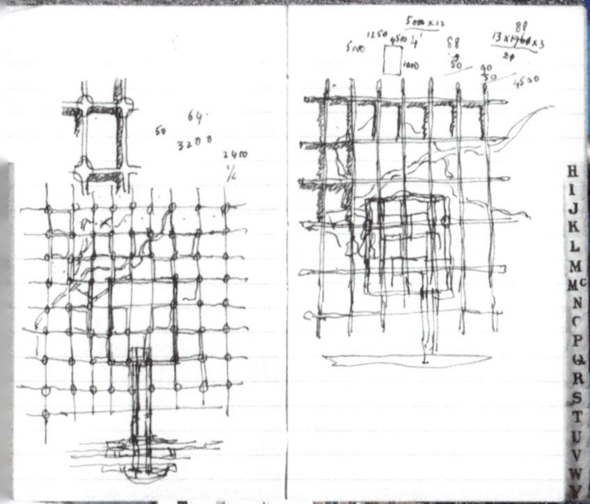

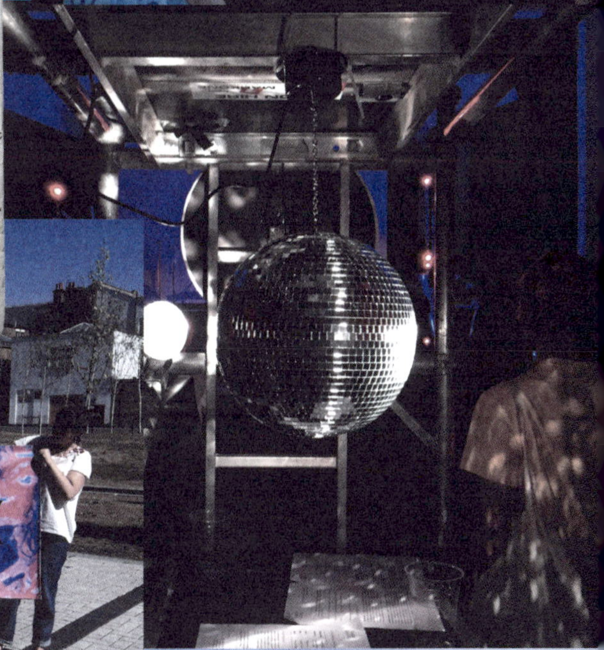

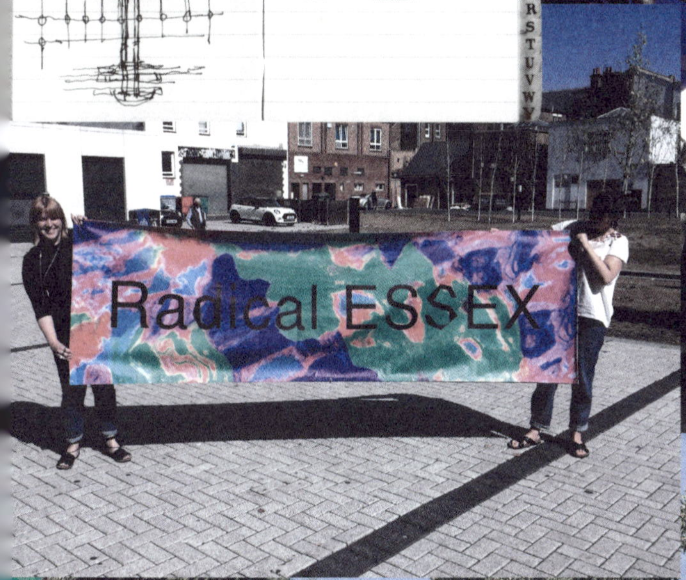
Radical ESSEX

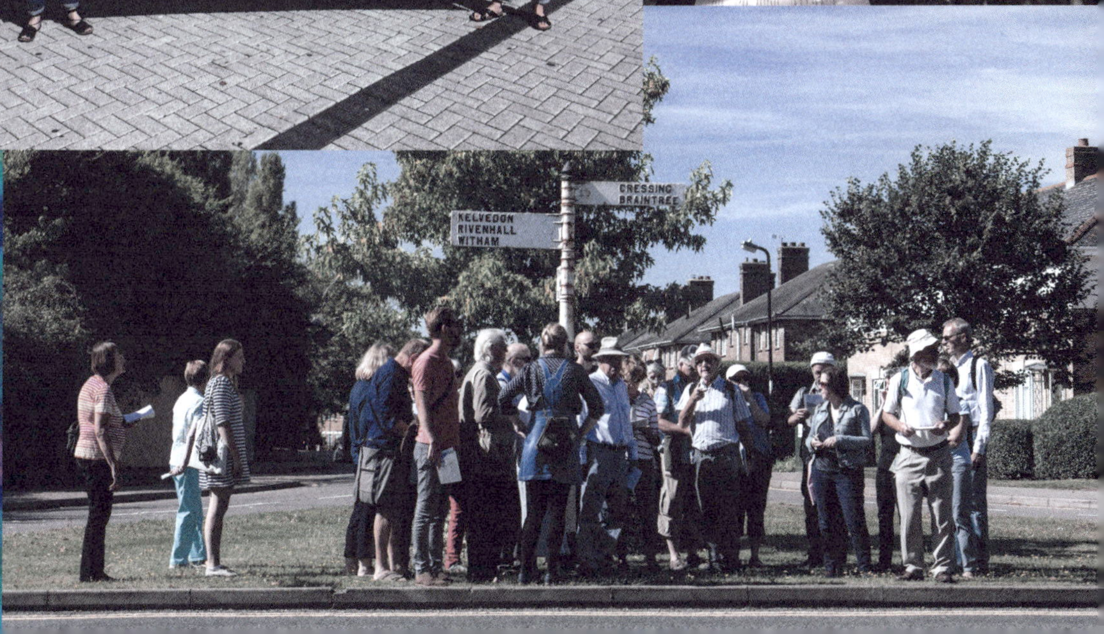
CRESSING
BRAINTREE
KELVEDON
RIVENHALL
WITHAM

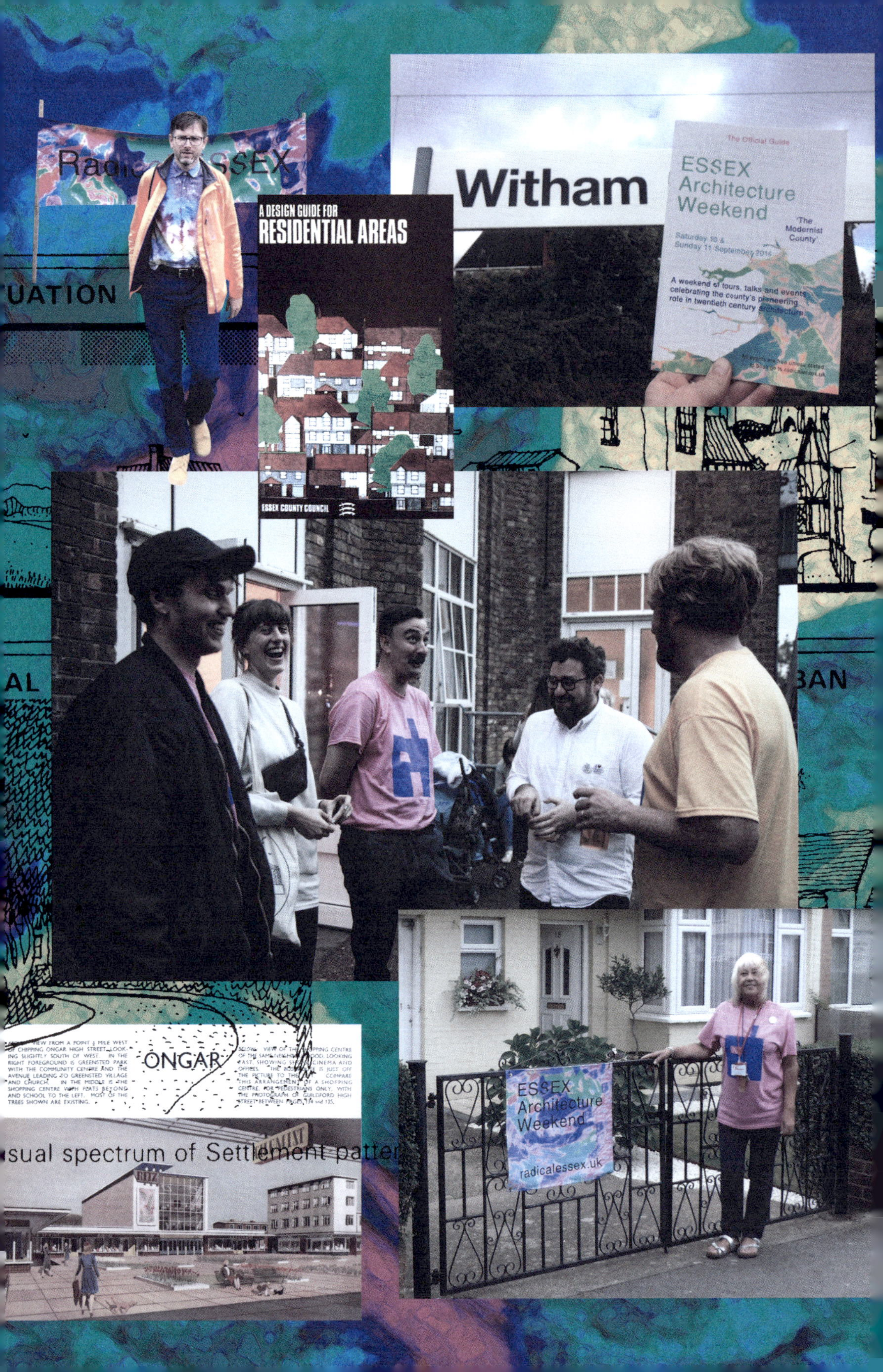

Witham
The Official Guide
ESSEX Architecture Weekend
'The Modernist County'
Saturday 10 & Sunday 11 September 2016
A weekend of tours, talks and events celebrating the county's pioneering role in twentieth century architecture
A DESIGN GUIDE FOR RESIDENTIAL AREAS
ESSEX COUNTY COUNCIL
UATION
AL
BAN
ONGAR
sual spectrum of Settlement patte
ESSEX Architecture Weekend
radicalessex.uk

Silver End Walking Tour

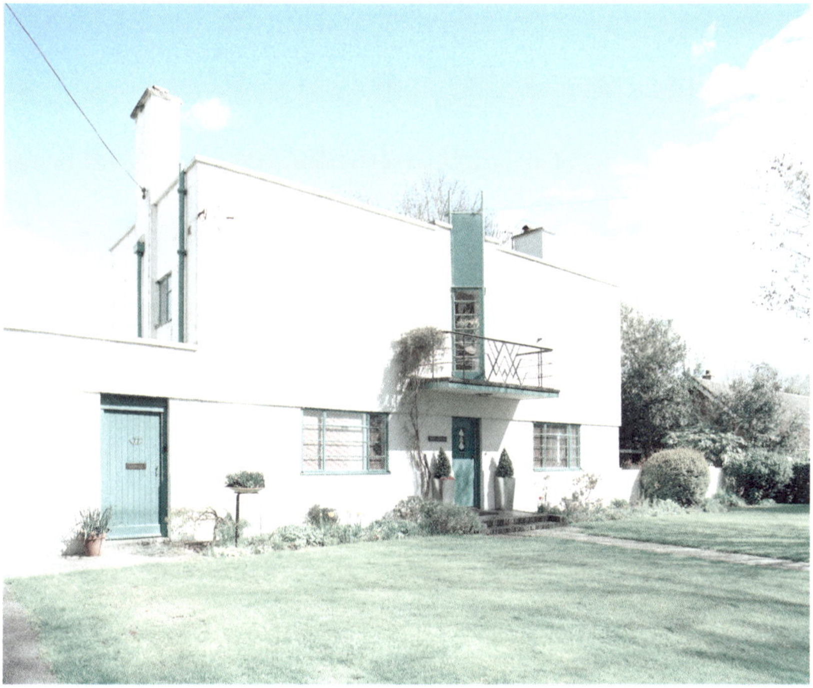

This walking tour guide was produced by Radical ESSEX in conjunction with Silver End Heritage Society on the occasion of ESSEX Architecture Weekend, 10–11 September 2016. Radical ESSEX is a project aiming to re-examine the history of the county in relation to radicalism in thought, lifestyle, politics and architecture.

Silver End Area Map

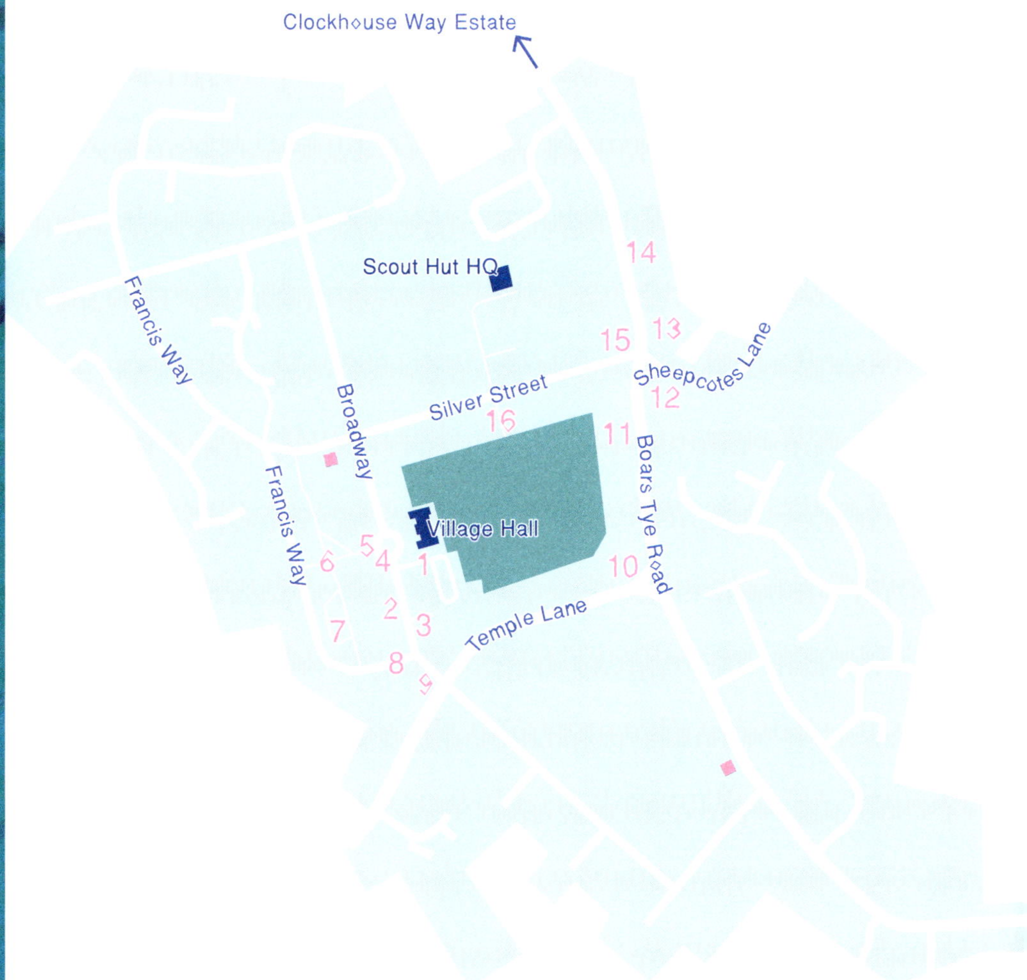

■ Red telephone boxes containing further information on Silver End village supplied by Silver End Heritage Society.

Silver End village was built in 1926, conceived by Francis Crittall to house his factory workers at Crittall Windows. The village master plan was designed by C. Murray Hennell. The houses were designed by Thomas S. Tait, Frederick MacManus and J. Miller stemming from the design of Britain's first Modernist building in nearby Clockhouse Way, Braintree. The traditional houses were designed by Hennell and C. H. B. Quennell, amongst others.

1 The tour starts at the shops adjacent to the Village Hall. Originally this was a 3 storey department store, catering to the needs of all residents, including a bakery, furniture store and butcher with meat supplied by Crittall's own farms. It came out as far as the edge of the present car park and had a colonnade shop front. The store was destroyed by a fire on 13 September 1952.

2 Turn to look across the road to the large brick building, Valentine House. This was originally the Silver End Hotel, comprising of 11 rooms plus bars, a restaurant and a function room. It was used by Crittall to accommodate clients and suppliers. Formally two large glazed earthenware tar pots stood by the main door. Following a fire at Christmas in the mid 1980s, it became a lively pub with an excellent carvery.

3 Walk to your left along the front of the car park to Jubilee House. Originally this was a bus shelter and public convenience but was pulled down in 1986 to build new premises for Fred Robinson, a local insurance broker.

4 Cross Broadway, walk along the front of Valentine House, keeping left at the roundabout to entrance of Memorial Gardens. Look across the roundabout. The Village Hall was designed by architect C. Murray Hennell and opened by the Lord Mayor of London on 10 May 1928. It is England's largest village hall with a main hall, sports courts, a stage and two smaller halls on the ground floor and committee rooms on both floors.

5 Turn round to face the gates of the Memorial Gardens. To the right of the gates was a thatched roof tea rooms and Mrs. Dunn's open all hours shop, which is now a private residence. The park gates show inscriptions of the Crittall family initials. Inside the entrance to the right there are the first of four notice boards, owned by Braintree District Council but now managed by Silver End Heritage Society with photographic displays. To the left under the trees is a memorial to Valentine Crittall, later Lord Braintree.

6 Enter the gardens and look ahead to a large white building. This is the Manors, Francis Crittall's home built in 1927 designed by architect Quennell. Note the blue plaque (top left). It is believed that the gardener and chauffeur lived in the bungalows.

7 Follow the garden path to the left towards the pond. Built in 1951 and designed by Walter 'Pink' Crittall with a Japanese inspired design, the pond included a pagoda. A memorial plaque is set in the wall nearby.

8 Continue towards the exit of the garden and turn left along Francis Way, towards Broadway. 5 Francis Way was the original telephone exchange. It is Modernist in style but the architect is unknown.

9 Turn right along Broadway to the crossroad with Temple Lane. Look across the road at the first house on corner with Valentine Way. 15 Temple Lane was the first house to be constructed in Silver End, designed by C. Murray Hennell. The foundation stone is low down on the right of the side door. The first six pairs of houses in Temple Lane are different to the others, numbered 1A–12A.

10 Continue left along Temple Lane, from the crossroad, to the T-junction with Boars Tye Road. This was the site of the original Crittall Manufacturing Company factory and Power House, now hidden behind a tall hedge to the right, and is all that remains of the larger complex that has been demolished. The Power House closest to the hedge, produced DC electricity for the houses (unusual for rural workers' houses in the 1920s) as well as for the factory. From here you can also see the unique Church of St. Francis and to the left opposite the junction was the site of the bus garage. The bus service was originally set up by the Crittalls. The factory canteen and picture house were also near the bus station, but are now demolished.

11 Cross the top of Temple Lane to the left and continue along Boars Tye Road. The large detached houses on the left were designed by C. Murray Hennell for the senior managers of the factory.

12 Stop before Silver Street/Boars Tye Road/Sheepcotes Lane junction and cross the road. Le Chateau was designed by

Thomas S. Tait of Sir John Burnet & Partners, built for Crittall's son Dan, who had an interest in steam locomotion and had a miniature railway in the garden. The house was later used for the '65 Club', a place for retired employees. It was also a location for the 1980s TV series 'The Nanny'. It is now a listed building.

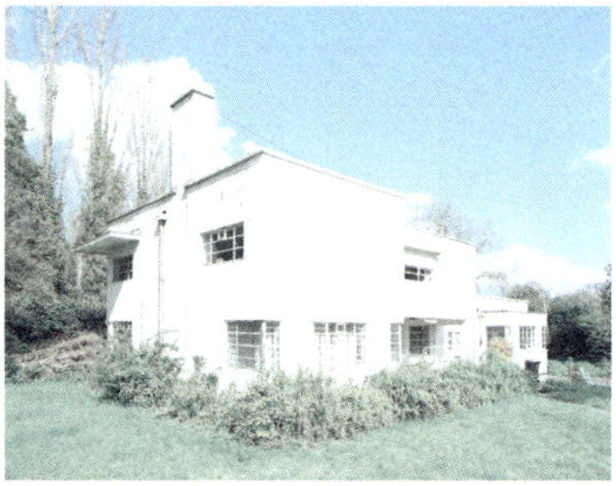

13 Cross over the top of Sheepcotes Lane.
Craig Angus was designed by Frederick McManus who was Tait's chief designer. It is also a listed building. Looking further down Sheepcotes Lane you will see the Roman Catholic church, designed by Martin Evans, built in 1966.

14 Continue along Boars Tye Road.
Wolverton was built in 1926 by Tait and McManus, beautifully restored and maintained by its present owners. Opposite is the Boars Tye farmhouse, the first the Crittall's bought. Dan Crittall moved here from Le Chateau with his wife and lived here until the 1980s. It then became a residential home.

15 Continue back along Boars Tye Road to the junction and turn right into Silver Street.
1–32 Silver Street were also designed by Tait and McManus. These are all listed buildings. Note the windows at number 4 and the original door and letter box at 5. One of Crittall's main concerns was the welfare of his workers. All houses were to have power, light, hot and cold running water, upstairs bathrooms and large gardens for the workers to grow produce. Apart from the Modernist movement styling, it is suggested that the flat roofs were used by Crittall to display how windows could be used. All houses were to have a view either of open countryside, sports fields or allotments, use of which the 'Guv'nor' encouraged. Employees could buy, part buy/rent or rent the houses but there was a strict 'pecking order'. They could only have a house deemed suitable to their position in the company. Greenfields Housing now owns many houses in the village and have recently replaced the windows and doors. The original village was designated a conservation area in 1983. It was covered by an 'Article 4 Direction' which removes 'permitted development rights'. The conservation guidance said that the windows and doors had to be steel, although more recently, aluminium is being allowed.

16 Continue along Silver Street to the junction with the entrance to the playing fields, cross over to the left and stop at entrance to the Village Hall sports field.
Here you can see evidence of the rail track that was used to bring the gravel from the area behind Temple Lane/Valentine Way to build the houses. The flat roofed houses at the lower end were built by Silver End Development Co. set up by Crittall to develop the village. These buildings are not listed. Continue along Silver Street to Broadway. Turn left at the crossroads and end back at the shops.

Silver End Heritage Society actively promote the village for its iconic architecture and unique social history. They run a Heritage Centre based in the Village Hall. For more information please visit www.silverendheritagesociety.co.uk

Photography: Catherine Hyland
Design: Fraser Muggeridge studio
Director: Joe Hill
Project Manager: Hayley Dixon
Project Assistant: Hannah Rose Whittle

www.radicalessex.uk
@RadicalEssex

FPG visit essex Firstsite ARTS COUNCIL ENGLAND VisitEngland
southend on sea Essex County Council Colchester RIBA Architecture.com Radical ESSEX

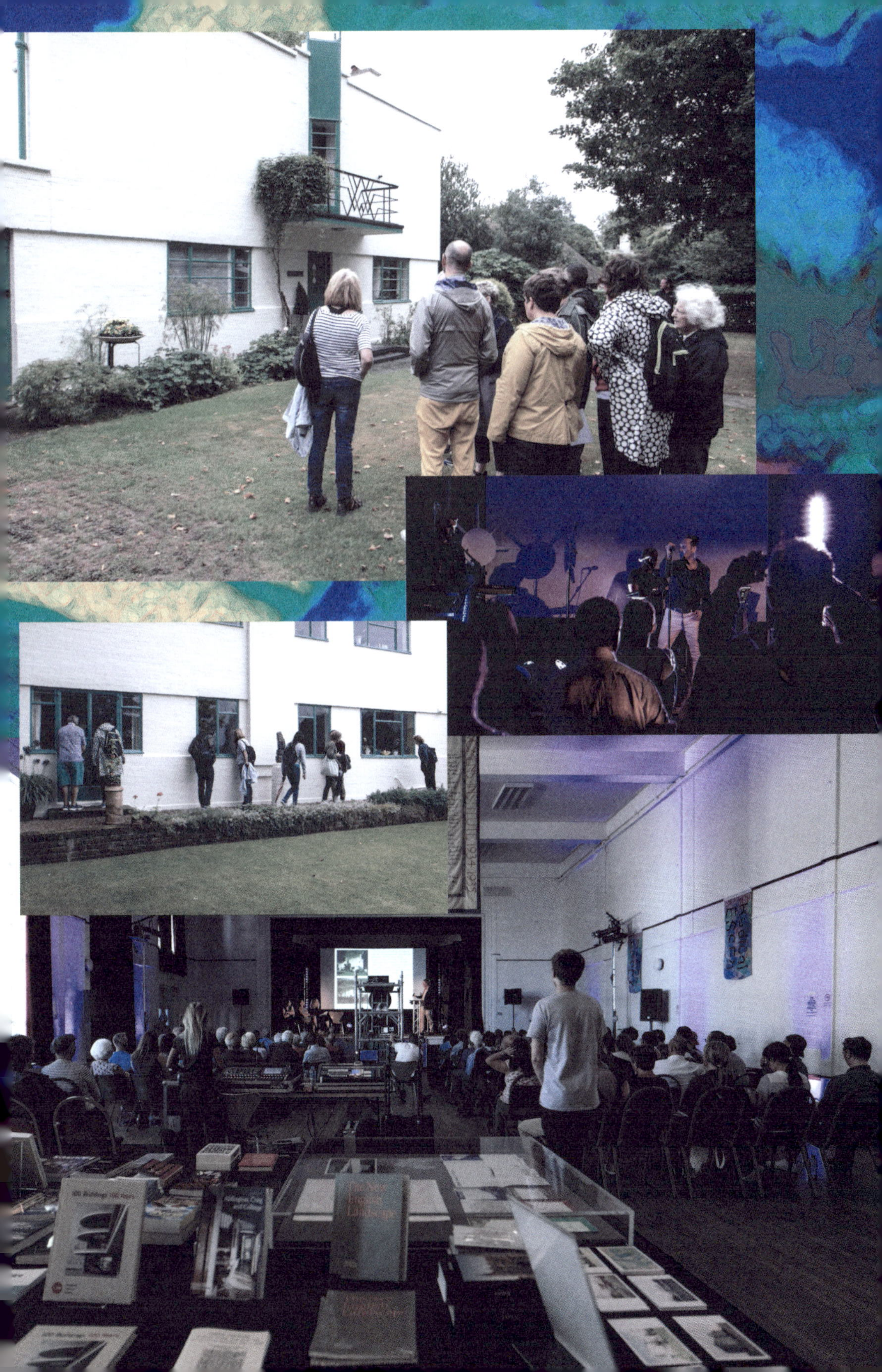

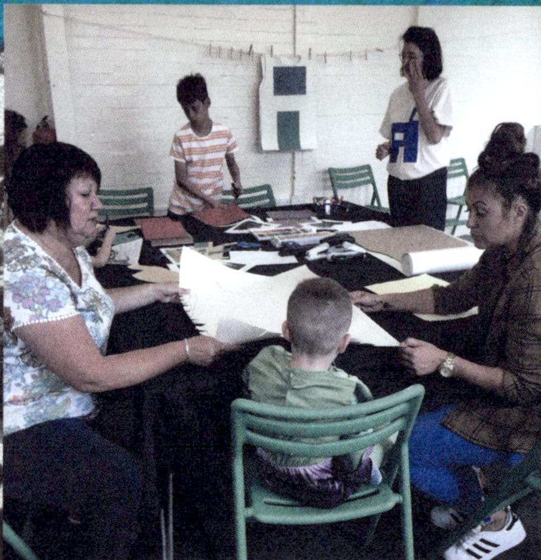

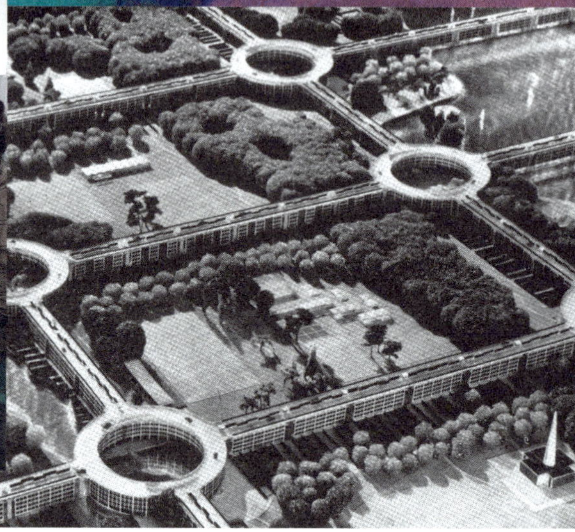

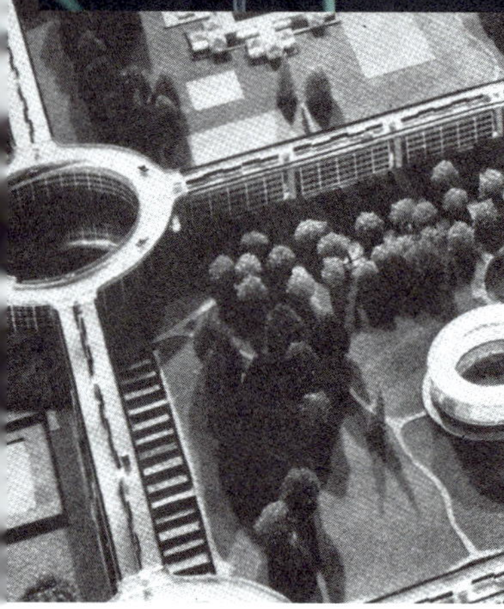

Essex Architecture Weekend 'The Modernist County'
Saturday 10 and Sunday 11 September 2016

Invitation to get involved!

Dear homeowner,

I am writing from Focal Point Gallery in Southend-on-Sea where, in collaboration with Heritage Open Days, VisitEngland and the Arts Council we are planning a weekend dedicated to the groundbreaking architecture of Essex, with particular focus to that in the modernist style. This forms part of the two year programme, Radical Essex.

Visitors will be invited to explore the architecture of Essex through walking tours, talks, and bus trips between three key modernist estates in the county, Silver End village, Bata Estate East Tilbury and Frinton-on-Sea. The talks and events programme will be based in Silver End village hall.

In addition to the estates we also acknowledge that there are a great deal of incredible individually designed modernist buildings within the county which we would also like to celebrate. As your property is one of particular significance to the modern movement we would like to speak with you regarding the possibility to include this as a place visitors could come to during this weekend in September. Any plans we make would be done only with your consent and collaboration, at this stage it would be wonderful to speak with you further to explain more about the project and how this might work.

Several homeowners have been approached who have agreed for their properties to be listed and either visited by appointment by members of the public or to show visitors the exterior of the properties, displaying the full breadth of the modernist architecture in Essex. Other buildings that will feature in the weekend include The Royal Corinthian Yacht Club in Burnham-on-Crouch and Labworth Café on Canvey Island. These proprietors are allowing the public to visit throughout the weekend.

If you are interested to ... ject
Manager for the event, ... 02 212932
... kend.
... We look

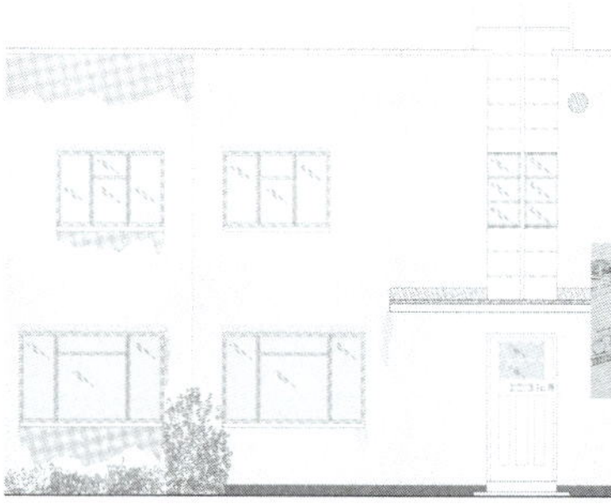

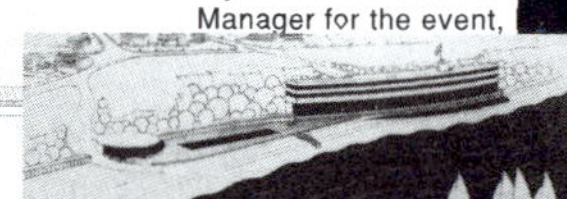

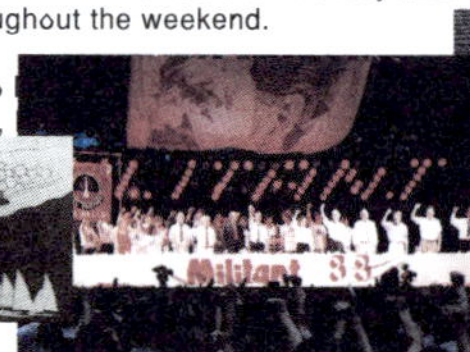

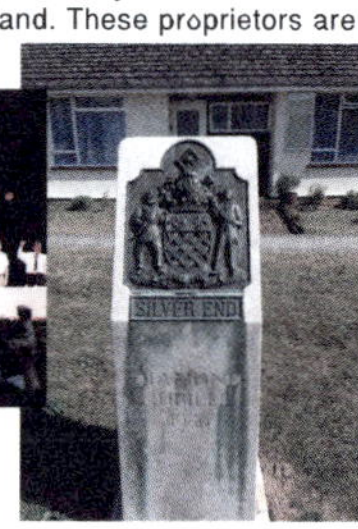

With best regards,

Joe Hill
Director, Focal Point Gallery

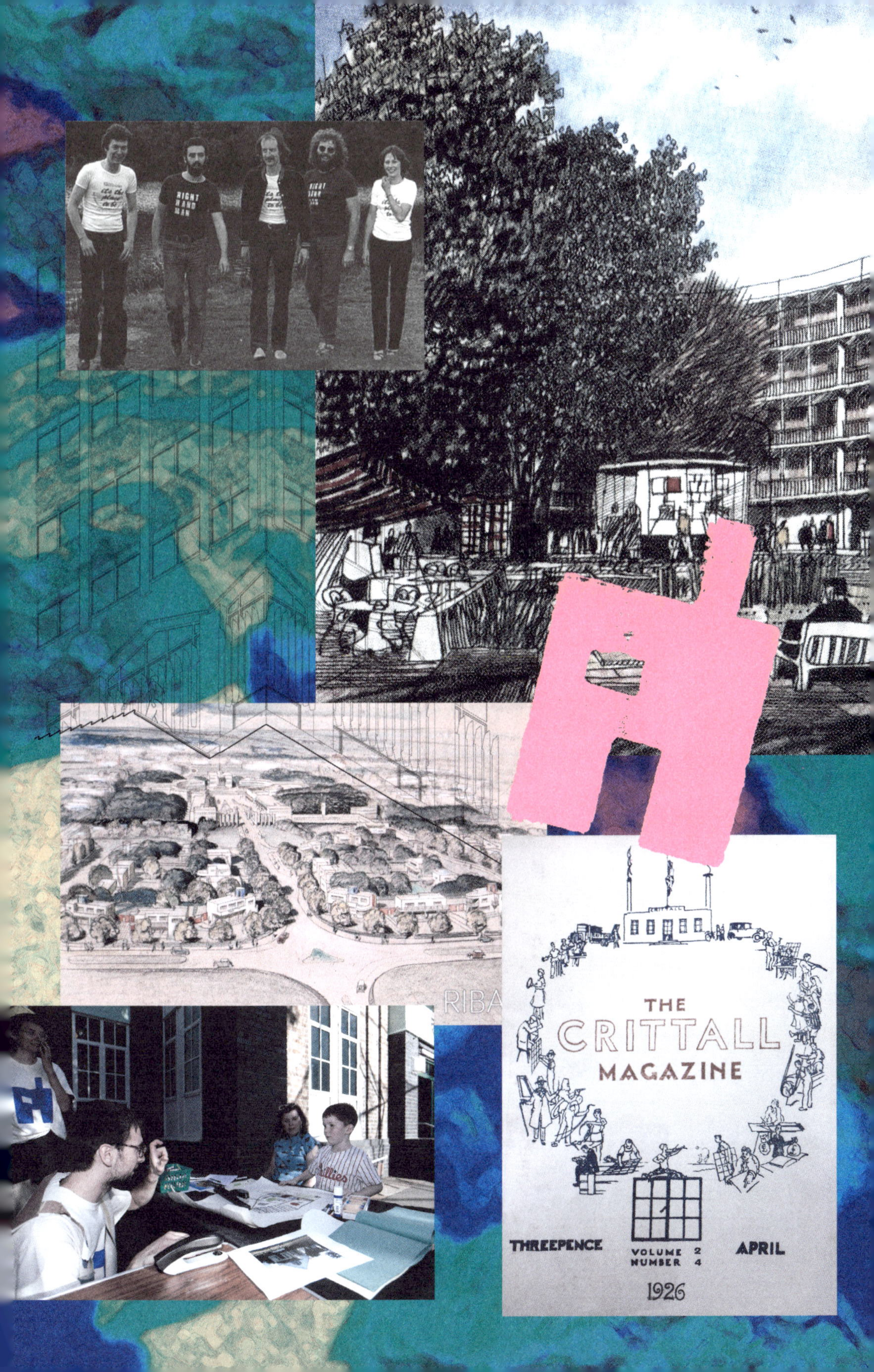
RIGHT
HAND
MAN
RIBA
THE
CRITTALL
MAGAZINE
THREEPENCE
VOLUME 2
NUMBER 4
APRIL
1926

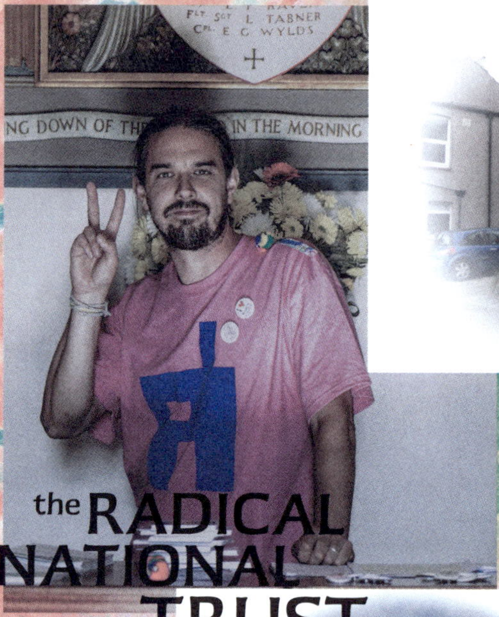

the RADICAL NATIONAL TRUST of SOUTH ESSEX

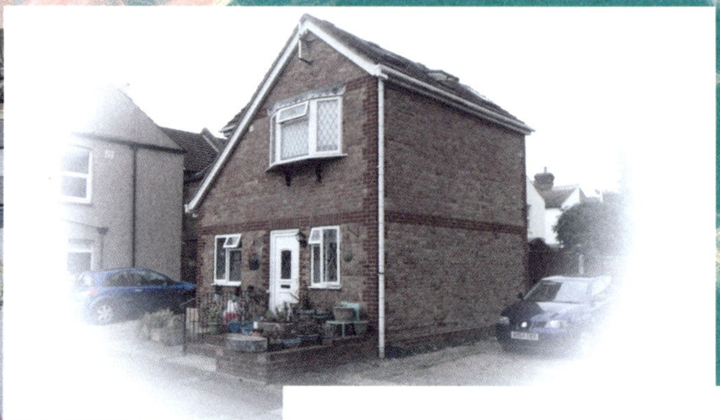

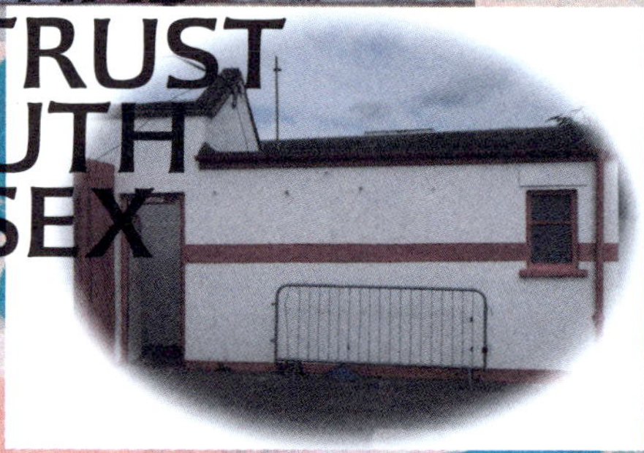

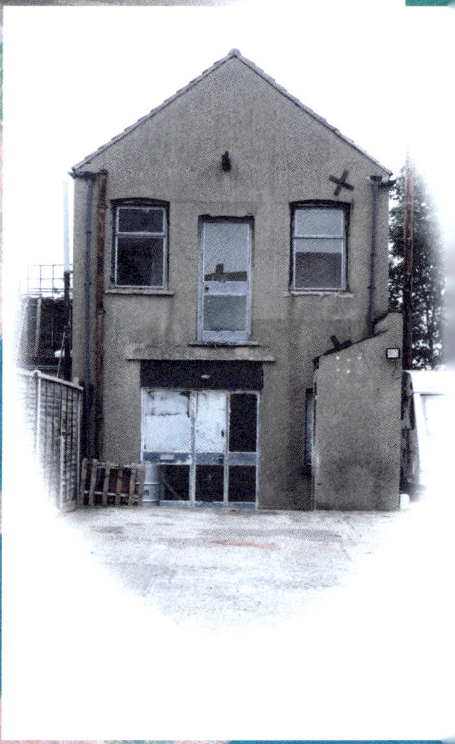

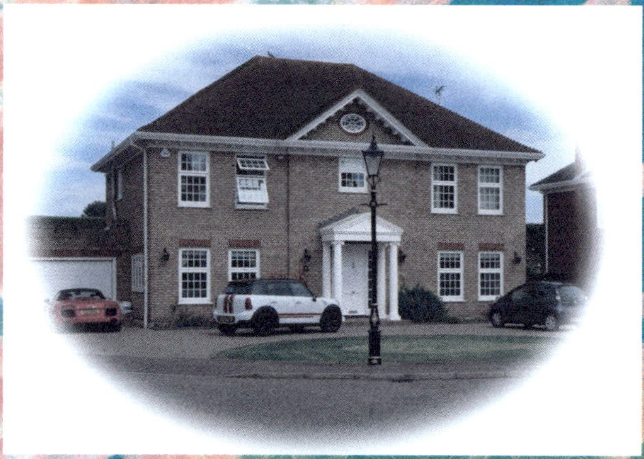

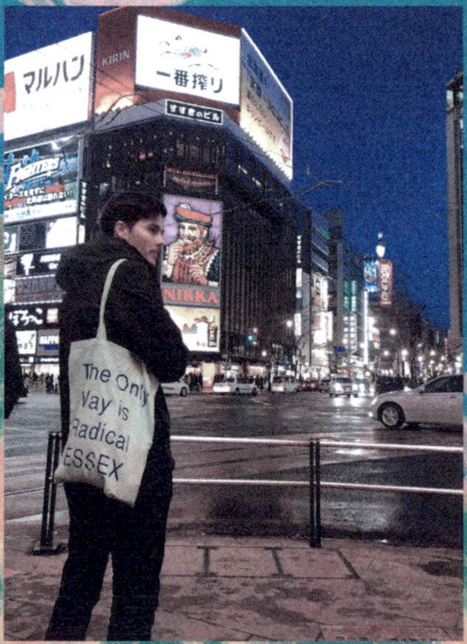

"The Trust aims to recognise the places where people *make* South Essex"

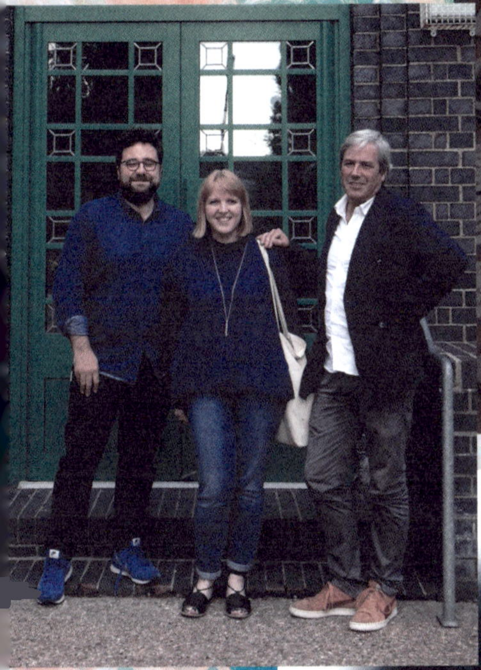

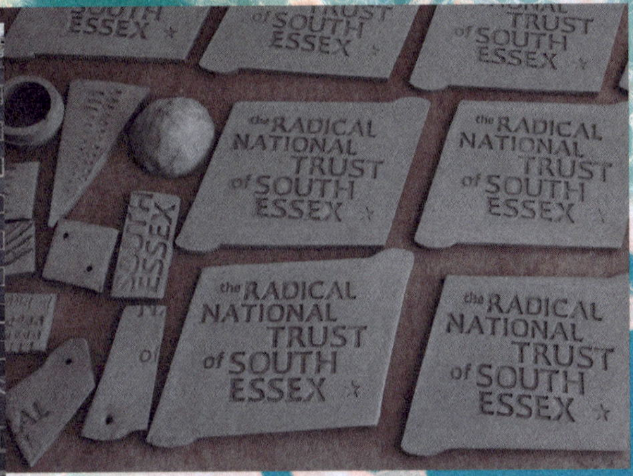
the RADICAL NATIONAL TRUST of SOUTH ESSEX
the RADICAL NATIONAL TRUST of SOUTH ESSEX
the RADICAL NATIONAL TRUST of SOUTH ESSEX
the RADICAL NATIONAL TRUST of SOUTH ESSEX
SOUTH ESSEX

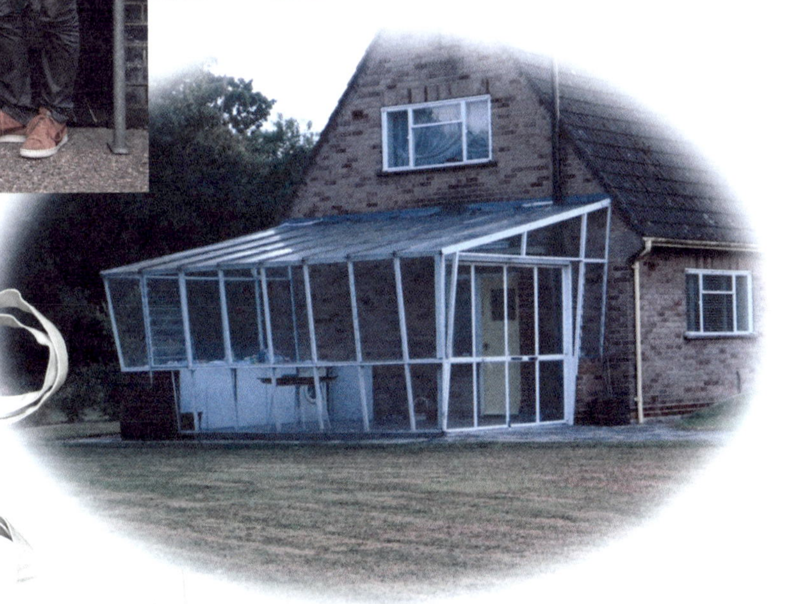

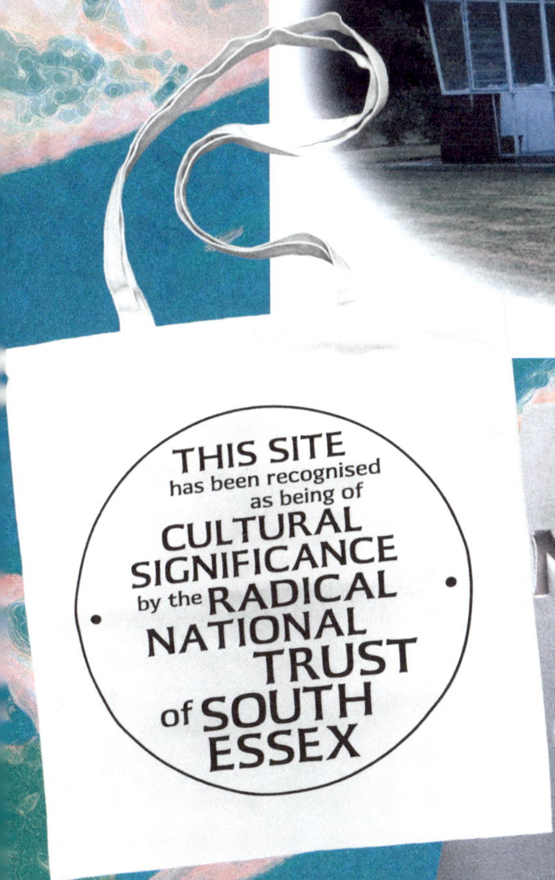
THIS SITE
has been recognised
as being of
CULTURAL
SIGNIFICANCE
by the RADICAL
NATIONAL
TRUST
of SOUTH
ESSEX

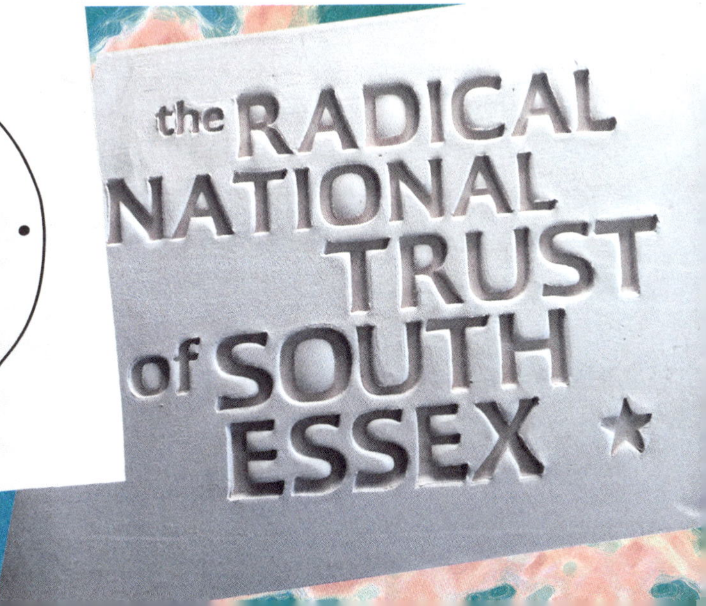
the RADICAL
NATIONAL
TRUST
of SOUTH
ESSEX

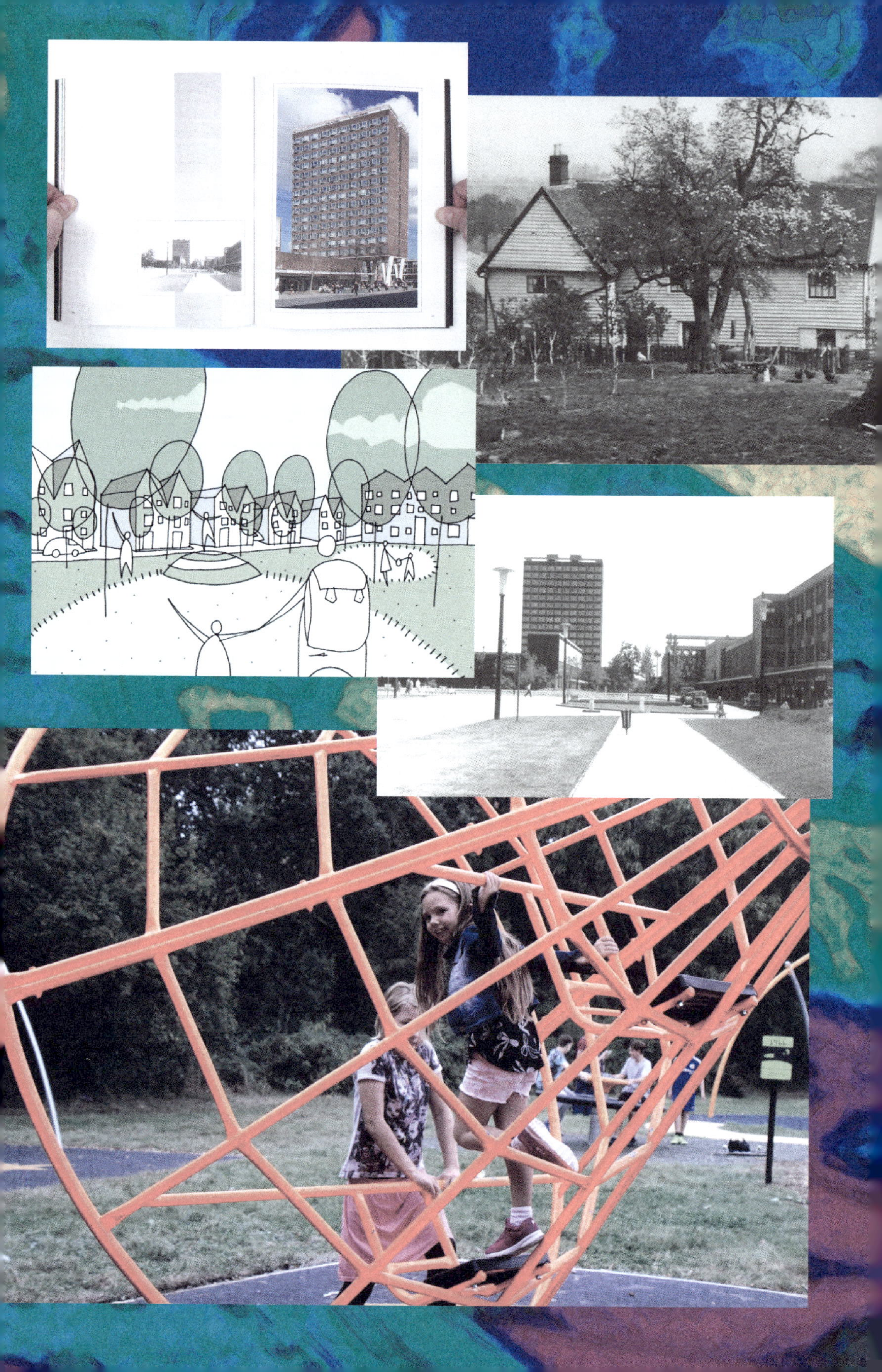

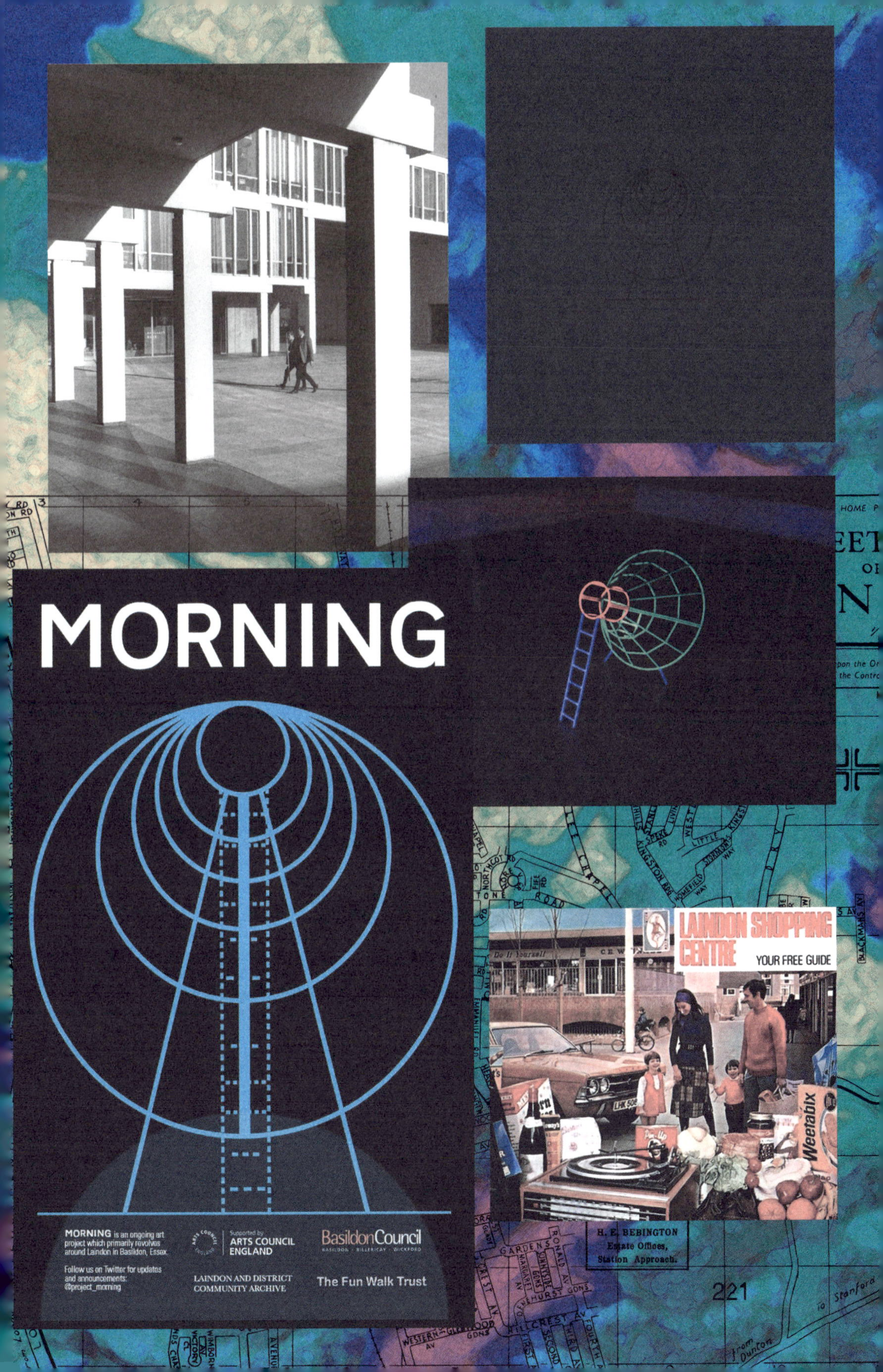
MORNING
MORNING is an ongoing art project which primarily revolves around Laindon in Basildon, Essex.
Follow us on Twitter for updates and announcements: @project_morning
Supported by ARTS COUNCIL ENGLAND
BasildonCouncil
BASILDON · BILLERICAY · WICKFORD
LAINDON AND DISTRICT COMMUNITY ARCHIVE
The Fun Walk Trust
LAINDON SHOPPING CENTRE
YOUR FREE GUIDE
Weetabix
H. E. BEBINGTON
Estate Offices,
Station Approach.
221

WHAT'S ON

I like to explore the edge of i

BGT horror hit comes to the Cliffs

Strippin Essex's

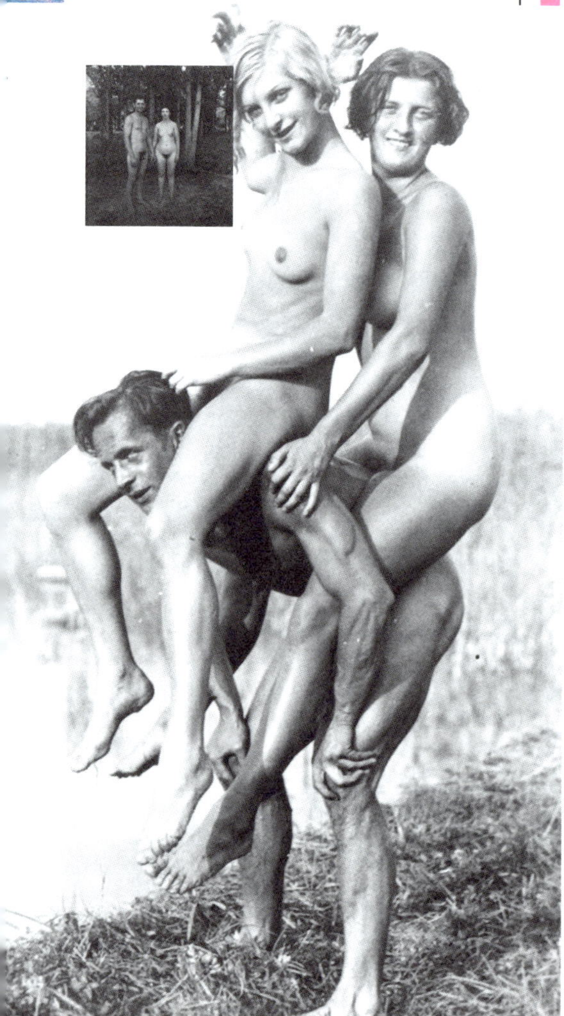

THE Circus of Horrors - a touring circus show which got to the finals of TV hit show Britain's Got Talent and has staged its own West End productions - is coming to the Cliffs Pavilion, with a new incarnation.

The Never-Ending Nightmare, promises to feature an an "amazing

By KELLY BUCKLEY

"BARE if you dare", so says the invitation being given to Joe Public, for the forthcoming event to be held at the Focal Point Gallery in Southend. It's a "performance lecture" about the history of social nudity in modern Essex from 1896-2017.

The invitation to get involved in the subject matter and strip off (or maybe just take off a shoe or a hat) is not meant to be sensationalist (of course), it's meant to be artistic (of course), and an interesting analysis of sorts, by way of sharing the project with the audience.

The project is another part of the h
laun
Galle
Site a
year.

Es
know
many
- arch
cultu
and t
proje
simu
relat
and U

On
has been radical, is that one of the first nudist colonies sprang up in the county. In the late 1800s, as a reaction to the industrialisation and chaste attitudes of Victorian society and inspired by the

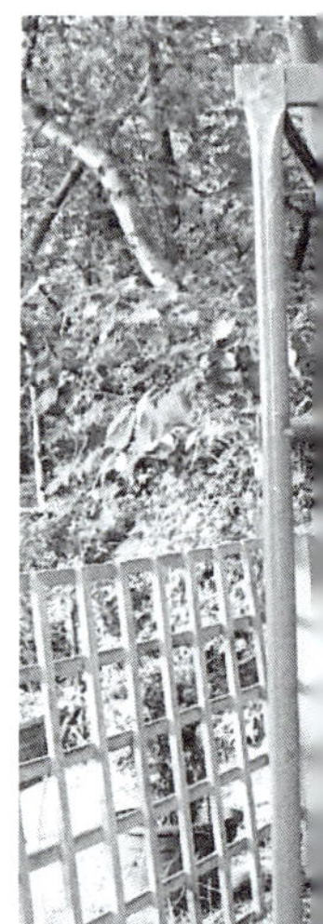

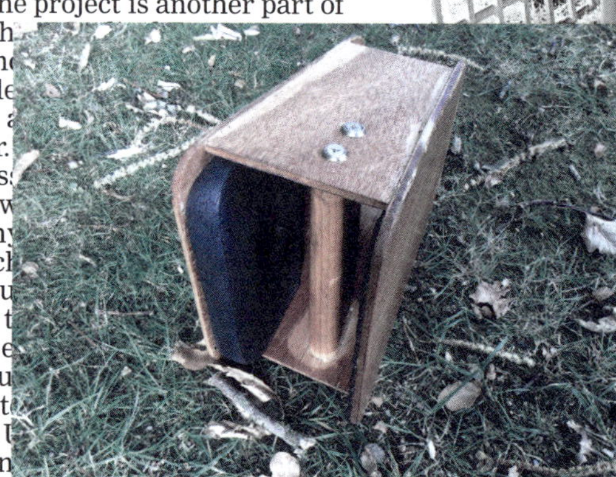

of research refl
shifting attitud
bodies".

He will attem
from Essex's Tc

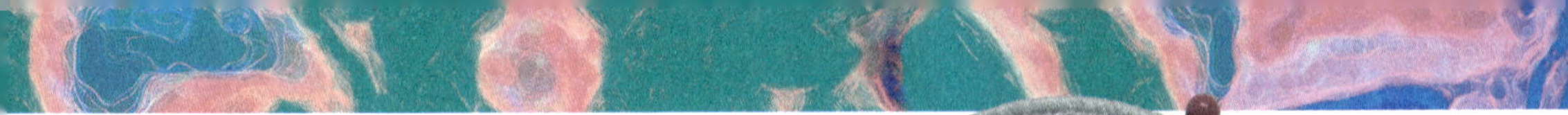

ropriate behaviour Damor

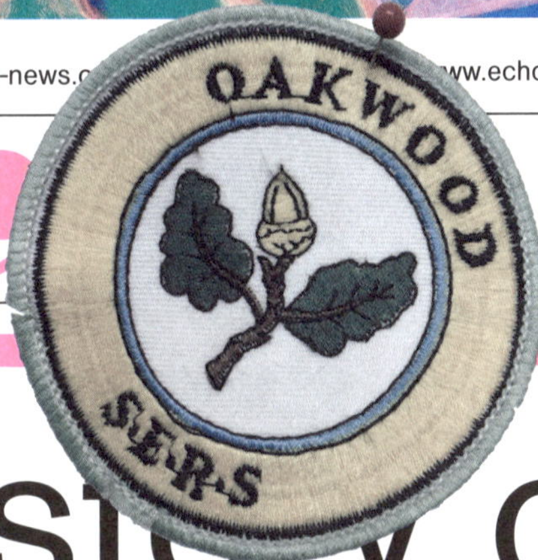

back hist of udist pioneers

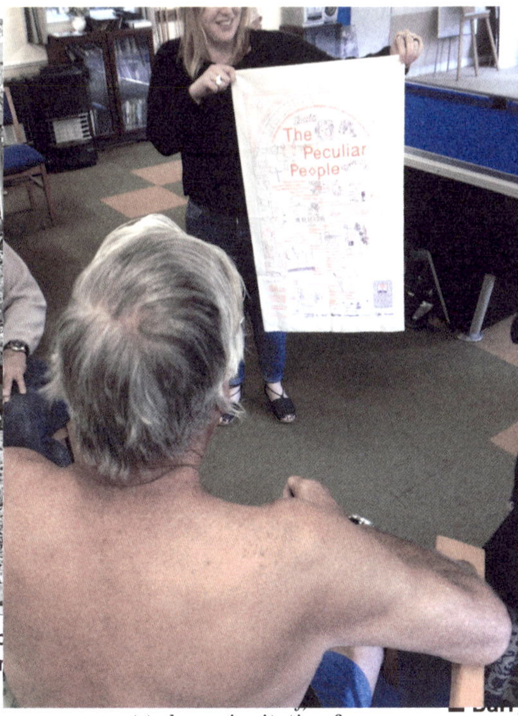

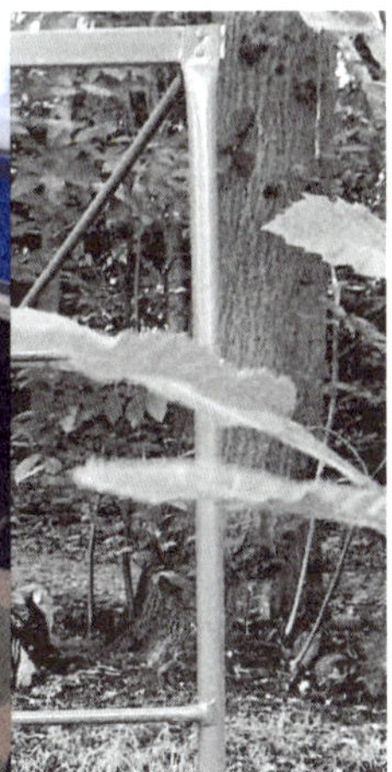

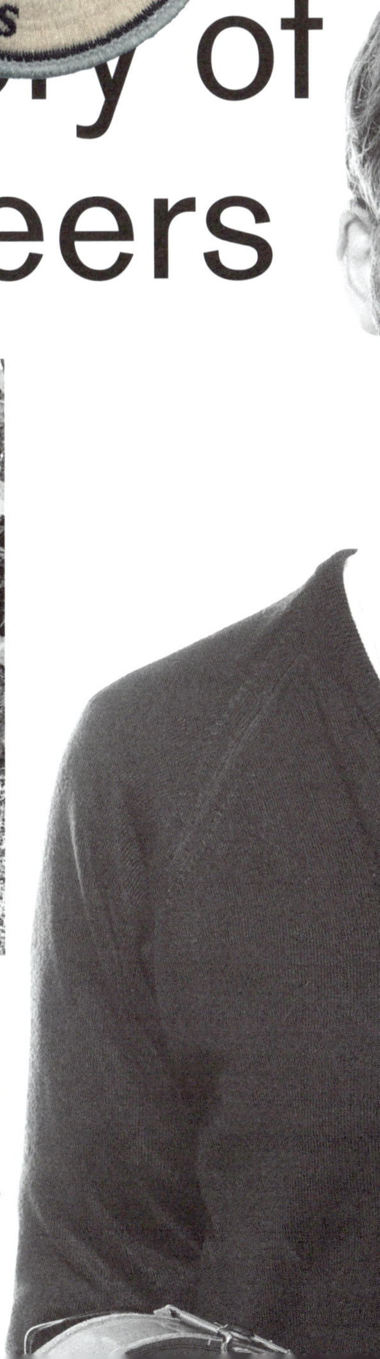

e remaining nudist
o Tolstoy

meant to be an invitation for anyone to attend, and bare if they dare, or not if they don't want to. It is an interesting discussion, and it will be as interesting if people choose not to participate in removing clothing, as it will be if they do.

ng
ss
d
s
ine
. via

y Sykes: An Amateur History of Social Nudity in Modern Essex, on Saturday at 7pm, with drinks from 5.30pm, at the Focal Point Gallery, Southend.

■ This performance lecture will be delivered within Torsten Slama's current exhibition of paintings and drawings of fantastical municipal landscapes.

■ From 4pm, Metal arts

NOTICE

tonight's talk

A CONFESSION: ANARCHY, ANONYMITY, HEALTH & EFFICIENCY

An Amateur History *of* Social Nudity *in* Modern Essex *1896-2017*

with Barry Sykes

7pm

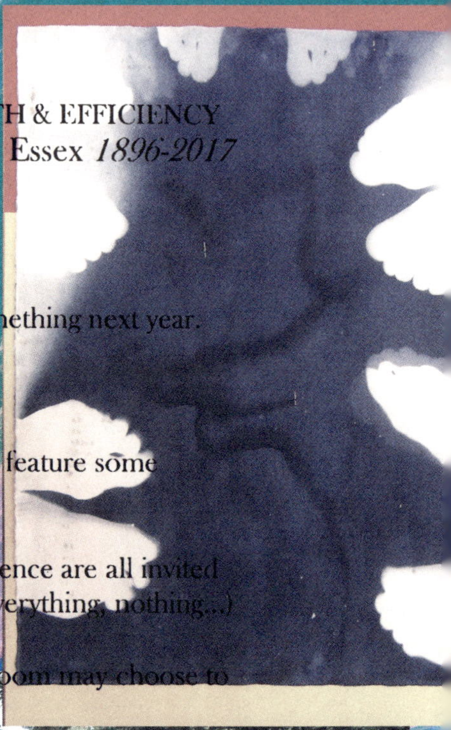

- *'A CONFESSION...'* is a work in progress for something next year.
- It will last about an hour
- Due to the nature of the subject matter the talk will feature some images of full-frontal male and female nudity.
- In keeping with the theme the speaker, staff & audience are all invited to be as *#BareAsYouDare*. (Remove a hat, shoe, everything, nothing...)
- Consequently, please be aware that anyone in the room may choose to remove some or all of their clothes.
- So please respect those around you, however you or they decide to participate.
- And therefore NO PHOTOGRAPHY please.
- Also, to be sure, please no phones out in the talk either.
- However, the gallery *will* be taking a photo from the back of the room behind the audience at the start and end of the talk, this will be announced.
- The talk will be followed by a short audience Q&A.
- Anything else, please ask an attendant.

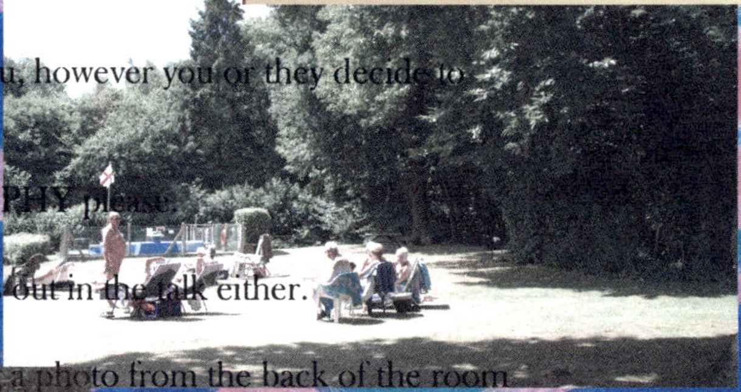

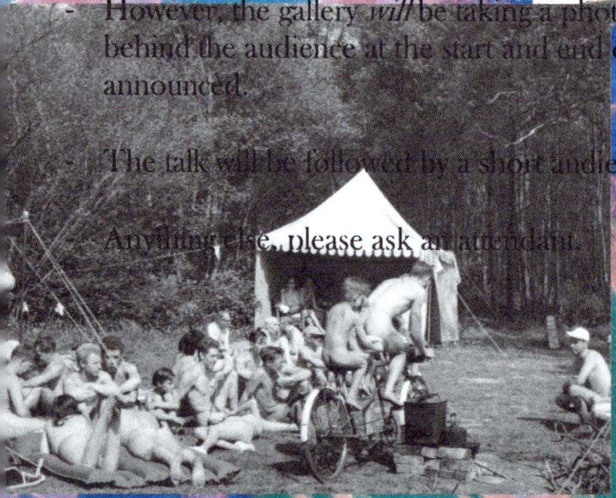

yellowad.co.uk **NEWS**

Tolstoy's nude awakening

ONE of the world's greatest ever novelists will feature in a free talk at the Southend Forum on Saturday.

Leo Tolstoy was a Russian writer and 'christian anarchist' best known for his novels War and Peace and Anna Karenina.

He is less well known as founder of the UK's first nudist colonies in Essex, at Wickford and Purliegh.

Essex-born artist Barry Sykes will host A Confession: Anarchy, Anonymity, Health And Efficiency; An Amateur History of Social Nudity in Modern Essex at 7pm.

Barry said: "This will be a performance lecture. Tolstoy's links to Essex and the two nudist colonies are not well known, so this a chance to explore some interesting ideas about place, anonymity and health in Essex."

The event, hosted by Radical Essex, will follow the first ever double-bill screening of Monster and Creature of the Estuary, in association with Metal and Focal Point Gallery.

Award-winning artist and filmmaker Eelyn Lee will present her latest film Creature of the Estuary at the Forum at 4pm.

www.radicalessex.uk/events
www.focalpoint.org.uk/about

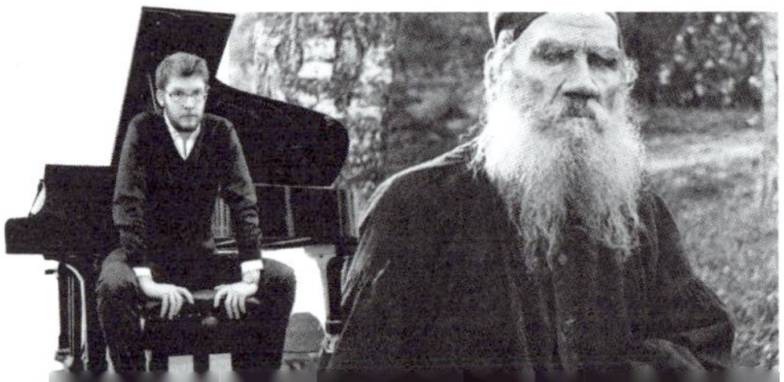

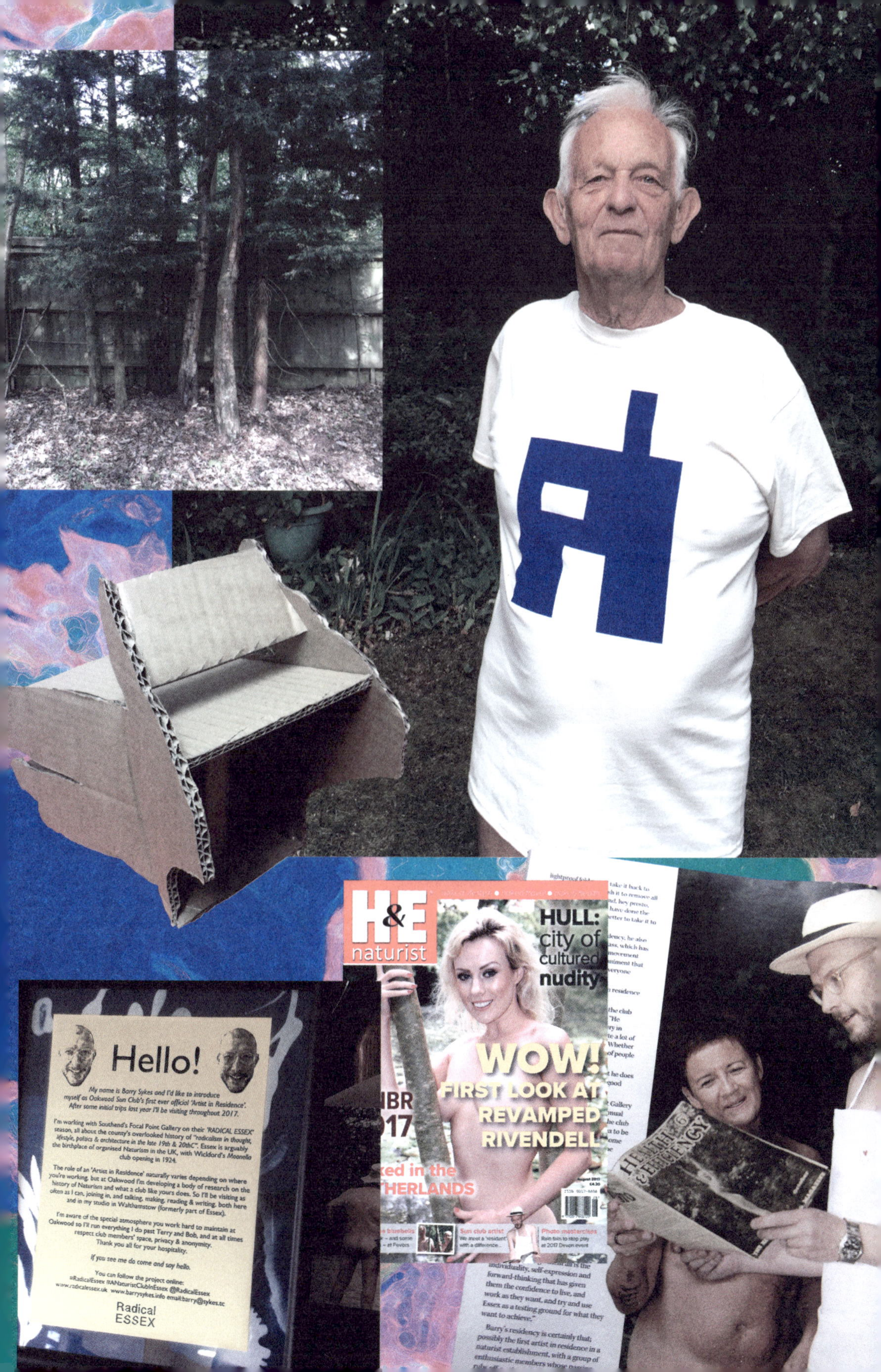
Hello!
My name is Barry Sykes and I'd like to introduce myself as Oakwood Sun Club's first ever official 'Artist in Residence'. After some initial trips last year I'll be visiting throughout 2017.
I'm working with Southend's Focal Point Gallery on their 'RADICAL ESSEX" season, all about the county's overlooked history of "radicalism in thought, lifestyle, politics & architecture in the late 19th & 20thC". Essex is arguably the birthplace of organised Naturism in the UK, with Wickford's Moonella club opening in 1924.
The role of an 'Artist in Residence' naturally varies depending on where you're working, but at Oakwood I'm developing a body of research on the history of Naturism and what a club like yours does. So I'll be visiting as often as I can, joining in, and talking, making, reading & writing, both here and in my studio in Walthamstow (formerly part of Essex).
I'm aware of the special atmosphere you work hard to maintain at Oakwood so I'll run everything I do past Terry and Bob, and at all times respect club members' space, privacy & anonymity.
Thank you all for your hospitality.
If you see me do come and say hello.
You can follow the project online:
#RadicalEssex #ANaturistClubInEssex @RadicalEssex
www.radicalessex.uk www.barrysykes.info email:barry@sykes.tc
Radical ESSEX
H&E naturist
HULL: city of cultured nudity
WOW! FIRST LOOK AT REVAMPED RIVENDELL
Sun club artist
We meet a 'resident' with a difference...
Photo masterclass
Rain fails to stop play at 2017 Devon event
£4.20
individuality, self-expression and forward-thinking that has given them the confidence to live, and work as they want, and try and use Essex as a testing ground for what they want to achieve."
Barry's residency is certainly that; possibly the first artist in residence in a naturist establishment, with a group of enthusiastic members whose

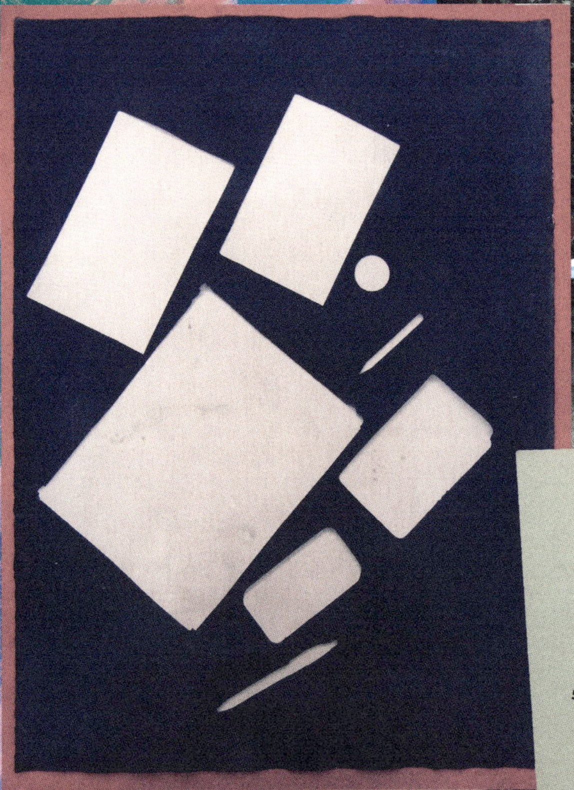

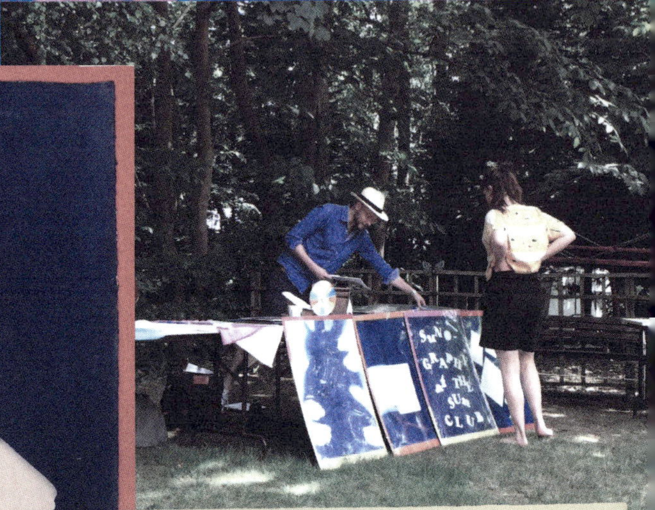

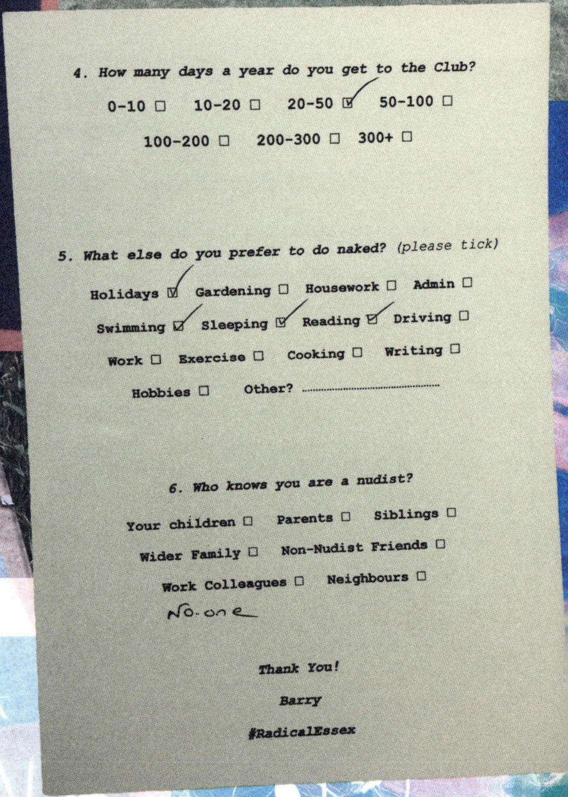

4. *How many days a year do you get to the Club?*

0-10 ☐ 10-20 ☐ 20-50 ☐ [✓] 50-100 ☐

100-200 ☐ 200-300 ☐ 300+ ☐

5. *What else do you prefer to do naked?* (please tick)

Holidays ☐ [✓] Gardening ☐ Housework ☐ Admin ☐

Swimming ☐ [✓] Sleeping ☐ [✓] Reading ☐ [✓] Driving ☐

Work ☐ Exercise ☐ Cooking ☐ Writing ☐

Hobbies ☐ Other? ....

6. *Who knows you are a nudist?*

Your children ☐ Parents ☐ Siblings ☐

Wider Family ☐ Non-Nudist Friends ☐

Work Colleagues ☐ Neighbours ☐

[No-one]

Thank You!

Barry

#RadicalEssex

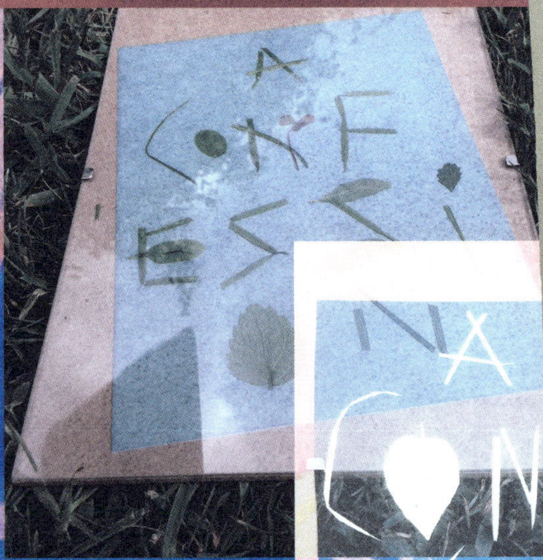

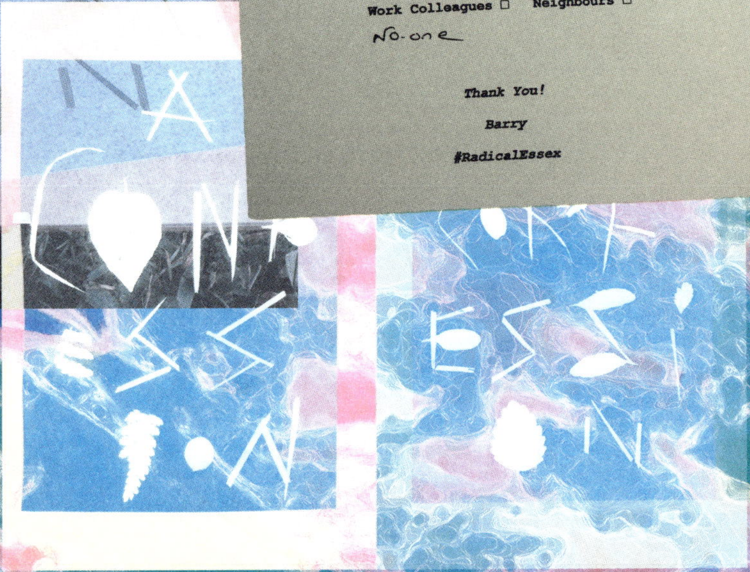

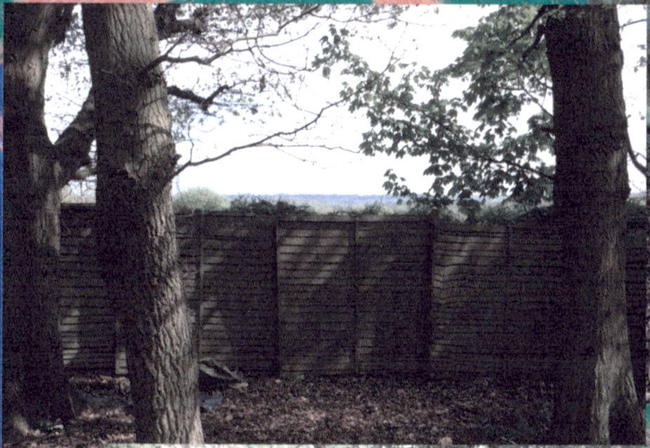

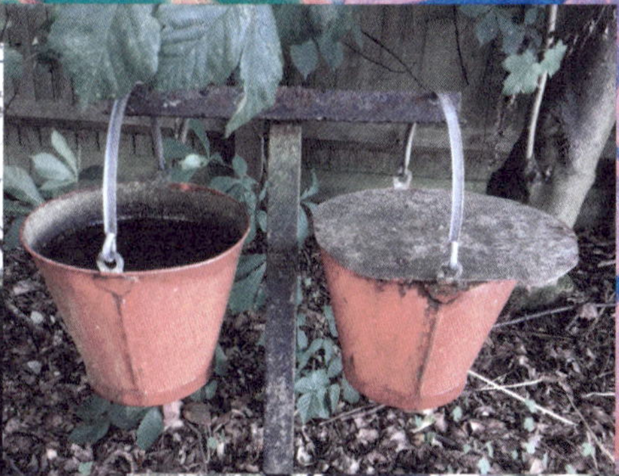

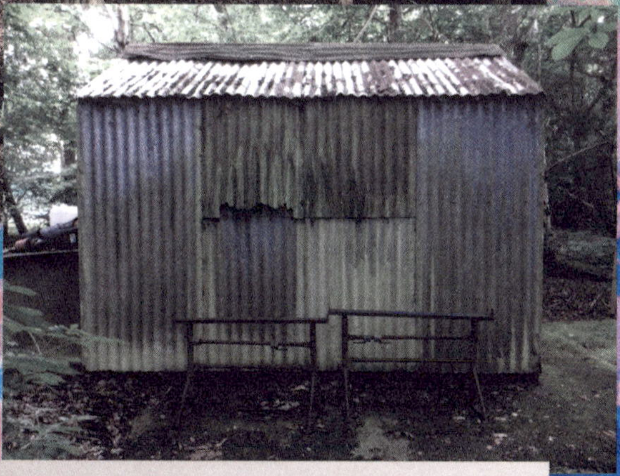

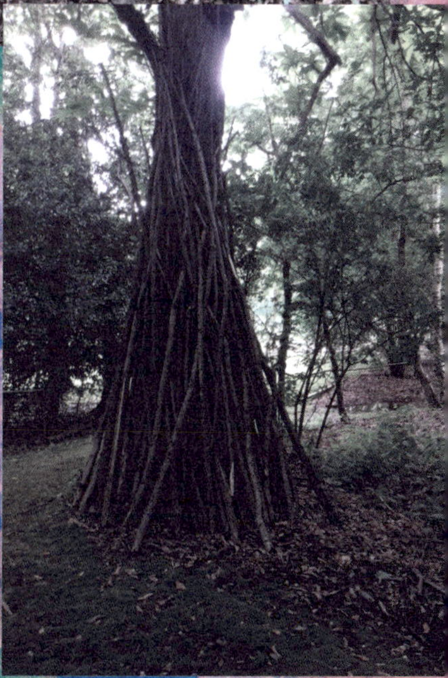

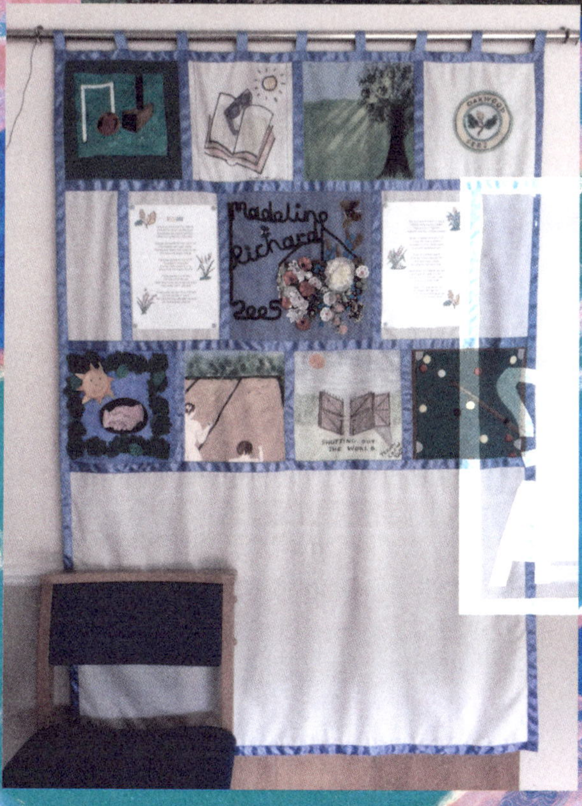
Madaline
Richard
2005

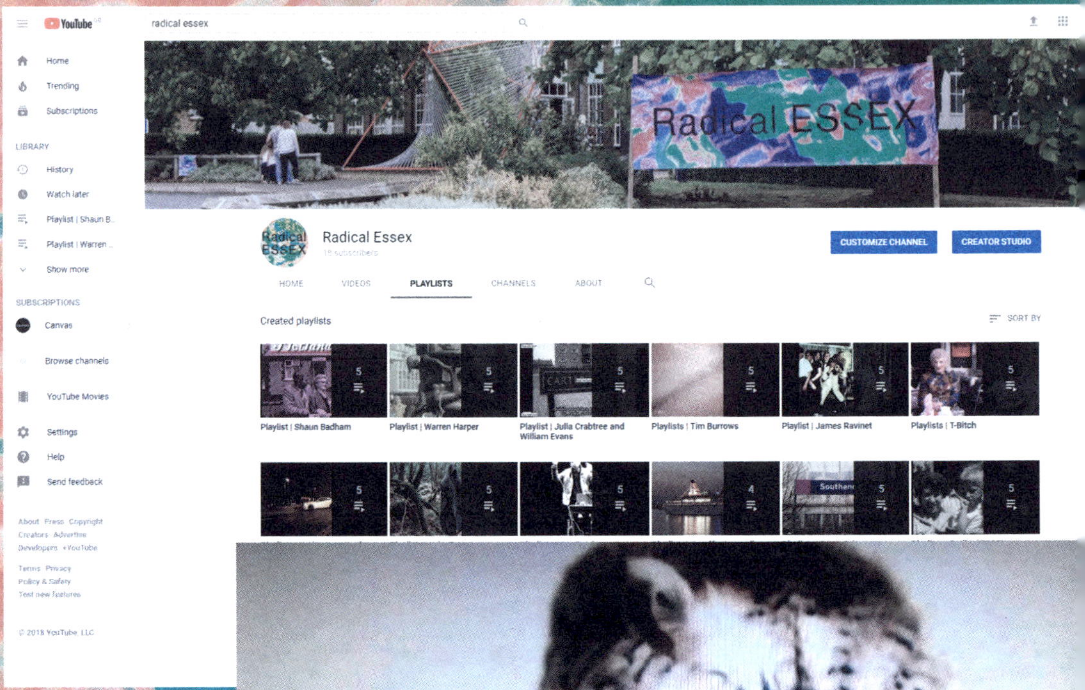

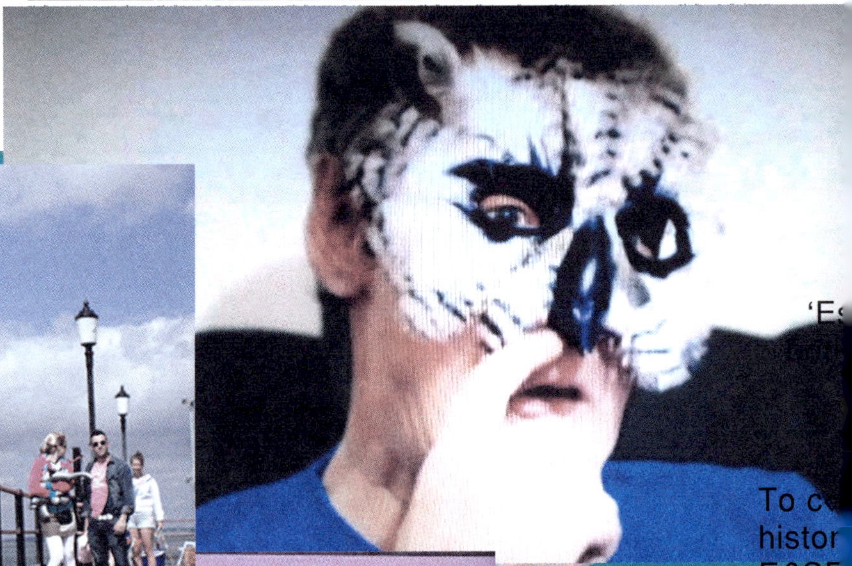

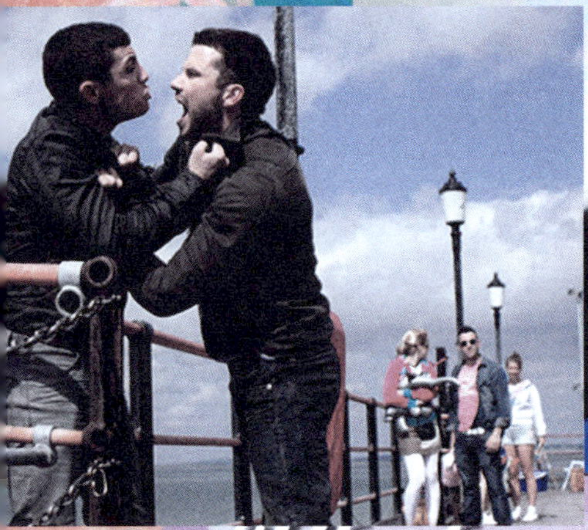

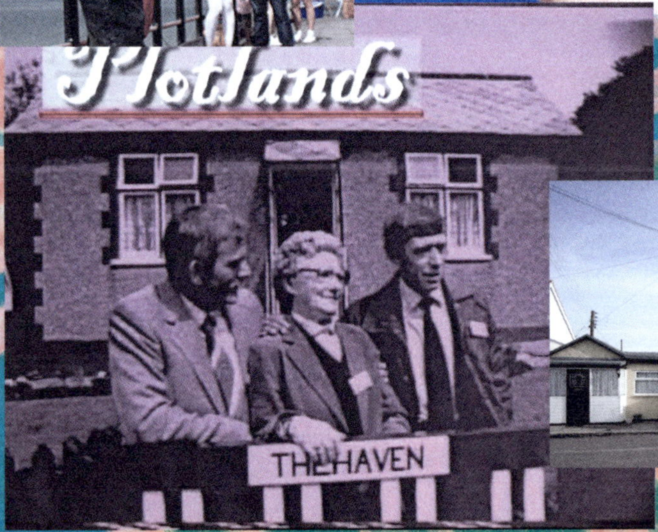

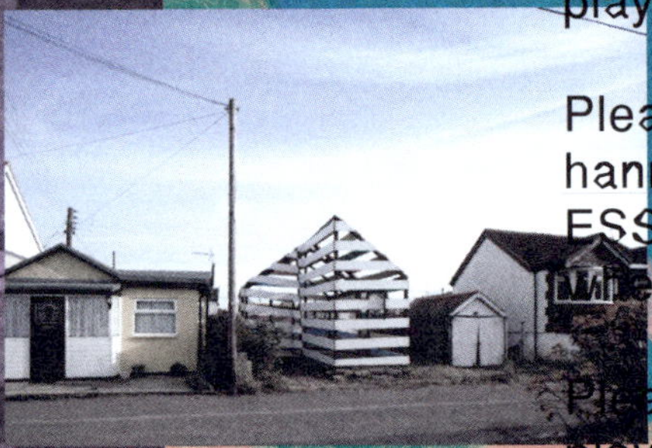

‘Es

To c
histor
ESSE
conte
wish,
this h
playli

Pleas
hanna
ESSE
when

Pleas
playli

Radical ESSEX

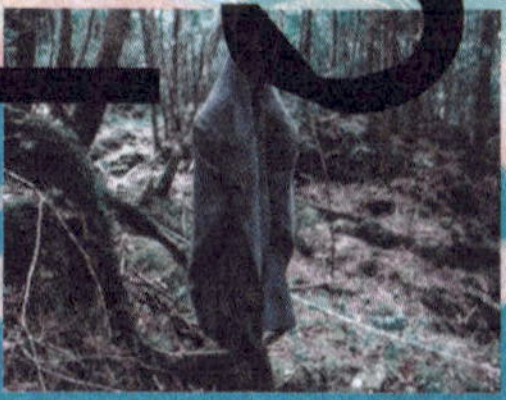

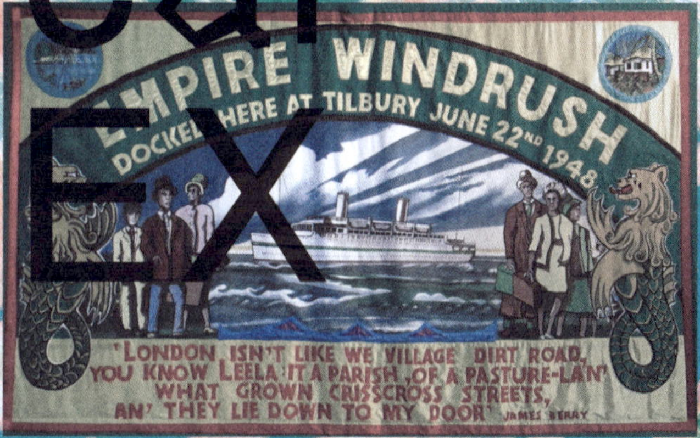

PLAYLISTS

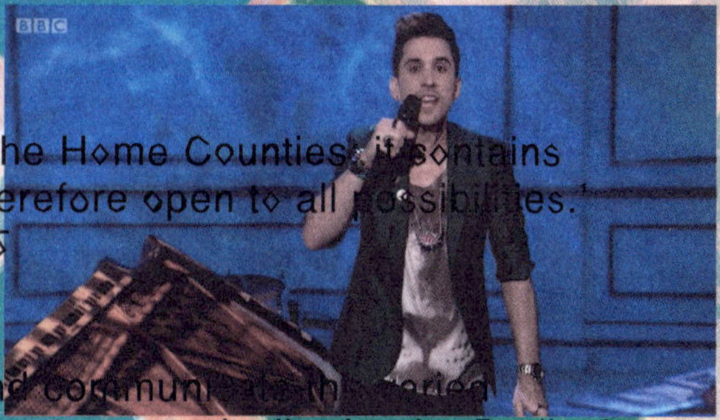

either part of East Anglia nor one of the Home Counties, it contains
and conservative elements, and is therefore open to all possibilities.'

Ken Worpole, 2015

e dialogue around Radical ESSEX and
county, we would like to invite you to curate a playlist for the Radical
pe channel. Examining your own perception of a radical Essex,
be relevant to the ethos of the project but can be as broad as you
your interests and ideas, direct or tenuous. Feel free to approach

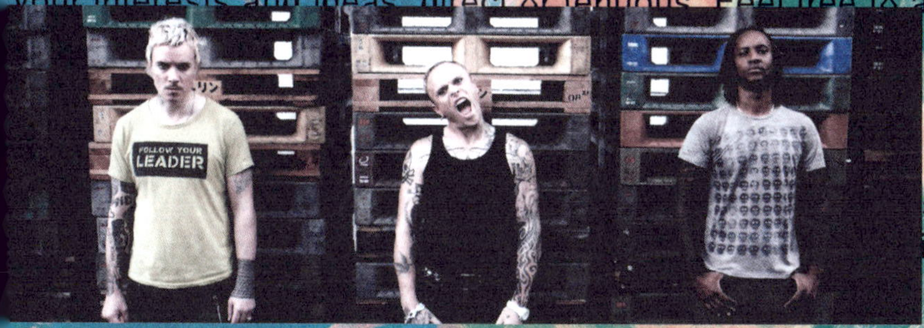

ion. The

through to
adical
in advance

s://www.youtube.com/channel/UCEJkd-wgxDC2OYVoHtkI23w/
previous Playlists.

I spent the morning with the Warden, Tim, who is SO excited about the event! But then so am I.

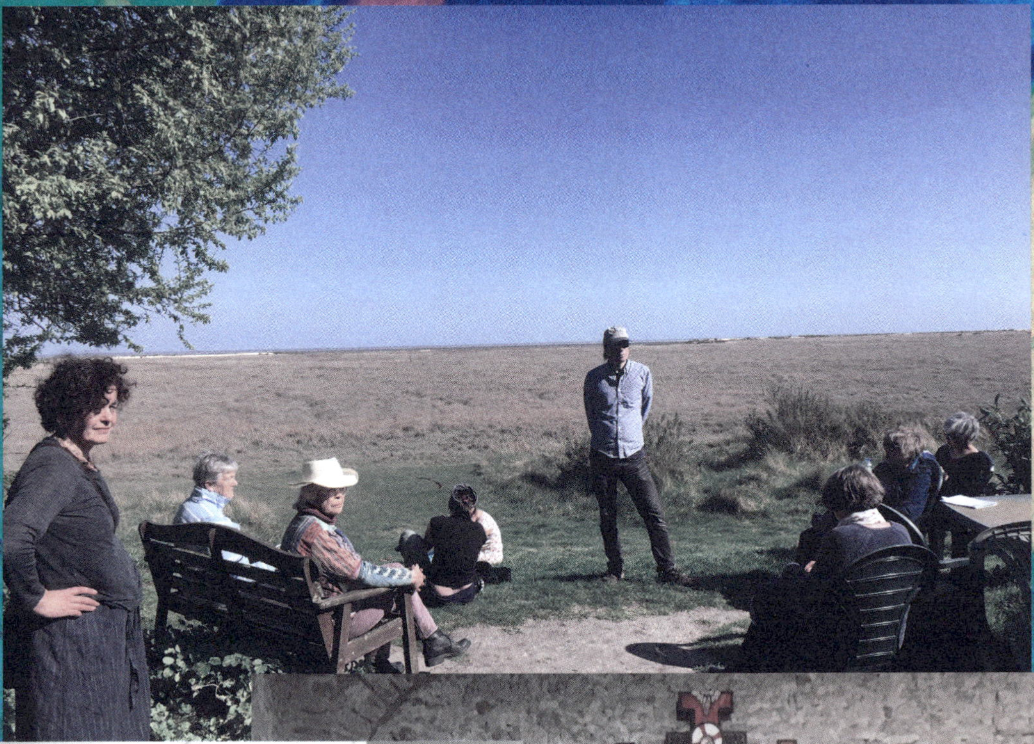

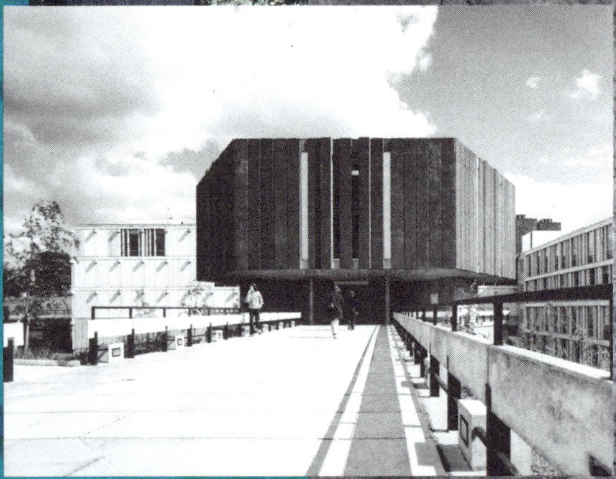

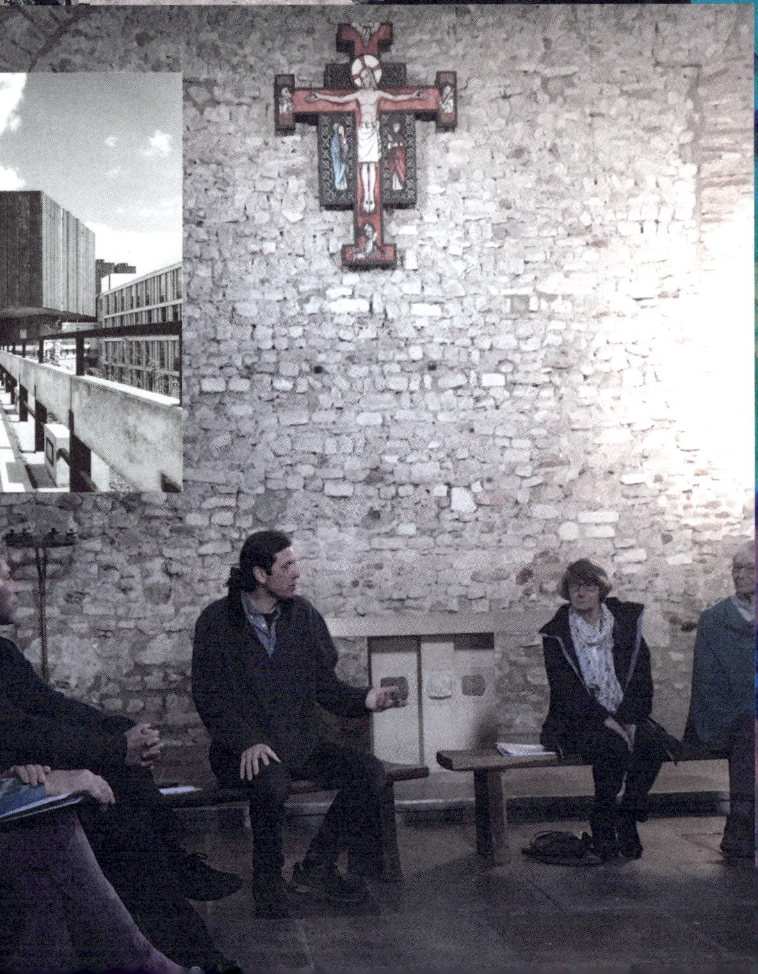

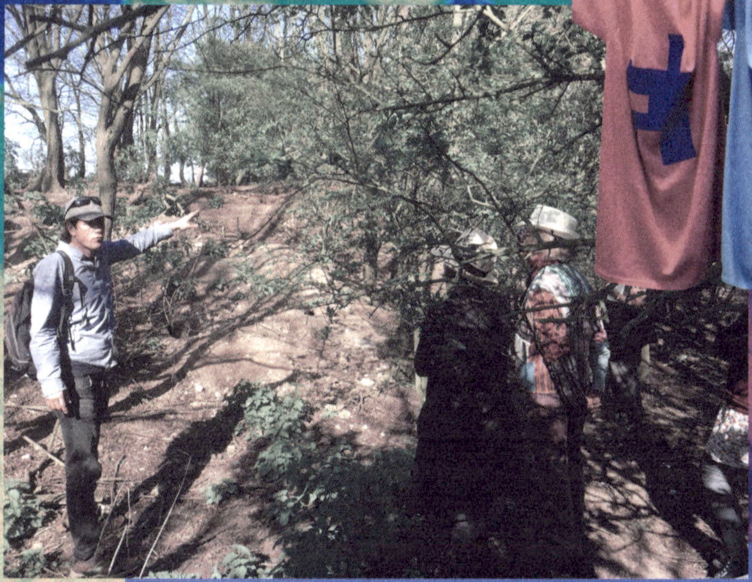

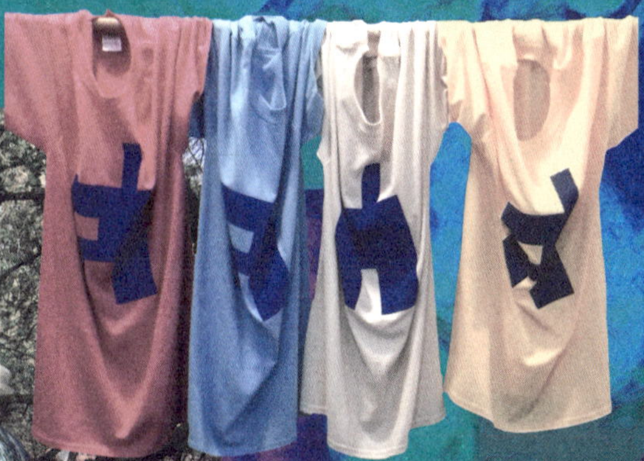

Jo and me had a fantastic research trip to The Othona Community. We have made a provisional booking at other partner organisation. I think it is the perfect venue: the people are lovely, many of the buildings are e Plus we can hold workshops/readings in St Peter's, the oldest church in England!!

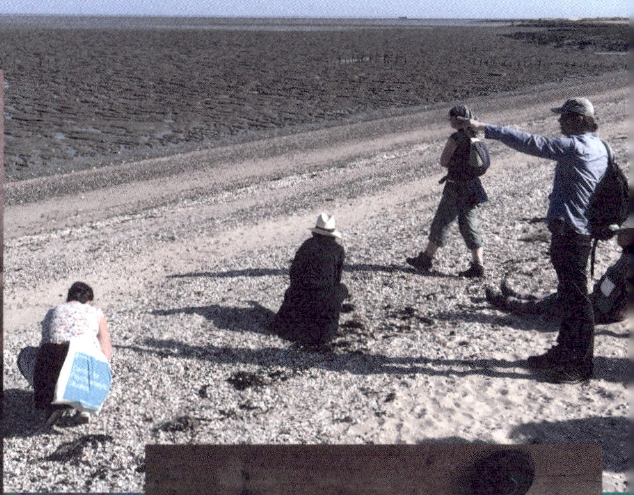

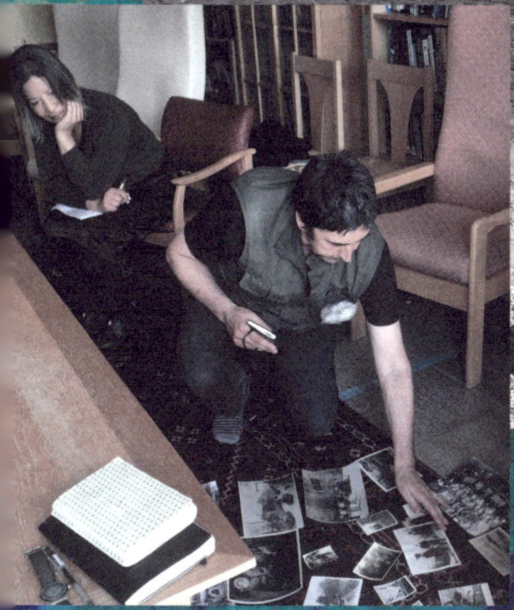

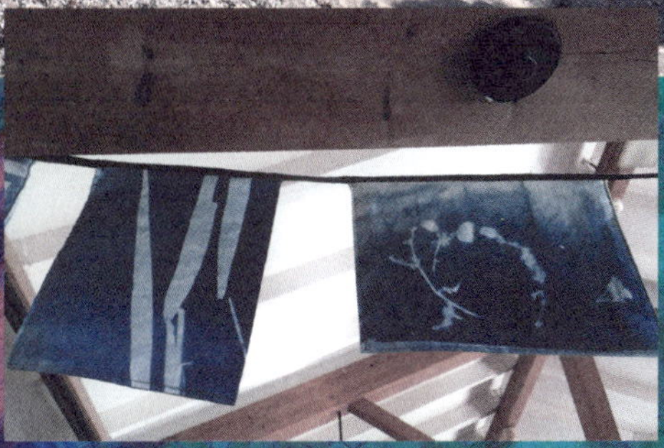

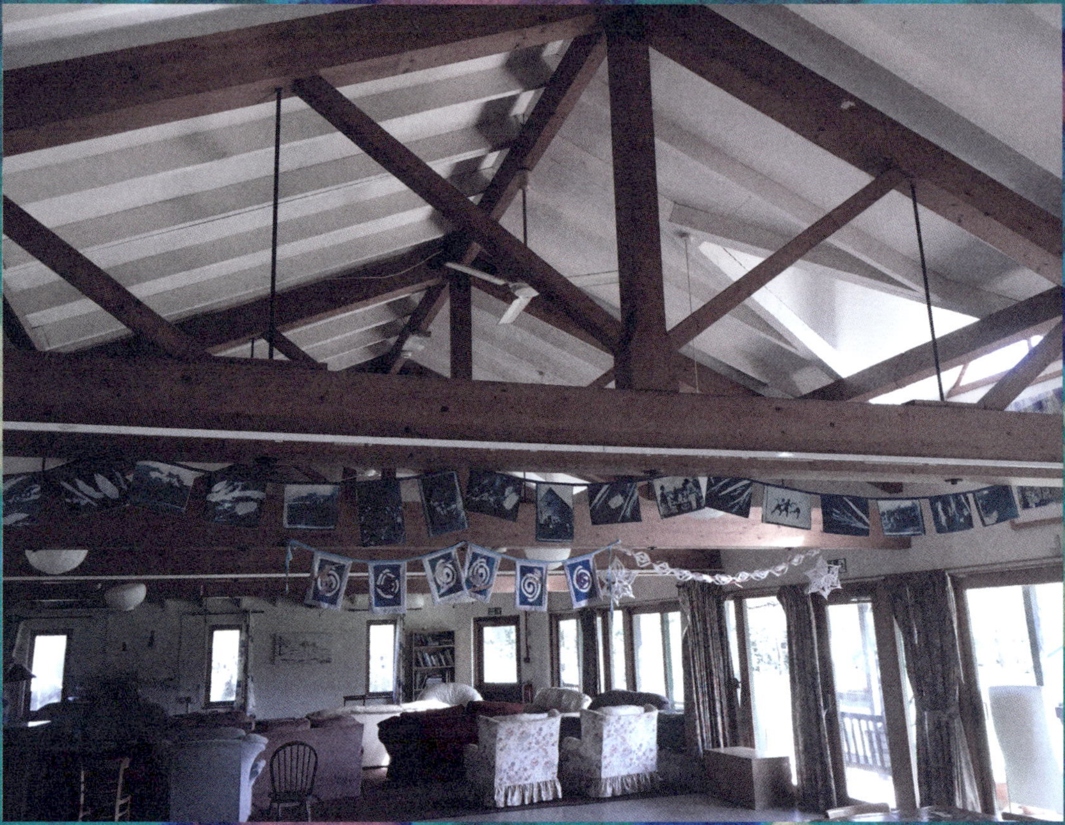

beginning of April for 2 nights - we just need to confirm dates with University of Essex creative writing team, th
constructions, i.e. straw bale, cob etc, they have an educational resources, including a beautifully restored pig st

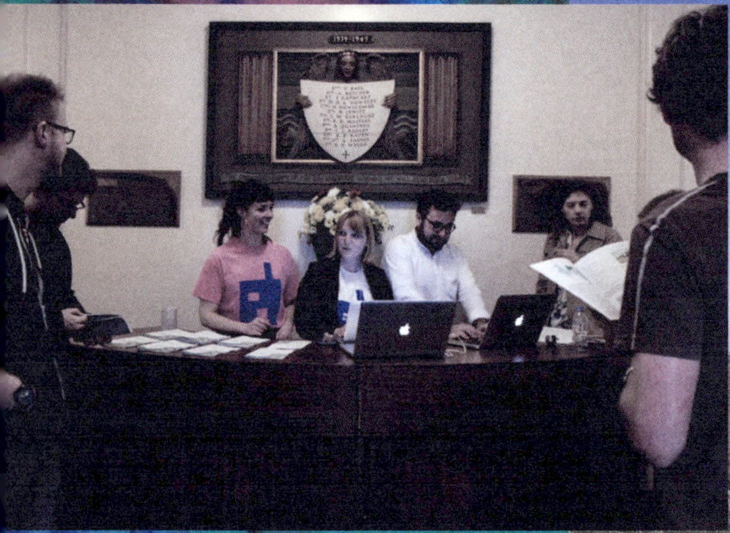

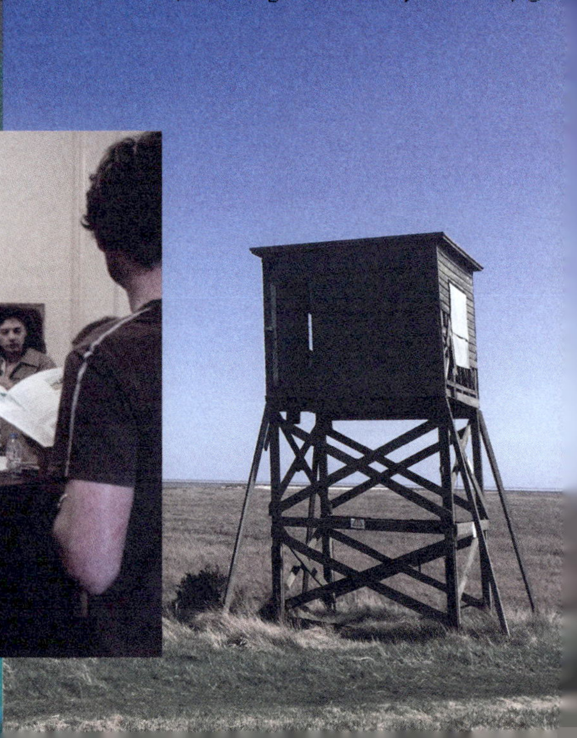

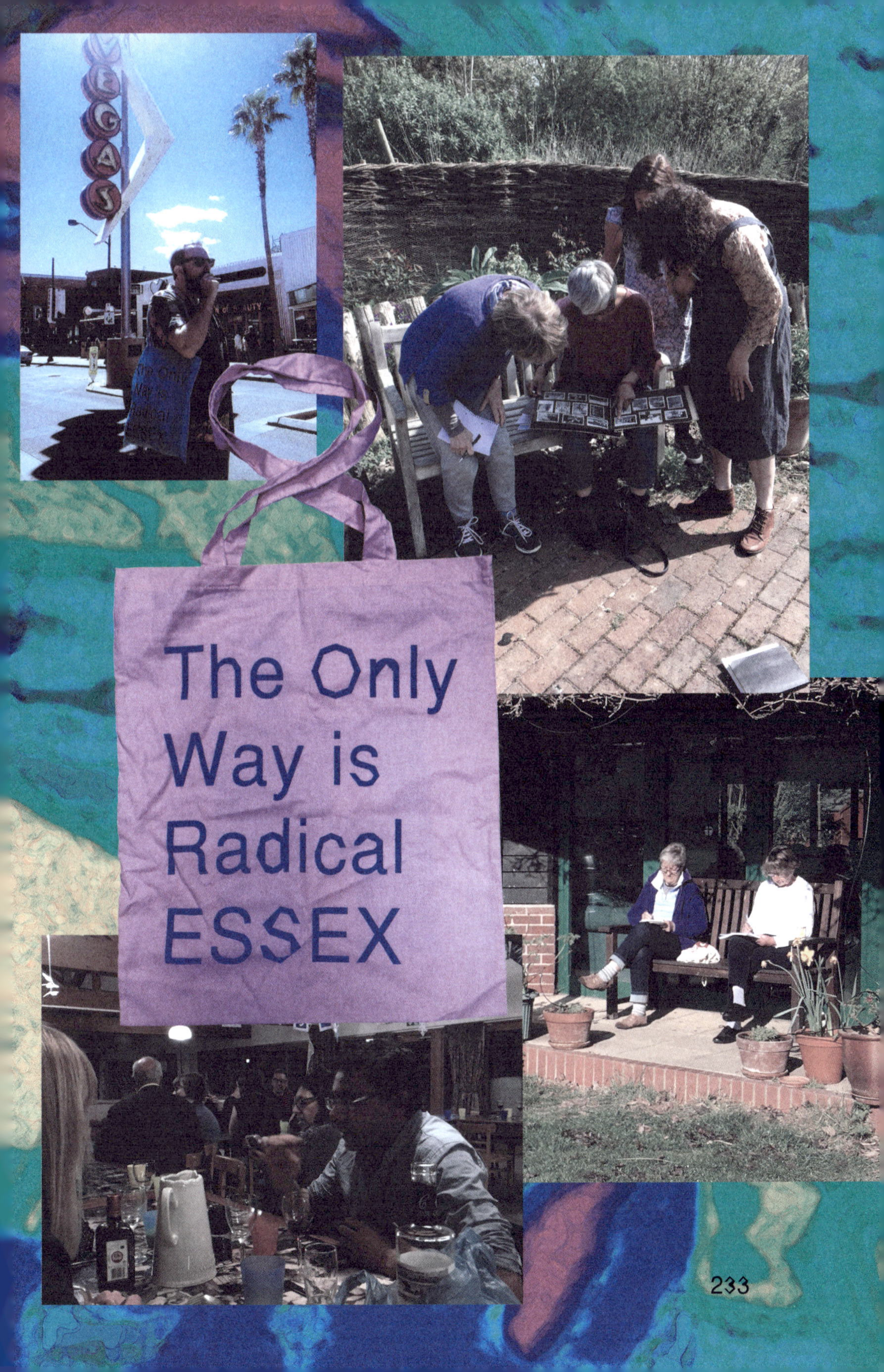
The Only
Way is
Radical
ESSEX

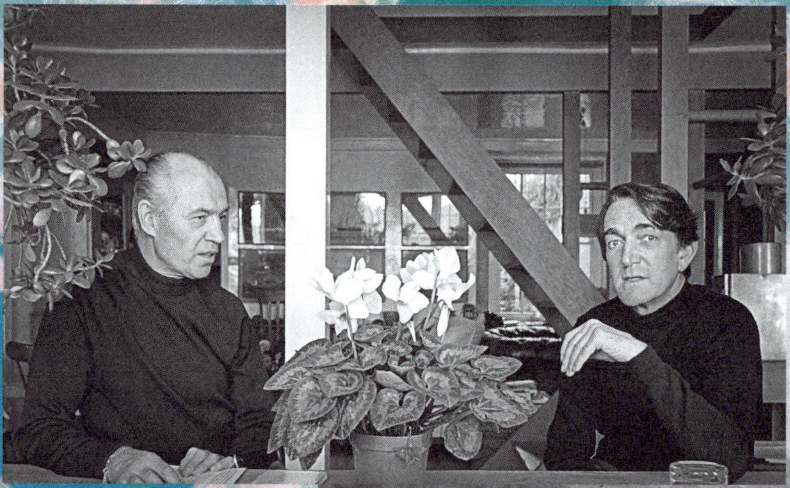

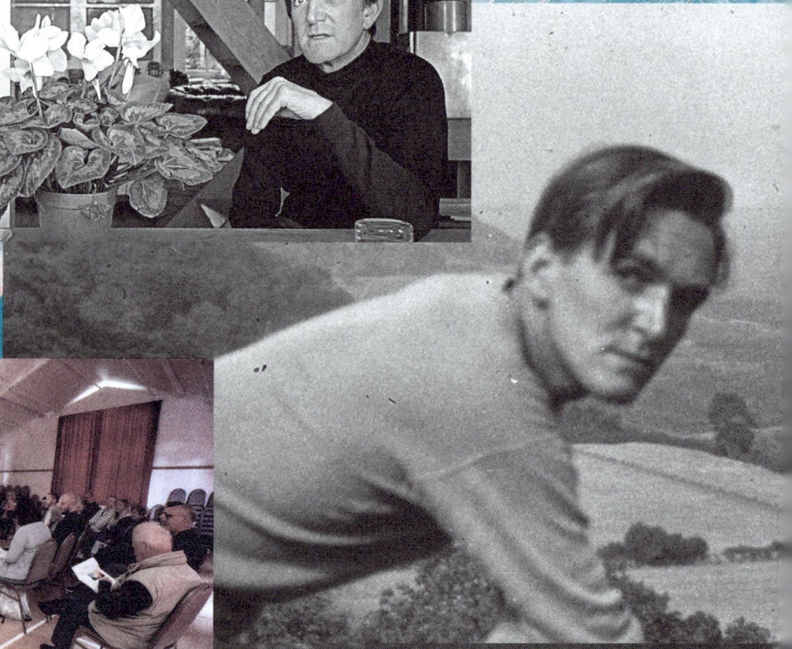

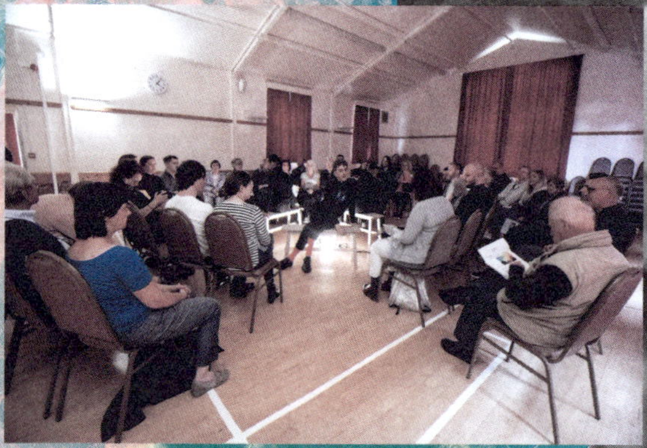

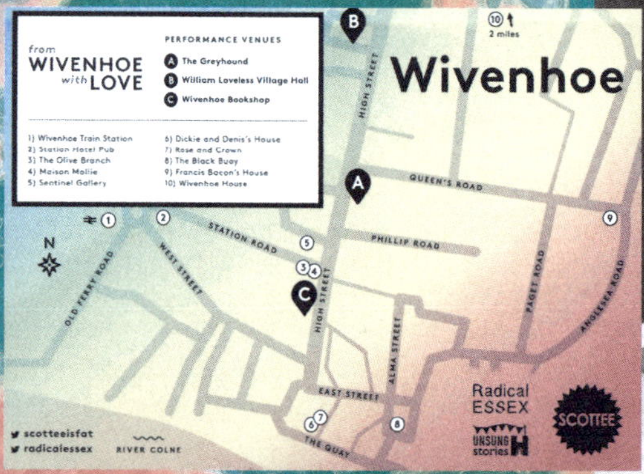
from
WIVENHOE
with LOVE
PERFORMANCE VENUES
A The Greyhound
B William Loveless Village Hall
C Wivenhoe Bookshop
1) Wivenhoe Train Station
2) Station Hotel Pub
3) The Olive Branch
4) Maison Mollie
5) Sentinel Gallery
6) Dickie and Denis's House
7) Rose and Crown
8) The Black Buoy
9) Francis Bacon's House
10) Wivenhoe House
Wivenhoe
2 miles
N
HIGH STREET
QUEEN'S ROAD
STATION ROAD
PHILLIP ROAD
WEST STREET
OLD FERRY ROAD
ALMA STREET
PAGET ROAD
ANGLESEA ROAD
EAST STREET
THE QUAY
RIVER COLNE
scotteeisfat
radicalessex
Radical
ESSEX
UNSUNG
stories
SCOTTEE

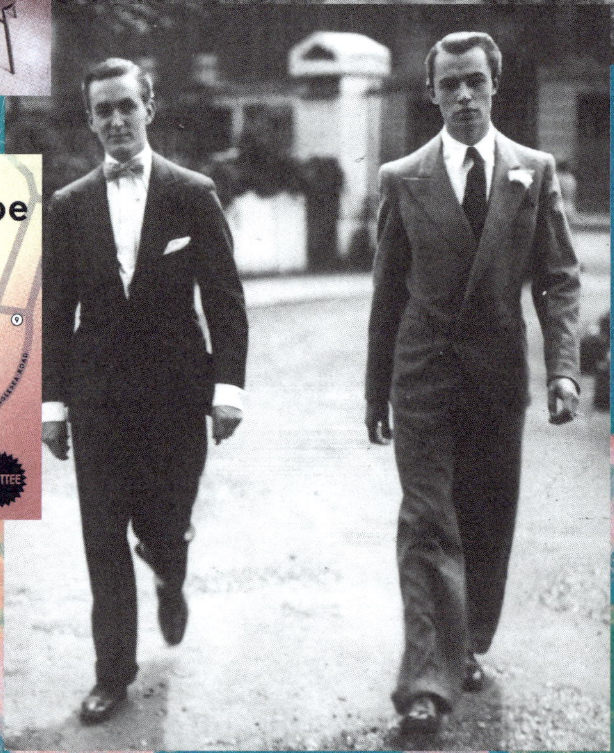

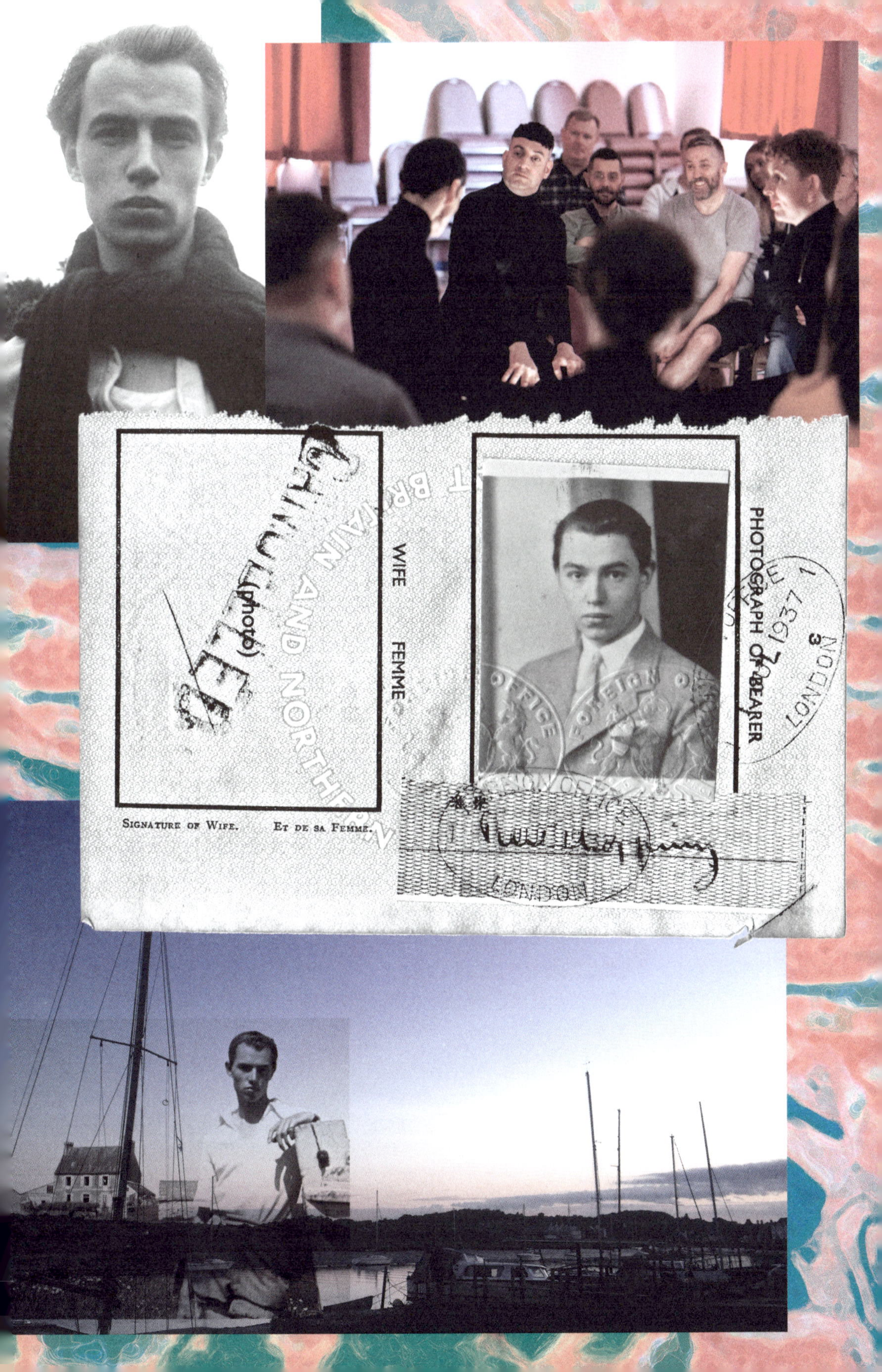
BRITAIN AND NORTHERN
(photo)
WIFE
FEMME
SIGNATURE OF WIFE.
ET DE SA FEMME.
PHOTOGRAPH OF BEARER
FOREIGN OFFICE
1937
LONDON

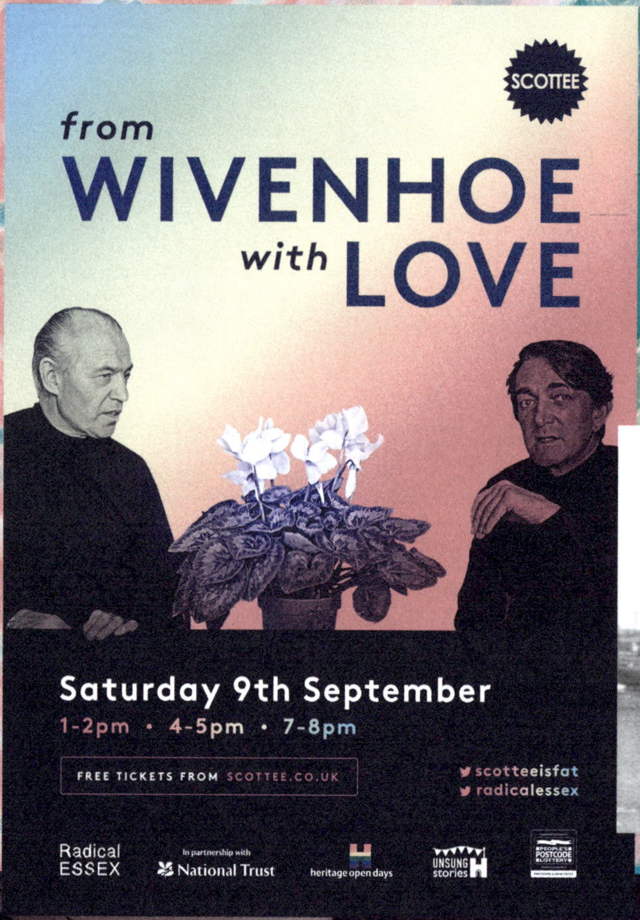
SCOTTEE
from
WIVENHOE
with LOVE
Saturday 9th September
1-2pm · 4-5pm · 7-8pm
FREE TICKETS FROM SCOTTEE.CO.UK
scotteeisfat
radicalessex
Radical ESSEX
In partnership with
National Trust
heritage open days
UNSUNG stories
PEOPLE'S POSTCODE LOTTERY

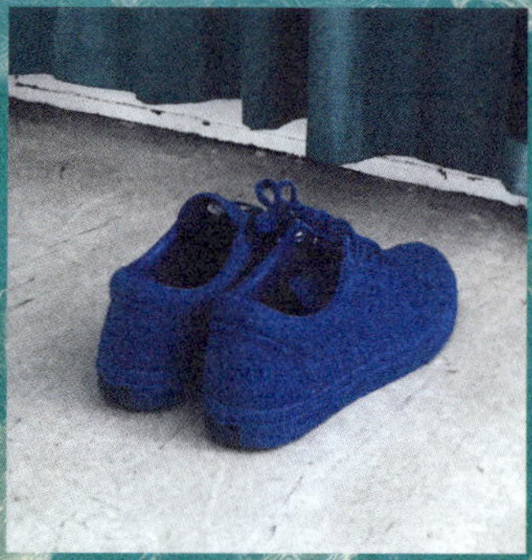

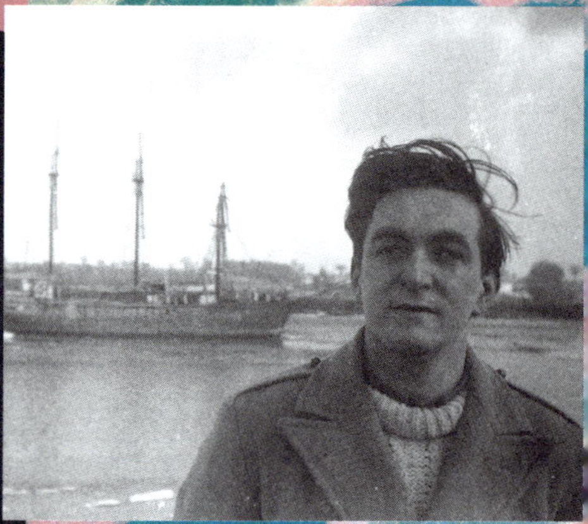

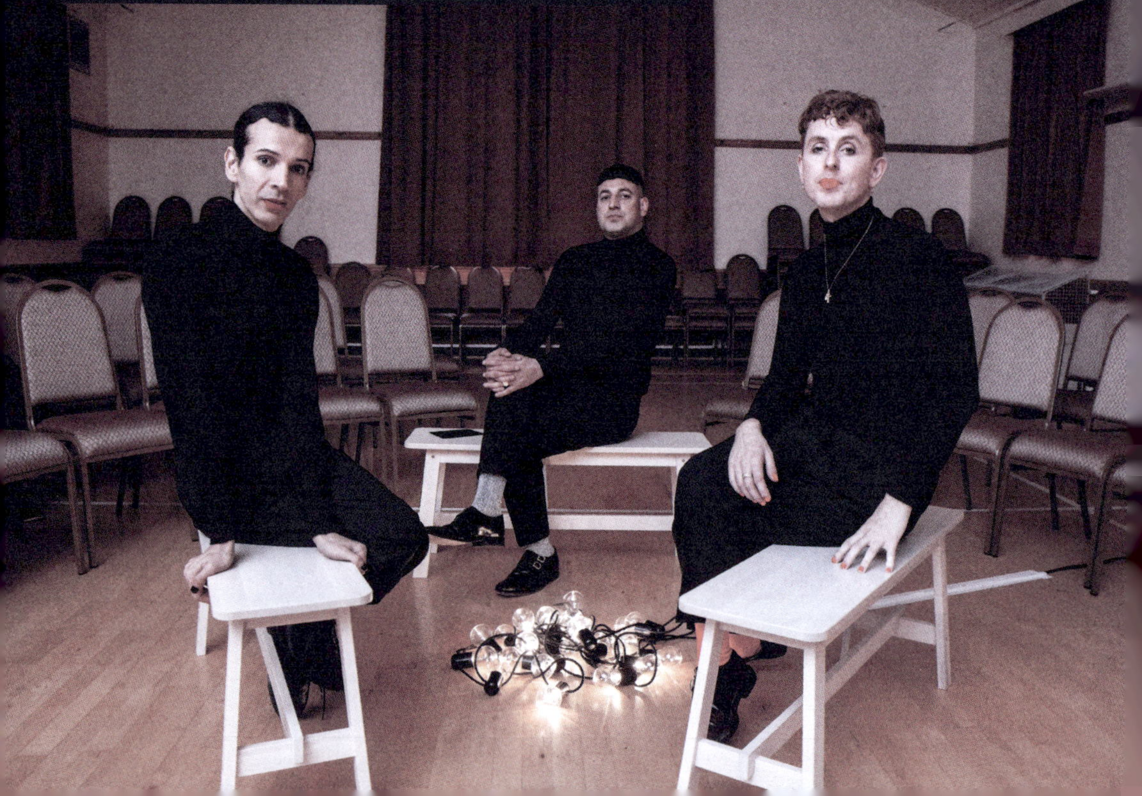

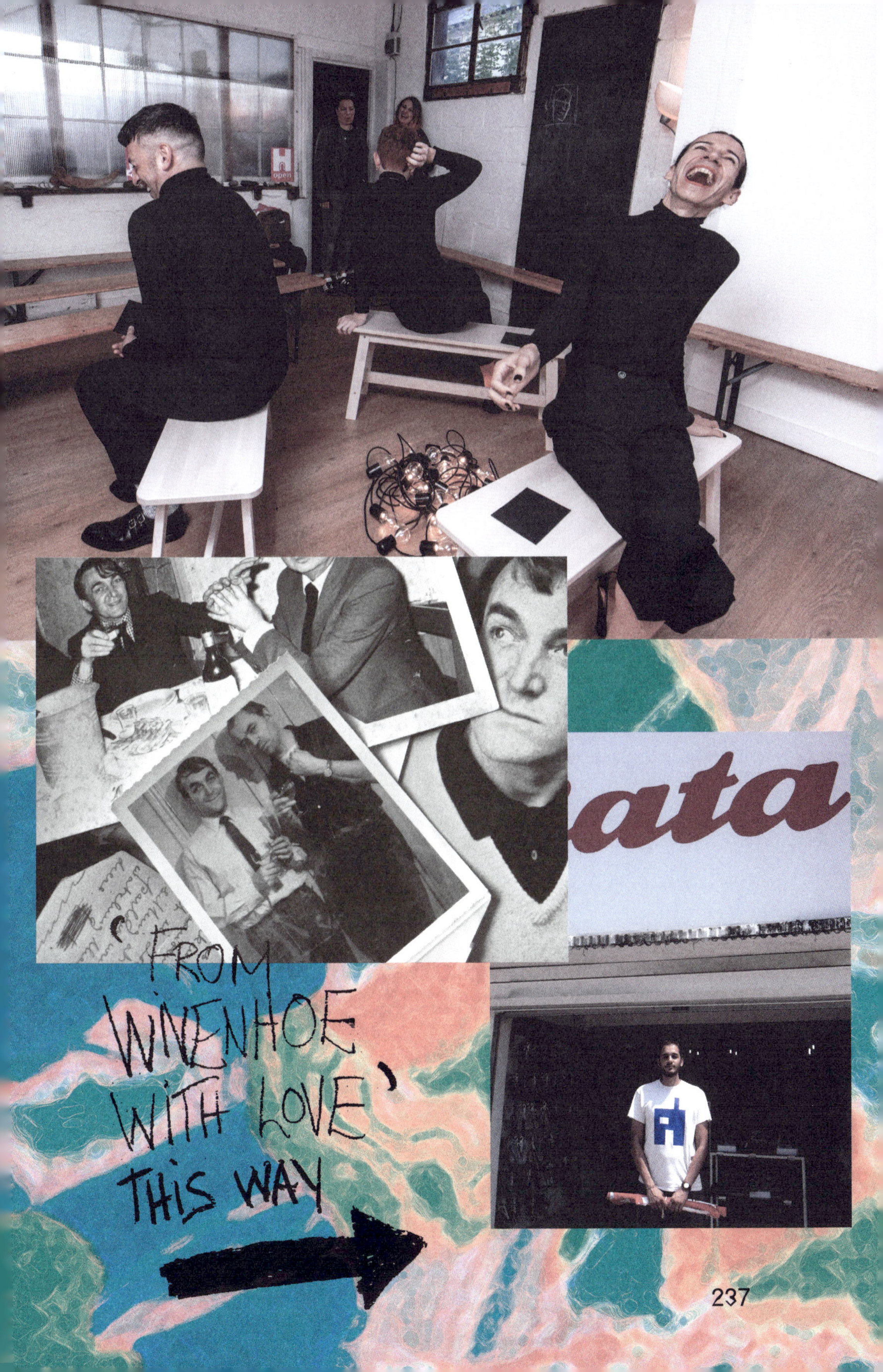
open
ata
'FROM
WIVENHOE,
WITH LOVE'
THIS WAY

Acknowledgements

The editors would like to give special thanks to the following for their contribution to the Radical ESSEX programme:

Rahil Ahmad, Albany Arts, Jennifer Lucy Allan, Arts Council England, Shaun C. Badham, Manuela Barczewski, Bata Heritage Centre, Beecroft Art Gallery, Teresa Bianchi, Hannah Black, Lisa Bone, Amy Botfield, Laura Bowen, Braintree District Council, Braintree District Museum, Kyle Buckle-Hodgson, Kelly Buckley, Nat Bullard, Graham Burnett, Tim Burrows, Matthew Butcher, Sharon Byrne, C2C, Aldo Caprini, Roxanne Carney, CCA, Rex Chen, Colchester Council, Mark Couzens, Julia Crabtree and William Evans, Catherine Croft, Curl la Tourelle Head Architects, Eileen Daly, Gillian Darley, Elizabeth Darling, Arnaud Desjardin, Dial House, James Dodds, David Doherty, Scott Dolling, Eva Duerden, Florence Dwyer, Paul Eastwood, Electric Belles, Essex County Council, Essex Heritage Trust, Essex Records Office, Essex Wildlife Trust, Ruth Ewan, Jes Fernie, Sue Finn, Firstsite, Alison Fogg, Fraser Muggeridge studio, Frinton and Walton Heritage Trust, Connie Gallagher, Ros Green, Ellen Greig, Karen Guthrie, Luke Hall, Dave Hanger, Warren Harper, India Harvey, HAT Projects, Owen Hatherley, Ruth Hazel, Wayne Head, Caspar Heinemann, Heritage Open Days, Charles Holland, Julie Hopkins, Tom Houghton, Catherine Hyland, Alice Jackson, Sam Jacob, La John Joseph, Alan Kane, Verity-Jane Keefe, PJ Kirby, Lina Lapelyte, Rachel Lichtenstein, Mary Lister, Jules Lubbock, Anna Lukala, Jon Lys Turner, Rachel McGivern, Jonathan Meades, Nando Messias, Metal, The Mighty Oak Brewing Company, Mem Morrison, Fraser Muggeridge, Jo Nancarrow, Mark Napier, Molly Nicholson, Christian Nyampeta, Oakwood Sun Club, Pallant House, Park Inn Palace, Simon Periton, Laura Phelps, Nina Pope, Alan Powers, Riah Pryor, Joanna Quinn, James Ravinet, Red Fox Brewery, RIBA East, Alex Rich, Penny Rimbaud, Sean Rowlands, Scottee, Holly Shuttleworth, Silver End Heritage Society, Silver End Scouts, Sound Choice Hire, Southend-on-Sea Borough Council, Speak and Spell, Spiralseed, Bob Stanley, Lindsey Strange, Suenos Guesthouse, Michael Sullivan, Stephanie Sutton, Barry Sykes, T-Bitch, Anya Tavkar, Mary Tebje, this is tomorrow, Milly Thompson, Ellen Thorogood, Thurrock Museum, Valerie Tinker, James Torble, Rachel Treliving, Karen Turnbull, Luke Turner, Twelve, Jess Twyman, University of Essex, Lauren Verney, VisitEngland, Visit Essex, Andrew Ward, the late Colin Ward, David Watkins, Jacob Watmore, Wivenhoe Bookshop, Wivenhoe House, Hannah Rose Whittle, Lucy Woodhouse, Ken Worpole, Simon Worthington, all homeowners who kindly opened their doors to us, and the whole team at Focal Point Gallery.

In memory of May Rippingale née Vaclavik

Radical ESSEX

This publication forms part of Radical ESSEX, a project re-examining the county in relation to radicalism in thought, lifestyle, politics and architecture, shedding light on the vibrant, pioneering thinking of the late-nineteenth and twentieth centuries. Led by Focal Point Gallery in partnership with Colchester Borough Council, Essex County Council, Firstsite, Southend-on-Sea Borough Council and Visit Essex, the project celebrates the crucial role Essex has played in the history of British modernism and its utopian ideologies.

The Scrapbook section is a creative interpretation of the wonderful and extensive visual material that has informed the research of the writers, artists, curators, editors and publishers working on Radical ESSEX, as well as documenting the projects that have been part of this programme. Great care has been taken to identify all image copyright holders correctly, however in the case of errors or omissions, please contact the publishers so that we can make corrections in future editions.

Images in this section are courtesy of the following:

1973 Essex Design Guide, Uosef Ahmadi, Shaun C. Badham, Manuela Barczewski, Bata Heritage Centre, BBC, the Trustees of the British Museum, Brotherton Lock, Kevin Bruce, Graham Burnett, Canvey Community Archive, Carnival Films/ITV, Channel 4, Chester River Press, Jason Coe, Cooking Vinyl/ The Prodigy, Niki Cornish, Gillian Darley, Emma Edmondson and Derek Pitt, Essex Records Office, Essex Wildlife Trust, ETV, Jes Fernie, Ellen Greig, Warren Harper, Heritage Open Days/Rahil Ahmad, Laindon District Community Archive, Anna Lukala, Jon Lys Turner, Alan Kane, Keith and Malcolm McQueen, The National Archives, Nina Pope and Karen Guthrie, Cedric Price Fonds, CCA, Gerhard Riebicke/Galerie Bob Niemann, Scottee, Silver End Heritage Society, Swan Housing, Barry Sykes, Quinlan & Francis Terry Architects, Mick Tesseras (image of Revolutionary Festival at University of Essex, 1969), Michael Thomas (image of University of Essex students debating in Square 4, 1968), Rosa Tyhurst, Special Collections, Albert Sloman Library, University of Essex (archive images of University of Essex), Ken Worpole and the editors.

This publication has been produced using public funding by the National Lottery through Arts Council England as part of the country-wide Cultural Destinations programme, a partnership with VisitEngland, supporting arts organisations to work with the tourism sector to deliver projects to maximise the impact culture has on local economies.

We are also grateful to Essex Heritage Trust for their additional support.

First published in 2018 by Focal Point Gallery in an edition of 1,000 copies
Second edition 2019

#87

Focal Point Gallery
The Forum
Elmer Square
Southend-on-Sea
Essex SS1 1NB
United Kingdom
www.fpg.org.uk

Edited by Hayley Dixon and Joe Hill
Editorial assistance by Hannah Rose Whittle
Copy edited by Eileen Daly
Designed by Fraser Muggeridge studio
Image research by Kyle Buckle-Hodgson
Copyright permissions by Tom Houghton

Essays by Tim Burrows, Gillian Darley, Charles Holland,
Rachel Lichtenstein, Jules Lubbock, Jess Twyman and Ken Worpole

Photography by Catherine Hyland

ISBN 978-1-907185-21-2

British Library Cataloguing-in-Publication Data
A full catalogue record of this book is available from the British Library

Distributed in the UK and Europe by
Cornerhouse Publications
Home
2 Tony Wilson Place
Manchester M15 4FN
United Kingdom
cornerhousepublications.org

Radical ESSEX
Director: Joe Hill
Project Manager: Hayley Dixon
Project Assistant: Hannah Rose Whittle

www.radicalessex.uk
@RadicalEssex